Susan Horner, Joanna Horner

Walks in Florence

Volume 2

Susan Horner, Joanna Horner

Walks in Florence
Volume 2

ISBN/EAN: 9783742803108

Manufactured in Europe, USA, Canada, Australia, Japa

Cover: Foto ©Andreas Hilbeck / pixelio.de

Manufactured and distributed by brebook publishing software (www.brebook.com)

Susan Horner, Joanna Horner

Walks in Florence

WALKS IN FLORENCE

By SUSAN AND JOANNA HORNER

WITH ILLUSTRATIONS

VOL. II.

CONTENTS OF VOL. II.

CHAPTER I.
San Firenze—Vicinity of Sta. Croce . . . . . . PAGE 1

CHAPTER II.
Sta. Croce—Architecture 15

CHAPTER III.
Sta. Croce—Monuments 25

CHAPTER IV.
Sta. Croce—the Pazzi Chapel—Inquisition . . . 40

CHAPTER V.
Sta. Croce—Frescos 49

CHAPTER VI.
Pia Casa di Lavoro—The Villani 76

CHAPTER VII.
Sta. Maria in Campo—Sant' Ambrogio 87

CONTENTS.

CHAPTER VIII.
The Protestant Cemetery, &c. 98

CHAPTER IX.
Convent and Church of the SS. Annunziata . 113

CHAPTER X.
Piazza of the SS. Annunziata—the Innocenti . . 129

CHAPTER XI.
Convent of Sta. Maria degli Angeli—Palazzo Ginori . . 135

CHAPTER XII.
Convent of San Marco 151

CHAPTER XIII.
San Marco—Library—Church . . . 171

CHAPTER XIV.
The Via San Gallo—The Palazzo Strozzi . . . 180

CHAPTER XV.
Palazzo Rucellai—Piazza Sta. Maria Novella . . 192

CHAPTER XVI.
Sta. Maria Novella 206

CHAPTER XVII.
Sta. Maria Novella—(*Continuation*) . . . 225

CHAPTER XVIII.
The Via della Scala—Bridges 239

CONTENTS.

CHAPTER XIX.
Via de' Bardi—Porta San Giorgio 254

CHAPTER XX.
Sta. Felicita to the Piazza Soderini . . . 274

CHAPTER XXI.
Fondaccio di Santo Spirito—San Felice . . 286

CHAPTER XXII.
Santo Spirito 295

CHAPTER XXIII.
The Carmine, &c. 304

CHAPTER XXIV.
The Boboli Gardens—Palazzo dei Pitti . . 321

PUBLIC GALLERIES OF FLORENCE.

THE ACADEMY:—
    First Room 332
    Second Room 352

THE PITTI GALLERY:—
    Large Rooms 367
    Small Rooms 399

TABERNACLES 408
MANUFACTURE OF PIETRA-DURA 412
EGYPTIAN MUSEUM.—ETRUSCAN REMAINS . . . 416
MUSEUM OF NATURAL HISTORY 440

VOL. II.

LIST OF ILLUSTRATIONS TO VOL. II.

MARZOCCO, BY DONATELLO . . . . . *Frontispiece.*

FRESCO BY GIOTTINO, ON THE STAIRCASE OF THE FILAR-
MONICA, VIA GHIBELLINA . . . . . *Face page* 76

ANNUNCIATION, BY LUCA DELLA ROBBIA, HOSPITAL OF THE
INNOCENTS 129

PORTA SAN NICOLÒ 254

FORMS OF ETRUSCAN VASES 427

WALKS IN FLORENCE.

CHAPTER I.

SAN FIRENZE.—PALAZZO GONDI.—LOGGIA DEL GRANO.
—PIAZZA CASTELLANI.—PONTE ALLE GRAZIE.—
VICINITY OF STA. CROCE.

THE Piazza di San Firenze, south of the Bargello, is in the shape of an irregular triangle. At one corner is the entrance to the Via de' Librai, a continuation of the Via del Proconsolo, which took its name from the book-stalls near the Badia, where the Benedictine monks probably formed the principal reading public of Florence. Beside the Bargello stood the Church of San Apollinare, long since demolished, which at one time gave its name to the piazza; here Beccheria of Pavia, Abbot of Vallombrosa, was executed in 1258. Beccheria was a notorious Ghibelline, whose faction had been defeated, and the leaders, Uberto degli Uberti and Mangia degli Infangati, beheaded in the Orto di San Michele.* Trusting, however, to the immunity of his sacred office, Beccheria ventured to enter Florence;

---

* See "Or San Michele," chap. xii. vol. i.

but was seized, charged with hatching plots against the State, put to the torture, and, in spite of his protests and appeals, beheaded in this piazza. His name has been immortalised by Dante, who placed him beside Count Ugolino among the traitors in the "Inferno:"—

> "Se fossi demandato altri chi v' era,
> Tu hai dallato quel di Beccheria,
> Di cui segò Firenze la gorgiera." *

The Church of San Firenze is supposed to occupy the site of a Roman Temple of Isis; but, more probably, of a building connected with the Amphitheatre. The remains of the foundations and of some broken columns were excavated in 1772, when a noble statue of a Roman senator was discovered, which is now in the Palazzo Gondi. San Firenze was one of the oldest churches in the city; but in 1640 it was ceded to the Fathers of the Oratory of San Filippo Neri, who undertook to enlarge the monastery attached to the church; the families of Magalotti and Mancini pulled down their towers to afford more room, and the work was commenced in 1646; but whilst it was still incomplete the last of the Serragli family died, and bequeathed his vast wealth to the Fathers with one condition, that instead of using it to enlarge their own dwelling, they should include all that had been already built in the church. The façade was added in 1732, and partakes of the bad taste prevalent in that century. The interior of San Firenze

---

* "If thou shouldst questioned be, who else was there,
Thou hast beside thee him of Beccaria,
Of whom the gorget Florence slit asunder."
Longfellow's Translation.

is handsome, and contains several modern pictures of merit.

The Palazzo Gondi is a good specimen of the architecture peculiar to Florence. It was built in 1501, after a design by Giuliano di San Gallo, who was employed by a wealthy merchant, Giuliano Gondi. The cortile is surrounded by graceful columns supporting arches, but is most remarkable for the staircase, with its fine balustrade, and curious variety of delicate ornamentation in animals and foliage. At the head of the interior staircase, leading to the principal apartments, is the statue of the Roman senator, taken from the supposed Temple of Isis. A magnificent chimney-piece, the work of Giuliano di San Gallo, adorns the large entrance-hall, round which are hung family portraits. The most distinguished of these are:—Maddalena, daughter of Simone Gondi, who married one of the Salviati, and who, by the marriage of her daughter Maria with Giovanni de' Medici delle Bande Nere, became the grandmother of Duke Cosimo I.; Giuliano de' Gondi, surnamed Il Vecchio, who was employed in various affairs of State by Catharine de' Medici, and by her sons, Charles IX. and Henry III., as well as by Henry IV. of France. Giuliano refused a pension offered him by the King of Naples for services he had rendered that sovereign, because he did not consider the citizen of a free republic could honourably accept money from a foreign prince. He founded this palace in 1501; and towards the close of his life he built the noble palace behind the archbishop's residence, which afterwards became the property of the Orlandini. The scruples of Giuliano do not appear to have been shared by his descendants, who were frequently in the pay of France, and were created

French generals, admirals, governors of provinces, and even archbishops. The celebrated Cardinal de Retz was of this family.

Passing behind the Palazzo Vecchio, we reach a piazzetta in which is the Loggia del Grano. This shelter for the corn vendors was built in 1619 by the Grand-Duke Cosimo II., whose bust is in front, and who employed the architect Giulio Parigi, a pupil of the still more celebrated Buontalenti. The Loggia del Grano is an elegant structure, consisting of a vaulted roof, resting on columns, with an upper chamber, lately converted into a theatre. The pavement of the loggia is raised a few feet from the ground, and here, until within a few years, was held the corn market.

A narrow street connects the Loggia del Grano with the Piazza de' Castellani or de' Giudici. At the right-hand corner, facing the river, stood the Castle of Altafronte, which was purchased by one of that name from the Ghibelline Uberti. The land attached to the castle extended some distance eastwards, and Altafronte bestowed a portion on the Franciscans, who thereupon commenced their church of Sta. Croce. The descendants of Altafronte sold the property to the Castellani, whose name has been erroneously supposed to refer to the office of Châtelain or Governor of the Castle of Altafronte. In 1558 the Grand-Duke Cosimo I. purchased the Castellani palace, which had risen on the site of the old castle, and removed thither the Tribunal of the Giudici a Ruota, which had previously held its sittings in the Bargello; the lawyers attached to this court had their chambers around the piazza. In 1860 the piazza underwent another change: the palace of the Castellani became a Government office, and opposite, where once stood a *tiratojo*, was built the Banca Toscana—the Bank of Florence. Several of these *tiratoji* once existed in the city, which, as the trade in woollen cloth diminished, gradually disappeared. The *tiratojo* in this piazza was attributed to Arnolfo di Cambio. On the parapet beside the river is a small tablet, with a Latin inscription, to the memory of a horse which belonged to the Venetian ambassador, and which was killed during the siege of 1529 by a shell from the Prince of Orange's camp, beyond San Miniato.

The bridge higher up the river, with its singular row of detached houses, was built in 1235 by Rubaconte da Mandella, a Milanese Podestà of Florence. He employed Lapo, the father of Arnolfo de' Lapi, for the work. This same Rubaconte caused Florence to be paved with large diagonal stones instead of brick. The bridge is thus alluded to by Dante, when describing the position of the Church of San Miniato on the hill above:—

"Come a man destra, per salire al monte
Dove siede la Chiesa, che soggioga
La ben guidata sopra Rubaconte." *

The bridge had originally nine arches, but in 1346 two were included in the mill-dam which was on the left bank of the river, but which has now been filled up to form part of the new quay. The little chapel on the right bank once

---

* "As on the right hand to ascend the mount
Where seated is the Church that lordeth
O'er the well-guided,† above Rubaconte."
Longfellow's Translation.

† La ben guidata—the well-guided—is ironically spoken of Florence.

contained an image of the Virgin and Child, which was held in peculiar veneration, and gave the name "Alle Grazie" to the bridge. It was founded in 1372 by one of the Alberti family, whose arms—the Fetters—are carved on a shield at the corner of their palace, opposite. There were likewise three chapels, dedicated to Sta. Caterina, Sta. Barbera, and San Lorenzo, but they have all disappeared. The small houses at intervals, which give this bridge its peculiar character, were built in the fourteenth century by ladies of distinction, under the direction of one Monna or Madonna Apollonia. These ladies, scandalised by the loose morality of convent life, immured themselves here, receiving their food through the windows, and were known as the Romite —female hermits—of the Ponte Rubaconte. Their number increased so rapidly, that they were at length obliged to remove into a convent near Sta. Croce, called, from their vows, the Murate, or Immured. The hermitages, thus abandoned, became the dwellings of poor artisans, and in one of them, in 1646, was born the poet Benedetto Mengini. He became a priest in Florence, and went to Rome, where he gained his celebrity under the patronage of Queen Christina of Sweden. He died in 1704.*

From the quay which bears the name of Alberti is seen one of the most lovely views of this neighbourhood: the weir, the suspension-bridge, and the Porta San Nicolò on the opposite bank; beyond, the heights of the Mozzi and Boboli gardens, skirted by the city wall with its Middle-Age towers; and still more distant, San Miniato al Monte

---

* These houses will probably be soon demolished in order to widen the bridge, and the chapel will be transferred to one of the adjoining houses of the Alberti.

and San Françesco, bounded by the ranges of mountains and forests of pine and beech of Vallombrosa.

The street leading from the Ponte alle Grazie to the Piazza di Sta. Croce was formerly composed of the palaces, towers, and loggie of the Alberti family, who were regarded with especial favour by Cosimo de' Medici and his descendants; the most celebrated was the author Leon Battista, who was also an artist, and constructed the fountain of Trevi at Rome for Pope Nicolas V. In the adjoining street, the Borgo Sta. Croce was the residence of the painter and author, Giorgio Vasari.

The Canto delle Colonnine, at the corner of the Borgo Sta. Croce, was originally part of a loggia of the Alberti; its projecting roof, resting on columns with quaint old capitals, was at one time the workshop of Nicolò Grossi, surnamed Caparra (pledge), so called by Lorenzo de' Medici because he refused to undertake any commission without receiving a part of the payment in advance. His delicately-wrought iron *fanali*, which adorn the external corners of some of the Florentine palaces, are among the finest works of the kind in existence. Near this spot was the Porta dei Buoi, in the second circuit of walls, called thus from the cattle market which was held here.

Opposite this loggia is the former church of San Jacopo tra Fossi, which stood between the ditches of the city walls, but which has long ceased to be used for sacred purposes. It was built on part of the site of the Roman Amphitheatre, which extended from San Jacopo to San Firenze. San Jacopo had three Gothic naves, and the principal entrance was in the alley leading from the Piazza dei Peruzzi to the Canto dei Soldani. In 1170 the church was bestowed on the Vallombrosian monks of San Salvi, whose monastery was outside Florence; but in 1531 they were deprived of San Jacopo, which was transferred to the Augustinians, as a reward for their adherence to the Medici.

Between the Palazzo Vecchio and the Piazza de Sta. Croce are houses belonging to the family of the Peruzzi. They were built on the site of the Roman Amphitheatre, whose circular form is retained in the piazetta, where shields bearing six pendant pears mark the former residences of the Peruzzi. In this amphitheatre, San Miniato, to whom the Lombards dedicated not less than thirty churches, was twice exposed to wild beasts in the reign of the Emperor Decius. The Via delle Burelle, or dungeons, immediately behind San Firenze, was so named from the dens of wild beasts which were kept here for the games of the circus; and as the dens were not destroyed till many centuries later, they were occasionally hired by the Signory from the Peruzzi and other families to whom they belonged, and used as State prisons, when there was an excess of prisoners. After the battle of Campaldino, in which Dante took part, seven hundred and forty human beings were thus immured. Yet, dreadful as this may sound, these caverns could not exceed in horror the prisons of the same, and even a later period, of the Tower of London, and of other European countries, where torture and cruel executions were as common as in Florence.

At the corner of the Via de' Cocchi, near the Via Anguillara and of the Piazza di Sta. Croce, was the Porta delle Pere, alluded to by Dante in the sixteenth canto of his "Paradiso:" the remains of a hinge on one side of the Palazzo Cocchi marks its exact position. Part of the quarter of the Peruzzi bears the name of Borgo de' Greci, and is supposed to have been so called when the Byzantine Emperor and his brother, the Patriarch of the Greek Church, were lodged here in 1436; in which year Pope Eugenius IV. held a Council at Florence in the hope of reconciling the differences between the Greek and Latin Churches; which Council is commemorated on a marble tablet in the choir of the cathedral. The Emperor and Patriarch were met by the Signory at the Porta San Gallo, and conducted hither with great pomp and ceremony. This supposed origin of the name Borgo de' Greci has, however, been disputed, as the street is said to have once been inhabited by a family of the name of Greci.

The Piazza di Sta. Croce was formerly the theatre for all public games, probably derived from old Roman days, when the games of the circus were exhibited in this neighbourhood. Here in the fifteenth century a famous tournament was held, which has been immortalised by Politian in a poem in honour of the feats performed by Lorenzo and Giuliano de' Medici. But the Piazza di Sta. Croce was especially used for the national game of *calcio*, or football, thus described by an author of the seventeenth century: " The games of the Florentine youth in spring are the *palla* and the *pome*—throwing the ball and wrestling; in summer, swimming; in autumn, the chase; and in winter, the calcio—football. The calcio is supposed to have been an ancient Roman game, since a Greek author, Julius Pollux, in a book written A.D. 177, and dedicated to the Emperor Commodus, describes it precisely as it has since been played in Florence. Though the name calcio—a kick—may lead to the inference that the game was played with the foot, the great force with which the ball had to be hurled obliged the player to use his hand. The number of players was fifty-four, young and active men, between the ages of eighteen and forty-five, as both strength and agility were required. All the ladies and gentlemen of Florence, as well as the populace, assembled to witness these games. The players adopted a costume which, whilst graceful, allowed the free use of their limbs. The season for the calcio was from January to March, both because the temperature was cool, and because it was the time of Carnival. When the two parties into which the fifty-four players were divided were ready for the onset, the Tuscan trumpets sounded; the balls were made of leather, and filled with air."*

This game was of sufficient importance to be noticed in various works of prose and poetry. During the siege of 1529, the Florentines, in order to defy the enemy, held the calcio here as usual, and even placed the trumpeters on the roof of Sta. Croce, exposed to the hostile missiles. Luckily for them, the unskilled gunners of those days vainly sent their shot in this direction from the Giramonte, or circle of hills beginning with the Poggio Imperiale, where the Prince of Orange had his camp. The last game of calcio was played in the Piazza di Sta. Croce in 1739.

The piazza was not always the scene of amusements. Here, in 1250, the first Parliament or meeting of the people was held; and here, in 1342, Walter de Brienne, Duke of Athens, when sheltered by the monks of Sta. Croce, convened a meeting of the populace to rouse the poor against the rich. The Priors of the Republic took alarm, and

---

* See "Discorso sopra il Giuoco di Calcio—Memoria del Calcio." Fiorentino, 1688.

offered De Brienne greater power and privileges on condition of his swearing not to infringe their liberties, and to hold the proposed meeting in the Piazza della Signoria, under the supervision of the Government; and Walter de Brienne accordingly rode forth, leaving his retreat among the friars, and with a hundred and twenty armed followers at his back, he started for the Palazzo Vecchio, there to commence his reign of terror.

The last great public spectacle in the piazza was held at the centenary of Dante's birth, 1864, when the statue of the poet, by the sculptor Pazzi, was unveiled in the presence of the King of Italy and of the assembled Florentine people. Deputations from all parts of the Peninsula, carrying banners, paraded the piazza—the Lion of Venice and the Wolf of Rome draped in mourning, because then forming no recognised part of the Italian kingdom, and none could then anticipate that in less than six years their deliverance would be accomplished.

The fountain in the piazza derives its waters from a source near Arcetri, and is carried to Sta. Croce across the Ponte alle Grazie. Around the piazza are palaces which once belonged to distinguished families—the Barberini, one of whom, Maffeo, was elected Pope in 1623, under the name of Urban VIII. He was the persecutor of his countryman Galileo, and was guilty of nepotism to as great an extent as any who ever occupied the pontifical chair. The Seristori Palace was built after a design by Baccio d'Agnolo, for one of the Cocchi family. The ground-floor has three arches, resting on little rustic columns; the upper storeys are adorned with columns of the Doric order. The Palazzo Stufa, once Antellesi, when it belonged to the Antella family, was designed by Giulio Parigi, and is covered with frescos, which were all executed in one month. Among the artists employed were Domenico Passignano, Matteo Rosselli, and Giovanni di San Giovanni. Their work is almost effaced, which may partly be attributed to the hasty execution. Traces may be discovered of three children supporting the shield of the Antella family over the door, which was painted by Giovanni di San Giovanni; an amorino with a swan, by the same artist, has been greatly admired, as well as an old man in the centre of the lowest tier of paintings, who is supposed to represent the father of Nicolò da Antella, the first owner of this palace. Within, are paintings by Pocetti; and in the garden behind, a statue by Giovanni Bologna. A marble disk outside, below the third window, counting from the Church of Sta. Croce, marked one of the extremities of the line which divided the parties engaged in the game of calcio. In an apartment beneath the roof of this palace, once in close proximity to the Inquisition which held its sittings in the Monastery of Sta. Croce, is now a Protestant school, established on the principles of the British and Foreign Schools of England, admitting the children of members of all persuasions.

South of the Church of Sta. Croce, and parallel with the river, is the Corso dei Tintori—the quarter of the dyers, who held horse-races here on the anniversary of Saint Onophrius. Young lads ambitious of being admitted into the guild were made to ride the horses, as a first step towards initiation. In the Borgo dei Tintori, beside the garden of the friars of Sta. Croce, at one time lived a painter, Il Rosso, a disciple of Michael Angelo. Vasari relates that Il Rosso possessed an ape, which became a great favourite with one

of his apprentices, called Battistino, who employed the
animal to steal the friars' grapes, by letting him down by a
rope into the garden, and drawing him up again with his
paws full of fruit. A friar who missed the grapes set a trap
for rats, but one day catching the ape in the fact, he took up
a stick to thrash him; a struggle ensued, in which the ape
had the best of it, and contrived to escape; the friar, however, summoned Il Rosso to appear before the judges, and
his favourite was condemned to have a weight fastened to
his tail. A few days afterwards an opportunity occurred for
revenge: the friar was performing mass in the church, when
the ape was made to climb the roof of his cell, and, in the
words of Vasari, he "performed so lively a dance with the
weight at his tail, that there was not a tile nor vase left
unbroken, and on the friar's return a torrent of lamentations
was heard, which lasted three days."

CHRONOLOGY.

	A.D.
Alberti, Leon Battista	1475—1520
Amphitheatre, Roman, excavated	1772
Baccio d'Agnolo	1462—1560
Beccheria, Abbot of Vallombrosa, executed	1258
Calcio, Game of, played last	1739
Cosimo II.	1609—1620
Council of Florence—Eugenius IV.	1436
Gondi, Palazzo, built	1501
Grano, Loggia del, built	1619
Grazie, Ponte alle, built	1235
,, ,, two arches diminished	1346
,, Chapel of the, founded	1372
Il Rosso	1496—1541
Mengini, Benedetto	1646—1704

WALKS IN FLORENCE.

	A.D.
Parliament of the people in Sta. Croce	1250
Passignano, Domenico	1560—1638
Retz, Cardinal de	1614—1679
Rosselli, Matteo	1578—1650
San Firenze ceded to the Fathers of the Oratory	1640
,, rebuilt	1646
,, façade built	1732
San Gallo, Giuliano di	1485—1547
San Giovanni, Giovanni di	1590—1638
Urban VIII., Pope	1623

CHAPTER II.

STA. CROCE.

Architecture.

WHEN St. Francis visited Florence in the year 1211, he found several brethren of his newly established Order, who had already formed themselves into a community beyond the Porta San Gallo. Their numbers rapidly increased; and when, in 1288, the family of Altafronte bestowed on them a tract of marshy land, with a hospital upon it, near the Arno, they removed thither, and built a small chapel, which they dedicated to St. Anthony. This chapel, consisting of one simple cross-vaulting, may still be seen beneath the choir of the Church of Sta. Croce. That same year, 1288, Pope Gregory IX., who had canonized his old friend Francis of Assisi, took this little community of Franciscans under his special protection.

The Church of Sta. Croce was commenced by the friars nine years later, on the Day of the Holy Cross—the 15th May, 1297—when the foundation stone was laid, and Arnolfo di Lapo was employed to make the design. As Arnolfo, who had at the same time been commissioned to undertake Sta. Maria del Fiore, laid the foundation stone of the Florentine Cathedral the following year, 1298, these two sacred edifices rose simultaneously.

Unfortunately for the early history of Sta. Croce, the archives of the monastery were nearly all destroyed by the floods from the Arno, which took place in 1333 * and in 1557; but the scanty records which remain inform us that in the year of the foundation, Cardinal Matteo d'Acquasparta, general of the Franciscan Order, proclaimed an indulgence to whoever should contribute money for the pious work.† We also learn that in 1320 the church, though still unfinished, was opened for public worship; that in 1334 Giotto was chosen master of the works; and that in 1371 a Board of six citizens was appointed by the Signory of Florence to superintend the building both of the Church of Sta. Croce and of the Cathedral. Political disturbances caused some delay, and the friars were obliged to resort to fresh devices to raise a fund for the continuation of their church: they were assisted by two of the guilds, or *arti*— the Mercatanti (merchants), and the Calimala (dealers in foreign wool), who undertook to collect the required sum.

The exterior of Sta. Croce has little left of the original construction. On the northern side is a porch, under which are some curious early monuments; the front, however, continued a wall of rough masonry. In the fifteenth century one of the Quaratesi family offered to defray the expenses of a handsome façade, but appended the condition that the arms of his family should be introduced among the ornaments; to this, however, neither the friars nor the Board

---

* This flood is recorded in a Latin inscription on a tablet on the Ponte Vecchio.

† Cardinal Matteo d'Acquasparta is mentioned by Dante in his "Paradiso," as having relaxed some of the severities of the Franciscan Order.—*Paradiso*, canto xii. v. 124.

would consent, and the munificent donator accordingly withdrew his gift of 100,000 golden florins, and assigned the money for the construction of another Franciscan Church, near San Miniato al Monte, which he dedicated to the Saviour, San Salvador.*

A layer of green and white marble, at the base of the façade, is all that remains on Sta. Croce to commemorate Quaratesi's generous intention. In 1834 Lorenzo Bartolini, the celebrated Tuscan sculptor, urged upon the Government the completion of the exterior of this noble church in a manner worthy of the interior; but want of funds again prevented the undertaking. Preparations were, however, made for a future façade, by the removal of a block of masonry in front of the church, popularly called the "Massa di Sta. Croce." This Massa was the remains of a campanile, commenced after a design by Françesco di Giuliano di San Gallo, in 1549, at the north-western angle of the edifice, and which was the second attempt, and failure, to erect a belfry for the church, after the first had been destroyed by a great storm in 1512. The Massa di Sta. Croce was left untouched for nearly two centuries, an ugly projection on the wall, frequently used as a hiding place for thieves. The present campanile, at the eastern extremity of the church, was built in 1842.

After the removal of the Massa di Sta. Croce, the design of the sculptor Nicola Matas was chosen for the new façade;

---

* This church is known as Michael Angelo's Bella Villanella, from its simplicity and beautiful proportions. The design was by Cronaca; but as he was only eleven years of age when Quaratesi died—1466— San Salvador was not built until many years after the death of the founder.

the expense was reckoned at 25,000 scudi (£5,600), a sum impossible to have been raised, had not an English gentleman who had long resided in Florence, the late Commendatore Sloane,* offered to advance as a loan 3,000 scudi (£700), and thus enabled the Government to begin the work. On the 21st August, 1857, the foundation stone was laid with great solemnity by Pope Pius IX., in the presence of the Grand-Duke Leopold II. and his family, and of an immense concourse of spectators. That same day the Commendatore Sloane converted his loan into a gift, and subsequently added to the sum, until, on the completion of the façade, his contribution alone became upwards of twelve thousand pounds sterling.

Matas raised upon Quaratesi's base of green and white marble, a facing in the same style of the old Florentine *igheronata*, which when mellowed by time will have a more agreeable effect than it has now. Over the three doors Matas has introduced pointed arches and canopies, crowning the whole with pinnacles of white marble. The statues and bas-reliefs were added by Giovanni Dupré of Sienna, Aristodemo Costoli, Françesco Giovanozzi, Luigi Fabbrucci, and Pietro Giusti. The relief above the central door is by Giovanni Dupré; it represents the Exaltation of the Cross, whilst above it, by the same artist, is a most beautiful statue of the Madonna. The rose window is left free, and the monogram of our Saviour in yellow on a blue ground is placed above the Madonna. Two angels in bronze support the cross at the apex of the central pinnacle. The gates are also in bronze;

---

* The Commendatore Françesco Sloane, an active and generous benefactor of Florence, died at his villa of Careggi, October, 1871.

the subject of the central gate is the Via Crucis, divided in twelve compartments from designs by Emilio Santarelli.

The façade was uncovered in the presence of Pope Pius IX. in May, 1863.

The interior of Sta. Croce is a good example of the style of Arnolfo di Lapo, more remarkable for ingenuity of construction than architectural invention.* He was required to build a church large enough to contain the vast numbers who sought the confessionals of the Franciscan friars. Cold and severely simple in his decorations, Arnolfo has, however, succeeded in leaving an impression of solemn grandeur, by vast space and long lines of perspective. The form is that of the old Roman basilica; the long nave and two short transepts make the Latin Cross. The eastern extremity is divided into nine chapels, the apse being only an enlargement of the central chapel.

The length of the nave is divided by seven pointed arches resting on octagonal columns; the clerestory above is supported by brackets, between which are windows of coloured glass. The ceiling of the nave and aisles is composed of beams, which were originally coloured in soft harmonious Saracenic tints, now in the process of restoration. The height of the columns and the wide span of the arches made it unsafe to impose any great superincumbent weight; Arnolfo therefore constructed gable roofs, with stone gutters to prevent water settling and causing decay. The pavement is brick, with many marble sepulchral slabs.

The architectural proportions of Sta. Croce have been injured by the removal of a step, which, like that of Sta.

---

* See " Cicerone von Jacob Burkhardt," 1860, p. 143.

Maria Novella, raised the pavement of one-third of the nave towards the eastern extremity. This part was further divided from the body of the church by a screen, such as is found in most English cathedrals, with gates—*regge*—which term was exclusively applied to the doors shutting out the congregation from the Holy of Holies, where the priests performed the sacred ceremonies. Dante calls the gates of Purgatory, *regge*.[*] The choir belonged to the wealthy family of the Alberti, whilst the chapels within the transepts and round the choir were the property of other distinguished Florentines, who caused them to be decorated with frescos, and placed iron gratings before those containing marble monuments. These frescos were painted by Giotto, Giottino, Memmi, Lippi, Taddeo Gaddi, &c. &c. In 1512, the storm which destroyed the first campanile and broke the roof of the church, likewise damaged the choir, which was still further injured by a flood in 1557. The friars, seconded by the Board of Works, petitioned the Grand-Duke Cosimo I. to be permitted to remove the screen, and carry the choir into the apse. Their request was granted, in spite of the remonstrances of the Alberti, who were thus deprived of all their rights within the church, except that of interment in the space once occupied by the choir. The chapels which had been attached to the choir were destroyed, and thus some valuable works of art were lost; an Enthronement of the Virgin, by Ugolino of Sienna, after lying neglected for centuries in the dormitory of the monastery, was sold for a mere trifle, and found its way in fragments to the Otley Collection in England.[†]

---

[*] "Purgatorio," canto ix., v. 134.
[†] See "Crowe and Cavalcaselle," vol. ii. p. 53.

When the choir was removed, the frescos on the lateral walls of the church were ruthlessly sacrificed to make room for chapels, constructed by Giorgio Vasari along the whole length of the nave, which were bestowed on families who had been deprived of their chapels around the former screen. All that remains of these paintings are the figures of St. John the Baptist and St. Francis, by Andrea del Castagno, near the Cavalcante Chapel. The Baptist is drawn with Castagno's usual dry hard outline, and has all the appearance of starvation given with characteristic realism. It was probably painted soon after the artist's return from Rome.

For many years banners were suspended over the illustrious dead, but, by order of the Signory, they were afterwards carried into the clerestory gallery, where they hung until very recently, when they were finally removed from the church.

One of the most beautiful objects in Sta. Croce is the pulpit of white Seravezza marble, which a wealthy Florentine merchant, named Pietro Mellini, commissioned Benedetto da Majano to execute about the year 1493.* Benedetto is much commended by Vasari for the skill he displayed in attaching this pulpit to one of the columns of the nave, in which he inserted a spiral staircase. The reliefs, surrounded by an elegant framework of marble, are especially beautiful. The scenes represented in five compartments are taken from the life of St. Francis :—Pope Honorius III. confirms the rules of the Franciscan Order; St. Francis passes unscathed through a fire, in the presence of the Sultan; he

* Near the little corridor of the Uffizi Gallery is a fine bust of Pietro Mellini by Benedetto da Majano.

receives the Stigmata at La Vernia, in the Casentino; his dead body is exposed in the Church of Assisi—one of the finest of the series; and, lastly, the martyrdom of his followers in Mauritania. Small figures, seated in niches of red marble, represent Faith, Hope, Charity, Fortitude, and Justice.

Over the western door is a bronze statue of St. Louis of Toulouse, which was formerly outside the church. This saint was the son of Charles of Anjou, King of Naples, and of Maria, a Hungarian princess, and nephew of King Louis IX. of France. When only fourteen years of age he with his two brothers were delivered as hostages to the King of Aragon, and he spent several years in captivity. The cruel treatment he received in Spain appears to have quenched all that might have existed of worldly ambition in his gentle nature, and on regaining his liberty Louis renounced the throne of Naples in favour of his brother Robert, and assumed the Franciscan habit. Two years later he was made Bishop of Toulouse by Boniface VIII., and died at the age of twenty-four. He was canonized by Pope John XXII. in 1317.* This statue is the last executed by Donatello, who did not value his own work greatly, and it is certainly one of his most inferior productions. He has represented St. Louis in the same attitude as he is painted by Taddeo Gaddi on one of the pilasters of the Capella Rinuccini, in the sacristy of this church. When Donatello was reproached for having made so indifferent a statue, he replied it was good enough for a man who had been so dull as to exchange a kingdom for a monastery.†

---

* See life of this saint in Mrs. Jameson's "Monastic Orders."
† See Vasari, "Vite dei Pittori—Donatello."

The rose window above has a Deposition in coloured glass, after a design by Lorenzo Ghiberti, and over this is a stone tablet containing the monogram of our Saviour, by San Bernardino, which was formerly outside the church. San Bernardino was born in 1380 of a noble Siennese family, and assumed the Franciscan habit at twenty-five years of age; it is related of him, that when preaching to the people he held a tablet before him on which the monogram of Christ was inscribed within a circle of golden rays. A man who earned his livelihood by the manufacture of cards and dice was reduced to sore distress by the reformation of manners produced under the influence of San Bernardino, who accordingly suggested, as a compensation, that he should manufacture tablets similar to that he had invented, and sell them to the people. The man took his advice and prospered. The original tablet was, by permission of the Signory, placed on the façade of Sta. Croce, with great ceremony, by San Bernardino, in 1437. Around it he caused to be inscribed in Lombard characters the following words:—"In nomine Jesu omne genu flectatur cælestum, terrestrium et inferorum."

CHRONOLOGY.

	A.D.
Arno overflowed	1333
,, ,, again	1557
Benedetto da Majano	1442—1497
Bernardino, St., born	1388
Church of Sta. Croce commenced	1297
,, ,, opened for public worship	1320

		A.D.
Church of Sta. Croce, choir destroyed		1557
,, ,, façade finished		1863
,, ,, Giotto, Master of the Works		1371
Francis, St., came to Florence		1211
Ghiberti, Lorenzo		1378—1455
John XXII., Pope		1316—1334
Louis, St., of France, died		1297

CHAPTER III.

STA. CROCE.

Monuments.

STA. CROCE has always been a favourite place of interment, but for many past years it has been reserved for the illustrious dead—the Westminster Abbey of Florence. The gates at the western extremity are surrounded by monumental slabs, most of which bear the names of remarkable men, belonging to the present and the last century. Two are dedicated to the Targioni Tozzetti, father and son, the elder of whom published his "Travels in Tuscany," "Viaggi in Toscana," with an account of the physical condition and natural history of his native province: the younger is well known as an eminent botanist and horticulturist. To the left of the entrance is a portrait in relief of the numismatician, Domenico Sestini, born in Florence in 1730, who travelled in the East, and made a collection of coins. He was afterwards appointed Royal Librarian by Princess Elisa Buonaparte, Queen of Etruria; and on the restoration of the Grand-Duke Ferdinand III., he was confirmed in this office. He died in 1835.

A small slab, higher on the wall, has the effigy of Daniel Manin, the Venetian patriot. By birth a Venetian Jew, whose family had become Christian, he received at baptism the name of their patrons, the Manins. Young Daniel early imbibed a hatred for Napoleon, to whose ambition Venice had been sacrificed at the Peace of Campoformio, when the last Doge, Manin, had been forced to abdicate. As he had been educated for the bar, he was well able to appreciate the evasions of the spirit, as well as of the letter of the law, and the unjust practices of the Austrian rulers, so intolerable to the educated classes of Italy. In 1847 he was arrested for having protested against the illegal acts of the Government. He was liberated by the people during the Revolution of February, 1848, and borne in triumph round the Piazza di San Marco. He then learnt that a constitutional government had been proclaimed at Vienna, and that he himself was chosen to lead the revolutionary movement in Venice. After the expulsion of the Austrians, he was elected President of the Republic. His courage, honesty, and zeal, united with moderation, as well as his great talents, enabled him to retain his influence over his fellow-citizens during the long siege. When Venice fell, Manin retired to Paris, where he died at the age of fifty-three, ten years before the liberation of his country from a foreign yoke had been accomplished. His remains were carried to Venice in 1870.

The first chapel to the right of the entrance belongs to the Buonarotti family. Here repose the remains of Michael Angelo, who died in Rome in 1564, in the ninetieth year of his age. Pope Pius IV. endeavoured to retain his body, but the Florentines had it secretly conveyed to his native city. The night after its arrival, it was borne to Sta. Croce by the members of the Florentine Academy, and his catafalque was displayed for several days to crowds of visitors. A funeral service in his honour was performed at San Lorenzo. The monument to Michael Angelo is from a design by Giorgio Vasari, and his bust was considered an excellent likeness. Allegorical figures of architecture, sculpture, and painting are represented, lamenting the loss of the great artist.

On the column facing this monument, above the vase for holy water, is an oval, or *mandorla*, within which is a marble relief of the Madonna and Child surrounded by cherubim, by Antonio Rosselino, erected to the Nori family. Beneath this spot lie the remains of Françesco Nori, Prior of the Republic, who fell in the Pazzi conspiracy, 1478, a victim to his attachment to the Medici, as he threw himself between Lorenzo and the assassin, and received the blow intended for Lorenzo. Leo X. granted an Indulgence to all who should pray for the soul of Françesco Nori.

The huge pile of marble erected to the memory of Dante Alighieri in 1829, was the work of Stefano Ricci, a tardy act of acknowledgment by Florence of her greatest poet, who died 1321.

The monument to Vittorio Alfieri was placed here by his widow, the Duchess of Albany. It is a good example of Canova's treatment of monumental sculpture. A graceful figure of a matron leaning on the tomb in a sorrowful attitude, is intended to represent the genius of Florence. Alfieri was born at Asti, in Piedmont, in 1749, of a noble family. He spent his early life in dissipation and in rapid journeys, visiting nearly all the countries of Europe: it was only after he had passed his twenty-fifth year that he attempted to write poetry, applying himself diligently to the study of

Italian and Latin; and in the course of fourteen years he produced as many tragedies. After his forty-eighth year he began Greek. He died in Florence, at the age of fifty-four, in 1803. A sincere patriot, and in his youth an ardent liberal, his aristocratic prejudices received too severe a shock by the violent democratic outbreak of the French Revolution, not to recoil in an opposite direction. His poetry constitutes an era in Italian literature, because he was one of the first to give expression to modern patriotic sentiments; but this evaporated in mere abstract denunciations of tyranny, and in aspirations after liberty, such as he supposed existed in ancient Greece and Rome.* Ugo Foscolo, in his poem, "I Sepolcri," supposes Alfieri meditating in this church:—

> "E a questi marmi
> Venne spesso Vittorio ad ispirarsi.
> Irato a' patrii numi, errava muto
> Ove Arno è più deserto, I campi e il cielo
> Desioso mirando; e poi che nullo
> Vivente aspetto gli molcea la cura
> Qui posava l' austero, e avea sul volto
> Il pallor della morte e la speranza.
> Con questi grandi abita Eterno, e l' ossa
> Fremono amor di patria."†

Near the tomb of Alfieri, and in front of the monument to Dante, the bones of the patriot and poet, Ugo Foscolo,

---

* See "I Poeti Italiani Moderni," with English Notes and Biographical Notices, by Louisa A. Merivale, pp. 1—3.

†   "And to these marbles
    Vittorio often came to be inspired;
    Irate with all his country's gods, he wandered mute
    Where most deserted is the Arno,
    With longing eyes beholding land and sky; and

brought from Chelsea in 1871, are laid temporarily, until some fitting monument shall be erected in his honour. Foscolo was an Ionian, of Venetian parentage. When a professor at Pavia, in 1808, he offended the Austrian government by his liberal and patriotic sentiments, and had to leave Italy for England, where he occupied himself in the study of Dante until his death in 1827.

Between the fourth and fifth chapels is the tomb of Macchiavelli. The great Florentine historian's last resting-place was without a monument until 1707, when Lord Cowper raised a subscription for this medallion. Nicolò Macchiavelli was born in Florence in 1467. He was appointed Secretary of the Republic, and was sent on embassies to the Courts of France, Germany, and Rome, and to Cesare Borgia, the son of Pope Alexander VI., of whom Macchiavelli gives a lively description in his correspondence with the Florentine Signory. His most important works are his "Istorie Fiorentine," "Discorsi sopra Tito Livio," and the "Principe." In his satire on the ambition of princes, contained in this last work, Macchiavelli maintained that a man who craves for power must not be troubled with conscientious and humane scruples, but must consent to be shamelessly selfish. Ugo Foscolo, in the "Sepolcri," alludes to Macchiavelli in these words:—

"Quando il monumento
Vidi ove posa il corpo di quel Grande

When no living sigh could soothe his care,
Here the austere man rested, and on his face was seen
The palour of death and hope.
With these great spirits he dwelt in the Eternal,
For with the love of country chafed their bones."

Che, temprando lo scettro a' regnatori,'
Gli allor ne sfronda, ed alle gente svela
Di che lagrime grondi e di che sangue," &c.

Beyond the fifth chapel is a portrait of the celebrated writer on Italian art, the Abate Luigi Lanzi, placed here by public subscription. Lanzi was born near Macerata in 1732, and belonged to the Order of Jesuits. He was appointed Conservator of Arts in Florence, and founded the collection of Etruscan antiquities. He died in 1810. The sixth chapel belongs to the old Florentine family of the Cavalcante. The monument is that of Benedetto Cavalcante, a friar of Sta. Croce; and the fresco, by Andrea del Castagno, is the last remnant of the paintings on the lateral walls of the church. Beside it is a group, in *macigno*—freestone—of the Annunciation, by Donatello, executed in 1411. Over it are four angels, carved in wood, holding back a curtain. Vasari bestows great commendation on this monument, and informs us that it was the first of Donatello's works which attracted public notice, and was the commencement of his fame. He especially mentions the figure of the Virgin, who, startled by the sudden apparition, bends timidly forward, her countenance bespeaking gratitude and humility: he also alludes to the draperies, and the lines of form in which Donatello endeavoured to emulate the antique.

Over the lateral door, next this group, is a lunette, con-

---

* "When I beheld
Where rests the body of that great man
Who, humbling the pride of rulers,
Strips of their leaves their laurels, and reveals
The tears and blood which drop from them," &c.

taining a fresco representing St. Francis and St. Dominick embracing. Above, is the organ.

Just beyond is a handsome monument in memory of Leonardo Bruni, surnamed Aretino from his birthplace in Arezzo. He was an exponent of the Aristotelian philosophy, as well as eminent jurist of the fifteenth century. After having filled the office of Apostolic Secretary to four Popes in succession, he became Chancellor of the Florentine Republic, and at his death, in 1444, his funeral expenses were defrayed by the Commonwealth; his monument by Bernardo Gambarelli, or Il Rossellino, is one of the finest in Sta. Croce. Leonardo is represented in a recumbent posture; angels hold a scroll. The eagle and the canopy are very beautifully composed. A lunette above contains a relief of the Virgin and Child, by Andrea Verocchio.*

Next the monument of Leonardo Aretino, is the bust of the eminent botanist, Pietro Antonio Micheli, who was born in Florence in 1679. He travelled throughout Italy for scientific objects, and published several works, the most important of which relates to "Cryptogamic Plants and Fungi." He died in 1737.

The last monument on this side of the Church is that of the natural philosopher, Leopoldo Nobili, born in 1784, and died in 1833. Nobili served as a soldier in Napoleon's Russian campaign, where he was taken prisoner by the Cossacks after the burning of Moscow. On his release and return to Italy, he devoted himself to scientific pursuits. He directed his principal attention to the study of magnetism,

---

* See engraving of this monument in Cicognara's "Storia della Scultura," tom. ii. tav. xxv.

and he threw fresh light on the discoveries of Volta, Oersted, and Ampère. Nobili was banished for political reasons in 1831, and found a refuge in France, from whence he returned to Florence in 1832.

The large monument in the south transept, lately erected to the memory of Don Neri Corsini, Marchese Laiatico, is by Fantacchiotti. The Marchese Laiatico took an active and honourable part during the political difficulties of 1848. Though an ardent liberal, he was personally attached to the late grand-duke, and desired to retain him on the throne of Tuscany; but Leopold II. relied more on Austrian soldiers than on the wise counsels of his best Italian friends. Don Neri Corsini was at one time Governor of Leghorn, where he made himself universally beloved; but when sent on a mission to the Court of St. James's, he was seized with small-pox, and died prematurely in 1859. A female, representing Florence, is pointing to a tablet on which Fame as a winged genius is inscribing the good deeds of the deceased.

On a bronze plate in the wall, near this monument, is an inscription by Bocaccio in memory of Françesco Barberini, an eminent jurist and poet, who died in the year 1300. He is chiefly known as the author of "A Discourse on Love."

In front of the last central columns of the nave, are modern monuments to two of the Alberti family, who had their burial vaults beneath this part of the church, the site of the ancient choir. That on the southern side, by the sculptor Santarelli, is to the senator Giovanni Vincenzio Alberti, who left a son, Leon Battista, the last of the family, by whom the Alberti became extinct, in 1836. The monument opposite, by Bartolini, is to commemorate the most distinguished man in the family, another Leon Battista, called the modern Vitruvius, who was born in 1398; he was eminent as a mathematician, natural philosopher, elegant writer, and orator. He published works on mechanics, painting, perspective, architecture, hydraulics, &c.

In the northern transept is a monument, by Fantacchiotti, to the celebrated musical composer Cherubini, born in Florence, 1760, where a mass composed by him at the age of thirteen was first performed. He spent most of his life in Paris, where he was appointed head of the Conservatoire de Musique, and where he died in 1842. He composed forty-two operas, and twenty-nine pieces of church music. In a recess is the monument to the Polish Countess Zamoyska, of the family Czartoryska, by the celebrated modern Tuscan sculptor Bartolini—one of his best works. She is seated almost upright on her bed, painfully emaciated, and with all the appearance of approaching death. The execution is admirable, but the representation of disease and dissolution is as unpleasing as it is inappropriate in a record of the life and immortality of the soul.

Returning to the nave, the first monument in the north aisle was erected to the celebrated engraver Raffaelle Morghen, by his pupils and friends, in 1854. Morghen was a Neapolitan, born in 1761, and he learned his art from his father, when engaged in taking engravings of the paintings discovered in Herculaneum. He studied under Volpato at Rome, and was afterwards appointed Professor of Engraving at Florence, by the Grand-Duke Ferdinand III. He died in 1833.

Near the monument to Morghen is that to Antonio Cocchi, who was remarkable as a physician, philologist, and antiquarian. He was also a Neapolitan, born in 1695, but educated at Pisa. He visited England, and became acquainted with Newton, Clarke, and other remarkable men. He died in Florence in 1758.

The monument to Vincenzio Filicaia follows. Filicaia was one of the best Italian lyric poets, and was born in Florence in 1642. He is best known to the English reader by his celebrated sonnet to his country:—

> "Italia, Italia! o tu, cui feo la Sorte
> Dono infelice di bellezza onde ai
> Funesta dote d' infiniti guai,
> Che in fronte scritti per gran doglia porta;
>
> "Deh! fossi tu men bella, o almen più forte,
> Onde assai più ti paventasse, o assai
> T' amasse men chi del tuo bello ai rai
> Par che si strugga, e pur ti sfida a morta!
>
> "Che or già dall' Alpi non vedrei torrenti
> Scender d' armati, nè di sangue tinta
> Bever l' onda del Po gallici armenti;
>
> "Ne te vedrei del non tuo ferro cinta
> Pugnar col braccio di straniere genti
> Per servir sempre, o vincitrice o vinta." *

---

* "Italy, Italy! thou on whom Fate
  The hapless gift of beauty has bestowed
  A fatal dowry of unceasing woes!
  Thou bearest suffering written on thy brow.

"Ah! hadst thou been less lovely or more strong,
  Or had they feared thee more or loved thee less
  Who, basking in thy beauty's rays, seem
  To dissolve, yet to a mortal combat challenge thee,

"Thou wouldst not then see pouring from the Alps
  Torrents of armed men, nor Gallic hordes
  Drink of the blood-stained waters of the Po;

"Nor wouldst thou see thy sons girt with a sword
  And use their arm to help a stranger's cause—
  Conquering or conquered—ever still to serve."

The next monument is to Carlo Marzuppini, also known as Carlo Aretino from his birth-place. On the pavement below is the monumental slab to Carlo's father, who was secretary to Charles VI. of France. Marzuppini was born in 1399, and was educated by learned Greeks. He was appointed secretary to Pope Eugenius IV., and afterwards Secretary to the Florentine Republic; he died in 1455, when he was honoured by a public funeral. This monument is the best example of the delicate and captivating style of work of Desiderio da Settignano, and is considered one of the three finest tombs of Tuscany. Marzuppini is represented lying on a sarcophagus with a book upon his breast. Genii at either end hold shields, and it is adorned with sphynxes, festoons, and various ornamental devices. The recess is crowned by a vase with a flame, and two graceful angels support garlands which hang down the sides of the arch. The lunette contains a representation of the Madonna and Child adored by Angels, in high relief. Although the whole surface is covered with elaborate ornament, yet, owing to the exquisite delicacy of the sculpture, the effect is extremely rich, without being overloaded.*

Count Vittorio Fossombroni, whose monument adjoins that to Marzuppini, was minister to the Grand-Dukes Pietro Leopoldo and Ferdinand III., and was distinguished for his efforts to improve the agriculture of Tuscany by drainage and irrigation. He died, at the age of ninety, in 1844.

The antiquarian and historian Giovanni Lami's monument follows. He was born in 1697, near Florence, and

---

* See " Tuscan Sculptors," Perkins.

became Professor of Ecclesiastical History; he was a man of vast learning, conversant with Latin, Greek, Hebrew, German, Spanish, and French, and he published several works against the Jesuits.

The last monument deserving notice is that of Galileo Galilei: born in 1564, immediately after the death of Michael Angelo, he died in 1642. He studied medicine when a boy, at Pisa, where the oscillations of a lamp in the cathedral awoke those reflections which led to his discovery of the pendulum; and at twenty-four years of age he was already far advanced in physical science, of which he became professor at Pisa in 1589. In 1592 he removed to Padua, where he held the chair of physics for many years, and invented the thermometer and telescope, for which the Venetian Republic granted him public honours. In 1612 he invented the microscope. But he had aroused the fears of the Jesuits and Roman inquisitors, and therefore was summoned to appear before their tribunal, who obliged him to abjure his so-called errors contained in his "Dialogo sui Due Grandi Sistemi del Mondo," and to take an oath never again to speak nor write on the movement of the earth. As he rose from his knees, he whispered to those near him, "E pur si muove,"—"nevertheless it moves." He was condemned to the prisons of the Inquisition, but his sentence was commuted by the Pope to a residence within the gardens of the SS. Trinità di Monte; he was at length allowed to return to Tuscany, and took up his abode in the neighbourhood of Florence. His latter days were saddened by domestic afflictions, and by the loss of sight. He died in 1642, at Arcetri, where our poet Milton visited him. It was many years later that his body was removed to

Sta. Croce. The forefinger and thumb were then cut off by a certain Giovanni Vincenzio, Marchese Capponi, who expressed a desire to possess the instruments with which Galileo had written his great works; on which Giovanni Targioni Tozzetti observed, touching the forehead of the corpse, "he would rather possess that contained within the head." Another finger was removed by the antiquarian Gori, which is now preserved in the Tribune, dedicated to Galileo, in the Museum of Natural History.

The pavement of Sta. Croce has many monumental slabs. The first disciples of St. Francis were buried near the centre, and their bronze effigies may still be traced, though worn by time and the footsteps of successive generations. One, richly ornamented with decorations by Ghiberti, was placed here in honour of Françesco Sansoni, of a Siennese family, though he himself was from Brescia; he was General of the Order of Minor Friars, and much esteemed by Pope Sixtus IV., to whom he offered fifty thousand of the brethren to fight in a crusade to the Holy Land. In the centre of the nave the English traveller may be interested to find the burial-place of John Ketterick, Bishop of Exeter, who died in Florence in 1419, when on a mission from Henry V. of England to Pope Martin V., then on his return to Rome from the Council of Constance. One of the oldest monumental slabs is in remembrance of Biordi degli Ubertini, 1358, a valiant defender of the Florentine Republic against the attacks of Fra Moreali, Count of Lando, and his Free Companies; another bears the name of Giovanni d' Aste, a follower of Sir John Hawkwood, who fought against Gian Galeazzo Visconti, 1392.

Giovan Françesco Megalotti, one of the Otto della

Balia, or Government of Florence, who died in 1377, has
"Libertas" inscribed on his slab: he distinguished himself
by his gallant defence of his native city against the Papal
troops. Another slab is to Lodovico degli Obizzi, who
died fighting against Milan, 1424.

Lorenzo Ghiberti is also said to have been laid in Sta.
Croce, though the exact spot is unknown. The historians
Villani are likewise buried here. Beyond the lateral door of
the northern aisle, beneath the outer porch, are two old
monuments—one to Françesco Pazzi, attributed to Nino,
son of Andrea Pisano; the other to Alamanni dei Car-
raccioli, who died 1337. In the cloister beyond the southern
aisle is a monument which was brought here from the
interior of the church, when the central choir was destroyed.
It was erected to Gastone della Torre da Milano, Bishop of
Aquileia, and is a fine monument in the old Tuscan style,
attributed to Agostino da Sienna. Gastone was the son of
Corrado della Torre, Lord of Milan, and in 1308 he was
created archbishop of that city by Pope Clement V. His
family was unfortunate; he himself suffered imprisonment, and was then sent into exile. In 1316 he was appointed Patriarch of Aquileia by John XXII., and came to
Florence, where he died the following year from a fall from
his horse. His monument was erected by the Torreani and
Bareucci families, with whom he resided, and who had their
arms sculptured upon it in commemoration of their good
deeds. The reliefs represent the Resurrection of our Lord,
and his Appearance to the Disciples at Emmaus. The eagle
above denotes the archbishop's Guelphic sympathies.

CHRONOLOGY.

	A.D.
Alberti, Leon Battista	d. 1472
" " last of the family	d. 1836
Alfieri, Vittorio	d. 1803
Alighieri, Dante	d. 1321
Andrea Castagno	d. 1457
Barberini, Françesco	d. 1300
Buonarotti, Michael Angelo	d. 1564
Bruni, Leonardo	d. 1444
Cherubini	d. 1842
Cocchi, Antonio	d. 1758
Corsini, Don Neri	d. 1859
Filicaia, Vincenzio	d. 1701
Fossombroni, Vittorio	d. 1844
Foscolo, Ugo	d. 1827
Galilei, Galileo	d. 1642
Lami, Giovanni	d. 1770
Lanzi, Luigi	d. 1810
Macchiavelli, Nicolò	d. 1467
Manin, Daniel	d. 1851
Marzuppini, Carlo	d. 1435
Micheli, Pietro Antonio	d. 1787
Nori, Françesco, murdered in the Pazzi conspiracy	1478
Nobili Leopoldo	d. 1833
Rossellino, Il, Gambarelli	1427—1478?
Sestini, Domenico	d. 1135
Targioni Tozzetti	d. 1783

CHAPTER IV.

STA. CROCE (*Continuation*).

The Pazzi Chapel.—Inquisition.

STA. CROCE has been frequently the scene of political meetings, as well as used for the delivery of orations on morals and philosophy; and not seldom severe denunciations were thundered from its pulpit against the rivals of the Franciscans—the Dominicans of San Marco and Sta. Maria Novella.

Outside the church, to the south, are arcades, within which are old frescos representing scenes from the life of St. Francis, by scholars of Taddeo Gaddi, of no great merit, but interesting from the representation of the Cathedral of Florence and other buildings as they appeared in early days. A flight of steps leads down to the cloister, which was built by Arnolfo di Lapo, and was for many years divided in two, but which has been recently restored to its primitive condition. Beneath the arcade are monumental slabs, most of which are modern.

In the midst of the court is a large and ponderous statue, intended to represent the Eternal, by Baccio Bandinelli. It once stood in the choir of the cathedral, forming part of a group, the remainder of which was the reclining statue of the Saviour, now in the Baroncelli Chapel of Sta. Croce. The ground enclosed by this cloister is paved with the gravestones of the monks. The beautiful portico on the eastern side, supported by Corinthian columns and pilasters, leads to the Pazzi Chapel, built after a design by Filippo Brunelleschi, and one of his most beautiful compositions. The work was executed at the expense of Messer Andrea de' Pazzi, a distinguished knight of the court of Réné, King of Naples, early in the fifteenth century, and he dedicated the chapel to his patron-saint, St. Andrew. Both the portico and chapel are adorned with coloured Robbia work, in which the arms of the Pazzi family—two dolphins and four daggers—are conspicuous. These arms, surrounded by a garland of fruit, form the central ornament of the cupola of the portico. Over the entrance-door, which is in beautiful proportions, is a medallion in blue and white Robbia ware, representing our Lord bearing his Cross, and beneath it the Eternal, with Adoring Angels. The Pazzi arms are borne upwards by angels. The door-posts and window-frames are decorated with garlands of oak-leaves, carefully executed. A favourite device of Brunelleschi's, the scallop, or pilgrim shell, is probably placed here in allusion to the crusading exploits of the founder of the family, who planted the first Christian standard on the walls of Jerusalem. The interior of the chapel, from its grand and symmetrical proportions, is as strikingly beautiful as the portico, though it is to be regretted that an unpleasant effect is produced by the contrast of the dark hue of the stone, of which the pilasters and arches are constructed, with the whitewash on the walls and vaulting of the roof. The cupola over the altar is peculiar in form, divided into two compartments; the circular windows are filled in with white and yellow glass. The Twelve Apostles in medallions of white and blue Robbia ware, the Four Evangelists in the later style of greater variety of colour, and the Pazzi arms, decorate the upper portion of the walls of the chapel; a narrow frieze, composed of lambs and cherubim, also in coloured Robbia ware, is carried round the building.

With the consent of the Pazzi this beautiful chapel was used by the monks as a chapter-house, and, in 1566, above four thousand friars were assembled here to listen to the new regulations for the Inquisition in Tuscany, issued by Pope Pius V., vesting all the power in the hands of one head Inquisitor, who was to be a Franciscan; the deputation from Rome was abolished, but every process was to be referred to the Roman consistory.

The larger refectory of the convent is entered from this cloister. At the farther end is a fresco covering the entire wall, attributed to Giotto, but supposed by Cavalcaselle to be by his scholar, Taddeo Gaddi. "Beneath a vast Crucifixion and Tree of Jesse, and four sides from the life of St. Francis and St. Louis, by some unknown Giottesque, a Last Supper is depicted. In this fresco the Saviour sits behind a long table in the midst of his disciples, and St. John falls fainting on his bosom. Judas alone is seated in front of the table, and places his hand in the dish. St. Peter, from his place at the side of St. John, looks sternly at the traitor, whilst the Apostles generally are distinguished by animated movement. Amongst the episodes depicted at the sides of the Crucifixion are St. Francis receiving the Stigmata, and the Noli me tangere. The wall, so adorned, has a fine and imposing aspect, though much of the background is damaged or repainted. The grandeur of the composition in the Last Supper is, however, marred by the somewhat weighty character of the figures and the large size of the heads. The eyes are drawn in close horizontal lines, and without corners, as was usual with Taddeo Gaddi; the foreheads are low, the necks broad, the heads short and coarse. Abruptness in the passage from light to shade, abuse of red in the shadows, a bold neglectful ease of hand in the drawing and colouring of the parts, draperies more arranged than natural, gay tones of vestment, are all peculiarities of Taddeo. The Crucifixion, on the other hand, is composed of figures remarkable for exaggeration of length, and without the just proportions which Giotto always succeeded in maintaining. Some of those in the foreground are indeed very feeble. This subject, with its attendant figures in the Tree of Jesse and side frescos, is executed, however, with a certain ease of hand, and betrays an artist of the middle of the fourteenth century, confident in somewhat slender powers, and sacrificing the great principles of art to boldness and rapidity of execution."*

The central subject is the Tree of Life, whose branches as scrolls spread on all sides, and are inscribed with rhymes declaring the attributes of the Saviour. Twelve prophets are at the ends of these scrolls. The Holy Spirit descends on Christ, and the pelican feeds her young on the top of the tree. St. Francis embraces it at the foot; St. Louis is seated beside it writing; the fainting Virgin is supported by St. John. To the right and left of this centre-piece the

---

* See "Crowe and Cavalcaselle," vol. L p. 364.

Saviour appears to St. Romanus; St. Benedict is at the mouth of his cave drawing up his food, and the Devil is flinging a stone at the bell by which the saint announced his hunger; Mary Magdalene is anointing the Saviour's feet; and below all is the Last Supper.*

The smaller refectory of the convent contains a fresco by Giovanni di San Giovanni, surnamed Manozzi, a painter of moderate attainments, but whose frescos possess more merit than his easel pictures. He was born in 1590, and was a pupil of Matteo Rosselli. The subject of this fresco is a miracle supposed to have been performed by St. Francis, in imitation of our Saviour, multiplying loaves of bread during a chapter of the Order.

A severe fire in 1423 destroyed the Dormitory of the Convent and a great portion of the building, which has also suffered at various times by floods from the Arno. The Infirmary and the Foresteria, or reception room for pilgrims or other strangers, extended in the direction of the Corso dei Tintori, where there were also extensive gardens. The Friars had once a fine library, commenced in 1426 from the bequest of a butcher, Michele di Guerdicio. It was united to the Laurentian Library by a decree of Pietro Leopoldo in 1766; but some of the manuscripts were kept back, and preserved in a part of the Monastery less exposed to floods than the original building.

When Cosimo I. became Grand-Duke of Tuscany, he filled a great part of the Monastery with the Spanish soldiers who accompanied his father-in-law, the Viceroy of Naples, to assist him in the conquest of Sienna; and, deaf

---

* See Lord Lindsay's "Christian Arts," vol. II. p. 240.

to the remonstrances of the friars, the Spanish prince made use of their gardens for his stud.

That part of the convent which is nearest the piazza contained the chambers where the Inquisition held its infamous Tribunals, from 1284 to 1782, when the Holy Office was suppressed. The Gate went by the name of Il Martello—the hammer—from the knocker employed to summon the porter; over it was once a fresco, long effaced, by Lorenzo de' Bicci. The two most celebrated trials by the Inquisitors within these walls were those of Cecco d' Ascoli and Pandolfo Ricasoli. Françesco Stabili, better known as Cecco d' Ascoli from his birthplace, born in 1257, was from his youth devoted to intellectual pursuits, especially the study of astrology. He was denounced by the Court of the Inquisition in Bologna for having maligned the Roman Catholic faith; and was condemned to a public penance, and to be deprived of all his astrological books. He accordingly removed to Florence; but there his enemies pursued him, and he was again summoned to appear before the Tribunal of the Holy Office sitting in Sta. Croce, where he was sentenced as a heretic to be burnt alive, at seventy years of age. His greatest crime was the prediction of the descent of Louis of Bavaria into Italy, and of the aggrandisement of Castruccio Castracani, Lord of Lucca; his condemnation was therefore caused by Guelphic influence; even Pope John XVII. exclaimed, in the presence of his court—"The Minor Friars have persecuted and murdered the prince of peripatetic philosophy."

Pandolfo Ricasoli was a man of great learning, who was celebrated in his day as a preacher and instructor of youth. He was, however, accused of immoral conduct with Faustina

Mainardi, a woman of low condition, who kept a girl's school, to which Pandolfo Ricasoli was spiritual director. He was brought before the Tribunal of the Holy Office, held that day in the Refectory of Sta. Croce, which was turned into a court of justice.* A scaffold, hung with black, as for a corpse, was placed in the centre of the hall, and the Inquisitors were seated around. Cardinal Giovanni de' Medici, the younger princes of the blood, the priests and nobles of Florence, with other persons holding places of authority, filled the remaining space. The two prisoners, in dresses painted with flames and demons, were made to kneel at the feet of the Grand Inquisitor, whilst a monk recited the accusations against them. Ricasoli and Faustina were condemned, and sentenced to be walled up alive in one of the dungeons of the Inquisition.†

It was not until 1782, as has been already stated, that this barbarous Tribunal was suppressed, and the Inquisition banished from Florence, by the order of Pietro Leopoldo I., when that part of Sta. Croce which had been assigned to the Inquisitors was converted into an Infirmary and Foresteria.

The Convent of Sta. Croce enjoyed the privilege of keeping one of the two urns which contained the voting balls for the election of the magistrates. One of these Franciscan friars, as well as a Dominican from St. Mark's, always assisted at the ceremony of election on the Ringhiera in front of the Palazzo della Signoria, where a solemn oath was administered to the new magistrates, who swore to

---

* A picture representing this scene is in the gallery of the Marchese Gino Capponi.

† See Napier's "Florentine History," vol. v. p. 499.

"leave the government as they found it, to do justice, and hate iniquity."

Sta. Croce has more than once offered an asylum to fugitives from justice; as in 1312, when the Monastery was selected by Walter de Brienne, Duke of Athens, as a residence, until he felt secure of his despotic power in Florence.

During the famous siege of Florence, in 1529, the friars were suspected of treachery. The accusation arose from the incaution of one of the monks, Vittorio Françeschi, who was much beloved by the lower orders from his preachings and consolations, and among whom he was known by the name of Fra Rigagolo: on his return to the city from one of his apostolic missions into the country, he was led from curiosity to examine the defences and guns. The suspicions of the soldiers and their commanders having been aroused, the Monastery of Sta. Croce was searched by night, but nothing found to justify the sacrilege. The Council of War who directed the operations of defence received another accusation against the monks, through the Tamburo, or Lion's mouth of Florence, by which they were declared to have had secret communications with the Pope, and even to have received the enemy's soldiers, disguised as Franciscans, within their walls. Fra Rigagolo was said to have himself opened the city gates to them. He was arrested and imprisoned in the Bargello, and finally executed within the building. Some hundred soldiers were quartered in the Monastery, and it would have gone still harder with the monks, had not Florence fallen a prey to the Medici, who regarded the Franciscans of Sta. Croce with more favour than the Dominicans of St. Mark.

During Napoleon Buonaparte's administration of Tuscany,

Sta. Croce was not suppressed, but its property was confiscated, and the monks only allowed an annual pension and their food. In 1809 a lay board of works was appointed to superintend the repairs of the church; and the manuscripts, pictures, statues, and reliefs, with all the objects of art, were confided to a commission for the preservation of artistic monuments. In 1814 the convent was restored to the monks, and it was only finally suppressed in 1871.

CHRONOLOGY.

	A.D.
Arnolfo di Lapo	1240—1311
Baccio Bandinelli	1493—1560
Brienne, Walter de, at Sta. Croce	1312
Brunelleschi, Filippo	1379—1446
Cecco d' Ascoli	1257—1327
Convent of Sta. Croce burnt	1423
" " suppressed	1871
Cosimo I.	1537—1575
Giovanni di San Giovanni	1576—1636
Giotto	1276—1337
Inquisition in Sta. Croce	1284—1782
Pazzi Chapel, assembly of monks	1565
René, King of Naples and Sicily	1409—1480
Ricasoli, Pandolfo, immured alive	1641
Rigagoli, Fra, accused and beheaded	1529

CHAPTER V.

STA. CROCE (*Continuation*).

Frescos.

THE frescos on the walls of the interior of Sta. Croce, from which the whitewash has been lately removed, are principally at the eastern extremity of the church. On the sides of the arch leading to the apse are represented the Twelve Apostles. To the right, St. Francis is receiving the Stigmata, or marks of our Saviour's wounds, in the rocky wilderness near La Vernia; the composition is nearly identical with that in one of the small paintings in the Florentine Academy, attributed to Giotto, but more probably by Taddeo Gaddi. To the left of the apse, the Virgin is represented in the *mandorla*, or *vesica piscis*, supported by angels. These frescos, if not actually by the hand of Taddeo Gaddi, must have been painted by one of his scholars.

The frescos in the interior of the apse have never undergone the process of whitewashing, and are the undoubted work of Agnolo Gaddi, the son of Taddeo, and the pupil of Giovanni da Milano and of Jacopo da Casentino: they were executed at the expense of Jacopo degli Alberti. The subject chosen is the origin and discovery of the Cross

The tradition is as follows :—When our first father Adam lay sick, his son Seth prayed for him at the Gate of Paradise, and received a branch of the Tree of Knowledge from the Archangel Michael, bidding him plant it on Mount Lebanon, and that when it bore fruit his father would be healed. Adam was, however, dead before his son returned, and Seth planted the branch on his grave, where it took root and flourished, till the days of Solomon. The wisest of men ordered it to be cut down, and used in building the Temple; but the builders rejected it as unsuitable in size and quality, and they threw it into a marsh, where it served as a bridge. When the Queen of Sheba came to Jerusalem, and was preparing to step upon the tree, she beheld in a vision the Saviour of the world suspended on it, and in place of walking over the bridge, she fell down and worshipped. Solomon accordingly ordered the tree to be buried deep in the earth on the spot whence afterwards arose the Pool of Bethesda, whose healing powers proceeded as much from the tree below it as from the angel who descended to trouble the waters. When the time of our Saviour's Passion drew near, the tree rose and floated on the surface, and the Jews seized upon it to make the Cross. After the Crucifixion the tree lay buried three hundred years, until Helena, the mother of Constantine, was inspired with a desire to discover the wood of the Cross, and she constrained a certain man, of the name of Judas, to show her where it was hidden; then Judas led the way to Golgotha, where, in answer to the prayers of Helena, three crosses appeared. The difficulty of distinguishing that of our Saviour from those on which the thieves were crucified was solved by the Bishop of Jerusalem, who caused a sick woman to touch all three, and when she came to the true Cross she was made whole. Helena caused the Cross to be cut in two; one half she enclosed in a silver shrine, which she left at Jerusalem; the other half she carried away to present to her son the Emperor Constantine; and she appointed the Feast of the Discovery or Invention of the Holy Cross to be celebrated every 15th of May throughout the whole world. Many years afterwards, Chosroes King of Persia subjugated all the kingdoms of the East, and when he came to Jerusalem, he carried away the portion of the Lord's Cross left there by Helena. He built a tower of gold and silver and gems, and placing the Cross beside him, commanded all people to worship him as King of kings, and Lord of lords. Then the Christian Emperor Heraclius arrived on the Danube with a large army, to fight against the son of Chosroes and recover the Cross; and they agreed to settle their dispute by single combat, in which the son of Chosroes was killed; and immediately his whole army was converted to Christianity, and were baptized. Heraclius seized Chosroes in his tower, beheaded him, and carried off the Cross, intending to restore it to Jerusalem. But when, mounted on his royal charger, he was about to enter the city by the gate our Lord had entered on an ass, the stones descended and made an impenetrable barrier; then an angel bearing the sign of the Cross appeared, and reproached the Emperor for his presumption. Heraclius accordingly dismounted, and presented himself barefoot with the Cross on his shoulder before Jerusalem, when, behold! the stones resumed their place, and he was thus enabled to enter and restore the precious relic whence it had been taken.

This legend is represented in eight divisions of the wall, and in the following order :—On the south wall, beginning from the top. 1. Seth receiving the branch from the angel, and planting it on the breast of Adam. 2. The Queen of Sheba adoring the tree, and King Solomon causing it to be buried. 3. The tree taken out of the Pool of Bethesda, and made into the form of a Cross. 4. The discovery of the Cross by Queen Helena, and the restoration of the sick woman. On the north wall :—5. The Cross carried in procession by Queen Helena and worshipped by the people. 6. The invasion of Chosroes, and the capture of the Cross. 7. The vision of Chosroes, the victory of Heraclius over the son of Chosroes, and Chosroes seated on his throne within his tower. 8. Heraclius carrying the Cross into Jerusalem; he is first seen on horseback, and afterwards, when admonished by the angel, he is on foot. In this last fresco there is a portrait of the painter, Agnolo Gaddi, at the right-hand corner; he wears a red hood, and has a small beard, according to the fashion of his time. Agnolo crowds his space with too many figures, but there is a certain dignity in all of them; the colour is clear and bright, and he gives animation and interest to the story. According to Cavalcaselle, "Agnolo composed better than his father Taddeo, and gave more repose and dignity, more nature and individuality to his figures. He did not exaggerate in the direction of slenderness, and his general outlines were at once more graceful, more true and grand than those of his father. As a draughtsman he was free and bold, defining everything equally, but he frequently failed to define form truly; and whilst the rest of his figures are still below the standard of Giotto, certain forms are purposely and persistently false.

The eyes are drawn according to a conventional model; the noses are straight and narrow, and expanded flatly at the end, and the mouths generally droop at the corners. . .
. . . In the drawings of hands and feet he bestowed more care; but he evidently never possessed the clear comprehension of the nature of the form he depicted. . . . . .
As a colourist Agnolo was bold. His tones are bright, clear, and transparent, and he shows a feeling for the true nature of harmonies. His idea of relief was greater than that of Taddeo."* The windows behind the apse are filled in with fine coloured glass.

Returning to the transepts, the first chapel south of the apse belonged to the family of Bardi, who, with the Peruzzi, —the owners of the adjoining chapel,—were the two great banking families of Florence during the fourteenth century. The walls of the Bardi Chapel are decorated with frescos containing scenes from the life of St. Francis. Ridolfi de Bardi, one of the sons of this house, though bred to arms, and a valiant soldier in the wars with the Ghibelline faction led by Louis of Bavaria, became finally a Franciscan monk. The frescos on the walls of the Bardi Chapel were executed by Giotto; but were covered with whitewash, and only disclosed in 1853. They were probably painted after 1310 (the date of the death of Bartolo de' Bardi, the father of Ridolfo). In the upper compartment, on the left, St. Francis is represented abandoning the world; below, he appears to St. Anthony of Padua at Arles; and still further down, is the death of St. Francis; his dead body surrounded by his weeping brethren. The portraits of

---

* See "Crowe and Cavalcaselle," vol. i. p. 469.

Arnolfo di Lapo and his father, who wears a black cap, are introduced in the left-hand corner of this fresco. On the opposite wall above, the Order of St. Francis is instituted; below, St. Francis passes through fire in the presence of the Sultan; and, in the third compartment, the body of the saint is translated from Sta. Maria degli Angeli, where he died, to Assisi, where he is buried. Ghirlandaio has followed this composition of the death of St. Francis in his fresco in the Sassetti Chapel of the SS. Trinità. On either side of the window are frescos, as well as on the vaulted ceiling. Beside the altar are St. Nicholas, St. Louis, St. Elizabeth of Hungary, and St. Clara. The rude altar-piece of this chapel has a figure of St. Francis painted on panel, with eight episodes on either side.

The Peruzzi Chapel is also surrounded by frescos of Giotto, which were covered with whitewash early in the eighteenth century, and restored in 1841 and 1863. The Peruzzis were generous patrons of the Church of Sta. Croce, and these frescos are the finest series ever executed by Giotto. The subjects represented are scenes from the lives of St. John the Baptist and St. John the Evangelist. The lunette above, on the left, represents Zacharias standing on the steps of the altar, waving a censer, with two lute-players and a piper behind; the angel appears to him under the portico of the altar. Two women are witnesses of the miracle, to which the younger appears to call the attention of the elder, who seems absorbed in thought and tremulous with fear. In the compartment below, St. Elizabeth lies on a bed, with two attendants, one of whom gracefully bends, and looks at a man, with a noble figure, who turns his back to the spectator. A partition, with an opening, separates this room from another, where Zacharias is writing the child's name on a tablet which he holds on his knee: he looks up at the infant, which is carried to him by a man and woman, behind whom are several other persons. The lowest fresco represents Herod seated, with two guests, behind a table under a rich portico, supported by slender columns with statuettes. Before Herod stands a soldier, who presents him with the head of John the Baptist. Salome dances gracefully to the sound of her own lyre and of a viol played by a youth, who stands to the left of the picture: two figures behind contemplate the dance. In another room Salome is kneeling before Herodias with the Baptist's head.*

On the opposite wall, is the Vision of Patmos—the Evangelist asleep on a solitary rock, and above him in a cloud is the Son of Man holding a scythe in his hand; on his right, the angel who calls on him to mow; the woman pursued by the dragon; the mystic child in its cradle; the angel and the four beasts—the whole is much damaged and repainted. In the compartment beneath is a very fine composition, representing the restoration to life of Drusiana —the saint is on the left of the picture, with a man kneeling beside him; two of his disciples, a cripple on crutches, and two spectators are behind; in the front kneel the relations or friends of Drusiana, who is rising from her couch, and is supported by one of the bearers; behind are the priests. There is a wonderful variety of emotions expressed in the countenances of the spectators, and simplicity and grandeur in the drapery. In the lowest compartment is represented

---

* See "Cavalcaselle," vol. i. p. 301.

the Resurrection of St. John. According to the legend, the favourite apostle of our Lord, being nearly ninety years old, ascended a lofty mountain, after he had commanded his disciples to dig a deep grave for him in the church. On his return from the mountain he found that they had done as he had ordered them, and, throwing his mantle into the pit, he descended and composed himself to sleep. His disciples believed he was dead, and at daybreak a crowd assembled to view the body; but when they looked into the grave, St. John had disappeared, leaving his sandals to prove that he had been there. The heads in this fresco are earnest in expression, the action natural, easy, and appropriate.

The Riccardi Chapel, which is next to the Peruzzi, formerly belonged to the Giugni family, and was also decorated with frescos by Giotto, representing incidents in the lives of the martyrs; they have, however, entirely disappeared. This chapel was bestowed on Joseph Buonaparte, the ex-king of Spain, and brother of Napoleon I., when he resided here: his monument and those of his family adorn the side walls. That to Julia Clary, the wife of Joseph, is by the Florentine sculptor Pampaloni. Bartolini was employed for the monument to Charlotte, their daughter, who was married to the only brother of Louis Napoleon, late Emperor of the French: she was much beloved, and died in 1839, aged thirty-seven.

Next to this chapel is that of the Soderini, which had formerly paintings by Taddeo Gaddi, of which no traces remain. The vaulted ceiling was painted in 1621, with incidents from the life of St. Andrew, by Giovanni di San Giovanni. The painting representing the Discovery of the

Cross, is by Jean Bilivert, 1576—1644; St. Francis distributing his possessions to the poor is by Passignano, 1560—1638; and of St. Francis in prayer, by Matteo Rosselli.

The last chapel is next to the door of the sacristy, and is called the Morelli Chapel; but it formerly belonged to the Velluti, and contains frescos on the right-hand wall, in a damaged condition, by a pupil of Giotto, representing incidents from the story of the Archangel Michael, to whom the chapel was dedicated by Gemma de' Velluti, a Franciscan nun. The frescos on the left wall give the legend of Sipontum, near the site of the modern Manfredonia, in Apulia, where it is recorded that a man named Galgano, or Garganus, lived in the fifth century, who was rich in pasture land, cattle and sheep. One of his bulls happening to stray, he set out with his servants in quest of him, and found him at the entrance of a cavern on the summit of a mountain overhanging the city of Sipontum. Enraged at the trouble the beast had given him, Garganus ordered that he should be slain; but the arrow discharged, instead of hitting the bull, returned to the bosom of him who sent it, who fell down dead. Garganus applied to the Bishop of Sipontum to explain this strange occurrence, and the bishop fasted and prayed for three successive days, at the end of which time the glorious Archangel Michael appeared to him in a vision, and informed him that the spot where the servant aimed at the bull was peculiarly sacred to himself, and commanded that a church should be built there, which order Garganus readily obeyed. The altar-piece of the Velluti Chapel is an Assumption of the Virgin, a good example of the work of Cristofano Allori. St. Thomas

Aquinas and two children are supposed to be by Passignano; this painting is very superior to that of Allori both in grace of composition and beauty of colour. The family of Velluti, to whom the chapel belongs, were Florentine merchants, who were employed on political missions to the Pope and Neapolitan sovereigns, and are now represented by the Duca di San Clemente.

The south transept terminates in a large chapel, belonging to the Baroncelli family, over which are recently-discovered frescos, in an imperfect condition—an old and young man, and Christ with the Doctors. To the right of the entrance is a monument, with the shield of the Baroncelli family, and within the arch are statuettes of the Annunciation, probably by Andrea Pisano. The monument itself is attributed to Nicolò Pisano, though some give it to Andrea. It is a beautiful specimen of monumental decorations of an early period. The inscription states that in February, 1327, this chapel was finished, and dedicated to God and the Virgin of the Annunciation.

The wall to the left is covered with frescos by Taddeo Gaddi, representing incidents from the life of the Virgin. As an example of an early work by this master, these frescos are especially interesting: they were probably executed while Giotto was in Naples. Taddeo has divided his subject into a lunette above, and five compartments below, separated by twisted columns and cornices. Within the lunette, Joachim, the father of the Virgin, is expelled from the Temple; below are the meeting of Joachim with his wife Anna, the birth of the Virgin, her presentation when a child in the Temple, where she is supposed to have been educated by the priests with other young girls, and lastly her marriage to Joseph. In the Presentation she is seen ascending the steps of the Temple; Joachim and Anna stand below; the High Priest above is prepared to receive her; on each side of the foreground groups of persons kneel, and on the right, behind these spectators, are two females beautifully drawn, and a man with a long beard seen in profile, who is supposed to be a portrait of the painter's father, Gaddo Gaddi; near him is another bearded man, dressed in white and wearing a cap, who represents Andrea Tafi, the worker in mosaic. In the Marriage of the Virgin there is a total absence of repose or order in the composition.

On either side of the window Taddeo Gaddi has painted the following subjects: The Annunciation; the Visitation; the Angels appearing to the Shepherds; the Adoration of the Shepherds; the Star appearing to the Wise Men; and their Visit to the Stable of Bethlehem. Within the pilasters supporting the arch are David with the head of Goliath, to represent the triumphs of the ancestor of the Saviour, and Joseph with his rod which has budded.

In the legend of the Virgin's life, it is related that there were many competitors for her hand. The high priest ordered every unmarried man of the house of David to lay a rod on the altar, and declared that he whose rod should give forth buds should be the husband of Mary; among the rivals was Joseph, an old man and widower, who had already sons and grandsons; his rod alone budded, and as it did so, a dove descended from heaven and lighted upon it. In all early pictures of the Marriage of the Virgin the traditional scene is represented of youths in despair breaking their rods, and even administering blows to Joseph, who receives them with the utmost equanimity.

Facing the larger frescos by Taddeo Gaddi is a fresco by Sebastian Mainardi, a pupil of Domenico Ghirlandaio, and one of his best productions, which has even been sometimes attributed to his master. The subject is the Virgin letting down her girdle to St. Thomas. According to the legend, the doubting apostle Thomas was absent when the Virgin ascended into heaven, leaving her tomb full of roses, to the wonder of all the apostles who were present. Thomas refused to believe the tale on his return, but when the grave was opened, he found it empty; and the Virgin, pitying the weakness of his faith, let down her girdle to him from heaven to remove all further doubt.

The altar-piece of this chapel is a very remarkable and authentic picture by Giotto, probably painted between 1299 and 1303, on the return of the artist from a visit to Rome, and before his departure for Padua. He has inscribed his name as follows: *Opus Magister Iocti.* The altar probably once stood where is Mainardi's fresco, and this picture was then opposite the fresco of Taddeo Gaddi; it has been reduced in size and set in its present ornamental framework. The painting is on five panels; the centre has the Coronation of the Virgin, who bends with modest grace and folded arms as the Saviour puts the crown on her head; the mild dignity of his expression and the earnest gaze of the four worshipping angels is very beautiful. In the lower half of the four compartments—two on either side—very lovely angels play musical instruments and sing hymns; above them are numerous heads of patriarchs, prophets, and saints in glory. Each is painted with characteristic portrait-like reality. In the five hexagons of the predella are the Saviour, St. Francis, the Baptist, St. Peter, and Paul the Hermit; they are delicately painted and varied in expression.

According to Cavalcaselle, " No traveller to Florence will have failed to visit Sta. Croce, or to study the Baroncelli altar-piece. It was long a standing piece for the critics of Giotto's style. It will therefore be needless minutely to describe the beauties of the principal group. . . . Let the student mark how admirably the idea of a heavenly choir is rendered—how intent the choristers on their canticles, the players on their melody—how quiet, yet how full of purpose —how characteristic and expressive are the faces, how appropriate the grave intentness and tender sentiment of some angels, how correct the action and movement of others—how grave yet how ardent are the saints, how admirably balanced the groups. Nor will he pass by without a less than cursory glance the five figures in the lower hexagons: the Ecce Homo, with a broad thorax and wasted arms, calmly grieving, but a type reminiscent of more distant times; the wild, austere, and emaciated Baptist, with his long unkempt locks, and arms reverently crossed on his naked breast; and St. Francis showing the stigmata. To perfect decorum and repose, Giotto added in this altar-piece his well-known quality of simplicity in drapery." *

Unfortunately, this interesting picture is half concealed by a heavy and awkward figure of the Saviour by Baccio Bandinelli, brought here from the cathedral with the statue of the Eternal which was placed in the cortile of the monastery.

---

* See " Crowe and Cavalcaselle," vol. I. p. 308.

To the right of the Baroncelli Chapel, facing the east, is another and larger, called the Chapel of the Holy Sacrament, which formerly belonged to the Castellani family, one of whom, a Prior of the Republic, founded this chapel, which he dedicated to St. Anthony, and which he caused an artist, of the name of Gherardo Starnina, to adorn with frescos. Gherardo, born in Florence in 1354, was a pupil of Antonio Veneziano, and the master of Masolino, the father of Masaccio. In 1378, soon after he had finished his work in this chapel, he joined in the riots of the Ciompi, or "Woodenshoes," of Florence, and was forced to quit the city. He travelled to Spain, where he became wealthy; but he returned to his native place in 1387, and after painting several frescos died there, in 1406. Until very recently all the paintings in the Castellani Chapel were buried in whitewash, with the exception of those on the ceiling. Vasari mentions that Starnina's paintings were thus concealed; it is even now, however, doubtful whether the recently-discovered frescos are all or any of them the work of this master. Cavalcaselle attributes them to Agnolo Gaddi.[*] He adds that the prophet in the recess, holding a scroll on which Hebrew lines are inscribed, is of a later date than those of the ceiling. Within the last two years, however, the careful and persevering efforts of a friar of the convent has brought to light some of the most interesting. The frescos appear to have been the work of more than one hand; those representing the histories of St. Anthony and St. Nicholas, though dramatic and powerful, are in the simple artless style of composition and drawing belonging

---

[*] See "Crowe and Cavalcaselle," vol. i. p. 454.

to an early period. The sleeve of the dress is curved, and the bent arm is without an elbow, the eyes are long and small, and the whole figures are Giottesque in treatment, reminding us of the frescos by Taddeo Gaddi in the Baroncelli Chapel, or of Agnolo in the apse of this church. The frescos representing the lives of our Saviour and of St. John the Evangelist belong to a more advanced period in art; they retain the simple narrative style in the composition, but with greater ease and freedom; the drawing and expression of the heads and figures is correct, noble, and often very beautiful; there is also more variety, and a closer approach to nature, with a fine disposition of drapery.

The History of St. Nicholas of Bari is to the right on entering the chapel; he was, as Mrs. Jameson observes, essentially the saint of the people. Above is represented the assistance he gave a poor nobleman who was without dowries for his daughters—St. Nicholas is throwing a purse of gold into an open window, that none might know from whence it came; he is seen restoring a sailor to life who had fallen overboard from a vessel which was conveying the saint to the Holy Land; he restores three children who had been cut to pieces and salted for provisions; he brings a lost child to his parents.

The most beautiful fresco of the series is that of the Life of our Saviour, near the window. Opposite is the Life of St. Anthony, born at Alexandria, A.D. 357, in affluent circumstances, but who joined a company of hermits in the wilderness. Here he was pursued by demons tempting him, all of whom he overcame, and, shutting himself up in a cavern, he lived twenty years in solitude. When he had reached ninety years of age, he flattered himself with the idea that no one else had passed a longer time in seclusion and the exercise of self-denial; but he was informed in a vision that a certain hermit called Paul had exceeded him in both. Anthony resolved to find him out, and was guided to his cavern by centaurs and satyrs. The hermits discoursed together with infinite delight, and a raven supplied them with bread, until Paul died, when two lions came to dig his grave, where Anthony buried him. Anthony retired, with a few other monks, to another solitary place, where he lived fourteen years, and, finally, his spirit was received by angels and carried to heaven. The last frescos on this side represent the life of St. John the Evangelist; they are very grand, and recall the frescos in the Carmine by Masaccio, which is not surprising if this work be by the hand of his master, Gherardo Starnina.

The monuments in this chapel have no interest, but there are two statues of Robbia work on a large scale, well executed. One represents San Bernardino, the other St. Dominick.

A handsome door to the left of the Baroncelli Chapel leads to the Sacristy and to the Capella del Noviziato, Chapel of the Novitiate, of the Medici. Within a lunette over the door is a fresco of the Madonna and Child, by Mainardi. This chapel is entered at the farther end of the corridor, on one side of which are windows, on the other monuments and a curious wooden Crucifix, attributed by some to Margheritone of Arezzo, 1236. It is said to have been presented by the artist to Farinata degli Uberti, the great Ghibelline leader, as a token of admiration for his having rescued his native city from the destruction threatened by his own party, in 1260, after the Ghibelline victory of Montaperti, when it was proposed to raze Florence to the ground; it was the single voice of Farinata degli Uberti which protested against so barbarous an act. Dante alludes to this when he makes Farinata, from his place in the "Inferno," utter these words—

> "Ma fu' io sol colà, dove sofferto
> Fu per ciascuno di tor via Firenze,
> Colui che lo disse, a viso aperto." *
>
> *Inferno*, canto x. l. 83.

The Chapel of the Novitiate, or Capella Medici, is dedicated to San Cosimo and San Damiano, and contains several beautiful works of art. There is a most exquisite specimen of Luca della Robbia's work over the altar: a Madonna and Child surrounded by cherubim, which have wonderful variety of expression; angels crown the Mother and Infant Christ; to the right is St. John the Baptist and St. Elizabeth with her lap full of roses; to the left St. Lawrence, St. Francis, and a bishop. There is also a lunette over the door facing the altar, with angels and a garland of fruit. To the right of the entrance is a very lovely shrine to hold the consecrated wafer, by Mino da Fiesole, brought hither from the Convent of the Murate, in 1815. Mino was born in 1433, and died in 1484; though called of Fiesole, he was really a native of Poppi, in the Casentino, and he was the intimate friend of Desiderio da Settignano. His style is sweet, refined, and graceful. This *Comunicatorio* represents angels waiting at the tomb of the Saviour. Opposite to this is another Robbia work of a

---

* "But there I was alone, where every one
Consented to the laying waste of Florence,
He who defended her with open face."
Longfellow's Translation.

Madonna and Child; and over the two doors on either side of the altar are representations in the same material of St. Dominick and St. Francis. A large monument on one side of this chapel to a young girl, Mademoiselle de Fauveau, is the work of a living sculptress of the same name. There are several good paintings on panel of the school of Giotto.

In this chapel the body of Galileo was laid, and remained for many years; when the great philosopher died in 1642, the Romish Church would not permit him a more honourable place of burial, and here were likewise brought the remains of Vincenzio Viviani, his favourite pupil, who died in 1703, and desired to lie beside his master. Viviani had succeeded in raising, by subscription, a sum of three thousand scudi for the monument of Galileo within the church, near the spot where Galileo had desired that his bones should repose, beside those of his ancestors; but it was only in 1757, at a meeting of the professors belonging to the University, of the members of the Florentine Academy, and of the Franciscan Friars of Sta. Croce, in the Pazzi Chapel, that it was resolved to disinter the remains of Galileo and Viviani, and bear them to their resting-place in the nave of the Church.

The Sacristy of Sta. Croce is a spacious square chamber, built by the Peruzzi family. It is surrounded by fine *intarsiatura* work, which was executed by Giovanni di Michele, a master carpenter, who lived early in the fifteenth century, along which was inserted the series of small pictures by Giotto or by Taddeo Gaddi, representing the lives of St. Francis and of the Saviour, which are now in the Florentine Academy. Some splendid illuminated books, church plate, and priests' vestments are exhibited here under glass. The south wall of the Sacristy is adorned with frescos by pupils of Giotto. The Crucifixion is attributed by Cavalcaselle to Taddeo Gaddi, though the frescos on either side, which were also assigned to him, are more probably by Nicola di Pietro or Gerini. One of the painted crucifixes on the wall is supposed to be by Cimabue, the other by Giotto. The Nativity, with Joseph and the patrons adoring the Child, St. Anthony of Padua, St. Bartholomew, St. Ambrose, and St. John the Baptist, painted on panel, is by Bugiardini, and was formerly in the Castellani Chapel. Bugiardini, born in 1471, was a pupil of Domenico Ghirlandaio, and worked under Mariotto Albertinelli and Michael Angelo, but never rose to great eminence. There are, besides, a Crucifix by Santi di Tito; a Vision of St. Thomas, by one of the school of Andrea del Sarto; and St. Anthony of Padua, by Perugino. Above the entrance-door is a fine head of Christ in Luca della Robbia ware; on the north side is a delicately carved lavabo, with St. Francis on the pediment, and above are paintings of the Saviour, and two small pictures set into the wood.

Separated from the Sacristy by a grating of finely wrought iron-work, is the Rinuccini Chapel, built by one Lapo di Rinuccini, towards the end of the thirteenth century. It is decorated with frescos by Giovanni da Milano, the favourite pupil of Taddeo Gaddi; which were, however, for a long time attributed to Taddeo himself. These paintings are superior in drawing, as well as composition, to those of Taddeo in the Baroncelli Chapel, and belong to a more advanced period of art. On the vaulted ceiling are painted St. Anthony, St. Francis, St. Andrew, and St. Louis; between them are half-length figures of the Apostles, and in the centre is the figure of the Saviour in relief, with the usual act of benediction.

On the walls are the lives of the Virgin and of Mary Magdalene. To the left, in the lunette above, is the Expulsion of Joachim from the Temple; below, as in the frescos by Taddeo in the Baroncelli Chapel, are the Meeting of Joachim and Anna, the Birth of the Virgin, her Presentation in the Temple, and her Marriage. In the lunette, on the right wall, the Magdalene is represented anointing the Saviour's feet; below, she is seated at the Saviour's feet in a beautiful and earnest attitude of attention; the Resurrection of Lazarus follows, and the Noli mi tangere; lastly, a monkish legend of the life of Mary Magdalene. The story of the Virgin is told with peculiar grace and truth to nature; but that of the Magdalene is perhaps superior in variety and interest. In the lunette where the Saviour, addressing Simon, points to the Magdalene at his feet, the attitudes of Simon and of the two Apostles, who have stopped eating to listen, are easy and natural; all the compositions are well ordered and the figures animated; where Mary is seated at the feet of Jesus, Martha is seen reproaching her, and pointing to the kitchen, where she is again represented occupied over the fire. In the Resurrection of Lazarus the painter descends to details which might as well be avoided, because unnecessary, and diverting the thoughts from the principal object of the picture: two of the disciples drag Lazarus from the grave, and the spectators hold their noses. The concluding legend is as follows:—Mary Magdalene, with her sister Martha and brother Lazarus, were set adrift in a ship by the heathen, and their vessel was driven to Marseilles, where, soon afterwards, arrived a certain prince with his wife, who came there to sacrifice to the heathen gods. They were, however, dissuaded from the act by the preachings of Mary Magdalene, and were finally converted to Christianity. Through her prayers, their wish for progeny was granted; but on their road to visit St. Peter at Jerusalem the princess died, after giving birth to a child. The prince left her body on a rocky island, with the infant beside it. Two years afterwards, when he had been confirmed in the Christian faith by the preaching of St. Peter, he quitted Jerusalem, and on his homeward way, landed on the island where he had left his dead wife and her child; he was surprised to find the child living, preserved by the prayers of Mary Magdalene; and his wife suddenly rose as he approached, and stretched out her arms to him. They all returned to Marseilles, where they were baptized by the Magdalene, and all the people of Marseilles and of the country around became Christians.

The altar-piece in the Rinuccini Chapel is also by Giovanni di Milano, and is a good specimen of the master; both that and the frescos bear the date of 1379. The predella represents the Magdalene in the Wilderness, St. John in the Island of Patmos, the Visit of the Magi, the Baptism, and St. Francis receiving the Stigmata.

Returning to the church, the first chapel to the left of the apse was once richly adorned with paintings by Giotto, all of which, however, have perished. It once belonged to the Tosinghi family, from whom it passed to the Spinelli, who bestowed a large portion of their wealth on the Monastery of Sta. Croce. Within the last few years it was purchased by the late Cavaliere Francesco Sloane, who so generously contributed to the façade of the church.

The second chapel is dedicated to St. Anne, and contains the remains of a celebrated composer and violinist, Pietro Nardini, born in Leghorn in 1725, and who died in Florence, 1796. The third chapel belongs to the Ricasoli family, and is dedicated to St. Anthony of Padua. The walls are painted in oil by the modern painter Luigi Sabatelli, and by his two sons, Françesco and Giuseppe. The subject is the Life of St. Anthony, a Portuguese and Franciscan monk, who taught Divinity at Padua. He boldly remonstrated with the tyrant of Padua, Eccellino; and after a time resigned the Professorship of Divinity to preach to the people.

At the entrance to the Ricasoli Chapel is a heavy stone, fastened by a chain to the wall, which is said to have fallen from the roof of the Church in 1698, without causing any injury; which miracle was attributed to the intercession of the Saints.

The adjoining chapel, dedicated to St. Lawrence and St. Stephen, belonged to the Pulci and Berudi families. The frescos were painted in the middle of the fourteenth century by Bernardo Daddi, who was a contemporary of Jacopo da Casentino, and disciple of Spinello Aretino, and was admitted into the company of Florentine Painters in 1355. "The only remaining frescos of Daddi that have been preserved are those of San Stefano, which represent the Martyrdom of San Lorenzo and San Stefano, and have been injured by time and retouching. They betray the weakness of an artist of a low order; not ignorant, however, of the laws of composition as they were known to most inferior Giottesques." *

---

* See "Crowe and Cavalcaselle," vol. ii. p. 6.

The fifth chapel belonged to the Conti Bardi, and is dedicated to St. Sylvester.

According to tradition, Sylvester was born at Rome in the fourth century, when the Emperor Constantine was still unconverted. He had been chosen Bishop of Rome, but fled from persecution, and dwelt for some time in a cavern near the summit of Monte Calvo. Whilst he was there, Constantine was seized with leprosy, and having refused to follow the advice of his false gods, who desired him to bathe in a bath of children's blood, St. Peter and St. Paul appeared to him in a vision, and bade him send for Sylvester, who would show him a pool in which, if he dipped three times, he should be cleansed from his leprosy. And when Sylvester came to the emperor, he explained to him who were Peter and Paul, and Constantine became a Christian from that day. Sylvester was then invited by the emperor to dispute with the Jewish rabbis, in order to clear away the doubts of his mother, the Empress Helena, who was then inclined to Judaism. One of the rabbis defied Sylvester to prove his faith by an exhibition of the power of God; and he whispered in the ear of a fierce bull, when the animal instantly dropped down dead. He then bade the Jew restore the bull to life, which he tried, but could not; upon which Sylvester made the sign of the Cross, bidding the bull rise, and go in peace, and the beast accordingly rose tame and docile. Then the Jews who were present believed, and were baptized. Some time afterwards, the priests of the heathen complained to Constantine, that since he had been baptized a great dragon had appeared in the moat of his castle, which had destroyed more than three hundred men by his envenomed breath; but Sylvester descended into the moat and exorcised the dragon in the name of Christ, and thus delivered the people from the double death of idolatry and the dragon.

The frescos in the Conti Bardi Chapel represent the principal incidents of this legend, and are by Tommaso Giottino, who was born in 1324, and was the contemporary of Gaddi. The subjects to the right, beginning from above, are the Conversion of Constantine, the Miracle of the Bull, and the Victory over the Dragon. The Miracle of the Bull is the finest composition. Constantine sits enthroned in the centre; the Jews and other spectators are behind the balustrades on the right and left, and the bull is rising from his knees at the word of Sylvester. The story is well told, and the composition has been most happily adapted from one very frequently engraved on the Consular diptyches of the Romans.*

Within this chapel is the tomb of Ubertini, a valiant captain, probably by Giottino, who painted the legend of Sylvester; it is unique among the monuments of the fourteenth century. The architectural design is that of the Pisan school; instead of the usual marble effigy recumbent on the sarcophagus, the deceased warrior is represented rising from the tomb at the Resurrection: angels blow a trumpet and hold the instruments of the Passion. The sarcophagus is of stone, but the rest is painted in fresco; a rocky wilderness is represented in the background. Ubertini rises in armour, "a pale but composed countenance; his hands joined in prayer; feature and attitude alike expressive

---

* See "Christian Art," Lord Lindsay, vol. ii. p. 279; also, "Crowe and Cavalcaselle," vol. i. p. 412.

and sublime. It is a daring and bold idea, and one only regrets that it has not been entirely wrought out in marble; the drawing is somewhat hard, and the colouring paler than in the adjacent frescos; but in a subject like this, such a defect becomes a merit."*

The Niccolini Chapel terminates the series at this extremity. It was here that the Company of the Laudesi, or Singers of Praise (to the Virgin), had their place of interment. The Company was composed of both men and women; and, in the early days of the Republic, they were in the habit of meeting near the Church of Sta. Reparata to sing hymns, as well as secular songs—*laudi vulgari*, as they were called; an inscription commemorating this custom is to be seen on the walls of the present Cathedral, on the side near the campanile. One of the latest members was Lorenzo de' Medici, who composed some of his most licentious poetry for this society, which excited the animadversions of Savonarola, and thus contributed to its dissolution. This chapel was only transferred from the Laudesi to the Niccolini family towards the end of the sixteenth century. It is richly decorated with coloured marbles; the statues of Moses and Aaron, of Chastity, Prudence, and Humility are by Francavilla, a mediocre sculptor of the school of Giovan Bologna. He was a native of Cambrai, but educated in Tuscany. The Assumption of the Virgin in the cupola was painted by Volterano in the seventeenth century.

The Chapel of St. Louis and St. Bartholomew, founded in the fourteenth century, occupies the northern extremity

---

* "Christian Art," Lord Lindsay, vol. ii. p. 282.

of this transept, facing the Baroncelli Chapel. It contains an old monument to one of the Bardi family, very similar in style to that of Ubertini by Giottino. Over the altar of this chapel is a crucifix by Donatello, one of his earliest works, and associated with an anecdote related by Vasari. Donatello, when young, studied painting under Bicci di Lorenzo, and executed this crucifix, which Brunelleschi, who ventured frankly to criticise the young artist's works, told him was more like a common peasant than the Saviour of the world. Donatello, considerably disconcerted, observed it was easier to find fault than to make another as good; Brunelleschi made no reply, but shortly afterwards invited Donatello to breakfast with him at his studio; and as Donatello entered the room, with his apron full of cheese and fruit from the market, the first thing he beheld was the crucifix Brunelleschi had just finished; the eatables fell to the ground, as he exclaimed with generous admiration, "Brunelleschi is capable of forming a Christ, but I can only make a peasant!"

CHRONOLOGY.

	A.D.
Baroncelli Chapel built	1337
Brunelleschi, Filippo	1379—1446
Bugiardini	1475—1554
Daddi, Bernardo, joined the Florentine painters . .	1355
Donatello	1386—1466
Francavilla	b. 1548 ....
Galileo	d. 1642
Gaddi, Agnolo	1333—1396
„ Gaddo	1259—1332

STA. CROCE.

	A.D.
Gaddi, Taddeo	1300—1366
Gherardo Starnina	1354—1406
Giotto	1276—1337
Giottino	alive in 1350
Giovanni da Milano	alive in 1366
Luca della Robbia	1400—1482
Mainardi, Sebastiano	alive in 1482
Margheritone di Arezzo	 1236
Mino da Fiesole	1431—1484
Montaperti, Battle of	1260
Nardini, Pietro	1725—1796
Pisano, Andrea	1273—1349
„ Nicolò	d. 1278
Santi di Tito	1536—1603
Tafi, Andrea	1250—1320
Viviano, Vincenzio	d. 1703

CHAPTER VI.

PIA CASA DI LAVORO.—BORGO ALLEGRI.—ACCADEMIA FILARMONICA.—HOUSE OF MICHAEL ANGELO.—THE VILLANI.

BEHIND the Church of Sta. Croce, and within the second circuit of walls, was the old mint, Zecca Vecchia, where the coinage took place, until the building for the same purpose in the Uffizi was finished. North of Sta. Croce is the Via de' Malcontenti, appropriately named, since along this street criminals were led to execution beyond the Porta alla Giustizia. They were accompanied by the Black Brothers, Confraternità dei Neri—instituted in 1361, who, like the Misericordia, devoted themselves to acts of mercy; the chief vocation of the Black Brothers was to administer the last consolations to those condemned to die, and they built a chapel beyond the Porta alla Giustizia, where they enclosed a cemetery for the burial of such unhappy persons.

At the end of the Via de' Malcontenti there once existed two convents, the Monticelli and the Monte Domini; both were suppressed during the French occupation, and the two buildings thrown into one became the Pia Casa di Lavoro, or workhouse of Florence.

The Franciscan nuns of Monticelli had their convent first outside the walls, on a rising ground beyond the Porta

Fresco by Giottino, on the staircase of the Filarmonica, Via Ghibellina.

Romana, whence the name; it was destroyed during the siege of 1529, to make room for the fortifications; the nuns were then conveyed within the town, and called their new habitation Monticelli. It was in the old Convent of Monticelli that Piccarda Donati, the sister of Corso Donati, and a cousin of Gemma Donati, the wife of Dante Alighieri, took the veil, as Sister Costanza. Piccarda became a nun to avoid a marriage with Messer Rossellino della Tosa; but her father Simone Donati and her brother Corso carried her forcibly from her refuge, and insisted on her union with Della Tosa. No sooner had the marriage ceremony ended, than Piccarda threw herself on her knees before the crucifix, entreating for protection, when she suddenly became so ill that her father was constrained to yield to her request, and to send her back to her convent, where she died in eight days. Dante has placed Piccarda in Paradise, in the moon, or lowest heaven, reserved for those who, however involuntarily, had broken their vows. The description of Piccarda is one of the most beautiful passages in the " Paradiso." To the question—

> " Grazioso mi fia, se mi contenti
> Del nome tuo, e della vostra sorte ?"

Piccarda replies—

> " Io fui nel mondo Vergine sorella !
> E se la mente tua ben mi riguarda
> Non mi ti celerà l' esser più bella ;
> Mi riconoscerai ch' io son Piccarda
> Che posta qui con questi altri beati
> Beata son nella spera più tarda." *
>
> *Paradiso*, canto iii.

---

* " Grateful 'twill be to me, if thou content me
Both with thy name and with your destiny?"

* * * * *

The Convent of Monte Domini, like that of Monticelli, was formerly outside the walls, and was removed hither during the siege of 1529. When the French converted both buildings into a workhouse for the aged and infirm, the name of Piccarda's convent was suppressed, and the Pia Casa di Lavoro is known as the Monte Domini; a school for indigent children has been lately added. The institution was in a neglected state under the late grand-ducal government, but the praiseworthy exertions of the Florentine municipality have made it a real charity, and the order, cleanliness, and cheerful, wholesome life within its walls, render it worthy the attention of all interested in the subject of workhouses.* No able-bodied man or woman is admitted; work, according to the ability of each individual, is required from all; a pleasant garden within the cloisters of the old convents is used for their recreation, and a playground is set apart for the young. Boys and girls receive a good education, and workshops are attached to the institution, which supply the means for teaching each child some branch of trade, before he is sent out to earn his own livelihood. The director, who has his office in the building, is ready at stated times to see any of the inmates, and to listen

---

"I was a Virgin Sister in the world,
And if thy mind doth contemplate me well,
The being more fair will not conceal me from thee;
But thou shalt recognise I am Piccarda,
Who, stationed here among these other blessed,
Myself am blessed in the lowest sphere."
Longfellow's Translation.

* The philanthropist, the Marchese Carlo Torrigiani, took especial interest in the welfare of this institution, and left money for the supply of good beds for the inmates.

PIA CASA DI LAVORO, ETC.

to complaints, with a view to redress every well-founded grievance. The person appointed is an educated gentleman, and he is assisted by a council. The fund for the support of the Pia Casa di Lavoro is supplied by the municipality.

The Via Ghibellina was thus named in 1261, in commemoration of the Ghibelline victory at Montaperti. The large building nearest the walls is the Murate, now the prisons of Florence, but formerly the convent of those nuns who left their hermitages on the Ponte alle Grazie to seek a more commodious dwelling. When Catharine de' Medici was a child of seven years of age, she was brought to the Murate, and placed under the protection of the nuns, during the siege of 1529.

A narrow, straggling, dirty street, crossing the Via Ghibellina, bears the pleasant name of Borgo Allegri; here the car was once kept which carried the Sacred Fire from San Biagio to the Canto dei Pazzi and to the Cathedral, on the Saturday before Easter Sunday. In this part of the borough, beyond the second circuit of walls, between San Pietro Maggiore and Sta. Croce, were gardens, in which, according to tradition, Cimabue had his first workshop or studio. Here he painted his Madonna enthroned, now in Sta. Maria Novella, a wonderful picture for the time; and here the painter was visited by King Charles of Anjou, when in Florence on his way from France to Naples. The story is thus related by Vasari: "Cimabue painted on panel a picture of our Lady, for the Church of Santa Maria Novella, which work was of greater size than any yet executed. . . . Whence it excited so much wonder in the people of that age, that it was borne in solemn procession with rejoicings and with trumpets from the house of Cimabue to the church, and he received great rewards and honours. It is said, as may be seen in records of the old painters, that whilst Cimabue was painting this panel in certain gardens near Sta. Croce, King Charles the Elder of Anjou passed through Florence, and, among the entertainments to do him honour by the people of the city, he was taken to see Cimabue's picture; as no one had until then obtained a glimpse of it, a vast crowd of men and women collected, making great signs of rejoicing whilst it was exhibited to the king, and pressing upon one another; and because of the joy this occasioned in the neighbourhood, the district was called Borgo Allegri (Joyful Borough)."

The Accademia Filarmonica and the Pagliano Theatre—the largest theatre in Florence—occupy the site of the Stinche Vecchia, the old prison, which succeeded that of the tower called Il Pagliazzo, in the Piazza di Santa Elisabetta. The Stinche was built in 1301, on ground which had belonged to the same Ghibelline family of Uberti who sold the land on the Arno to Altafronte. Just as the building was ready for use, the Florentines had subdued a powerful family or clan, at some distance from the city, whom they brought captives to Florence, and these were the first occupants of the prison, which was thenceforward called by the name of their castle, the Stinche. In later times, only debtors were confined here, and finally all prisoners were lodged in the Bargello. Among the men of note who were imprisoned in the Stinche was Carnesecchi, when he wrote a piteous appeal for the means to provide himself with sufficient food, addressed to the Grand-Duke Cosimo I., already mentioned in the National Library.

On the staircase of the Accademia Filarmonica are the

remains of a singular old fresco, supposed to have been painted by Giottino, called the Scimia della Natura. It represents an allegory of the Expulsion of the Duke of Athens, whose portrait is the tall figure to the right; St. Anna enthroned is supported by angels on either side; she points to the Palazzo Vecchio, represented as it then stood. The saint presents the banners of the City of Florence to the new guardians, who, clothed in armour, kneel and do her homage. The dethroned duke tramples on the symbols of justice and law, and clasps a monster emblematical of treason, a hoary human head with the tail of a scorpion,—the usual symbol of the Gentile or heretic, and significant of the hatred with which the tyrant was regarded.*

A tabernacle outside the Accademia Filarmonica, at the corner of the street, refers to the former prison; it is a good example of the powers of Giovanni di San Giovanni, and represents a Florentine merchant bestowing alms on the prisoners, who are looking through the bars of the windows; the Saviour and two saints stand beside the charitable donor, and angels hover above.

Near the Filarmonica a street crosses the Via Ghibellina, called the Via del Diluvio—the Street of the Flood—a continuation of the Via del Fosso. All this quarter was subject to floods from the Arno, when the Piazza di Santa Croce formed a peninsula, or island, in the river. In the Via del Fosso, the Palazzo Conte Bardi is an interesting specimen of Florentine architecture, and was probably an early work of Brunelleschi; twelve slender columns support round arches in the court. The external ornaments on this

---

* See illustration to this chapter.

palace are among the earliest specimens extant of the mural painting peculiar to Florence.*

Behind the Pagliano Theatre is a small piazza in front of the Church of San Simone, which was built by the Benedictines of the Badia, in 1209, on the site of a little oratory which stood in their vineyard; the church was restored in modern taste in 1630. Here was buried the Florentine painter, Raffaellino del Garbo. An ancient record informs us that in 1294 the Comune assigned twenty lire for deepening the fosse from the Porta Ghibellina to the Porta San Simone, which stood near the present church.

Nearly opposite the Pagliano Theatre is the house of Michael Angelo Buonarotti. The marbles, terra-cottas, and other objects of ancient art contained in the first room were collected in the beginning of the seventeenth century by the Senator Filippo Buonarotti. In the gallery beyond, the same senator caused the events in the life of his great ancestor to be commemorated by frescos of a size disproportionate to the dimensions of the room, and therefore, though they were painted by the best masters of the day, it is difficult to form an opinion of their merits. Fourteen of the subjects are allegorical. A fine seated statue of the sculptor by one of his scholars is placed near the entrance; at the farther end of the gallery is a mezzo-relievo of Hercules and the Centaurs by Michael Angelo. Politian suggested the subject, and the work was executed with so much ability as to astonish all who beheld so near an approach to the antique. The sculptor himself set a high value on this relief, and would never part with it, but, even

---

* See "Der Cicerone," pp. 158—170.

in old age, took pleasure in its contemplation.* Beside this is a picture of the Virgin with Saints, attributed to Michael Angelo. The room beyond is surrounded by a fresco representing the ancestors of the sculptor. The most interesting part of this house is a light closet, whose existence had been forgotten, until accidentally discovered by the wife of the last Buonarotti. This cabinet appears to have been the study of Michael Angelo, where we may suppose him to have written his noble sonnets, and designed his great works in sculpture; his crutch is on the wall, and his slippers on the desk; and a portrait, probably recently placed there, is thought to represent Vittoria Colonna.

In a fourth room, his first model for the statue of David is exhibited among several others of inferior interest; such as that for the group of Hercules and Cacus, which he was not allowed to execute; also a copy of the antique group, now under the Loggia de' Lanzi, representing Ajax supporting the body of Patroclus. In all these little models we can perceive the true comprehension of the grand in nature, and the powerful invention as well as skill of the great artist.

Returning to the entrance, a door to the left leads to a room containing a collection of drawings, many of which are original designs by Michael Angelo. No. 123 is a Madonna and Child, in which the artist has combined grace and tenderness with his usual strength of treatment. On a sheet of paper, covered with sketches for his picture of the Last Judgment (No. 114), is some of his writing. This room also contains a very lovely Venetian picture.

---

* See "Life of Michael Angelo Buonarotti," by Herman Grimm.

In the court below is a slab of sandstone with the figure of an Etruscan warrior in relief, nearly nude; his hair hangs loosely down his back; he holds a spear in one hand, and a lotus flower with a little bird on a stalk in the other; this slab was discovered at Fiesole, and, from the Egyptian rigidity of the figure, it may be supposed to belong to a very early period.

Leaving the house of Michael Angelo, the visitor arrives at a small street between the Via Palagio and the Via Ghibellina called the Via Giraldi, in which are the remains of the Church of SS. Procolo e Nicomede, one of the oldest in Florence; it belonged to the monks of the Badia, but was suppressed by the Grand-Duke Pietro Leopoldo. Opposite were the houses of the Villani family, where lived the celebrated chroniclers of that name. Their residence is now included in the Palace of Prince Borghese in the Via Ghibellina.

Giovanni and Matteo Villani were born early in the fourteenth century; the elder brother filled many honourable offices in the State, such as Master of the Mint, and Commissioner appointed to superintend the construction of the Gates of the Baptistery, and the Campanile of the Badia. He was, however, falsely accused of peculation, and thrown into prison. Though acquitted and released, it was only to meet with fresh misfortunes: he became a partner in the mercantile house of Buonaccorsi, which was involved in the bankruptcy of the Bardi and Peruzzi, occasioned by Edward III. of England repudiating his debts, incurred for his invasion of France. In 1339, Edward issued a decree suspending all payments to creditors of State, not excepting his "*beloved* bankers Bardi and Peruzzi of Florence." The debt was accordingly never paid.* Giovanni Villani died of the plague in 1348. His Treatise on the Gold Florin is little known; his most famous work is his Chronicle, the first ten books of which bring the history of his country down to the year 1303; but he had not completed more than two books of the second part when his death interrupted the work. The best edition is that of 1587, made by Baccio Valori, whose house and bust have been described in the Via degli Albizzi. Giovanni's son Matteo made a copy of his father's work, which became the property of the celebrated translator of Tacitus, Bernardo Davanzati, and is now in the Riccardi Library of Florence. Another Matteo, the brother of Giovanni, continued the Chronicle until 1363, when he also died of the plague. His son, Filippo Villani, who wrote a commentary on the "Divina Commedia" of Dante, added forty-two chapters to the Chronicle of his father and uncle, bringing the history down to 1365. The Chronicle has not only the merit of being a minute and faithful record of the times in which the Villani lived, but it is considered a model for elegance of style and purity of language; in both of which, however, Filippo is greatly inferior to those who preceded him. The remains of Giovanni, of his brother Matteo, and of his nephew Filippo, repose side by side in the vaults of Sta. Croce.

The last division of the Via Ghibellina, opposite the Bargello, where once stood the residences of the formidable Counts Guidi, bears the name of Via del Palagio. This powerful family were expelled from their possessions in the

---

* "Storia del Commercio e dei Banchieri di Firenze," dal Commendatore Simone Peruzzi, p. 471.

Casentino by the Florentines in the year 1400. The district of the Casentino, behind the mountains of Vallombrosa, contained the principal cities of the Guidi—viz., Palagio and Montemezzano; they were united in one community, under the name of Palagio Fiorentino, and annexed to the Republic.

CHRONOLOGY.

	A.D.
Athens, Duke of, driven from Florence	1343
Buonarotti, Michael Angelo, born	1475
,, ,, died	1564
Cimabue, Giovanni, born	1240
Crecy, Battle of	1346
Donati, Corso, died	1308
Edward III. of England began to reign	1327
,, ,, died	1377
Ghibelline, Via, named	1261
Giottino	1324—1356
Guidi, Counts, conquered by Florentines	1400
Montaperti, Battle of	1260
Monticelli, Convent of, founded	1269
Poitiers, Battle of	1356
San Simone, Church of, built	1209
,, ,, restored	1630
Villani Giovanni died	1348
,, Matteo died	1363
,, Filippo died after	1404

CHAPTER VII.

STA. MARIA IN CAMPO.—BANCA NAZIONALE.—SAN MICHELE DEI VISDOMINI. — PALAZZO DINO CAMPAGNI.—HOSPITAL STA. MARIA NUOVA.—SANT' AMBROGIO.

IN the Via del Proconsolo, between the Via degli Albizzi and the Piazza del Duomo, is a small church, Sta. Maria in Campo, so called from having been built on a field outside the first circuit of walls. The name is also said to have been derived from the site having been that of the Campus Martius of the Florentines. Until 1216 the church belonged to the bishops of Fiesole, and a miraculous image of the Virgin was brought hither from the Cathedral of Fiesole in 1529; but Sta. Maria in Campo was claimed likewise by Florence, and was a constant subject of dispute between the Fiesolan and Florentine diocesans. On the northern side of the little piazza, a house formerly belonging to the Vannini family was the scene of a curious custom on the Feast of St. John the Baptist: a man in a costume to represent the Baptist was led on a car throughout the city, and stopped before this house, from the window of which was lowered a basket with wine, bread, and confectionery. This custom ceased in 1749, and the car only carried a banner, which was presented to the victor at the races held on St. John's Day.

Turning to the right, on leaving the Via del Proconsolo, the first street is the Via dell' Orivolo, or Sun-Dial. The large palace recently built on the foundations of what was the Palace of the Pazzi, where the conspiracy against the Medici was hatched, is the Banca Nazionale of Florence, built after a design by Professor Cipolla, a Roman architect. The sculpture over the doors of *putti*, or boy-genii, is from a design by Girolamo Bastiniani, a Florentine, and are spirited and well-executed. Here, when a palace of the Pazzi, the members of the Accademia degli Apatisti, a literary club, were in the habit of meeting to discuss absurd and trivial questions, which, as described by Goldoni, were only calculated to display much idle pedantry; the Abate Giovanni Lami was, however, once the President, and the Grand-Duke Cosimo III. took the society under his special protection. In 1783 it was merged in the Accademia della Crusca.

The Vicolo Folco Portinari, formerly Via de Pappe, conducts to the Via Sant' Egidio, and the Hospital founded by the father of Dante's Beatrice. At the farther end of the Via Sant' Egidio is the small Church of San Michele dei Visdomini, near which stood the Porta dei Visdomini, and the Porta a Balla, in the first and second circuit of walls. There were formerly two paintings of Andrea Orgagna in this church, one representing Paradise, in which he introduced the most deserving citizens of the Republic; the other Hell, in a part of which he placed the Duke of Athens and his followers, as well as all who had acted contrary to the public interest; therefore a common gibe between Florentines was, "You are painted in the Inferno of San Michele." The church was modernised in 1655.

The palace of the old chronicler Dino Compagni is in the Via Sant' Egidio, and was inhabited by the late Commendatore Sloane. Dino Compagni was born in the middle of the thirteenth century; his "Chronicle" begins in 1280, and ends in 1312. It includes the history of the Bianchi and Neri factions, which commenced at a period when the Guelphs were predominant in the State, but who were thus divided among themselves. The Bianchi, who were inferior in numbers to the Neri, recalled the Ghibellines, in order to obtain equal power with their rivals; and it was when parties were thus evenly balanced that the Florentine Constitution was framed: the Arts or Guilds were formed, and the Priors were chosen from the most influential citizens. Just as peace appeared possible, Charles of Valois arrived in Florence, ostensibly to reconcile contending parties, but really to sow dissension by adopting the side of the Neri, and banishing the Ghibelline supporters of the Bianchi, among whom were the fathers of Petrarch and of Dante.

On a tablet, in a house of the Via Sant' Egidio, is recorded that here Lorenzo Ghiberti cast the bronze Gates of the Baptistery in 1403.

Between the years 1285 and 1288, Folco Portinari was engaged in founding the Hospital of Sta. Maria Nuova. The building originally occupied the space a little in advance of the present Hospital, to the left of the church. Among the archives there still exists the contract, dated 1285, by which Folco Portinari became the owner of land beyond the walls of the city, which he had purchased in the parish of San Michele dei Visdomini, and on which he proposed to build his Hospital. According to tradition, the good work was first suggested to him by his servant, Monna Tessa, or Madonna Tessa, who had already begun it by receiving and nursing the sick in a room of her master's house. Folco Portinari was soon obliged to increase the size of his Hospital from the number of afflicted persons who applied for admittance. At his death, in 1288, the Signory ordered the same honours to be paid to him as to one of themselves, and his merits are recorded on a tablet near the high altar of the church attached to the Hospital. A relief, inserted in the wall of the cloister, leading from the outer porch to the office-room of the Commissary, is supposed to represent Monna Tessa. In the year 1300, part of the adjoining Monastery of Sant' Egidio was added to the Hospital, and assigned to male patients, whilst that part which had been built by Folco Portinari was reserved for women. During the Plague of 1348, large gifts and rich legacies were bestowed on this institution, which, according to Villani, added at that time twenty-five thousand golden florins to its funds. The building was altered to its present form by Buontalenti and Giulio Parigi in 1641. The loggia had been already built by Buontalenti in 1612.

The church was consecrated by Pope Martin V. in 1458. Over the central door is a Coronation of the Virgin in high relief by Dello, an artist of the fifteenth century; the angels on either side were painted much later by the scholars of Pomarancia. To the right of the door is a fresco by Lorenzo de' Bicci, the same artist who was employed in the Cathedral. This painting represents Michele da Panzano, Governor of the Hospital, attired in a black monastic dress, kneeling at the feet of Pope Martin V. to receive the confirmation of those pontifical privileges which had already been granted to the Hospital. The Venetian cardinal, Antonio Cordera, is seated with the other cardinals in Consistory; and Pope Eugenius IV., likewise then a cardinal, is attired in the blue dress of the Canons of San Giorgio in Alge. To the left of the door, another fresco represents the same governor, Michele da Panzano, receiving a Brief from Pope Martin V., in front of the Church of Sta. Maria Nuova. Panzano kneels and kisses the pope's hand; he wears a priest's vestments; behind him are the officials belonging to the Hospital, all in the monastic habit. The Panzani were a branch of the Ricasoli family, and were called Panzano, after a stronghold in their possession. They must have been people of importance in Florence when Michele was made the first Governor of Portinari's Hospital; and one of the family fought in the battle of Montaperti. The daughter of Firidolfi da Panzano married a Ricasoli in 1818, thus renewing the connection between the families, after an interval of eight hundred years.

The frescos in the rest of this compartment, under the loggia or porch in front of the Hospital, are by Antonio della Pomerancia, a painter of the sixteenth century. The fresco at the farther extremity is an Annunciation by Taddeo Zucchero, of the same period, but is much damaged.

Within the church, to the right of the entrance, a plain monument marks the spot where Folco Portinari was buried. In a picture by Hugo Van der Goes the groups of children are portraits of the family of Folco; a penitent Magdalene is by Andrea del Castagno; over the altar is a Crucifix, attributed to Giovan Dologna; and behind it is a fine Luca della Robbia; there are, besides, a Madonna by Cristofano Allori, the Nativity and Flight into Egypt by Veneziano, and Sant' Egidio discovered in his Cave by the King of France, by Giunto Gemignano. Sant' Egidio, who first showed his piety by healing a sick man, is an appropriate saint for a hospital.* On the *cassa*, or shrine, there is a Madonna and Angels by Fra Filippo, and the Missal belonging to the church has admirable miniatures by Cosimo Rosselli, painted between 1460 and 1470.

In the gardens of the Campo Santo, beside the cloister where is the likeness of Monna Tessa, are the remains of a once beautiful fresco of the Last Judgment, by Fra Bartolommeo, finished by his friend Mariotto Albertinelli. It is now protected by a shed; and though a great part of the painting is effaced, enough remains to prove its excellence. The drawing, expression, and movement of the heads and figures, which can still be traced, are full of life, beauty, and grace. Christ is seated above—a dignified figure with a sad countenance; he is surrounded by cherubim. On either side are the Apostles, whose heads have great variety as well as grandeur; St. Peter and the Virgin are nearest the Saviour: below, the archangel Michael stands in the centre (but this part of the painting is almost wholly destroyed); an angel, looking down, has a wonderfully beautiful expression, and the two angels who blow their trumpets as they descend, give the idea of rapid movement by their outspread wings and flying draperies. The lowest part of this fresco is, as usual, divided by the accepted and the rejected; among the last, one gazing upwards with

---

* See "Legends of the Monastic Orders," by Mrs. Jameson, p. 31.

a look of despair, and another walking with his hands raised, are powerfully drawn.

In the Cloister, beyond the monument of Monna Tessa, is a small tabernacle by Giovanni di San Giovanni.

In the first room of the Hospital there is a Madonna with Saints by Il Rosso. The Hospital contains about two thousand beds, and is attended by twelve medical professors; there is a supply of instruments, and a library of five thousand volumes, founded by the celebrated mathematician, Vincenzo Viviani, the pupil of Galileo, is attached to the institution. Among its treasures are some interesting manuscripts relating to the history of Florence, one of which is the original autograph copy of the works of Scipio Ammirato.

By the Via Sant' Egidio the visitor reaches a piazzetta in which meet the Via dell' Orivolo and the Via Pietra Piana, leading to the old Church of Sant' Ambrogio.

Sant' Ambrogio di Pietro Piana is one of the oldest churches in Florence. The convent attached to the church was the first containing nuns in Florence. They, as well as the monks of the Badia, were Benedictines, until during the French occupation of the last century, part of the immense building was destroyed, and the nuns were expelled. A few years afterwards the convent was bestowed on the nuns of the Sacré-Cœur, who still inhabit it. There are between forty and fifty Sisters, who never leave the walls, and are occupied with needlework, chiefly making priests' garments. Some have attained a great age; and even those in middle life have been twenty-eight years thus immured. There is nothing of artistic interest in the dilapidated building, except an old fountain in the Cloister, next the Refectory.

The Church of Sant' Ambrogio was rebuilt by Giov. Batt. Foggini; and Luigi Ademollo, a Milanese painter, within this century decorated the façade, nave, and choir with representations of the life of St. Ambrose and of our Saviour. Here Andrea Verocchio, the master of Leonardo da Vinci, was buried; but the greatest treasures of this church are the fresco by Cosimo Rosselli, and the marble altar by Mino da Fiesole, both of them in the Capella della Misericordia, to the left of the high altar. The fresco of Cosimo Rosselli is esteemed his finest work; it was painted in 1476, and represents a miraculous chalice, containing the sacramental wine, which was conveyed to the Archbishop's Palace after it had been converted into the real blood of the Saviour. Though much injured by a fire which took place in this chapel, enough of the painting remains to give an idea of its excellence. There is great variety of movement, and many of the heads have the air of portraits. In a group to the left, the figure facing the spectator is said to be a portrait of Pico della Mirandola, whose likeness is also in the small room of Tuscan painters in the Uffizi Gallery. The head in this fresco appears to have been retouched. Pico was a younger son of the Lord of Mirandola, born in 1463. He acquired proficiency in Latin, Greek, Arabic, Hebrew, and Chaldee, besides various sciences; and, after visiting the universities of France and Italy, settled in Florence, where he devoted himself to the study of religion and Platonic philosophy. He died in 1494. The female figures in Rosselli's fresco are dignified and graceful, and some of them, as well as the children, very lovely. The different impression made by the miracle, on young and old, is admirably given.

The paintings on the ceiling of the chapel are almost wholly destroyed.*

The richly carved marble altar to the right is that by Mino da Fiesole. The Infant Saviour is represented standing in the cup; adoring saints are on either side. The arch above is covered with delicate foliage, interspersed with the heads of cherubs; the Eternal is seen above. The *gradino*, or predella of small figures below the altar, is almost concealed by the table with candles and decorations in front. In the centre a priest holds up the chalice, and worshipping multitudes are on either side.

Descending the church on the same side with the Chapel of the Misericordia, there is a finely carved wooden statuette of St. Sebastian by Leonardo Tassini. Along the whole length of the nave, on either side, is a series of shrines or arches of carved stone, beneath which are pictures and altars. In the third from the entrance, a painting on panel is likewise by Cosimo Rosselli; the Madonna in glory surrounded by cherubim and angels; the Eternal above, and below, St. Ambrose and St. Francis, with a landscape background. The picture is wanting in force, but the predella is extremely beautiful. It represents scenes from the life of St. Francis: the Confirmation of his Order, by Pope Honorius III.; St. Francis receiving the Stigmata; his Death, surrounded by his disciples.

In a shrine on the opposite side of the nave is a Descent from the Cross, by one of the school of Giotto. The expression of the Magdalene, who receives the body of the Saviour from Nicodemus, is full of beauty, in spite of

---

* See "Crowe and Cavalcaselle," vol. ii. p. 183.

exaggeration. The Virgin, St. John the Baptist, and St. Catherine, stand passively by, as spectators.

In the next shrine there is a picture attributed to Giotto, but with little probability. It is called the Madonna del Latte, as the Virgin is suckling the Child. To the right is St. John the Baptist; to the left St. Bartholomew with his knife. There is a certain dignity in this composition, and the picture is in tolerable preservation. In the third shrine is a much-damaged picture, but good in drawing and composition. The subject is St. Benedict, who is attired in black, and seated; an angel leads to him the youthful Tobit, symbolical of the human pilgrim; St. Nicholas on the left has his three balls in his hand.

In the Via de' Pilastri, nearly opposite the Church of Sant' Ambrogio, is a house which in 1639 was the scene of one of the most horrible tragedies of Florentine history. In the reign of the Grand-Duke Ferdinand II. there lived here an elderly Florentine gentleman, Giustino Canacci, who had been twice married, and his second wife, Caterina, was celebrated for her beauty and virtue. Jacopo Salviati, Duke of San Giuliano, was among her admirers, which excited the jealousy of his duchess, Veronica Cibo, a Princess of Massa. She determined to get rid of one she thought a rival, and Caterina, having unfortunately incurred the hatred of her step-son, Bartolommeo Canacci, he consented to guide three assassins, hired by the duchess, to this house, where Caterina was one evening entertaining some of her friends. Here they murdered her, with her maid, who remained beside her mistress when the rest of the party had taken flight. Caterina's head was then cut off and carried to the duchess, who concealed it in a bason of clean linen, which it was customary to place in her husband's apartment on the first day of the year. The duke uncovered the bason, and nearly fainted away on seeing its contents. Though the crime was of so heinous a nature, Bartolommeo Canacci alone suffered punishment; he was seized and beheaded, whilst the rest of the culprits escaped; the duchess left Florence, in greater dread of the fury of the populace than of the justice of the tribunals. Crime in high places had little to fear, when Ferdinand himself entertained and employed the assassin Fra Paolo to get rid of troublesome persons.* A well in the Via de Pentolini still exists into which the body of Bartolommeo Canacci is said to have been thrown.

CHRONOLOGY.

	A.D.
Cosimo Roselli	b. 1416—d. 1484
Dino Compagni began his "Chronicle"	1280
,, ,, ended ,,	1312
Ferdinand II.	1621—1670
Hospital of Sta. Maria Nuova built	1285—1288
,, Church of Sta. Maria Nuova, consecrated by Pope Martin V.	1456
Mino da Fiesole	b. 1431—d. 1486
Pico della Mirandola	b. 1463—d. 1494
Plague of Florence	1348
Sta. Maria in Campo belonged to the Bishops of Fiesole until	1216
Sta. Maria, Miraculous Image brought to	1529
San Michele dei Visdomini modernised	1655
Verocchio, Andrea	b. 1432—d. 1488

* See vol. I.—" Bargello."

CHAPTER VIII.

THE PROTESTANT CEMETERY.—STA. MADDALENA DE'
PAZZI.—THE PANCIATICHI GALLERY.—THE CAPPONI
GALLERY.—GAME OF PALLA E MAGLIO.

FROM Sant' Ambrogio a wide street leads to the modern Piazza of Massimo d' Azeglio, which contains a large public garden, with seats for the accommodation of the public. On one side is a new theatre, or circus, called after Prince Umberto. Near this piazza lies the old Protestant Cemetery of Florence, once beyond the Porta Pinti, and under the shelter of the ivy-covered walls, both of which have been included in the recent demolitions. The greater number of the tall old cypresses which crowned the summit of the mound have been cut down, and the picturesque beauty, as well as seclusion of the spot, which were so congenial to the feelings of mourning friends, no longer exist. It is now protected by a neat iron railing, within which have been planted cypresses and various shrubs, which it is to be hoped will, in time, restore some of its former beauty. The mountains of Vallombrosa and Fiesole are not quite shut out by the row of houses rising on all sides, and the order and care bestowed by the municipality, into whose hands it has fallen by purchase, leave no room for complaints. The white marble monuments, to each of which is attached a little garden of roses or other flowers, give a peculiar loveliness to this cemetery, far removed from gloom, and in the spring-time, the remains of the departed seem to repose under a shower of sweet blossoms. Among the monuments raised to those whose names are known to the world, may be mentioned Elizabeth Barrett Browning, Mrs. Trollope and her accomplished daughter-in-law, the poet Arthur Clough, and the American divine Theodore Parker.

Returning to the Piazza Massimo d' Azeglio, and passing the Teatro del Principe Umberto, we arrive at the Via della Colonna, which leads to the Borgo Pinti. To the left is the Convent of Santa Maddalena de' Pazzi; to the right the Palace of the Marchese Panciatichi. Strangers have only lately been permitted to enter the sacred precincts of this convent, where a fresco in the chapter-house, representing the Crucifixion, is the finest work of Perugino. As the chapter-house is now separated from the convent, the privacy of the nuns is still held sacred.

The saint from whom the convent derived its name, was a lady of the Pazzi family, who took the veil, and lived and died in a convent on the other side of the Arno, opposite the Church of San Frediano. She was canonized, for her singular piety, by Pope Alexander VIII. in 1670.[*] The sisters were then transferred to their present habitation, which previously, since 1220, had been occupied by Cistercian monks who employed Perugino, when on a visit to Florence, to paint the fresco. It was at this period that he likewise painted the Madonna and Child with the Baptist and St. Sebastian,

---

[*] See Mrs. Jameson, "Legends of the Monastic Orders," p. 475.

for the monks of San Domenico in Fiesole, now in the tribune of the Uffizi Gallery. Perugino's chief patrons were the Gesuati, or monks of St. Justus, whose monastery was just beyond the Porta Pinti, and whose skill in painting on glass, displayed in the windows of the Florentine cathedral, was probably derived from Flanders.*

In the fresco of the chapter-house of Sta. Maddalena de' Pazzi, the influence of the Florentine on the Umbrian School may be clearly perceived—the union of dramatic power with grace and tenderness. The subject is divided in three compartments. In the centre the Saviour hangs on the Cross, and the Magdalene kneels below; in the compartment to the right are St. John, the beloved disciple of our Lord, and St. Benedict; in that to the left are the Virgin and St. Bernard. The composition is perfectly simple, and is in harmony with the solemnity of the scene represented. A beautiful landscape background unites the three compartments. A winding river skirts a range of low hills, resembling the country in the neighbourhood of Orvieto, where Perugino was at this time engaged to paint with Pinturicchio. Tall trees with light foliage crown the summit of the hill behind St. Bernard. But the attention of the spectator is rivetted by the majestic and touching beauty of our Saviour's head, over which the shadow of death truly seems to pass. It is encircled with a green fillet, and a purple cloth is bound round the loins. The body has none of the meagreness of Perugino's usual work, but is drawn and coloured with great breadth and softness. The Magdalene,

---

* This art seems to have been successfully practised by the Cistercian Order. The fine glass in the choir of Lichfield Cathedral was brought from a Cistercian nunnery near Liège.

attired in black, with a red mantle lined with green over her shoulders, gazes upwards at the Saviour, her countenance calm in the repose of entire trust that her sins are forgiven. St. John is truly represented as the apostle of Love. He is clothed in green, whilst St. Benedict wears the original black habit of his Order. The Virgin is also in black, with a purple mantle. She stands with her hands meekly clasped, and with lips apart, the image of resignation, and of deep, unspoken grief. A beautiful sketch for this figure by Perugino is among the drawings exhibited in the Uffizi. St. Bernard, the founder of the Cistercian branch of the Benedictines, is in white, beside the mother of our Lord.

The entrance to the present Convent of Sta. Maddalena de' Pazzi is in the Borgo Pinti. To the right is a chapel, built by a cousin of San Filippo Neri, the founder o. the Order of the Oratory; he at first intended to dedicate his pious work to San Filippo, but he changed his mind when the canonization of his cousin was delayed, and the chapel was therefore instead dedicated to Santi Nereo ed Achilleo. The walls are covered with frescos by Bernardo Pocetti, which are among the best works of this artist. The original design for the cupola is among the drawings exhibited in the Uffizi. A picture by Passignano commemorates the Martyrdom of the Saints. Beyond this chapel is the outer cloister of the monastery. The Ionic columns in front of the church are by Giuliano di San Gallo, and, as Vasari states in his life of San Gallo, were intended to imitate the antique. The church does not contain any picture of extraordinary merit, except the Coronation of the Virgin by Cosimo Rosselli, painted in tempera, and treated with much grandeur. The Virgin is very dignified and lovely; she bends gracefully to receive the crown; an angel below the Saviour bears the lily and the emblems of the Passion. Behind the Virgin other angels carry musical instruments; a garland of cherubs surround the principal group, with prophets and saints; St. Peter and St. John kneel in the centre; John the Baptist is to the right. This picture appears to have been painted contemporaneously with the fresco in Sant' Ambrogio. In the sacristy is an excellent copy of a Madonna by Luca Giordano, the original of which is in the choir. In the left transept is the Sepulchre of Sta. Maddalena de' Pazzi, whose body was embalmed, and is preserved under glass in the convent. There is also an interesting picture of Sant' Ignazio and San Roch by Raffaellino del Garbo, who painted the Miracle of the Loaves and Fishes for the refectory of the convent. This artist was a pupil of Filippino Lippi, and contemporary of Lorenzo di Credi, 1466—1524. Of early promise, he appears to have disappointed the hopes of those who expected to see him a great artist, and affectation and mannerism prove him to have been more the mechanic than the man of genius.* The remaining pictures within the church are a Coronation of the Virgin, by Fabrizio Boschi, who painted the Tabernacle at the corner of the Bargello; an Annunciation, by Botticelli, but too much defaced or too dark to be visible; and pictures by Matteo Rosselli, Santi di Tito, and others of inferior name. The pavement of coloured marbles before the high altar is worthy of notice; and within the choir are the paintings by Luca Giordano, already referred to.

---

* See "Crowe and Cavalcaselle," vol. iii. p. 416, and Vasari, "Vite dei Pittori," vol. vii. p. 191.

Opposite the Convent of Sta. Maddalena de' Pazzi is the
fine palace built by Ammanati, with gardens attached to it,
which belonged to the family of Simone di Firenzuole. The
Panciatichi, to whom the palace next Sta. Maddalena de'
Pazzi belongs, is a very ancient family of Pistoia, who carry
their history back to the eleventh century. They owed
their greatness to Imperial favour, and first settled in
Florence in 1352. The rich collection of paintings belonging to the present representative of the family are, most of
them, on sale, as well as a valuable collection of objects of
virtù; the prices asked are high, and when any of the
treasures, which fill twenty-six rooms of the palace, are sold,
they are immediately replaced by articles of equal value.
Every picture has a ticket with the name of the artist, and the
date of his birth. One of the most interesting pictures here
is the Madonna della Stella, by Fra Bartolommeo. The
beauty and tenderness expressed in the countenance of the
Virgin, who bends reverentially to kiss the head of her
infant, is truly exquisite. A Magdalene, evidently the portrait of a young lady, by the same master, is likewise very
beautiful. Both these paintings have been long in the Panciatichi family. Near the Madonna is a good specimen of
Baldassare Peruzzi, a late acquisition: the subject is a
Holy Family, the Virgin reading. It is in a fine old Florentine frame of carved dark wood, picked out with gold. Two
pictures are attributed to Joas Cleef, called Il Pazzo—the
Mad—mentionéd in Walpole's "Lives of the Painters"
among artists in England during the reign of Queen Mary.
The pictures here by Cleef represent an Entombment, and
Christ crowned with Thorns, both very powerful. The
Madonna and Child, with St. John the Baptist, painted in

chiaroscuro by Andrea del Sarto, is a *replica* of the picture in the Pitti. A portrait of Baccio Valori is by the same artist. Baccio, born in 1467, was one of the chief adherents of the Medici, and was in great favour with Pope Clement VII. After the accession of Duke Cosimo I., he joined Filippo Strozzi in his attempt to liberate Florence from the new sovereign, and was taken prisoner after the battle of Monte Murlo. He was led through the streets of Florence on a pony, exposed to the insults of the multitude, who had already demolished part of his house in the Via degli Albizzi, and he was executed in the court of the Bargello, 1537. The finest portrait in this gallery is that of Piero Soderini, by Leonardo da Vinci. Soderini, born in 1450, was created perpetual Gonfalonier of the Republic in 1502, which office, however, he only held ten years. Though a strong opponent of the Medici, he was a man of mild and unpretending character, and a patron of Art and Literature. When the Medici returned to power, he was banished, and ended his days in Rome.

A beautiful picture by Mariotto Albertinelli represents the Child seated on a pedestal with the head of Joseph appearing behind; the Virgin, a lovely figure, stands beside him, and lays her hand on the head of the Christ; in the background is a landscape with monks. There is also in another room a very small but beautiful Annunciation, by Albertinelli. A singular rather than beautiful composition, by Fra Filippo Lippi, represents angels offering grapes and corn, typical of the Resurrection, to the Infant Christ, who is seated on the lap of the Virgin; the charm of this composition consists in the thoughtful, earnest expression in the face of the Virgin, and timid doubt in that of the Child, who shrinks from the angel, yet seems to desire the gifts. A picture containing a multitude of figures, also by Fra Filippo, represents the betrayal of a small fortified town or *castello* in a war between Sienna and Arezzo; there is much animation in the figures, especially in the groups of fighting horsemen in the landscape behind.

Two most exquisite small paintings, by Andrea Mantegna, represent St. John the Baptist and St. Peter; and in the same room is a Deposition, by Crivelli, the precursor of the Bellini and of Titian; it is rich in colour and gilding, as well as highly finished, and forcible, if somewhat exaggerated in expression. A very finely coloured portrait, by Titian, represents Laura, one of the three wives of Alfonso of Ferrara, the brother of the celebrated Leonora of Tasso. A large and valuable picture by Garofalo, belonging to a friend of the Marchese Panciatichi, is on sale here. The subject is a Madonna and Child in glory, with angels; and below, three saints. There are several pictures by Sustermans, among them a group of three children of the family—1577 —and a portrait of a lovely princess of the house of Medici —1597—with another of her mother, who strongly resembles her daughter. There are likewise interesting portraits of Neri di Gino Capponi—1568—and of Francesco Valori, who was torn to pieces by the mob, because a follower of Savonarola; his monument is in the cloisters of the Badia. The portrait of a boy is by Correggio. A likeness of Metastasio is by Pompeo Battoni, who died in 1787. In the same room are two lovely heads by Guido Reni, representing Diana and Endymion. There are several splendid landscapes by Rosa di Tivoli and Salvator Rosa, and a small cabinet, painted by this last artist in sea-pieces, and landscapes. His finest picture in this collection is a battle-piece, which unites his usual power and animation with a finish, light, and clearness unusual in his works. A portrait of Salvator Rosa by himself, in a black cloak and hood, and a torn glove on one hand, is one of the most powerful pictures here, both in expression and colour.

There are several bronzes of merit in the gallery; two by Giovan Bologna, the Arno and the Tiber; and a shepherd carrying a lamb on his shoulders; but the finest is a small but noble group by Donatello, of David springing on Goliath, with his sword raised to slay him. The giant struggles to rise, his head is thrown slightly back, the stone is in his forehead, his mouth is open as if uttering a cry, and he grasps the earth with both clenched hands; the curve of his body, and the muscular action of his legs as he strives to rise, are grandly composed, and true to nature: in wonderful and graceful contrast is the easy, light, and slender figure of David, who with one hand seizes his enemy by the hair, and with the other grasps his sword raised to strike.

In an upper storey of the palace is displayed a rich collection of objects of virtù. On one table is a large set of the black Wedgewood ware; cups and vases of blue Sèvres, agate, and rock-crystal, are on other tables; a long gallery is lined with glass cases, containing guns, pistols, and swords, the old manufacture of Brescia and Pistoia; and one richly ornamented pistol is the work of Benvenuto Cellini. A gold vase has delicate silver figures, copied from the antique. The largest and most valuable part of this collection are blue enamelled bronze vases from China, with various Chinese and Japanese curiosities; among them a figure in complete armour made of iron and silk; a black iron mask is on the face, and the shoes have so high a polish as to resemble fine jet or glass.

The Panciatichi Palace was built by Giuliano and Antonio di San Gallo for their own abode: when Napoleon Buonaparte was in Florence, in 1796, he lodged in this palace, then the residence of the French minister.

In the Borgo Pinti, near where was once the Porta, is the Palazzo Gherardesca, inhabited by a collateral descendant of Count Ugolino della Gherardesca, of Pisa, celebrated by Dante in his "Inferno." This palace contains little of interest beyond the beauty of its gardens; but it formerly received within its walls the historian Bartolommeo della Scala—1430—the son of a poor miller from Colle, on the road to Sienna, who was patronised by the Medici.

The Via della Pergola crosses the Via della Colonna and the Via della Mandorla; the Pergola, or Bower, was probably at one time in the midst of gardens. Here is the fashionable theatre or opera-house of Florence. The first theatre in the Uffizi, built by Buontalenti for the Grand-Duke Francis I., was abandoned in the seventeenth century, and applied to other uses. The passion for theatrical amusements, however, induced some young dilettanti to form themselves into a company, which assumed the name of Accademia degli Infuocati, and adopted as their emblem a bombshell ready to burst; they gave dramatic representations at the house of their patron Don Lorenzo, the son of Ferdinand I., which was on the site of the Palazzo Corsini, Via del Parione. After Don Lorenzo's death they hired a house in the Via del Cocomero, now Ricasoli, where is the present Teatro Niccolini; but the number of performers increasing, part of them separated, and purchased a *tiratoio* of the

Guild of Wool, in the Via della Pergola, on which they constructed a theatre of wood. Such was the beginning of the Florentine opera house. In the Via della Pergola, a tablet marks the house where Benvenuto Cellini cast his Perseus, as described in his Memoir.* Cristofano Allori had also a house here.

At the end of the Via della Mandorla, joining the Via San Sebastiano, is a large house, a detached portion of which in the Via della Mandorla is decorated with sculpture, the residence of Andrea del Sarto, when he returned from France, and afterwards of Federigo Zucchero.

In the Via San Sebastiano—so named after the Pucci Chapel in the opposite Church of the SS. Annunziata, is a group of Luca della Robbia work over a door leading to an elegant though small cloister, adorned with frescos by Pocetti, which once belonged to the Confraternity of San Piero Maggiore.

Towards the centre of the street is the Palazzo Capponi, the largest palace, with the exception of the Pitti, in Florence. The gardens behind join those of the Gherardesca. The palace is still inhabited by the last representative of the elder and most celebrated branch of the family, who is revered and beloved by his countrymen, and hardly less held in honour by every stranger visiting Florence.

The Capponi were in the fourteenth century a powerful *popolano* family, belonging to the Arte della Seta—Guild of Silk—and inhabited the quarter of San Frediano beyond the river. They were always found taking part against the turbulent nobles of the city, ready to check,

---

* The Perseus is under the Loggia de' Lanzi.

as far as in them lay, the undue aspirations for power of ambitious citizens, and fearlessly maintaining the liberties and greatness of Florence. Gino Capponi, born 1360, first gave importance to his family, by successfully directing a war which gave Pisa to Florence. Of his three sons, the descendants of one settled at Lyons in France, where they were noted for benevolence, but this branch became extinct in 1797. A descendant of another founded the Riccardi library of Florence, and is still represented by the Marchese Capponi, who inhabits a palace in the Via Bardi. From the eldest Neri is descended a long line of patriots, the last of whom is the present Marchese Gino Capponi.

The palace in the Via San Sebastiano was built after a design by Fontana. On a magnificent staircase, within the right wing, is a modern statue of Piero Capponi, who made himself famous by his bold defiance of Charles VIII. of France. A narrow staircase, in the left wing, leads to the library, rich in manuscripts, and to the picture gallery, containing a large collection of paintings, and where the ceilings are painted in fresco. Among the most interesting is a portrait of Piero Capponi in the second room, probably taken from authentic sources, by Angiolo Allori. Another good picture, by a recent artist, Sabatelli, represents Piero tearing the treaty in the presence of the King of France. Nearer the window is a fine, though small, picture of St. Jerome, by Carlo Dolce; and facing the light another St. Jerome (No. 114), attributed to the school of Albert Dürer, though corrected in the catalogue to Pinturicchio, a beautiful and highly finished picture. The Infant Christ and St. John the Baptist conversing, in the rocky background, are most lovely, and the expression of the saint is very fine.

In a third room is a picture, by Gardini, of Pandolfo Ricasoli and his companion in guilt listening to their sentence by the Inquisition, pronounced in the Refectory of Sta. Croce before a crowd of witnesses. A Last Communion of St. Jerome is by Andrea del Castagno; a very sweet picture of the Madonna and Child, No. 173, is by Marco d' Oggione, a pupil of Leonardo da Vinci; above it is a fine Christ in the arms of Nicodemus, by Andrea del Sarto. No. 160 is a good portrait of a gentleman, with a little girl holding a flower, of the Venetian school. But the gem of the collection is a Communion of St. Jerome, by Filippino Lippi, a most exquisite miniature; the expression of the saint, of the priest who places the wafer in his mouth, and of the attendant monks, is true to nature, forcible and earnest; and every detail of the accessories is finished with the utmost delicacy. In a fourth room is a portrait of the present Marchese Gino Capponi when young; a fifth room contains some excellent portrait-heads. A large bed of state is shown in a room near the entrance, with rich carving, cherubs, &c., in wood gilt.

Nearly opposite the Capponi Palace is the Palace of the Velluti-Zati, Dukes of San Clemente, formerly among the merchant-princes of Florence, and inventors of velvet. They were employed at various times on important political missions abroad, and received the title of Dukes of San Clemente from one of the popes. This palace was inhabited by Charles Edward, the Young Pretender, and afterwards by the English minister at the Court of Florence.

Proceeding westward, we arrive at an old Dominican convent, directly behind San Marco, now used by the government, and therefore cleared of anything it might have possessed of artistic value. Nearly opposite is the oldest botanical garden in Europe, which was enclosed by order of the Grand-Duke Cosimo I., to prevent the nuns being disturbed at their devotions by the noisy sounds of the game of "palla e maglio," at that time a favourite pastime of the Florentines. The game was introduced from Naples in the fifteenth century, and the ground chosen for this diversion was between San Marco and the walls, where there were no buildings at that time, except the Convent of the Dominican nuns and the Studio Fiorentino, or Academy for Artists, erected from a dying bequest of Nicolò d' Uzzano. The *maglio* was a bat by which the ball was sent to a given distance. The amusement appears to have had some analogy with our game of cricket. Pall Mall was probably named after it. For a full description the reader is referred to " L'Academie Universelle des Jeux," printed at Amsterdam in 1756.

CHRONOLOGY.

	A.D.
Albertinelli, Mariotto	b. 1475—d. 1520
Allori, Angiolo	b. 1511—d. 1580
" Cristofano	b. 1577—d. 1621
Ammanati	b. 1511—d. 1589
Andrea del Sarto	b. 1488—d. 1530
Battoni, Pompei	b. 1702—d. 1787
Bologna, Giovan	b. 1525—d. 1608
Boschi Fabrizio	b. 1570—d. 1642
Capponi, Neri, founded the greatness of his family	1360
" Neri di Gino	d. 1568
" Piero	d. 1496
Castagno, Andrea del	b. 1409—d. 1477

Cellini, Benvenuto	b. 1500—d. 1570
Cistercian monks established in the Via della Colonna	1230
Cleef, Joos	b. 1500—d. 1536
Correggio	b. 1494—d. 1529
Crivelli flourished	1450—1476
Dolce, Carlo	b. 1616—d. 1686
Donatello	b. 1383—d. 1466
Fontana	b. 1634—d. 1714
Fra Bartolommeo	b. 1469—d. 1517
Garofalo	b. 1481—d. 1559
Giordano, Luca	b. 1632—d. 1705
Lippi, Fra Filippo	b. 1400—d. 1469
„ Filippino	b. 1460—d. 1505
Neri, San Filippo	b. 1515—d. 1595
Panciatichi settled at Florence	1352
Passignano	b. 1558—d. 1638
Pazzi, Sta. Maddalena dei, canonized, and nuns transferred to the Via della Colonna	1670
Perugino, Pietro	b. 1446—d. 1524
Peruzzi, Baldassare	b. 1481—d. 1536
Pinturicchio	b. 1454—d. 1513
Raffaellino del Garbo	b. 1466—d. 1524
Rosa di Tivoli	b. 1613—d. 1649
Rosa, Salvator	b. 1613—d. 1673
Rosselli, Cosimo	b. 1439—d. 1506
San Gallo, Giuliano di	b. 1443—d. 1517
„ Antonio di	b. 1482—d. 1546
Scala, Bartolommeo della	b. 1430—d. 1495
Soderini, Piero	b. 1450—d. 1514(?)
Sustermans	b. 1597—d. 1681
Valori, Baccio	b. 1354—d. 1427
„ Francesco	b. 1439—d. 1498
Vinci, Leonardo da	b. 1445—d. 1519

CHAPTER IX.

CONVENT AND CHURCH OF THE SS. ANNUNZIATA.

THE Convent and Church of the SS. Annunziata was built by the Servi or Serviti, an order of monks founded in 1239 by seven rich and noble Florentines, who were in the habit of meeting daily to sing the "Ave Maria," or evening service to the Madonna, in the Chapel of San Zenobio, on the site of Giotto's Campanile. Their piety was so conspicuous, that the women and children as they passed them would exclaim, "Guardate i Servi di Maria," "Behold the Servants of the Virgin." This religious fervour at length led them to retire from the world, and to devote themselves wholly to the service of the Madonna. They selected for their retreat a poor and wretched cottage near the Porta dei Peruzzi, on the site of the present Church of Sta. Croce; but finding an abode so near the city unfavourable to contemplation, they removed to the summit of Monte Senario, one of the Apennines, about seven miles north of Florence, where their monastery, in the midst of its dark woods, is still visible from many parts of the city.

---

* See Mrs. Jameson's "Monastic Orders."

The Convent and Church of the SS. Annunziata was built in 1250, on the site of the ancient oratory, by one of the seven original founders of the order. At that period this quarter of Florence was outside the third circuit of walls, and was known as Cafaggio, Campo di Faggio—Field of Beech. The convent has nothing remarkable in its structure; but the church, altered and embellished at different periods, is handsome and very richly decorated. The entrance was originally towards the north.

The atrium or portico of the church faces the piazza, and is composed of seven arches, raised on slender Corinthian columns. The central arch was erected by Leo X., after a design by Antonio di San Gallo, and in 1512 it was decorated with a fresco representing Faith, Hope, and Charity, by Jacopo Carucci da Pontormo (1493 —1588); but of which unfortunately little now remains. Pontormo was only nineteen years of age when he executed this fresco; and Michael Angelo esteemed the work so highly, that he declared, "If the youth continued in this path he would raise painting to the skies." There are three doors under the portico; that to the left opens on the cloister and leads to the convent; to the right is the entrance to the Chapel of the Pucci family, dedicated to San Sebastiano. It was founded about the year 1300, and was adorned with frescos by Pocetti, in the seventeenth century. It formerly contained an altarpiece—the Martyrdom of St. Sebastian, by Antonio Pollajuolo (1426—1498), which is now in the National Gallery of London, as it was sold by the Marchese Pucci in 1857. The picture is one of Pollajuolo's most celebrated works.

The central door under the portico opens on the cortile,

or court of entrance; over this door is a lunette, containing a mosaic of the Annunciation, by David Ghirlandaio, who, inferior to his brother Domenico in painting, excelled him as a mosaicist. The cortile is surrounded by an arcade, according to the old basilican type,* here a late addition made by the Medici; it is decorated with frescos, most of which are preserved under glass. They are best seen in the morning light. The earliest of the series, by Alessio Baldovinetti (1422—1499), represents the Nativity, and is painted at the back of the Chapel of the Annunciation. Alessio made use of a strong vehicle, composed of yolk of eggs mixed with varnish, by which he hoped to preserve his paintings from the weather, but unfortunately it peeled off, and the colours disappeared, as may be seen in this fresco, of which Vasari writes, that it was executed with such pains that every wisp of the straw thatch of the cottage can be counted; he imitated the effect on stone caused by rain and ice in the ruined walls, and faithfully copied from nature the root of a great ivy, painting the different colour of the two sides of the leaves, &c. A close imitator of nature, the outline drawing here, which is discovered by the destruction of the painting, is very pure and correct. The Virgin kneels in prayer before the Infant, who lies on the ground. St. Joseph is plunged in thought, his hands clasped over his right knee; two shepherds advance towards the group, and a serpent behind them is retreating through a hole in the wall, symbolizing the sin of our first parents departing with the birth of the Saviour. The Annunciation to the Shepherds is represented to the

---

* See "Christian Art," Lord Lindsay, vol. L p. 13.

left of the picture, with a beautiful landscape background; a frame painted in medallions surrounds the composition.* The genuine works of Alessio Baldovinetti are very rare.

Next this fresco is the Life and Miracles of San Filippo Benizzi, by Cosimo Rosselli and Andrea del Sarto, in six compartments, preserved beneath glass. This saint joined the Servites in 1247, fifteen years after the foundation of the order; he had begun life as a physician, and had studied in Padua and at Paris, before he returned to Florence to practise his art. In obedience to a vision which appeared to him whilst attending mass in the Chapel of the SS. Annunziata, he resolved to abandon the world, and he retired to Monte Senario, where he became distinguished as a preacher, and ultimately rose to be General of the order; he died in 1285. Leo X. granted him the title of *beato* † in 1516, but he was not formally canonized until 1671. It was on the occasion of his beatification that this cortile was decorated with frescos. The first of this series was painted by Cosimo Rosselli (1439—1506 ?), and represents the saint assuming the habit of the order. It is not a picture of superlative merit, nor even the best specimen of the master. The five other compartments, representing the miracles of San Filippo Benizzi, are by Andrea del Sarto, and painted after 1548. Vasari relates that the sacristan of the convent, one Fra Mariano, when he engaged Andrea's services, ingeniously contrived, by rousing his

---

* See " Crowe and Cavalcaselle," vol. ii. p. 375.

† The decree of beatification did not confer the privilege of being invoked as an intercessor and portrayed in the churches; it was merely a declaration that the person so distinguished had passed a holy life, and been received into bliss—*beato*, " blessed."

jealousy of his brother-artist Franciabigio, to get as much as possible from him at the smallest remuneration. The first fresco by Andrea del Sarto represents San Filippo, on his road to the Papal Court at Viterbo, dividing his cloak with a leper. Next to this is one of the best of the series, —the saint, with three of the brethren, is on his way to Monte Senario, and is persecuted by the insults and gibes of a party of loose fellows; a storm arises, and these men take refuge under a tree, where they are killed by the lightning, while San Filippo and his companions pull their cowls over their heads, and quietly pursue their way. This fresco exhibits Andrea's versatility in composition, as well as his skill in landscape. In the fourth fresco, San Filippo heals a woman possessed with a demon; the incident is rendered with simplicity, the interest of the spectators is well-sustained, and there is neither coarseness nor exaggeration in the attitude and expression of the afflicted person. These three frescos were the first Andrea executed, and excited so much admiration that he was at once ordered to commence the two last of the series,—the Miracle performed on the death of San Filippo, and children healed of disease by touching his garments. In the first, a friar leans over the dead body, while groups of spectators are gathered together on either side, in the foreground; the priests in the background suspend their chant in astonishment, as they witness the miracle: a child is lying dead on the floor, but, revived by the touch of the saint's bier, he rises to life. The other fresco, in which children are brought by their parents to touch the garments of San Filippo, is remarkably well composed. A priest stands in a doorway, and lays the clothes on the head of a child, who kneels beside his mother; to the left a cripple receives charity; to the right an aged man approaches, leaning on his staff, supposed to be the portrait of Andrea della Robbia, personally known to Andrea del Sarto, and father of the more celebrated Luca.* An admirable bust of Andrea del Sarto, in the centre of the arcade, is by Raffaelle da Montelupo, a pupil of Michael Angelo, and is placed over his grave.

The opposite side of the cortile, also protected by glass, contains two other frescos by Andrea del Sarto, one by Franciabigio, another by Jacopo da Pontormo, and the last by Il Rosso Fiorentino.

The Visit of the Magi, and the Birth of the Virgin, are by Andrea. The former was intended for a continuation of Baldovinetti's Nativity. In the foreground, among the followers of the kings, Andrea has introduced several portraits. To the right, the figure facing the spectator is the sculptor, Jacopo Sansovino; the head seen in profile is the musician, Françesco Ajolle; the figure leaning on the arm of Sansovino is Andrea himself. The Nativity of the Virgin is one of Andrea's finest compositions. The picture is divided into two groups, of which Joachim, who sits meditating, forms the connecting link; St. Anne is the centre of attraction in the group to the right, the infant Virgin in that to the left. The females in attendance are singularly graceful and dignified. When Jacopo da Empoli, about 1570, some years after the death of Andrea, was copying this fresco, an old lady who was on her way to mass paused beside his easel, and pointing to the central figure, informed him, that was the portrait of the painter's

---

* See "Crowe and Cavalcaselle," vol. iii. pp. 546—550.

wife. After conversing with Jacopo some little time, she acknowledged herself to be Lucretia, the beautiful widow of a hatter, whom Andrea married, and who became the torment of his life.

The Marriage of the Virgin is by Françesco di Cristofano, better known as Franciabigio (1482—1525), a pupil of Albertinelli, and friend of Andrea del Sarto. He painted this fresco in 1513. The High Priest marries Joseph and Mary before a noble palace, covered with reliefs of Scripture subjects. The despair of the unsuccessful suitors is well represented. Franciabigio had nearly finished his painting on the eve of a great festival of the Church, some touches were still wanting, when the monks, impatient to display the work, removed the screens. The wrath of the artist knew no bounds; he hastened to the convent, and, seizing a hammer, nearly obliterated the heads of the Virgin and of several other persons, to the great amusement of his companions, none of whom could be persuaded to restore what the master had destroyed. To this day the fresco, although the best work of Franciabigio, has remained in the condition in which he left it.

The adjoining fresco, the Visitation of Elizabeth to Mary, is by Jacopo da Pontormo, the pupil of Andrea del Sarto, who executed it in 1516. Vasari praises the work, and says that Pontormo painted it in a new manner, and was especially successful in the flesh, referring particularly to the boy seated on the steps. The Assumption of the Virgin, the last of the series in the cortile, is by Il Rosso Fiorentino (1496—1541), who painted it in 1513, when only seventeen years of age. Il Rosso afterwards visited Rome and Venice, and proceeded to France, where he painted for

Francis I., and was appointed by that monarch superintendant of the works at Fontainebleau. The Madonna is surrounded in the heavens by a crowd of angels; the Apostles stand below; St. James, who wears the dress of a pilgrim, is the portrait of Françesco Berni, the satirist; and the smile Franciabigio has given him is probably in allusion to the style of comic poetry which he invented, and which has been called after him Bernesca.

The Church of the SS. Annunziata is composed of a single nave, with five chapels on either side, two short transepts, and a circular choir, surmounted by a cupola. The whole is richly decorated with paintings, stucco, and gilding. The Assumption of the Virgin on the ceiling of the nave is by Baldassare Françeschini, called Il Volterrano (1611—1689), one of the best painters in fresco of his day, and a pupil of Matteo Rosselli (the best colourist of the Revival), and of Giovanni di San Giovanni. The cupola of the tribune is also by him. Twelve frescos along the whole length of the nave, on the wall beneath the ceiling, are by Cosimo Ulivelli (1625—1704), a pupil of Il Volterrano. Before the church was as much decorated as it now is, it was customary to suspend from the roof waxen images of living eminent persons. This privilege was only granted to citizens entitled to the highest magisterial offices, or to foreign sovereigns. The effigy of Lorenzo de' Medici, by Andrea Verocchio, was thus suspended in the dress he wore when he miraculously escaped death from the daggers of the Pazzi. To remove any such effigy was considered the greatest insult and disgrace; and if one fell to the ground it was thought an evil omen. The images of Florentine citizens were hung on one side of the church; those of Popes and foreign potentates on the other. When the SS. Annunziata was altered to please modern taste, these effigies were transferred to the outer cortile, but in the reign of Pietro Leopoldo they were wholly removed.

There are few pictures of any importance in this church. The first chapel, to the right of the entrance, contains the last work of Jacopo Chimenti da Empoli (1554—1640). The subject is the Virgin with St. Nicholas and other saints. Jacopo was a diligent copyist of the paintings of Andrea del Sarto, and one of the best masters of his period, which was that of the reformed Florentine School. This picture has, however, been so much meddled with, that it is difficult to recognise the hand of the master.

The second chapel has a good altarpiece by Piero Dandini (1646—1712), a Florentine painter of considerable merit, patronised by the Grand-Duke Cosimo III., but negligent in the finishing of his works.

In the fifth chapel, on this side, is the tomb of Orlando de' Medici, who lived in the fifteenth century, but was in no way distinguished except having been knighted by the Emperor Frederick III. in the Florentine Cathedral. The monument is, however, a fine example of the sculpture of that period, and is attributed to Simone, by some supposed to have been the brother of Donatello.

The sixth chapel contains the grave of the painter Giovanni Stradone; his bust is by his son Scipio. Strada, Stradanus, or Stradone, born at Bruges in 1536, and much employed in Rome, where he worked in conjunction with Daniele da Volterra, was a member of the Florentine Academy, and died in Florence in 1605.

The nave is terminated on either side by richly sculptured

marble organ galleries, with altars below, the work of Francesco Silvani.

In the eastern transept is a chapel containing the tomb of Baccio Bandinelli, the vain, ambitious, feeble rival of Michael Angelo, of whom so many diverting anecdotes are related by Benvenuto Cellini; he was laid here in 1529: the monument was executed by himself; the subject is a Pietà; the Saviour resting in the arms of Nicodemus, whom Bandinelli intended for his own portrait. His profile, and that of his wife, in relief, decorate the frieze to the back of the monument.

The tribune is approached from the nave by a lofty arch, on either side of which are monuments; that to the right is to the memory of the Senator Donato dell' Antella, and is by Giovan Battista Foggini. Antella, after enjoying his worldly possessions and dignities to advanced life, became a priest, and bestowed all he had on the Servites, with the condition that his money should be expended on the decoration of the church. He died in 1666. The opposite very striking monument was erected to the memory of Angiolo Marzi Medici, and is the work of Francesco di San Gallo. Angiolo Marzi was a notary of San Gemignano, and began his career as secretary to Piero Soderini, Gonfalonier of the Republic. Accommodating his views to the times, he became a faithful adherent of the Medici faction, when Soderini was expelled in 1512; and he accompanied Cardinal Giulio de' Medici when he assumed the tiara as Clement VII. Marzi was afterwards appointed Secretary to Duke Alexander, and still later to Cosimo I., who allowed him to add the name of Medici to his own, and to adopt the Medici balls in his coat of arms. He is here represented in the dress of a bishop, with a mitre on his head, and reclining on a couch. He died in 1546, and his remains repose beneath this monument.

The tribune, or choir, is circular, and surrounded by chapels. The cupola above was built about the middle of the fifteenth century, after a design by Leon Battista Alberti, and at the expense of Luigi Gonzaga, Marquis of Mantua, surnamed the Turk, who reigned from 1444 to 1478. He was one of the first generals in Europe, but was still more celebrated for his taste in the fine arts, and for his patronage of artists at his court.

The high altar in the centre of the choir, or tribune, is raised several steps, and has a splendid *ciborio*—pyx—carved in wood by Baccio d' Agnolo, 1543. Baccio also executed the *intarsiatura*, or wood mosaic, of the choir. Immediately behind the altar is the Capella del Soccorso, where lie the remains of Giovan Bologna. He selected this place himself, and decorated it at his own expense, with the intention that any Fleming rendering good service to sculpture or architecture, might likewise be buried here. The altarpiece of the chapel, the Resurrection of our Lord, is by Domenico Cresti (1558—1638), called Passignano, from his birthplace, near Florence. The Crucifix and bronze reliefs were executed by pupils of Giovan Bologna, under his directions. The two small statues of Active and Contemplative Life are by Francavilla, the French artist, who made the statues on the bridge of the SS. Trinità. The frescos on the vaulted ceiling, which are nearly effaced, are by Bernardo Pocetti. In the adjoining chapel is a good altar-piece by Angelo Bronzino, representing the Resurrection. The next chapel contains a painting attributed to

Perugino, but more probably by one of his pupils; the Virgin is seated on a throne, surrounded by four saints; it is much injured by restorations.

The cloister and sacristy are approached through the western transept. The latter is a handsome apartment; the marble frame round the door, within the room, is delicately sculptured in the style of Benedetto da Majano.

Descending the nave to the left of the high altar, the fifth chapel from the entrance, on this side, contains an altar-piece by Perugino (1446—1524), representing an Assumption of the Virgin. The contemporaries of Perugino accused him of repeating his early pictures in his later works; and he defended himself by maintaining that he only copied what had already obtained the approbation of the public; his reputation, however, suffered in consequence, and he quitted Florence to return to Perugia. Giannicolo Manni, his pupil, is said to have painted a great part of this picture. The fourth chapel—Capella del SS. Crocifisso—has an altarpiece by Stradone, which is esteemed his finest work. In the third chapel is a copy of Michael Angelo's Last Judgment, by Alessandro Allori (1533—1607). Alessandro was the father of the more celebrated Cristofano. The head, seen above the body covered with a white sheet, is supposed to be a portrait of Michael Angelo.

The last chapel is called the Chapel of the Annunciation. It was constructed by Piero, son of Lorenzo the Magnificent, after a design by Michelozzi, and contains the so-called miraculous painting of the Annunciation, attributed by some to a certain Bartolommeo, by others supposed to be by Pietro Cavallini, the disciple of Giotto, who practised the art of mosaic as well as painting. Vasari

CONVENT AND CHURCH OF SS. ANNUNZIATA.

states that Cavallini was born at Rome in 1279, and died in 1364; but others assign an earlier date to this artist, and believe him to have been the architect of Edward the Confessor's shrine in Westminster Abbey, erected by Henry III., 1269, as well as of the crosses to the memory of Eleanor, Queen of Edward I. There is a repetition of this picture of the Annunciation, also by Pietro Cavallini, in the Church of San Marco; but that belonging to the SS. Annunziata is said to have been finished by an angelic hand, when the artist had fallen asleep and dreamt that he was unworthy to paint the mother of our Lord. This picture is considered so sacred that it is only exhibited on great festivals of the church, when the crowd of worshippers renders it impossible for any stranger to obtain a glimpse; at all other times it is invisible. The wooden Crucifix in this chapel is by Giuliano di San Gallo, and the marble image of the infant Jesus is by Baccio Bandinelli. The head of the Saviour over the altar is a good work of Andrea del Sarto. The silver lamps and rich decorations, in pietradura, or Florentine mosaic, were made at the expense of the Grand-Duke Cosimo I., and of his son, Ferdinand I. Ferdinand is represented in a relief, on his knees, invoking the aid of the Holy Virgin.

The Cloister of the SS. Annunziata was built by Simone Pollajuolo, "Il Cronaca," towards the end of the fifteenth century. It is surrounded by frescos, chiefly by Bernardino Barbatelli, called Pocetti, who was born in Florence, 1542. In a lunette over a door in this cloister is Andrea del Sarto's most celebrated work, the Madonna del Sacco, so called from Joseph being represented leaning on a sack of corn. Vasari declares that "for drawing, grace, beauty of colour, liveliness, and relief, no artist had ever approached this fresco," and though this praise appears exaggerated, the work, even in its present ruined state, possesses, a simple grandeur and nobleness of conception and execution which has rarely found its equal. Françesco Bocchi, a friend of Giovan Bologna, who wrote a guide to Florence,* relates that Michael Angelo was such an admirer of this work, as well as of other paintings by Andrea del Sarto, that he observed to Raffaello d' Urbino, "There is a little man (*homocetto*) in Florence who, if he is employed in works of magnitude, will make you sweat for it—*ti farà sudar la fronte;*" which observation, however (always granting the high merits of Andrea del Sarto), was, if true, an amusing piece of egotism in the great sculptor, as well as in the writer who recorded it, and must have sprung as much from jealousy for the honour of the city he belonged to, as from any just comparison between Andrea and Raffaelle.

The Company of St. Luke, or Confraternity of Artists, which was instituted in 1350, at one time held their meetings in an oratory of the Hospital of Santa Maria Nuova, but in the middle of the sixteenth century they were transferred to a chapel within this cloister. In the small vestibule leading to the chapel is a well-executed crucifix in bronze, and a very sweet low relief of the Madonna and Child, with two angels, by Mino da Fiesole. The ceiling of the chapel is painted in fresco by Luca Giordano, who was born in Naples 1632, and died 1705. Over the altar is a fresco by Vasari—St. Luke painting

---

* "Le Bellezze della Città di Firenze da M. Francesco Bocchi, da M. Giovanni Cinelli ampliate ed accresciuto." Firenze: 1677.

the Virgin. Three other frescos decorate the walls—The Trinity, by Angelo Bronzino; a Madonna and Saints, by Jacopo Pontormo; and Solomon building the Temple of Jerusalem, by Santi di Tito. Two marble busts, by Montorsoli, the pupil of Michael Angelo, are over the doors of the chapel—one represents the Saviour, the other his own portrait. The statues around are copies from the frescos of the Sistine Chapel in Rome, and are by the pupils of Michael Angelo. The small fresco, in monochrome, above these statues, are by Pocetti. Several celebrated artists are buried beneath this chapel—Jacopo Pontormo, Franciabigio, Benvenuto Cellini, &c. The last buried here was Lorenzo Bartolini, whose graceful works in sculpture are frequently met with in Florence.

CHRONOLOGY.

	A.D.
Alberti, Leon Battista	b. 1398—d. 1480
Allori, Alessandro	b. 1533—d. 1607
Baccio d' Agnolo	1543
Baldovinetti, Alesso	b. 1422—d. 1499
Bandinelli, Baccio	d. 1529
Benizzi, San Filippo	b. 1232—d. 1285
,, ,, his Beatification	1516
,, ,, frescos by Andrea del Sarto of	1548
Berni, Françesco	d. 1536
Bologna Giovan	b. 1525—d. 1608
Bronzino, Angiolo	b. 1502—d. 1570
Cavallini, Pietro	b. 1279—1364 (?)
Chapel of S. Sebastiano founded	1300
Church of SS. Annunziata founded	1250
Company of St. Luke founded	1350
Cronaca, Simone Pollaiolo	b. 1454—d. 1509

128   WALKS IN FLORENCE.

	A.D.
Dandini, Piero	b. 1646—d. 1712
Empoli, Jacopo Chimenti da	b. 1554—d. 1640
Foggini, Giovan Battista	b. 1715—d. 1783
Franciabigio	b. 1482—d. 1525
,, ,, his fresco in the SS. Annunziata	1513
Franceschini, Baldassare, Il Volterrano	b. 1611—d. 1689
Giordano, Luca	b. 1632—d. 1705
Gonzaga, Luigi, Marquis of Mantua	b. 1444—d. 1478
Michelozzo de' Michelozzi	b. 1396—d. 1470
Mino da Fiesole	b. 1431—d. 1486
Marzi Medici	d. 1546
Passignano	b. 1558—d. 1638
Perugino, Pietro	b. 1446—d. 1524
Pocetti, Bernardo	b. 1542—d. 1612
Pollaiolo, Antonio	b. 1426—d. 1498
Pontormo, Jacopo Carucci da	b. 1493—d. 1588
Rosselli, Cosimo	b. 1439—d. 1500
Rosso, Il	b. 1496—d. 1541
San Gallo, Giuliano di	b. 1443—d. 1517
,, Francesco di	b. 1482—d. 1546
Servites, Order of, founded	1239
Silvani, Gherardo	b. 1570—d. 1675
Stradone, Giovanni	d. 1605
Ulivelli, Cosimo	b. 1625—d. 1704

CHAPTER X.

PIAZZA OF THE SS. ANNUNZIATA, AND HOSPITAL OF THE FOUNDLINGS—"INNOCENTI."

THE piazza in front of the Church of the SS. Annunziata is adorned by two handsome fountains, placed here in 1643. They are composed of a mixture of bronze and marble, and represent sea-monsters, executed by Pietro Tacca, of Carrara, a pupil of Giovan Bologna, who lived in the early part of the seventeenth century. He also cast the equestrian statue of the Grand-Duke Ferdinand I. in the centre of the piazza, which was modelled by Giovan Bologna in his old age, and was placed here six months after his death. The bronze was supplied from cannon taken from the Turks at Bona, in Africa, by the knights of St. Stephen, a military order instituted by Cosimo I. Ferdinand was the second son of Cosimo, and was educated for the church; but on the death of his brother Francis* he ascended the throne of Tuscany, and as he was less cruel than his father, though not less eager for territorial aggrandisement, he was not quite as much hated by his subjects.

---

* Francis I. and his wife Bianca Capello died within a few hours of one another at Poggio a Cajano, in 1587.

On either side of the piazza are arcades of very elegant proportions, raised several steps. That to the left of the church was built by the monks of the adjoining convent of the SS. Annunziata about the year 1520, after a design of Antonio Giamberti di San Gallo, a brother of Giuliano di San Gallo. The houses beneath this arcade are let out to private individuals. The arcade to the right of the church was built after a design of Filippo Brunelleschi. It is decorated with medallions of the Della Robbia school, representing swaddled infants, varied in form and expression, and charmingly executed. Beneath the arcade are busts of the Medicean grand-dukes, and over the doors are lunettes, one of which is modern, the other a fine fresco by Il Graffione, a pupil of Alessio Baldovinetti,* representing the Eternal surrounded by angels. The central door leads into the cortile of the Foundling Hospital—Spedale degli Innocenti—round which are again images of swaddled infants, the cock of the Bigallo, and the gate of the Art of Silk. This institution, one of the earliest of the kind, was founded in 1421, when Giovanni de' Medici was gonfalonier, who was stimulated to this good work by an eloquent appeal from Leonardo Aretino.† The management was confided to the Guild of Silk, and the building was constructed by Françesco della Luna, after a design of his master Brunelleschi, upon gardens and land belonging to the Albizzi family. The hospital was opened in 1444, and gradually acquired additional funds by the successive incorporation of smaller analogous institutions previously exist-

---

* See Vasari, "Vite dei Pittori," vol. iv. p. 106.
† The monument of Leonardo Aretino is in Sta. Croce.

ing.* It was liberally endowed by the Medici and succeeding grand-dukes. During the reign of Pietro Leopoldo, 1765—1790, the Innocenti underwent some important reforms. Most of the boys admitted to the charity are brought up as field labourers, but receive aid from the institution until the age of eighteen. The girls can claim marriage dowries, and are under the guardianship of the institution until the age of thirty-five; but when younger, they are sent out as domestic servants, or are educated for a trade. Between seven and eight thousand foundlings are annually supported, though few are actually maintained within the building. The larger number, soon after admission, are dispersed among the peasantry living round Florence, who are paid for their maintenance until they are old enough to return to the institution within the city.

There are several interesting pictures in the Commission-room of the Innocenti, the pious gifts of artists and their patrons. One of the most important is by Filippo Lippi, 1412—1469, in which a boy-angel brings the Christ-child to the Madonna. It is almost a *replica* of one in the room of early Tuscan masters in the Uffizi Gallery; this picture is, however, superior in refinement, grace, and fresh harmonious colour. Instead of two angels there is but one; the head, throat, and hands of the Virgin are exquisitely modelled, and the figure of the Child is drawn with the utmost care and delicacy. Another very fine picture in this room is by Piero di Cosimo, 1460—1521, the master of Andrea del

---

* An institution in the Via della Scala was converted into the Convent of San Martino, but remained long in possession of a fine piece of Robbia ware, representing swaddled infants, which is now in the Bargello.

Sarto; Elizabeth of Hungary is here represented offering roses to the Christ-child, who is seated on his mother's knee. Groups of saints are on either side. The Virgin is sweet and tender in composition, and the drawing good. A predella, divided into four parts, is by Domenico Ghirlandaio. The subjects are: The Marriage of the Virgin, The Presentation in the Temple, The Baptism, and The Entombment; the last is especially fine. This predella originally belonged to the altar-piece of the Church of the Innocenti. The other pictures are: The Martyrdom of St. John, by Ghirlandaio; an Annunciation, by Piero di Cosimo; the same subject by Pietro Cavallini, who, as already mentioned, painted the sacred picture in the SS. Annunziata; and a Madonna gathering children beneath her mantle, by an unknown master, probably painted in allusion to the object of this institution; the children are extremely lovely, playful, and tender.

Near the entrance to the Church, within the cloister, is a most exquisite relief in Robbia work, representing the Annunciation. The angel, with look inspired, bends reverentially before the meek and lovely Virgin; a vase of lilies is between them, and a garland of cherubs' heads, beautiful and varied in their infantile expression, surrounds the group.*

The only picture of merit within the church is the altar-piece—The Adoration of the Magi, by Domenico Ghirlandaio, executed in 1498, his greatest work on panel. The Virgin, a calm, dignified figure, holds the Child tenderly on her knee; Joseph stands near, with the usual accompaniments of the ox and the ass; the principal

---

* See illustration at the beginning of this chapter.

Annunciation, by Luca della Robbia.—Hospital of the Innocents.

Page 139. II.

king, a noble old man, kneels reverently and kisses the Child's foot; the second king, a beautiful youth, with long fair hair, holds a jewelled glass cup in his hand; his cloak falls from his shoulders in majestic folds; behind him are three fine portrait-like heads. On the opposite side are groups of persons, evidently portraits, who represent the followers of the Magi, and in the far distance is seen the Annunciation to the Shepherds, who are feeding their flocks on a hill. The Murder of the Innocents is represented to the left, where a winding road leads up to a convent and a church. The shed over the Holy Family is supported by pilasters with rich arabesques, and beyond is a river and mountainous landscape, a town and church with a spire. Two shepherds look over the wall. The group of the Murder of the Innocents has evidently formed a study for Raffaelle in his composition of the same subject, especially that of a mother escaping with a child in her arms, whilst an older one is running towards the river. One mother is seated on the ground, whilst a third attempts to fly from a soldier, who holds her back by her hair, and raises his arm to strike. Two of the Innocents, clothed in white, typical of their having entered into glory, and with bleeding wounds, kneel before the Saviour, and are presented to him by St. John the Baptist and St. John the Evangelist; these children, who form the most beautiful part of the picture, are, however, attributed to Fra Filippo Lippi. In the midst of the group to the left of the Virgin, and the fourth figure from the side of the picture, is Ghirlandaio's own portrait. The colour is full and simple; the details are carefully finished, and there is great power and precision in the drawing, but, above all, a wonderful grace and truth of expression.

CHRONOLOGY.

	A.D.
Aretino, Leonardo	b. 1369—d. 1444
Bologna, Giovan	b. 1525—d. 1608
Brunelleschi, Filippo	b. 1377—d. 1444
Cavallini, Pietro	b. 1279—d. 1364 (?)
Cosimo, Piero di	b. 1460—d. 1521
Fountains in the Piazza di SS. Annunziata	1643
Ghirlandaio, Domenico	b. 1449—d. 1493
,, ,, his altar-piece in the Innocenti	1498
Innocenti Hospital founded	1421
,, ,, opened	1444
Lippo, Fra Filippo	b. 1412—d. 1469
Robbia, Luca della	b. 1400—d. 1481

CHAPTER XI.

CONVENT OF STA. MARIA DEGLI ANGELI.—IL CASTEL-LACCIO.—CINQUE LAMPADE.—VIA RICASOLI.—VIA DELLA SAPIENZA.—PIAZZA DI SAN MARCO.—VIA CAVOUR.—MARUCELLIANA LIBRARY.—PALAZZO RICCARDI.—PALAZZO MARTELLI.—PALAZZO GINORI.

FROM the Innocenti, the Via dei Fibbiai, where lived Andrea del Castagno, leads to the Via degli Alfani. In this street was formerly one of the most considerable monasteries of Florence, known as the Sta. Maria degli Angeli: the roughly-hewn wall at the corner is the remains of an unfinished building designed by Brunelleschi, with the intention of enlarging the church; from its octagon form, resembling a fortress or castle, it has obtained the name of the Castellaccio, or the ugly castle. The monastery was founded about 1293 by a certain Fra Guittone, of Arezzo, assisted by Don Fridiano, the prior of the Calmaldolese monastery in the Casentino.

Fra Guittone, of Arezzo, was one of the Gaudenti, or Jovial Friars, mentioned by Dante in his "Divina Commedia." Guittone was a poet, and first brought the Italian sonnet to perfection; he left behind him the earliest specimens of Italian letter-writing. One of his most celebrated letters was addressed to Florence, beginning, "O queen of cities, court of justice, school of wisdom, mirror of life, and mould of manners! whose sons were kings reigning in every land, or were above all others, who art no longer queen but servant, oppressed and subject to tribute! no longer court of justice, but cave of robbers, and school of all folly and madness, mirror of death and mould of felony," &c., &c.

Dante mentions Guittone in his "Purgatorio," where another poet, Buongiunta, of Lucca, addresses the author in these words:—

> "Ma di, s' io veggio qui colui, che fuore
> Trasse le nuove rime, cominciando,
> '*Donne ch' avete intelletto d'amor?*'
> Et io a lui: 'Io mi son un, che, quando
> Amore spira, noto; et a quel modo
> Che detta dentro, vo significando.'
> 'O Frate, issa veggio,' diss' egli, 'il nodo
> Che 'l notaio,* e Guittone, e me ritenne
> Di quà del dolce stil nuovo, ch' i' odo.
> Io veggio ben, come le vostre penne
> Diretro al dittator sen vanno strette
> Che delle nostre certo non avvenne;
> E qual più a gradire oltre si mette,
> Non vede più dall' uno all' altro stilo.'
> E quasi contentato si tacette."†
>
> *Purgatorio*, xxiv. 49.

---

* Jacopo da Lentino, or "'the Notary,'" was a Sicilian poet who flourished about 1250, in the later days of the Emperor Frederick II. See notes to "Dante," Longfellow, p. 431.

† "But say if him I here behold who forth
    Evoked the new-invented rhymes, beginning
   '*Ladies that have intelligence of Love!*'

CONVENT OF STA. MARIA DEGLI ANGELI, ETC.

Dante apparently did not place a high value on Guittone's verses, or at any rate esteems him inferior to another poet, Guido Guinicelli, who is supposed to speak thus to the friar:—

> "Così fer molti antichi di Guittone;
> Di grido, in grido, pur lui dando pregio,
> Fin che l' ha vinto l' ver con più persone." [b]
>
> *Purgatorio*, xxvi. 124.

The spot chosen for Sta. Maria degli Angeli was outside the Porta a Balla, on the same ground of Cafagiolo—Campo di Faggio, Field of Beech—on which the SS. Annunziata was also built, and the foundations were laid with great pomp and ceremony by the bishop, the gonfalonier, and other magistrates of Florence. The wealth of the monastery rapidly increased by donations in money and land. During the plague of 1348 all the monks perished, and a fresh supply were sent

---

> And I to him: 'One am I who, whenever
> Love doth inspire me, note, and in that measure
> Which he within me dictates, singing go.'
> 'O brother, now I see,' he said, 'the knot
> Which me, the Notary, and Guittone held
> Short of the sweet new style that now I hear.
> I do perceive full clearly how your pens
> Go closely following after him who dictates,
> Which with our own, forsooth, came not to pass;
> And he who sets himself to go beyond,
> No difference sees from one style to another.'
> And, as if satisfied, he held his peace."
>
> *Longfellow's Translation.*

[b] "Thus many ancients with Guittone did;
From cry to cry still giving him applause,
Until the truth has conquered with most persons." [a]

---

[a] See Longfellow's translation and notes.

from the Hermitage of Calmaldoli, who soon gained a reputation for industry in embroidering priests' vestments, and in illuminating liturgies and choral books. Whilst the Ciompi riots were raging in the city, many Florentines brought their treasures for security to this monastery, but it was unhappily attacked and plundered by the mob. The enlargement of the church, for which Brunelleschi was employed, was commenced with funds bequeathed for that purpose by one Matteo degli Scolari in 1424; but the Government used the money for a war with Lucca, and the Castellaccio was left as a monument of their unfaithful discharge of a dying man's request. The Grand-Duke Cosimo I. proposed to turn it into a drawing academy, but changed his intention; the roof was allowed to fall in, and the work of Brunelleschi was left a ruin. It is now the studio of the sculptor Signor Pazzi, who composed the statue of Dante, which is in the centre of the Piazza di Sta. Croce, and who has just completed a fine statue of Savonarola.

The pious lives of the monks of Sta. Maria degli Angeli induced Pope Boniface IX. to grant plenary indulgence to every person dwelling within the precincts of the monastery; and the Florentine Republic cancelled all their debts. Early in the fourteenth century, a Neapolitan, Ambrogio Traversari, celebrated for his learning, was chosen General of the Order. Whilst yet a simple monk, he persuaded the prior to allow a new academy for the study of Greek and Latin to hold its meetings within their walls; and here Cosimo, afterwards Pater Patriæ, and his brother Lorenzo, sons of Giovanni de' Medici, with Gino Capponi, Landini, Bernardo Pucci, and others, who afterwards became celebrated, received their education. When Pope Eugenius IV. came to Florence in 1435, Ambrogio was sent with several eminent citizens to meet him at Leghorn. Besides his reputation for learning, and as a reformer of morals within the monasteries, Ambrogio was known for his skill in music and embroidery.

Not long ago there was a beautiful group of Luca della Robbia over the doorway leading to the former monastery, but this, with other works of art within the building, have been removed. A few frescos still remain; one by Ridolfo Ghirlandaio in the cloisters, and two Crucifixions by Andrea del Castagno; that by Castagno, in the first cloister, represents the Saviour life-size, between the Virgin and St. John; St. Benedict is next to the Virgin, and St. Romualdo by St. John; the Magdalene is at the foot of the cross. The figure of Christ is in good proportions, and the action well studied. The second Crucifixion, in the fifth cell of the second cloister, is without the Magdalene. All this part of the building has been incorporated into the Hospital of Sta. Maria Nuova, and is partly used for lecture-rooms. Opposite Sta. Maria degli Angeli is the fine palace of the Counts della Porta, once Palazzo Guigni, to which family it had descended from the family Da Firenzuola. The palace was built after a design by Ammanati, upon the remains of the ancient Convent of Sta. Margherita, which was inhabited by Camaldolese nuns. Between this and the Canto alla Catena, called so from the Alberti arms—the Fetters—on a house there, was one of the celebrated *tiratoj* of the Guild of Wool. At the corner of the Via del Castellaccio, leading into the Via de' Servi, is a tablet marking the dwelling of the sculptor Benedetto da Majano. In the Via de' Pucci, between the Via de' Servi and the Via

Ricasoli, is the Palace of the Marchese Pucci, whose family contributed to the decorations of the Church of the SS. Annunziata; within the palace is a gallery of pictures, including some good Botticelli's, but difficult of access, since the marchese has given strict orders to refuse admittance to all strangers. At the corner of the Via Ricasoli, formerly Cocomero, is a tabernacle before which hang five lamps, well known throughout Florence as the "Tabernacolo delle Cinque Lampade."* In the house to which it is attached lived Andrea Tafi, the author of the miraculous picture of a Madonna and Child, contained within the tabernacle. Buffalmacco and Giotto were likewise inhabitants of this dwelling. The little palace adjoining was built by Buontalenti, and belonged to Serguidi, the Secretary of the Grand-Duke Francis I.

In the Via Ricasoli, opposite the suppressed Convent of San Nicolò, lived Donatello.

Returning to the Piazza della SS. Annunziata, the large palace to the left of the Via Ricasoli belongs to the Manelli family, who date their origin back to Roman times, and at whose expense the Ponte Vecchio was built; but their history belongs to the Oltr' Arno. In one of the houses under the arcade in the piazza, opposite the Innocenti, lived, until 1528, the painter Françesco Rustici. Here he entertained his companions at supper; and a story is related that on one occasion Andrea del Sarto brought hither a dish of sausages and jellies, built up to resemble the Baptistery, with quails in the midst, to represent the priests in the choir.

---

* The Cinque Lampade formed the subject of tales by Sacchetti and Bocaccio.

In the Via della Sapienza, adjoining the Monastery of the
SS. Annunziata, a building was commenced, intended for a
college to instruct youth in science and letters. The money for
this purpose was provided by the will of Nicolò Uzzano,
and the trust confided to the Consuls of the Mercanzia.
But the college was never finished, and all that remains of
Uzzano's bequest is the name Sapienza given to the street,
and his arms on the outer walls of the monastery. The
incomplete building was used by the Grand-Duke Cosimo I.,
partly to contain the lions of the State, partly as a stable for
his horses. The opposite side of the street is now chiefly
occupied by sculptors who have their studios here, and of
whom Dupré, who executed the principal statues and reliefs
for the façade of Sta. Croce, is the most remarkable. The
corner house of the Piazza di San Marco is the Accademia
delle Belle Arti, which contains the finest collection of pictures by the early masters, and has also lecture rooms for
the professors of the Florentine University. The building
was originally the Hospital of St. Matthew, founded by one
Lemmo, who confided the care of it to the Consuls of the
Guild of Merchants of Exchange, " del Cambio," to which he
himself belonged, and of which St. Matthew was the patron
saint. The arms of Lemmo and of the Guild of Exchange
still remain on the walls, and a fresco within one of the
rooms, by Andrea del Sarto, commemorates the ward for
sick women. Leopold I. converted this hospital into the
Academy of Fine Arts. A row of low houses once occupied
the side of the piazza facing the church, one of which was
inhabited by the beautiful Bianca Capello, when she fled
hither with her husband from Venice ; and here she was
first seen by the Grand-Duke Francis I.—an event which

led to the murder of Capello, and to his widow becoming Grand-Duchess of Tuscany. On the western side was the Nunnery of Sta. Caterina, divided by the Via degli Arazzieri, now demolished for a Government building, and beyond it, towards the north, was the Giardino Medici di San Marco, where Lorenzo the Magnificent instituted a school or academy for young painters and sculptors. The place was sacked in 1494, when Piero de' Medici was driven from Florence, but restored to its original purpose by Giuliano de' Medici in 1512. Under Cosimo I. the funds for its support were withdrawn, but it was again restored by Prince Antonio, the son of the Grand-Duke Francis I. and Bianca Capello; here he was allowed, by the succeeding Grand-Duke Ferdinand I., to end his days unmolested. Ottaviano de' Medici, the ancestor of the Neapolitan branch of the Medici, occupied the Palace at one time, and bestowed a part of it on the Scalzi, or Barefooted Friars, for whom Andrea del Sarto painted the frescos in the cloister.

The Via Larga, or Cavour, extending from the walls to the Via Martelli, or Piazza del Duomo, is a wide street of palaces. Near where once stood the Convent of Sta. Caterina, were the houses of the Marucelli family, one of which contains the Public Library. Seven members of this family filled the office of Priors of the Republic, and Françesco Marucelli, an accomplished scholar, who died in 1703, bequeathed his valuable library to his native city. The number of volumes on all subjects is now nearly twelve thousand, arranged partly in rooms on the ground-floor, partly on the first floor of the palace. The governors propose to confine this library as much as possible to subjects relating to Art, and to increase the collection of engravings, which is very meagre compared with the Uffizi, or with other public collections in Europe, for the present collection hardly exceeds six thousand. One of the most interesting volumes here contains the portraits of the first members of the Accademia del Cimento, drawn in crayon by Il Padovannino, an artist of the Venetian School, who was famous for his accurate likenesses; he was born in 1562, and died 1617. This little volume contains upwards of twenty portraits, beginning with the painters; the sculptors follow, next the poets, and lastly the philosophers. The most remarkable are—Annibale and Agostino Caracci, Michael Angelo da Caravaggio, Guercino, Cesare d'Arpino, Simon Vouet, and Galileo Galilei, which last seems to convey a far more lifelike, and therefore truer idea of the man, than the portraits of him in oil. The forehead is singularly high; the small blue eyes are full of animation, and, though the features are coarse, there is nobility and dignity of soul in the calm serious expression of the great philosopher.

A copy of Dante, painted in Florence in 1481, by Lorenzo della Magna, and illustrated by Botticelli, is the most perfect extant, except that in the Riccardiana Library; eighteen of the twenty illustrations are to be found in this volume.

A folio volume contains specimens of various early masters of engraving, beginning with nielli, or impressions made from engravings on a silver plate. There does not, however, appear to be any examples of the inventor of this art, Maso Finiguerra; they are chiefly by Peregrini and Da Cesena, or Da Cesio, of the sixteenth century, who also bears a high reputation; the Combat of Giants in

a Forest, is a well-known engraving by Antonio Pollaiolo;
several are by Robetta, one of which is the Visit of the
Wise Men; another by the same artist, of a mother pointing to some object beyond the picture, whilst a pair of
lovely children listen to her, is a charming composition, full
of nature and grace. Robetta was a Florentine engraver,
born about 1460, of whom little is known except that he
belonged to one of those numerous societies in Florence,
the members of whom called themselves La Compagnia
del Pajuolo—(stock pot), who supped by turns at one
another's houses, bringing their own food. Andrea del Sarto
belonged to this club, of which, from the anecdote related
of Andrea's contribution to a supper at his house, Rustici
was probably also an associate.* The Calumny of Apelles,
by an unknown engraver, with the names of the allegorical
personages inscribed, throws light on Botticelli's composition
in the Gallery of the Uffizi. There are several very fine
specimens of the works of Andrea Mantegna; four dancing
nymphs beautifully drawn, light and graceful in movement,
and very lovely in features and expression; Judith with the
Head of Holofernes is a magnificent composition. The
rest of this volume contains principally German and French
engravings.

Among the Florentine engravings are several from Michael
Angelo's Last Judgment; a splendid copy of the great
sculptor's group of Christ sinking between Nicodemus and
Mary, which is behind the high altar of the Duomo, but
which is reproduced here with a landscape background;

---

* See above at p. 140. Also Bryant's " Dictionary of Painters and
Engravers."

the Dream of Human Life, by Michael Angelo, of which the oil-painting is in the National Gallery of London; a portrait of Baccio Bandinelli, displaying some of his groups of sculpture. One volume contains engravings from the designs of Raffaelle, Michael Angelo, and Baccio Bandinelli, by the celebrated Venetian engraver, Agostino Musi, born 1490, and a pupil of Marc Antonio; among these engravings is one from Michael Angelo's celebrated cartoon, now lost, of Soldiers bathing; also a copy of the Apollo Belvedere, as it must have appeared before the restorations were added. The remainder in this volume are again German prints. Another contains engravings by a German named Kruger— 1576—from the paintings of Andrea del Sarto.

The English school is only represented by Houbraken's illustrations of Birch's Lives.

Not far from the Marucelliana Library, at the corner of the Via Guelfa, is the house once inhabited by Bernadetto de' Medici, the son of Ottaviano de' Medici, and brother of Pope Leo XI. He was a patron of art and letters.

At No. 37 in this street lived and died the modern poet, Giovan Battista Niccolini. He was born in 1782, at a period when Tuscany, following the example of France, was attempting to introduce reforms into her administration, and when the Inquisition was at length abolished, and the instruments of torture publicly burned. Niccolini was connected, by his mother's side, with Vincenzio Filicaia, whose Ode on Italy is read by every Italian scholar. Whilst studying at Pisa, in 1799, he became one of the most ardent advocates for a republic, but necessity obliged him to seek the means of gaining a livelihood, and he therefore could only take a passive interest in politics. In 1807 he was appointed Professor of History and Mythology in Florence, under the auspices of Elisa Buonaparte, Queen of Etruria, who was an enthusiastic admirer of all that belonged to ancient Greece. The subjects for his muse were taken from classical story, and elicited the warm eulogiums of Ugo Foscolo. His aim in all he wrote was to inspire his countrymen with the ancient spirit of freedom, to expose the impostures of priests, and the turpitude of princes. The "Foscarini" was acted at the theatre which now bears Niccolini's name, in the Via Ricasoli, then Cocomero, where it was received with enthusiasm, as well as throughout Italy; Niccolini's words, addressed to the foreigner, French and Austrian, "Repass the Alps and you will again become our brothers," were everywhere repeated. His most famous tragedy is "Arnaldo da Brescia," in which he reproduced Dante's idea that the temporal power of the Pope was inconsistent with the office of a Christian bishop and head of the Church. Niccolini died on the 20th September, 1861.

At the farther end of the Via Cavour is the Palazzo Riccardi, formerly Medici, one of the noblest structures in Florence. It was in 1430 that Cosimo il Vecchio, the Pater Patriæ, began this magnificent palace, after a design by Michelozzo Michelozzi. He chose the site near the Church of San Giovannino, then a little oratory built where once existed houses belonging to a great-uncle of Cosimo. The lower part of the palace consists of bold, roughly hewn stones, usual in Florentine architecture, which unites an appearance of solidity and strength with light and shadow, so essential to beauty under the glare of a southern sun. Above, is the equally characteristic broad overhanging roof supported by brackets. The windows are extremely beautiful, arched, and with a column in the centre; they were designed by Michael Angelo, who added to those in the lower storey the grating with that peculiar projection outwards, which has been called *inginnocchiata,* or the kneeling. Iron rings are attached to the sides of the windows for the purpose of holding banners or for illuminations, whilst those below were for torches. The larger rings were used to tie the horses of visitors to the palace. In the corner is one of Nicolò Caparra's beautiful *fanali,* lanterns—inferior, however, to that on the Pazzi Palace. No sooner was the Medici Palace finished than the death of Cosimo's favourite son, Giovanni, plunged the owner into the deepest sorrow. The broken-hearted father caused himself to be carried through all the rooms, exclaiming that his home was now too large for his family.

When Charles VIII. of France visited Florence, he inhabited this palace; here also Giovanni de' Medici, the son of Lorenzo the Magnificent, returned as Pope Leo X., accompanied by the Emperor Charles V. It was in this palace that Duke Alexander, the Moor, was murdered by his own cousin Lorenzino, and his successor, the Grand-Duke Cosimo I., caused the wing in which the murder was committed to be pulled down, when a lane called Del Traditore—the Traitor—connected the Via Cavour with the Via Ginori. This was afterwards blocked up by stables built by the Riccardi, who bought the palace in 1659 from the Grand-Duke Ferdinand II.; but the Riccardi were only allowed to build their stables here on condition that an empty space should be left above, where had been the room in which the ancestor of Ferdinand was assassinated, and that the public should be allowed a free passage across the court of the palace to the Via Ginori. The sarcophagi around this court were the same which once stood outside the Baptistery, and the statues and other antiquities were collected by the Riccardi, and brought here in 1718. A rich library of rare works, collected by the Marchese Vincenzio Capponi, was brought to the Riccardi on the marriage of his daughter with one of that family. The library, with the palace, is now public property. In one room there is a ceiling gorgeous with carving and gilding; in another, a fine fresco by Luca Giordano, a Neapolitan painter, born in 1632, whose merits lay rather in a fertile invention, facile execution, and brilliant colouring, than in taste or beauty of composition.

The greatest treasure of the palace is the old chapel painted in fresco by Benozzo Gozzoli, which, both from its excellent state of preservation and intrinsic merits, is one of the most valuable as well as interesting works of art in Florence.

Benozzo Gozzoli, born in 1400, was a pupil of Fra Angelico, and though he possessed a mind less exalted than his master, he had merits which entitle him to a high place in Art. He was most successful in landscape, and his compositions are varied, and display marvellous ingenuity in the arrangement of numerous figures. This chapel had originally no window, but was lighted by silver lamps. The altar-piece is supposed to have been the picture of the Madonna to whom angels bring the infant Christ, by Fra Filippo Lippi, now in the room of old masters in the Gallery of the Uffizi. On either side of the altar, Benozzo Gozzoli has painted angels worshipping; those nearest the altar kneel in natural and graceful attitudes; their heads are bent, their countenances absorbed in earnest devotion, and their hands are clasped in prayer or crossed on their bosoms; behind them, angels approach on foot, whilst others descend from the heavens, and nestle in the tall branches of the trees or gather roses in a lovely garden; birds of various kinds are introduced in these compositions. On the angles of the walls, within the chapel itself, are seen the shepherds leaving their flocks to follow the Star of Bethlehem; these are beautifully composed. The rest of the walls is covered with innumerable figures, who represent the visit of the Wise Men of the East, most of whom are portraits of distinguished men; that of Gozzoli himself and of other painters are introduced amidst the crowd of followers to the right of the altar; in the foreground are Cosimo Vecchio and his brother Lorenzo, the ancestors of the two branches of the House of Medici. The youth on horseback in front was probably intended for Lorenzo the Magnificent; the Emperor of the East faces the window, and in the corner, on the wall to the left, is seen the grey-bearded head of the Patriarch of the Greek Church. The second youth on horseback may possibly be a portrait of Giuliano, Lorenzo's brother; he has a hunting leopard seated behind him, and another held in leash below. The landscape background is enlivened with groups of persons, as well as every description of animal, and in the distance are other groups.

Next the Palazzo Riccardi is the Church of San Giovannino, or San Giovanni Evangelista, on the site of the Oratory built in fulfilment of the will of Giovanni di Lando de' Gori, at the corner of what was once the Via degli Spadai, or Swordmakers, afterwards de' Martelli, from the family of that name who had their houses in this neighbourhood.

The body of the murdered Duke Alexander was concealed in this church in 1536. When the Jesuits came to Florence, under the patronage of Eleanora di Toledo, the wife of the Grand-Duke Cosimo I., this Oratory and the adjacent houses were given to them, on the site of which to build their church; and Bartolommeo Ammanati, the celebrated architect and sculptor, gave his whole patrimony to furnish the means. He had married Laura Battiferi, a lady who was remarkable as a painter and poetess as well as for her literary attainments: Ammanati and his wife are buried in the Chapel of St. Bartholomew in this church, where is a picture, by Bronzino, of Christ and the Apostles: an old woman behind is the portrait of Laura Battiferi.

The Via della Forca, behind the Via Martelli, contains the Palazzo Martelli, belonging to a descendant of one Roberto Martelli, whose greatest distinction is having been the patron of Donatello, whom he received as a boy into his house, and treated like a son. As a token of his gratitude Donatello afterwards presented him with a statue of St. John the Baptist, still in the possession of the family, one of the master's best productions. The figure is full-length, with emaciated limbs, and clothed in the garment of camel's hair. The effect of long fasting is given by the pinched nostrils and large eyes; the lips are apart, showing the teeth, and the eyebrows are raised; the details are highly finished. In the same room with this statue is a very fine bust of St. John the Baptist when a youth, by Donatello; the round forms and the surface given to the marble is extremely beautiful, and there is a peculiar sweetness in the expression of the mouth and half-closed eyes; the throat and hair are carefully modelled. This bust was conveyed to the

Baptistery in 1541, to grace the ceremony of baptism of the eldest son of the Grand-Duke Cosimo I. and Eleanora of Toledo.

In the Via della Forca is a very lovely image of the Madonna and Child and St. John, by Mino da Fiesole. It is in rather flat relief, but is a particularly sweet example of this artist's works.

At the corner of the Via della Forca and the Via Cerretani is a tablet, pointing out the former residence of the poetess Corilla, who was crowned in Rome.

In the Via de' Ginori, behind the Palazzo Riccardi, and running parallel with the Via Cavour from the Piazza di San Lorenzo to the Via degli Arazzieri, is the Palazzo Ginori. The family of Ginori, which has given many remarkable and patriotic citizens to Florence, is descended from one Gino Benvenuto, who settled in Florence in this district, near San Lorenzo, about the year 1304. The Marchese Carlo Ginori, who died in 1757, instituted the manufacture of porcelain near Florence, which is still celebrated throughout Europe. He began by collecting all the different earths of Tuscany; and he freighted a ship in which he sent out young men to collect models not only from the principal manufactures of Europe, but from China. They also imported rare plants from the East, which were introduced into Italy, as well as gold fish from China. His porcelain manufactory was opened in 1740, and was enlarged and improved by his son, the Marchese Lorenzo Ginori.

The Palazzo Ginori contains a small but select collection of pictures. The most valuable is a very fine painting, by Luca Signorelli, of the Holy Family. The Madonna stands behind a wall or ledge, on which the infant Christ bends to kiss the little St. John, who kneels, and whose countenance is most lovely, expressive of child-like innocence and reverence. To the left, in the landscape background, St. Jerome is represented, to the right, St. Bernard, with a church on a hill. Another picture of a Madonna and Child is by Botticelli—a very sweet and good example of the master; over this is another doubtful picture, by Signorelli. Some landscapes by Albani, and a highly finished head of an old man by a German artist, with one or two other pictures, are all contained in this room; in the ball-room, beyond, are some interesting sketches by Paolo Veronese, and a good portrait by Sustermans.

CHRONOLOGY.

	A.D.
Alexander, Duke, de' Medici, began to reign	1532—murdered 1537
Ammanati, Bartolommeo	b. 1511—d. 1560
Angeli, Sta. Maria degli, founded	1293
,, ,, church enlarged	1424
Andrea del Castagno	b. 1409—d. 1480
Arpino, Cesare d'	b. 1560—d. 1640
Baccio Bandinelli	b. 1487—d. 1559
Battiferri, Laura	d. 1589
Benedetto da Maiano	b. 1490(?)—d. 1550
Boniface IX., chosen Pope	1389—d. 1404
Botticelli, Sandro	b. 1437—d. 1515
Buffalmacco	b. 1262—d. 1340
Buonarotti, Michael Angelo da	b. 1474—d. 1563
Capello, Bianca, Grand-Duchess	b. 1579—d. 1587
Capponi, Gino, founder of the family	d. 1420
Caracci, Annibale	b. 1560—d. 1609
,, Agostino	b. 1558—d. 1602
Caravaggio, Michael Angelo da	b. 1569—d. 1609

CONVENT OF STA. MARIA DEGLI ANGELI, ETC.

	A.D.
Charles VIII. of France, at Florence	1494
Ciompi Riots	1378
Donatello	b. 1383—d. 1466
Eugenius IV. came to Florence	1135
Galilei Galileo	b. 1564—d. 1642
Ghirlandaio, Ridolfo	b. 1485—d. 1560
Ginori porcelain manufacture opened	1740
Giordano, Luca	b. 1632—d. 1705
Giotto	b. 1276—d. 1336
Gozzoli, Benozzo	b. 1400—d. 1478
Guercino	b. 1590—d. 1666
Houbraken, Jacob	b. 1698
Landino	b. 1424—d. 1504
Leo XI., Pope	1605
Marucelliana Library founded	1703
Medici, Cosimo de', Pater Patriæ	b. 1389—d. 1464
Michelozzi, Michelozzo	b. 1396—d. 1478
Mino da Fiesole	b. 1431—d. 1486
Niccolini, Giovan Battista	b. 1782—d. 1861
Padovannino, Il	b. 1502—d. 1617
Peregrini da Cesena, his first engraving	1511
Pollaioli, Antonio	b. 1426
Riccardi or Medici Palace founded	1430
Robetta, engraver	b. 1460 (?)
Rustici, Françesco, painter	b. 1595—d. 1625
Tafi, Andrea	b. 1213—d. 1294
Traversari, Ambogio	b. 1378—d. 1439
Uzzano, Nicolò	b. 1382—d. 1417
Vouet, Simon	b. 1582—d. 1641

CHAPTER XII.

CONVENT OF SAN MARCO.

IN the year 1290 some monks belonging to a branch of the Vallombrosian order, called Silvestrini, came to Florence. The name was derived from their founder, one Silvestro Gozzolini. They procured for themselves an Oratory close to the city walls, and there in 1299 they built a large church and monastery, which were consecrated under the name of San Marco Nuovo, to distinguish the edifice from San Marco Vecchio, outside the Porta San Gallo. The piety of these monks won the respect and reverence of the Florentine citizens, which continued until the year 1400, when the city was ravaged by the Plague, and the friars, instead of becoming more earnest in the presence of so terrible a calamity, relaxed the severity of their discipline, and thus greatly diminished their influence with the people. An equal laxity of morals displaying itself in the convents of the Dominican order, a monk of Sta. Maria Novella was appointed to attempt a reformation; and in 1405 the Monastery of San Domenico, on the slopes of Fiesole, was assigned for the members of this reformed community; who, however, a few years later, 1435, were permitted by Pope Eugenius IV. to return to Florence.

The Signory ceded to them the little monastery of San Giorgio on the Costa, Oltr' Arno; but meantime no such reform appearing to have taken place among the Silvestrine monks, the Pope and Signory decided that they should yield their larger and more important monastery to the Dominicans. The exchange was made in two solemn processions, moving from San Marco and San Giorgio, preceded by the clergy and people singing canticles.

The Dominicans found San Marco in a state of dilapidation, for the entire dormitory had been consumed by a great fire the previous year, and part of the roof of the church had fallen in. The monks were therefore obliged to build wooden cabins to protect themselves from the weather, until Cosimo de' Medici offered to restore the building, and entrusted the work to Michelozzo Michelozzi. This architect demolished the whole edifice, with the exception of the refectory and church; he then commenced building the cloisters and the library above, and also enlarged the church, sacristy, and refectory, and built a dormitory to contain forty-four beds over the outer cloister, the walls of which were painted in fresco by Fra Angelico and his brother. This pious and accomplished monk was born about 1387 at Vicchio in the Mugello, a district beyond Fiesole. He was baptized by the name of Guido; but at twenty years of age he and his brother assumed the Dominican habit at the convent below Fiesole, and took the names of Fra Giovanni and Fra Benedetto. The angelic temper and blameless purity of Fra Giovanni's life procured him the epithet of "Angelico," to which was afterwards added the title of "Beato," so that the name which has been handed down to posterity is "Beato Giovanni, *detto* Angelico da Fiesole." Both brothers were sent for several years to the Dominican Convent at Cortona under the care of the Master of the Novices, the Beato Fra Lorenzo di Ripa Fratta. They were early distinguished as illuminators of choral books, and Fra Angelico left several frescos on the walls of the Convent of Cortona. On his return to Florence, in 1436, he began his frescos in San Marco, most of which are admirably preserved to this day. Some of the first works he executed are the lunettes in the outer cloister.*

Facing the entrance from the piazza is a fresco of the Crucifixion by Fra Angelico. St. Dominick kneels at the foot of the cross, which he embraces, looking upwards at the Saviour with an expression of deep grief. Above the door, leading to the sacristy and the church, Fra Angelico has painted St. Peter Martyr, with his forefinger pressed against his lips to impose silence. The knife buried in his shoulder conveys the history of his martyrdom. In a second lunette, over the entrance to the chapter-house, St. Dominick is represented holding a book and a whip of nine tails, emblematic of the stern discipline of the order. A third, over the portal, leading to the Great Refectory, exhibits the Saviour rising from the sepulchre. Over the entrance to what was formerly the Foresteria, or guest chamber, are two Dominicans who welcome the Saviour, in the garb of a pilgrim, a staff in his hand, and his hat hanging over his shoulders. Over a fifth entrance is a fresco, much damaged, of St. Thomas Aquinas, who is regarded by the

---

* This cloister, and the cells above, now form a kind of museum, open daily to the public on payment of a franc.

Dominicans as the most learned of their order, as St. Peter Martyr is considered the most holy.

The other frescos with which the walls of this cloister are adorned exhibit incidents in the life of San Antonino, and are of a later date.* They are by a variety of masters, but several of the best are by Pocetti (1542—1612), and are interesting as representations of old Florence and its neighbourhood. On the east side of the cloisters, Antonino is represented as a boy, praying before the crucifix at Or San Michele; a most graceful composition: on the south he appears, when bishop, in a procession, about to enter the Duomo, the façade of which is represented before the decorations attributed to Giotto were removed. Savonarola, his cowl drawn over his head, is also introduced; he is seen in profile standing amidst a group of monks and other spectators. The compartment immediately on the left, when entering from the piazza, exhibits a bride entering the Duomo, and San Antonino driving away the crowd of curious spectators: the bride is worthy of Ghirlandaio. A fourth fresco, also by Pocetti, on the northern side, has Dante da Castiglione (the hero of the Siege of Florence in 1530), and his wife, kneeling before Antonino (a slight anachronism, as Antonino died in 1459), to invoke the aid of his prayers for the blessing of offspring. In the distance appears the villa of Dante da Castiglione with the little village of Cercina, still to be seen in its primitive simplicity on the slopes of Monte Morello. All these, besides a few others, are by Bernard Pocetti. The compart-

---

* For a sketch of the life of Bishop Antonino, see chapter describing Or San Michele.

ment to the left of the entrance to the Great Refectory, representing the body of San Antonino surrounded by a crowd of mourners, is by Matteo Rosselli (1578—1650), and is a very good composition. This painter was much employed by the Grand-Duke Cosimo II., and excelled in fresco.

The Refectory contains a very good, though damaged fresco by Giovanni Antonio Sogliani (1492—1544), a pupil of Lorenzo Credi. St. Dominick is seated with his brother monks around a table, and two angels bring them food. According to the legend, when St. Dominick was residing with forty of his brethren in the Convent of St. Sabina, at Rome, some of their number who had been sent out to buy provisions returned with nothing but a small quantity of bread. St. Dominick ordered them to sit down in the Refectory, and having pronounced the usual blessing, two youths clad in shining garments appeared, carrying a basket of bread, and a pitcher of wine.* Above this is painted the Crucifixion. St. John and the Virgin stand on either side of the Cross, and beyond are seen, kneeling in adoration, St. Antonino and St. Catherine of Sienna, who, among the Dominicans, was the type of female sanctity and self-denial. The date of this fresco, 1536, is inscribed upon it.

The Chapter-house of this convent has the Crucifixion painted in fresco by Fra Angelico. The crucified Saviour is the feeblest part. The good and the wicked thief are suspended on either side. The fainting Virgin is supported by the two Marys and by St. John. Beyond this group are

---

* See Mrs. Jameson's "Legends of the Monastic Orders."

St. John the Baptist, St. Mark kneeling, St. Lawrence, and St. Cosimo and St. Damian, the patron saints of the Medici family. St. Cosimo is said to be the portrait of Nanni di Banco, a friend of the artist, who executed some of the statues around Or San Michele. To the right of the cross are all the Fathers and Doctors of the Church—St. Dominick, St. Augustine, St. Jerome, and St. Ambrose; St. Francis, St. Bernard, St. Anthony, St. Peter Martyr, St. Thomas Aquinas, &c. The most beautiful portion of the fresco is the group around the Mother of our Lord. The heads are throughout full of character. The kneeling St. Jerome is peculiarly grand. The background was probably once blue, but in its present state is a dull red. At the base of the fresco, St. Dominick supports a framework containing the Tree of Life, with medallion-portraits of the different monks of the order. Prophets, sibyls, and saints are around. A pelican, the ancient symbol of our Saviour, looks down upon the cross.

Two large carved Crucifixes, suspended against the side walls of the Chapter-house, on either side, are wonderfully executed, though painfully realistic.

At the foot of the stairs leading to the cells above, is the smaller Refectory of the convent. It contains on one side a Last Supper by Domenico Ghirlandaio, painted subsequent to a Cenacolo which he executed for the Church of Ogni Santi in Florence, and exhibits the same arrangement; the Saviour in the centre of a double-winged table, and Judas alone on the opposite side, between Christ and the spectator. The fresco has suffered by time and damp, but is very interesting, and exhibits great attention to details. A lunette outside one of the doors which opens from this Refectory into a small inner cortile, has a beautiful fresco by Fra Bartolommeo, representing the Meeting of Christ and the Apostles at Emmaus. As one of the saints is recorded by Vasari to have been the portrait of a monk who was prior of the convent between 1505 and 1506, we can probably assign this work to a period when Fra Bartolommeo was about thirty years of age. It is one of his masterpieces for tenderness and grace, as well as for richness of colour.*

At the head of the stairs leading to the cells above this cloister, is a very beautiful fresco by Fra Angelico of an Annunciation, in which subject this master peculiarly excelled, and he has therefore made numerous repetitions in his fresco and distemper paintings. The angel Gabriel bends before the Virgin, with his arms reverentially crossed on his breast. The Virgin's figure is slender; she stands gracefully, and, as Lord Lindsay remarks, "she has a look of naïve curiosity mingled with modesty and humility." A park paling encloses a meadow with flowers, which is supposed to have an allegorical meaning relating to the Church of Christ. Facing the Annunciation is a Crucifix, with St. Dominick embracing the cross, almost a repetition of that below, but inferior in merit.

The old Dormitory of the convent was built over three sides of the cloister, and for some time was not divided into cells, but was arranged like the ward of an hospital, with beds on either side. On the walls, over the beds, Fra Angelico, assisted by his brother Fra Benedetto, executed a series of lovely frescos, with subjects selected from the life

---

* This fresco is in so dark a position that it will probably be shortly removed to the chapel of the Giovanali, adjoining Savonarola's cell.

of our Saviour. The division into cells was an after-thought, though the alteration appears to have been made shortly after the execution of these works.

Proceeding down the long corridor, the entrance to which nearly faces the head of the staircase, the cells on the left contain frescos entirely by the hand of Fra Angelico, while those on the right of the corridor are chiefly by Fra Benedetto, although many were designed by his more gifted brother. Two of these only are the entire work of Fra Angelico, namely, a " Via Crucis," Christ bearing the Cross; in which He is represented younger than usual, the mother aged, and full of suffering, a Dominican monk contemplating the scene; and another of the Baptism of our Lord: John the Baptist advances eagerly to perform the sacred rite, while two angels kneel on the left of the fresco; these last are especially beautiful. The first subject to the left of the corridor is a " Noli me tangere." The expression of reverence in the eyes of the Magdalene and in her action tells the story admirably. Immediately beyond is a Pietà. St. Dominick gazes at the body of the Saviour. In the third cell is an Annunciation, a most simple and lovely composition; St. Peter Martyr is represented as a spectator. The fourth cell has the Crucifixion. In the fifth, the Virgin and St. Joseph adore the Infant Christ; St. Peter Martyr and other saints also worship.

Nearly opposite this cell is a fresco in the corridor (once a tabernacle in the dormitory), in remarkably good preservation—an Enthronement of the Virgin, the " Madonna del Trono." The Infant Saviour, seated on her knee, is very finely painted, and with more majesty than the artist usually imparts to this subject. On either side stand saints: St.

Mark, St. Thomas Aquinas, St. Lawrence, and St. Peter Martyr on the right of the picture; St. John the Evangelist, St. Cosimo, and St. Damian clothed in red, and St. Dominick, on the left. The saints have very expressive countenances.

Returning to the cells, the sixth cell on the left contains the Transfiguration, a magnificent composition. The Saviour is here represented as a majestic figure in long flowing white drapery, his arms extended. The disciples below are overpowered by the dazzling light; St. John, in the centre, is a very graceful figure; above are the heads of Moses and Elias, beneath are St. Dominick and the Virgin. The seventh cell has Christ buffeted. He is again represented in white, seated, and meekly enduring this persecution. The Virgin and St. Dominick appear below, seated on a step; the first absorbed in thought, the other reading. The eighth cell has the Resurrection; a very lovely angel, seated on a tomb, points upwards with his finger; he addresses the three Marys and St. John, who with looks of wonder gaze into the empty tomb. Fra Angelico had painted his own portrait kneeling below in the left-hand corner. The ninth cell has the Coronation of the Virgin. Lord Lindsay especially commends this fresco.* The Virgin is represented as in a vision, seated in the clouds, and meekly bending to the Saviour, who with both hands holds the crown destined for his mother. Her hands are crossed on her breast, and in her countenance is expressed deep and intense joy. St. Paul, St. Peter Martyr, St. Francis, St. Dominick, St. Benedict, and St. Thomas Aquinas are beneath, in groups of three on either side, and look up,

---

* See Lord Lindsay, "Christian Art," vol. iii. p. 185.

with outstretched arms, as if eager to attain to heavenly
bliss.* The tenth cell has the Presentation at the Temple.
The Infant Jesus rests in the arms of Simeon. The Virgin
holds out her hands to receive her child again., Joseph
stands behind with a basket of offerings. St. Peter Martyr
kneels in front to the left. The Beata Villana kneels on the
right.† The eleventh cell contains the Enthronement of
the Virgin; a very inferior production.

The end of this corridor was formerly divided by a partition wall and door from the corridor on the southern side,
and included the cells of the younger monks—Giovanati—
who had just passed through their novitiate. The prior's cell
was at the farther end, and he thus had them under his
immediate supervision. Each of these cells contains a
fresco of the Crucifixion, apparently the work of Fra
Benedetto.

The prior's cell, divided into two small chambers, is
reached by passing through what was formerly a chapel
raised three steps above the corridor. A marble tablet at
its entrance records that Leo X., after visiting the convent
in 1516, as a tribute to the memory of the pious Savonarola,
granted an indulgence of ten years to whosoever visited the
inner cell.

Two wonderfully fine frescos by Fra Bartolommeo are
represented here; both represent the Madonna and Child.
That facing the entrance was brought hither from a villa

---

* See Crowe and Cavalcaselle, "Italian Painters," "Life of Fra
Angelico," vol. i. p. 581—583.
† La Beata Villana, a Dominican nun of remarkable sanctity, who
lived in the eighteenth century, and is buried in the church of Sta. Maria
Novella.

a few miles distant from Florence; the other has been greatly injured by an attempt to remove it. Both are noble compositions, above life-size. The drawing is in grand proportions, the colour good. Raffaelle himself never attained greater success in the representation of womanly tenderness and childlike innocence, combined with dignity, and a holiness almost divine. This chamber also contains two excellent imitations of old terra-cotta busts by an artist, Girolamo Bastiniani, who died recently (1868). One is intended for Savonarola; the other for his admirer and friend, the poet Girolamo Benivieni.*

The two small cells within have a more than usually historical interest, from having been occupied by Girolamo Savonarola when he was prior of this convent. Born at Florence, in 1452, of a noble Paduan family, he assumed the Dominican habit at the age of three-and-twenty. In 1482 he came to Florence, and entered the Convent of St. Mark's. About this time he began to preach, but neither his manner nor his language gained him many auditors. He was soon afterwards sent on a religious mission to Lombardy, where he remained several years, and where his earnest zeal and rare mental powers attracted public notice. At Reggio he happened to meet Pico della Mirandola, the friend of Lorenzo de' Medici, who at once conceived such an admiration for his eloquence and powers of mind, that he persuaded Lorenzo to recall him to Florence. Savonarola accordingly returned to St. Mark's in 1489, and a few

---

* Girolamo Bastiniani, a modern Florentine sculptor, who died young, and exhibited remarkable powers in imitating the execution of Middle-Age Art. A bust by him was sold by a dealer in Paris, as a genuine antique work, at the enormous price of 12,500 francs.

months later was appointed prior of the convent. Lorenzo de' Medici was not long in discovering that the stern virtue of the Dominican monk was above corruption. Even while attending Lorenzo on his death-bed, according to popular tradition, Savonarola with his usual inflexibility left Lorenzo unshriven, because he refused to show repentance for his past misdeeds, by sanctioning the restoration of Florentine liberty. Savonarola's steadfast moral courage and earnest pleadings for the cause of duty obtained for him an unbounded influence over the multitude, and, although he denounced their errors in unmeasured language, his sermons in the Duomo were thronged with eager listeners. He, however, committed the fatal mistake of believing that the regeneration of the city could be effected by a foreigner and a monarch, and he welcomed Charles VIII. of France, in the hope of finding that love of republican virtue and liberty in a feudal king, which his exhortations could not awaken in the breast of an ambitious citizen. Charles entered Florence as a conqueror, rather than protector; and at the solicitation of the Signory, Savonarola, discovering his error too late, had to use his eloquence to persuade him to depart from the city. The Dominican was no theological reformer, but exhorted both clergy and laity to greater purity of morals and politics, and was eager to give liberty on a sounder basis to the Florentine Commonwealth. For this end he first suggested the Council of Five Hundred, for whose accommodation Cronaca designed the Great Hall in the Palazzo Vecchio. Savonarola's persistent defiance of the orders sent him by Pope Alexander VI. to desist from preaching, finally brought him into conflict with certain parties in Florence, headed by the Franciscans, who became so violent that, in 1490, he and two brother monks were dragged from the Convent of St. Mark's to the Palazzo Vecchio, where they were judged and condemned by the Great Council he had himself helped to institute. His death only converted the stern reformer into a saint and martyr; and his relics were preserved and hidden until the name of Savonarola was revered as one of the greatest of Florentine citizens. In the prior's cell which he long inhabited are preserved his hair-shirt, rosary, a small portion of the wood from the pile on which his body was burnt, and the chair on which he sat. A desk made in exact imitation of that which he used, as the original was falling to pieces, contains a copy of some of his sermons in his small, but wonderfully distinct handwriting; also some other religious books, with his annotations on the margin. Upon this desk is his wooden crucifix, and on the wall a portrait of him, attributed to Fra Bartolommeo. The inner cell contains the copy of a picture executed within half a century after Savonarola's execution, representing the Piazza della Signoria on the fatal 29th May.

Retracing our steps to the head of the stairs, which leads from the cloister to the dormitory, the cell exactly facing the staircase was formerly occupied by the good Archbishop Antonino, before Pope Eugenius IV., at the suggestion of Fra Angelico, raised him to the episcopate of Florence. On the wall of this cell is a fresco by Fra Angelico, of Christ's descent to Limbo. Adam and his companions are represented meeting the Saviour with eager anxious faces. The vestments of the archbishop, a mask of his face, and his portrait in crayon by Fra Bartolommeo, also two church books in his handwriting, are preserved here. Opposite the window is a Genealogical Tree of the monks of the convent, in which the name of Savonarola is nearly obliterated by the kisses of his admirers. Above it is a good canvas portrait of Fra Lorenzo Ripa Fratta, taken at a later period. He was master of the novices, and accompanied Fra Angelico and his brother to Cortona, when they first assumed the Dominican habit. The cell beyond contains another fresco, by Angelico, of the Sermon on the Mount. Judas has a black glory round his head, the symbol of a virtue which is dead, a custom derived from the Greeks, and still adopted by the devout painters of Mount Athos. The adjoining cell has a fresco of the Temptation. Opposite these, and next the staircase, is a cell now used as the private apartment of the inspector of the Museum. As long as the monks occupied this part of the convent, this was used as a penitential cell, and was surrounded by a stone bench, with iron rings attached to the walls, to which the refractory monks were fastened. The adjoining cell has a fresco of the Crucifixion. Beyond the entrance to the library are several other cells on either side. The first on the left is divided into two, and contains an exquisite reliquary, with a panel by Fra Angelico, transported hither lately from the Sacristy of Sta. Maria Novella. It is called the "Madonna della Stella," from a star over the head of the Virgin. She carries the Child tenderly on her bosom; his cheek rests against her own. The sweet seriousness of the mother, and the playfulness of the Child, is rendered with great truth and nature. Angels worship on either side, and swing censers. The Eternal, surrounded by cherubim, looks down from above. Beneath, two angels seated on the ground play organs; a vase containing flowers in the centre. The angel on the left is singularly beautiful. Beneath the whole are represented St. Dominick and Peter Martyr. It is altogether a wonderful little miniature, painted with the utmost delicacy and finish. The jewels with which it was encrusted have been all removed. The fresco in this cell, also by Fra Angelico, represents the Betrayal of Judas, and Peter cutting off the ear of Malchus. The inner cell contains another reliquary, painted by Angelico, and likewise brought hither from Sta. Maria Novella. The subject is the Coronation of the Virgin; angels around play musical instruments, saints kneel at the foot of the throne. The predella below is most exquisite. Joseph and Mary worship the new-born Infant; angels hand in hand move in a mystic dance, while two of these play musical instruments. The adjoining cell has a fresco of Christ in the Garden, the three Apostles asleep, and Martha and Mary waiting at the entrance of a house. A third reliquary, also by Fra Angelico, represents his favourite subject of the Annunciation; and below, the worship of the kings. On the predella are the Virgin and Child, and saints with their names inscribed. The following cell contains a fresco of the Last Supper. The Saviour walks round the table, and places the wafer in the mouth of his disciples. Judas is again represented in a black glory, and two other apostles kneel in the foreground. The Virgin is on the left of the painting. The next fresco has Christ fastened to the cross by two soldiers; the Virgin and St. John on the left; St. Peter, the rich man, and a soldier, on the right. The last cell in this corridor contains a fresco of Christ on the cross between the two thieves, which is treated much in the manner of the fresco in the chapter-house. The three cells on the opposite side also contain frescos, but they are much damaged. The last cell on the right, adjoining the church, has an inner chamber raised several steps. An inscription over the entrance records that it belonged to Cosimo de' Medici, who built it for himself, in order that, when visiting the convent, he might converse in greater privacy with St. Antonino, and the two brothers Fra Giovanni the Beato Angelico, and Fra Benedetto.* Here lodged Pope Eugenius IV., in 1432, when he assisted at the consecration of the church. It contains a very fine fresco of the Visit of the Magi, by Angelico, in excellent preservation. Opposite this is a good canvas portrait of Cosimo Vecchio, by Pontormo, transported hither recently from the Uffizi Gallery; also a very interesting terra-cotta bust of Bishop Antonino, lately found in a neglected condition in a corner of the convent, and placed here by the inspector, Signor Rondoni.

CHRONOLOGY.

	A.D.
Cosimo II., Grand-Duke	1609—1621
Dominick, St.	1170—1221
Dominicans came to San Marco	1435
Eugenius IV., Pope	1431—1447
Fra Angelico	1387—1455
,, began his frescos in San Marco	1436
Fra Bartolommeo	1475—1517
Ghirlandajo, Domenico	1449—1494
Leo X., Pope, visited San Marco	1516
Michelozzi, Michelozzo	1391—1472

* The dormitory could not have been then divided into cells, but open the whole length, like the ward of an hospital, as described above.

	A.D.
Nanni di Banco	1420
Pocetti, Bernardo Barbatelli, Il	1542—1612
Rosselli, Matteo	1578—1650
Sant' Antonino	1389—1459
San Domenico di Fiesole given to Silvestrine monks	1405
San Marco first built	1299
Savonarola, prior of San Marco	1489
Silvestrine monks came to Florence	1290
Sogliani, Giovan Antonio	1492—1544

CHAPTER XIII.

SAN MARCO (*Continuation*).

Library—Lower Dormitory—Church.

THE Library of San Marco was built after a design by Michelozzo Michelozzi, and Cosimo de' Medici contributed a fine collection of MS. which had once belonged to Nicolò Niccoli,* the friend of Poggio Bracciolini. Nicolò had desired in his will that sixteen learned Florentine citizens should be appointed to decide where his library could be placed, so as to render it most extensively useful; but, after his death, his property was found burdened with such heavy debts, that no one seemed willing to accept the trust until Cosimo de' Medici offered to settle with the creditors, and at the same time fulfil the wishes of his deceased friend respecting the disposal of his library. Nicolò Niccoli left about six hundred MSS., of which Cosimo retained two hundred for his own private use—the nucleus of the Laurentian Library. He then bestowed the remaining four hundred MSS. of Niccoli's collection on the friars of San Marco, but added a few volumes of his own, in order to secure for himself and his heirs a right over the whole collection.

---

* See chapter on "Laurentian Library."

The Library of San Marco was further enriched by contributions from Sienna and Lucca, as well as by private gifts from Florentine citizens and from various monks of the convent. In 1453 the room was injured by an earthquake, but Cosimo and his son, Piero il Gottoso, took immediate steps for its repair. The library received large additions during the exile of Piero de' Medici, the son of Lorenzo the Magnificent, when the monks purchased the Medici collection after its confiscation, by order of the Signory. Two years later, 1498, after the execution of Savonarola, the Signory not only deprived the Dominicans of the volumes they had so lately sold them, but even laid hands on the rest of their library, and refused to restore the property until the monks consented to their conditions. Soon afterwards the Dominicans were obliged to sell some of their MSS. to pay their debts, and the larger number were purchased by Cardinal Giovanni de' Medici (Leo X.), who carried them to Rome. The monks of San Marco were the first in Italy to allow the public free access to their library.[*]

The shelves of the cabinets which line the walls of the room are now nearly empty, for the few monks who remain (1872), not above twenty, have removed many volumes to that part of the convent which is still reserved for them.

The cross transept at the end of the long room was formerly closed, and contained books forbidden by the Church, but it is now open to the public, and within the cases are some of the most valuable illuminated MSS. of the collection. There are several imitations of the old convent-chairs

---

[*] See "San Marco, Conventi del Padri Predicatore in Firenze, &c., dal Padre Vincenzo Marchese, Dominicano." Firenze: 1853.

in the library; the rings at the extremity of the arms, carved out of the same block of wood, were intended to afford the friars the sleepy amusement of twirling them round as they dozed; even Savonarola's chair, which is preserved in his cell, is of the same description, though the rings have broken away with age.

A numerous collection of choral books, brought here from various convents, lately suppressed in Florence and its neighbourhood, have been added to those already belonging to San Marco. They are arranged under glass, in cases down the centre of the long room. About twenty-four of these books are the property of the convent, and fourteen were illuminated by Fra Benedetto, the brother of Fra Angelico. A very beautiful Psaltery is adorned by paintings of Fra Eustachio, who also illuminated some of the choral books in the Cathedral, and whom Savonarola introduced into San Marco in 1496. The date of the Psaltery is 1505. Fra Eustachio's illuminations are remarkable for the care bestowed on the smaller decorations round every page, and his delight in painting children. Several of the finest choral books are from the Badia of Florence; one is painted by Monte di Giovanni, of the fifteenth century; another is by Giovanni Boccardini, of the sixteenth. Several of the volumes are from the Carmine, Santo Spirito, Ogni Santi, Monte Uliveto, and Sta. Elisabetta in Capitolo, a suppressed nunnery of Franciscans, not far from Sta. Croce. One of the books from Sta. Maria Nuova is decorated by Bartolommeo del Frosino, a goldsmith. Among the most beautiful missals in this collection is that which formerly belonged to Maria Antoinetta, wife of the last Grand-Duke Leopold II., and which is illuminated by

Fra Angelico. It was a marriage present from her husband. The margins of the volume have unfortunately been woefully clipped, probably by some modern bookbinder. Two of the missals are illuminated by Sor. Plautilla Nelli and her sister, who were nuns of St. Catherine of Sienna, living in a convent adjoining San Marco, where is now a government building in the Via Cavour. A subterranean passage once existed which afforded a communication between the convent and monastery; Savonarola encouraged the nuns in miniature-painting, as an occupation which might prevent the demoralisation produced by idleness. The missals from Sta. Maria Novella are all inferior in execution.*

Parallel with the library was once a terrazza, or balcony, now enclosed so as to form another chamber, in which are collected three or four hundred banners, sent to Florence in 1865, on the sixth centenary of the birth of Dante. They were carried in the procession which, led by the King of Italy in person, paraded the streets of Florence to celebrate the union of the peninsula, the fulfilment of the great poet's aspiration: the Venetian and Roman banners are veiled with crape, as both cities were then panting for that liberty which they soon afterwards obtained. A fine bust of Dante Alighieri, by the sculptor Pasquale Romanelli, stands on a pedestal at the end of the gallery. Several relics of the poet and patriot Ugo Foscolo are exhibited here. His remains were brought from England in 1871, and on opening the coffin in Sta. Croce, before reinterment, the features of the poet were found unaltered.

---

* The Cavaliere Rondoni has lately published a catalogue of the choral books.

On the ground floor, adjoining the inner cloister, was the Dormitory for the Novices; it is now used for the meetings of the Accademia della Crusca. Over the doors admitting to the former cells are lunettes painted in fresco, portraits of Dominican monks, by Fra Bartolommeo, and executed towards the end of his life, in 1516. They have almost the force and richness of colour of the Venetian school. Unfortunately, they are much injured. Of the eight lunettes, five only are by the *frate*. That farthest removed from the entrance of the corridor represents St. Dominick with a star above his cowl, and a lily in his left hand, whilst his right imposes silence; the second, Peter Martyr, holds a palm-branch and red book; the third is reading out of the book bound in red—he has a wonderfully fine head; the fourth is preaching; the fifth and sixth are by an inferior hand; the seventh, also by Fra Bartolommeo, represents a bare-headed monk, with rays diverging from his head—he holds the City of Florence in his hand; the eighth is of more recent date, probably the seventeenth century, but is not without merit.*

The Church of San Marco has been several times altered and embellished. It consists of a simple nave, with chapels on either side and a square tribune richly decorated. The design is by Piero Françesco Silvani, an artist who lived in the seventeenth century, so that very little exists of the church as it appeared when Savonarola was prior of the convent. A few traces of fresco, said to have been by Pietro Cavallini, remain on the left wall of the nave.

---

* See Crowe and Cavalcaselle's remarks on these frescos, vol. iii. p. 468.

On the *facciata* outside is St. Dominick with his dog, which Mrs. Jameson alludes to, as a typical statue of this saint, "familiar to strangers visiting Florence." Over the principal entrance within the church is suspended a wooden Crucifix, painted by Giotto, with a gold ground; this is supposed to be the same which established Giotto's superiority over Cimabue, and called forth the lines in the "Purgatorio:"—

> "O vanagloria delle umane posse
> Com' poco verde in su la cima dura
> Se non è giunta dall' estati grosse!
> Credetto Cimabue nella pintura
> Tener lo campo, et ora ha Giotto il grido
> Si che la fama di colui oscura."
> *Purgatorio*, xi. v. 91—96.*

Vasari mentions this Crucifix with commendation, and supposes it to have been painted after Giotto's visit to Naples and Rome.

The first altar to the right of the entrance contains an Annunciation by Pietro Cavallini, which is never exhibited without special permission from the Pope. Over the fourth altar in the chapel of the Ricci family, is a large mosaic of a Madonna, brought hither in 1609 from the Oratory of the Porta Santa and presented by Michael Angelo to the Ricci.

---

* "O thou vain glory of the human powers
How little green upon thy summit lingers
If't be not followed by an age of grossness!
In painting, Cimabue thought that he
Should hold the field, now Giotto has the cry,
So that the other's fame is growing dim."
Longfellow's Translation.

The arch over the last chapel on this side is crowned by a statue of San Zanobius; it is placed too high to judge of its merits; but opposite is a good statue of Sant' Antonino, by Giovan Bologna. A door to the right of the high altar leads to the sacristy and convent. The sacristy contains a statue of Sant' Antonino, by Montorsoli, a pupil of Michael Angelo. The Chapel of the Holy Sacrament, to the left of the high altar, contains paintings by Bernardo Pocetti, Santi di Tito, Jacopo d'Empoli, Passignano, Bilivert, Salsetti, and Curradi, all of them good artists of the sixteenth and seventeenth centuries; but none of these pictures are of great interest, and the chapel is so dimly lighted, they are not easily seen.

The left transept is entirely occupied by the Chapel of Sant' Antonino, and contains the remains of the good bishop. The walls are covered with frescos by Passignano, who was the pupil of Federigo Zucchero; he was the friend of Cigoli, and the Master of the Caracci. On the right wall is painted the interior of San Marco, as it appeared when the body of the saint was exposed to public view, and his panegyric pronounced from the pulpit. On the opposite wall is represented the procession when the body of Sant' Antonino, borne on the shoulders of four bishops, was carried to its last resting place in this chapel: the fresco is in Passignano's best manner, when he approaches Paolo Veronese. Behind the altar is a painting by Bronzino, representing the Fathers of the Church leaving Limbo. The marble statues on either side of St. Philip and St. John the Baptist, are by Francavilla, who worked under Giovan Bologna. The bronze reliefs of scenes from the life of Sant' Antonino are by Fra Domenico Partigiani.

On the left wall of the nave are inscribed the names of Poliziano, Pico della Mirandola, and Girolamo Benivieni: The remains of the two last repose in one coffin. Angelo Poliziano, born at Monte Pulciano in 1454, early acquired a reputation for his acquaintance with Greek and Latin literature. He was at one time tutor to the sons of Lorenzo the Magnificent, and died in 1494. Girolamo Pico della Mirandola was born in 1403; while still a child, he was a prodigy of memory and learning, and his mother provided for him the best instructors, so that at ten years old he was compared to the first poets and orators of Italy. He studied canon law in Bologna, and passed seven years in the most celebrated universities of Italy and France, in order to acquire greater perfection in Latin, Greek, Arabic, Hebrew, and Chaldee. In 1486 he proceeded to Rome; on his return to Florence he bestowed all his worldly possessions on a nephew, and passed the rest of his days in retirement, surrounded by his books and friends, until on the 17th November, 1494, the day that Charles VIII. of France made his triumphal entry into Florence, Pico della Mirandola died, at the age of ninety-one. Girolamo Benivieni, born in 1453, was a poet who endeavoured to restore the study of the Italian language. He was buried by his friend Pico in 1542, having attained his eighty-ninth year.

Beneath the pulpit of San Marco is a stone which marks the burial place of the Lapi family, a name rendered famous by the historical romance of Massimo D'Azeglio, founded on the life of Nicolò de' Lapi, of which, the obsequies to Bindo, the young son of Nicolò, in this church, is so graphically described.

CHRONOLOGY.

	A.D.	
Bartolommeo, Fra, last fresco in San Marco .		1516
Benvieni, Girolamo	1453	1542
Cavallini, Piero	....	1364 (?)
Cimabue	1240 (?)	1302 (?)
Eustachio, Fra, at San Marco		1496
Foscolo, Ugo	1776	1827
Francavilla	1548	
Giotto	1276	1337
Leo X., Pope	1515	1521
Library of San Marco injured by earthquake .		1453
Michelozzi Michelozzo.	1391	1472
Montorsoli	1507	1563
Pico della Mirandola	1403	1494
Piero de' Medici		1496
Savonarola executed		1498

CHAPTER XIV.

THE VIA SAN GALLO.—THE PALAZZO STROZZI.

NEAR where formerly stood the Porta Pinti, and as far as the Porta San Gallo, the old Walls have been demolished, and the new Boulevard has received the name of the Viale Principe Umberto. Beyond the Porta San Gallo is a meadow or grove, where once stood an hospital for the reception of children abandoned by their parents; still earlier, the ground belonged to Dante Alighieri, who is said often to have rested here to meditate. The triumphal arch in front of this public garden was erected to commemorate the entrance of Francis II., the husband of the Empress Maria Theresa, who received Tuscany in exchange for his hereditary Duchy of Lorraine, which was ceded by the Pragmatic Sanction of 1737 to Stanislaus of Poland, and later to France.

The Porta San Gallo was built in 1284, and received its name from a neighbouring church, dedicated to San Gallo.* Before the siege of 1529, this gate was closed, and a postern opened at a little distance for the use of the public. It was again closed by the Grand-Duke Cosimo I., when he for-

---

* Giuliano di San Gallo rebuilt this church, and thus obtained the name of San Gallo.

tified this part of the city, but was finally reopened in 1661. On the side facing the country is a curious antique head carved in the stone, and within the arch is a lunette containing a fresco of the Virgin and Child and St. John the Baptist, painted by Michele, the pupil of Ridolfo Ghirlandaio. The high towers, which once rose above all the gates of the city, were demolished by the Grand-Duke Cosimo I., and a broad roof raised on pilasters erected in their stead to protect the cannon placed there; the Porta San Nicolò and the Porta Pinti were alone left in their original state, whilst the Porta di Faenza, following the Porta San Gallo, was included in the Fortezza del Basso.

The Via San Gallo runs parallel with the Via Cavour. Near the Porta are the Convents of San Rocco and Sta. Caterina, which last has been converted into an Hospital for Incurables. Next San Rocco is San Clemente, once a convent of Augustinian nuns, under the special patronage of the Medici, and where two daughters of Duke Alexander ended their days. San Clemente is now joined to the suppressed Convent of Sta. Agata, and they form together a Military Hospital. Nearly opposite the entrance to the Via delle Ruote is the Church of San Giovannino dei Cavalieri, which belonged to the nuns of the Order of St. John of Jerusalem. This church possessed several fine pictures, which have all been recently removed to the public galleries.

In the Via delle Ruote is the Church of Sta. Maria dei Battilani, where the Florentine insurgents of the thirteenth century, called the Ciompi, held their meetings, led by Michele di Lando the Wool Carder. Casa Baci, in this street, is the house built by the artist Santi di Tito for himself, and where he died in 1603.

Returning to the Via San Gallo, the Church dei Pretori formed a refuge for secular priests who happened to arrive as strangers in Florence. On the pavement, at the entrance, is a singular epitaph over the grave of a Florentine wit, the parish priest Arlotti. The inscription is to this effect:—
"This sepulchre was constructed by the Piovano Arlotti for himself, and for all who may desire to enter." "Questa sepoltura il Piovano Arlotti la fece fare—per sè e per chi ci vuol entrare."

At the corner of the Via Silvestrino is the beautiful Palazzo Pandolfini, built after a design by Raffaello of Urbino; the architect was Françesco di San Gallo, who was employed by Giannozzo Pandolfini, Bishop of Troy. The cornice and projecting roof are considered models of proportion in Florentine architecture. The Ionic windows on the first story are extremely beautiful; but the Doric windows below have less strength and solidity, and greater elegance, than is usually characteristic of this style.

The Pandolfini were originally from Signa, half-way between Florence and Pisa: they fought on the Guelphic side in the battle of Montaperti, 1260, and afterwards became distinguished as Florentine citizens, filling the office of Priors and Gonfaloniers of the Republic, and were sent on important missions abroad. Giannozzo, Bishop of Troy, who built this Palace, was highly favoured by Pope Leo X., who appointed him his legate to the army sent against Françesco della Rovere, Duke of Urbino. The King of Naples made him Bishop of Troy, a title also conferred on his nephew Ferdinand.

On the opposite side of the Via San Gallo is the Lunatic Asylum of Florence, San Bonifazio, founded in 1377 by one

Bonifazio di M. Ugolotti Lupi, Marquis of Soragna, a valiant captain, who served the Florentines in a war against Pisa in 1362. He built this hospital for the sick, which was afterwards converted into a lunatic asylum.

Not far from San Bonifazio is Sta. Apollonia, founded in 1339 for Camaldolese nuns. The door of the church was renewed in the sixteenth century after a design by Michael Angelo. In the Refectory is a Cenacolo by Andrea del Castagno; the composition is very original, vigorous, and powerful, especially the head and attitude of St. Thomas, who is looking upwards in meditation. In a chapel off the spacious church is another Cenacolo by Bronzino, painted in 1561. There is much sweetness in the expression of the angels below, and in the female figures on either side, typical of Religion. The church, which is now used as a magazine for military stores, is built in the same style as the Church of San Felice Oltr'Arno; the tribune, or gallery for the nuns, extends half over the church, and is supported by six stone pillars; the ceiling is very handsome, of wood, and richly gilt; the altars are supposed to have been designed by Michael Angelo.

· Parallel with the Via San Gallo is the Via Sta. Reparata, once popularly known as the Campaccio, because here was the Jews' Cemetery. The Church of San Barnaba, at the corner of the Via San Zanobi and the Via Guelfa, was founded in 1309 in commemoration of the Battle of Campaldino, won by the Guelphic faction, in 1289, in which Dante fought. Near the suppressed Convent of San Barnaba, Luca della Robbia was born in 1388.

The Piazza della Indipendenza beyond was laid out in 1845; a small marble tablet over the entrance to some houses in a street leading to the Fortezza del Basso marks the model lodging-houses for poor artisans, built by the late Marchese Carlo Torrigiano, who died in 1865. At the north-western angle of this Piazza is the house once inhabited by the accomplished authoress, Theodosia Trollope, daughter-in-law of the more celebrated Mrs. Trollope. Both died in Florence, and were laid in the Protestant Cemetery of the Borgo Pinti. Theodosia Trollope published, in the form of letters to a London periodical, the most accurate account of the last revolution in Tuscany, which led to the formation of the Italian kingdom.

The Fortezza di San Giovanni Battista, or Del Basso, was commenced in 1533 by Duke Alexander dei Medici, at the instigation of Filippo Strozzi, in order to repress any attempt of the Florentines to recover their liberty: it was finished by Alexander's cousin, the Grand-Duke Cosimo I. Strozzi himself furnished the means for the subjugation of his fellow-citizens, and he was among the first incarcerated in that fortress, which he had intended for others, and where he died by violence; some suppose by his own hand, but more probably, murdered by the order of Duke Cosimo.

In the Via Nazionale, leading from the Piazza della Indipendenza to the Piazza Vecchia di Sta. Maria Novella, is a large Tabernacle in Luca della Robbia Ware, probably by one of the nephews, as it is highly coloured, and inferior in composition to the works of his uncle.

Amidst the narrow streets in this quarter of the town, entering the Piazza Madonna, or Campo dei Corbellini—as it is called in old chronicles of the city—and behind the Church of San Lorenzo, is the Via dell' Amore, which had its name from a romance by Macchiavelli: here was the

Palace of Vincenzo Viviani, the astronomer, mathematician, and favourite pupil of Galileo Galilei. He received a pension from Louis XIV. of France in 1622, and died in 1702, at eighty years of age. The bust of Galileo is over the door, and inscriptions in his honour are placed on either side. Galileo left Viviani his Library, which has since passed to the Hospital of Sta. Maria Nuova.* In the Campo dei Corbellini lived the Gaddi family, Gaddo, Taddeo, and Agnolo, of the schools of Cimabue and Giotto ; and the Via Melarancio, at the corner of the Via dell' Amore, was so called, from the pomegranates in their garden. The Palace of the philosopher Poggio Bracciolini was in the adjoining Via del Giglio, leading to the Via Panzani, and here lodged our English poet, Milton, when he came to Florence to visit Galileo Galilei.

The irregular space which forms the Piazza Vecchia di Sta. Maria Novella was once a usual meeting-place for both the Guelphic and Ghibelline factions. The Via Panzani and the Via Cerretani lead from the Piazza Vecchia to the Church of Sta. Maria Maggiore. Nearly opposite this church is the Albergo di Firenze, on the site of the houses of Nicolò de' Lapi, the Florentine citizen, who has been immortalised by the romance of Massimo D'Azeglio. Sta. Maria Maggiore is supposed to have been founded in the sixth century, and the first building to have been an exact copy of the Basilica of the same name in Rome. The Florentine Sta. Maria Maggiore was made a Collegiate Church in 1021, with a condition attached, that all the canons should be of noble blood. In 1311 the building was restored after a

---

* Among the recent alterations in Florence a splendid market is nearly completed in this immediate neighbourhood.

design by Arnolfo di Cambio, and decorated with frescos by
Paolo Uccello, Spinello Aretino, Agnolo Gaddi, Masaccio,
Sandro Botticelli, Lippi, Bugiardini, &c., but all these paintings have disappeared. In 1515 Leo. X. bestowed the
patronage of this church on the Chapter of the Cathedral,
and the canons of Sta. Maria Maggiore ceded their rights to
the Carmelite friars of Mantua, who were transferred here
from their monastery at San Barnaba in 1521. Within the
cloister was buried Ser. Brunetto Latini, a celebrated philosopher, the master of Dante Alighieri and of Guido Cavalcante. He died in 1294, after having filled the office of
Prior of the Republic. In the Piazza beside this church is
the Palazzo delle Cento Finestre—Hundred Windows—
where lived the painter Cigoli.

Behind Sta. Maria Maggiore is the beautiful Palazzo
Orlandini, built early in this century, but including within
its walls the original Palace of the Gondi, and that of the
Beccuti, who represent the extinct family of the Orlandini,
and in whose house lodged Pope John XXIII. after he had
been deposed by the Council of Constance.

Between the Via Cerretani and the Piazza di San
Gaetano is the Via Rondinelli, where the family Rondinelli
had their residence, one of whom became the husband of
Ginevra, who was buried and came to life again, as related
in a former chapter.* The Church of San Gaetano was
built on the site of San Michele Bertoldi, one of the most
ancient churches in Florence, but it contains nothing of interest. Opposite is the Palazzo Antinori, where once was
Ridolfo Ghirlandaio's finest work, a Spasimo, or Christ

---

* See "Piazza del Duomo."

bearing his Cross, now removed to the Academy. The palace was built in the fifteenth century after a design by Giuliano di San Gallo for one of the Boni family, from whom it came to the Antinori.

The Palazzo Corsi, belonging to the ancient family of that name, is in the Via Tornabuoni. It was designed by Michelozzo Michelozzi, but has lately been renewed, and the ground-floor let out in shops. Beyond is the magnificent Palazzo Strozzi, which was commenced in 1489, after a design by Benedetto da Majano, for the wealthy merchant Filippo Strozzi the elder, who was dissatisfied with the dimensions of the small though solidly-built palace, which still remains in the Piazza delle Cipolle, behind the dwelling of Prince Strozzi. The merchant had his shop in the Via Porta Rossa, and his child, the younger Filippo, who ended his days in the Fortezza del Basso, was carried to the foundations of the new palace and made to drop a small coin in the ground to bring good fortune to the inhabitants. Il Cronaca continued the work begun by Benedetto da Majano, but neither the architect nor the owner lived to see it finished.* The Cortile, with its beautiful columns, was wholly designed by Il Cronaca. The uppermost story is surmounted by a gallery supporting the roof, which, where complete, projects beyond the walls, casting a broad shadow beneath, characteristic of Florentine architecture. The rough masonry below gives the usual appearance of strength or solidity to the building. At the corner is a peculiarly elegant Fanale, the work of Nicolò Caparrà. This delicately wrought-iron ornament, used for the purpose of fire-works

---

* See " Vasari Vite de' Pittori," vol. viii. pp. 117—120.

or illuminations was, it may be remembered, a privilege only conceded to distinguished Florentine citizens.

The suite of reception rooms is adorned by a very choice collection of pictures and sculpture. In the first room is a portrait bust by Mino da Fiesole, of Nicolò Strozzi, the father of the elder Filippo. The forehead is narrow and the lower part of the face heavy, but is not wanting in intelligence. Near it, is a portrait of Lorenzo Strozzi. A small Annunciation, by Filippino Lippi, is extremely beautiful. A bronze statuette on a table of St. John the Baptist is by Donatello, and on one side there is a copy of Michael Angelo's celebrated Pietà at Rome, by Giovan Bologna. Two fine Carlo Dolce's, and David, by Guido Reni, are also worthy of notice. In the next room is one of the most celebrated busts by Desiderio di Settignano, of Marietta Strozzi, who married one of the family of the Este of Ferrara. The grace, refinement, delicacy of finish, and fine surface, are all characteristic of this artist: the bust is cited by Vasari. Facing the window is the *Puttina*, the portrait of a little girl feeding her dog, by Titian. She is in a white dress, with a pearl necklace, and a girdle or châtelaine of jewels. She stands on a balcony, with a landscape background. The picture, though very charming from the childlike animation and grace, united with great elegance in the composition, has been probably much repainted; in a letter of the Countess of Pomfret to Lady Hertford, in the middle of the last century, she describes La Puttina as in "so ruined a condition" that she expresses a hope that "a good copy may be made before the original wholly disappears." This little girl was a niece of Luisa Strozzi, who was celebrated for her beauty and misfortunes.

Beside the Puttina, another lovely young girl of the family is by Leonardo da Vinci. A portrait of Giuliano de' Medici, the brother of Lorenzo de' Medici, who was murdered by the Pazzi, is by Pollaiolo; it was taken after death. A small and early picture of a Holy Family is by Andrea del Sarto; the Virgin resembles the most celebrated Madonna of Andrea in the Pitti. A large family picture is by Sustermans. The Garden of Gethsemane, a small picture by Perugino, is in composition like the larger in the Academy, but whilst the Academy picture has more of Raffaelle in the drawing, this is quite in the manner of Perugino.

In the third room is the bust of Filippo Strozzi the Elder, by Benedetto da Majano. Though more refined and intelligent-looking than his father, judging by the bust, Filippo has the same narrow forehead and peculiar elevation of the head. Above it hangs the portrait of Filippo Strozzi the Younger, the friend of the Grand-Duke Cosimo I., who ended his days in the Fortezza del Basso. This picture is a fine copy of the original by Titian, which is in Vienna. Filippo is dressed in a cloak trimmed with fur, and in the graceful but nervous action of the hand, and, in his whole bearing, the character of the feeble but accomplished gentleman is well given. The portraits of his three sons, the brothers of Luisa Strozzi, are good pictures, by Alessandro Allori; Piero, the eldest, is in armour: he spent the days of his exile in France, protected by Catherine de' Medici, who saved him from the attempts at poison of Cosimo I. Roberto, the father of the "Puttina," is beside him. Leone, the prior of Capua, is on the other side of their father, and beyond him is Filippo, a son of Piero, who served as a French general. A round picture over the door, of a Madonna worshipping the Child, is by Perugino or Pinturicchio, and opposite is a Holy Family by Lorenzo Credi.

In the last room are two exquisite little landscapes by Salvator Rosa, and graceful portraits of two youths; one represents Cardinal Bembo, and is by Angelo Bronzino: he stands facing the spectator holding a book, and leaning on a table: the other, a still more interesting portrait, is the poet Ludovico Martelli, by Raffaelle. These portraits are placed near one another, to prove how Bronzino could approach the great master. A good portrait of Pope Paul III. is by Paolo Veronese; a large picture of card-players is by Caravaggio; and opposite, there is a good picture, by the living painter Gordigiani, of the present Princess Strozzi.

CHRONOLOGY.

	A.D.
Apollonia, Church of Sta., founded	1339
Arnolfo di Cambio	b. 1232—d. 1310
Barnaba, Church of Sta., founded	1309
Bembo, Cardinal	b. 1470—d. 1547
Benedetto da Majano	b. 1442—d. 1497
Bonifazio, San, founded	1377
Botticelli, Sandro	b. 1447—d. 1510
Bronzino	b. 1535—d. 1607
Brunetto Latini	1294
Bugiardini	b. 1481—d. 1556
Campaldino, Battle of	1289
Caravaggio, Michel Angelo da	b. 1569—d. 1609
Castagno, Andrea	b. 1409—d. 1480 (?)
Cigoli, Ludovico Cardi	b. 1559—d. 1613
Ciompi Riots	1378

THE VIA SAN GALLO.—THE PALAZZO STROZZI. 191

	A.D.
Dolce, Carlo	b. 1616—d. 1686
Fortezza del Basso commenced	1533
Galileo Galilei	b. 1564—d. 1642
Ghirlandaio, Domenico	b. 1449—d. 1493
„ Ridolfo	b. 1485—d. 1560
Guido Reni	b. 1575—d. 1642
Il Cronaca, Simone Pollaiolo	b. 1459—d. 1508
Leo X., Pope	b. 1475—d. 1521
Lippi, Fra Filippo	b. 1400—d. 1469
„ Filippino	b. 1460—d. 1505
Lucas van Leyden	b. 1494—d. 1533
Maria Maggiore, Church of Sta., made collegiate	1021
„ restored by Arnolfo di Cambio	1311
Martelli, Ludovico	b. 1499—d. 1527
Masaccio	b. 1401—d. 1443
Montaperti, Battle of	1260
Orcagna, Andrea	b. 1329—d. 1375
Perugino, Pietro	b. 1446—d. 1524
Pragmatic Sanction	1737
Raffaellino del Garbo	b. 1476—d. 1534
Raffaello d'Urbino	b. 1483—d. 1520
Salvator Rosa	b. 1615—d. 1673
San Gallo, Francesco di	b. 1498—d. 1570
„ Porta di, built	1284
Santi di Tito	b. 1538—d. 1603
Spinello Aretino	b. 1308—d. 1400
Strozzi, Filippo	b. 1488—d. 1538
„ Piero	b. —d. 1558
„ Palazzo, commenced	1489
Sustermans	b. 1597—d. 1681
Titian	b. 1477—d. 1576
Uccello, Paolo	b. 1349—d. 1436
Viviani, Vincenzo	b. 1622—d. 1703

CHAPTER XV.

PALAZZO RUCELLAI.—SAN PANCRAZIO.—VIA TORNA-
BUONI.—SS. TRINITA.—PALAZZO CORSINI.—PIAZZA
STA. MARIA NOVELLA.

OPPOSITE the Palazzo Strozzi, a corner house between two streets bears a shield, with the lion rampant. Here lived and died Robert Dudley, Duke of Northumberland, the son of Queen Elizabeth's favourite, the Earl of Leicester, and of Amy Robsart, the unhappy heroine of Sir Walter Scott's "Kenilworth." As his mother's marriage was never acknowledged, and he was not allowed to bear his hereditary title, although his possessions were restored to him, he quitted England in 1612, and sought a refuge in Tuscany at the court of the Grand-Duke Cosimo II., who appointed him chamberlain to the Grand-Duchess, sister of the German Emperor Matthias. At her request the Emperor created Dudley a Duke of the Holy Empire, with the title of Duke of Northumberland. He was a man of great learning and accomplishment; his chief studies were mathematics and nautical science, and he designed the Mole at Leghorn, besides publishing works of value on navigation, &c.

The narrow street to the left is the Vigna Nuova, in which is the Palazzo Rucellai, with its beautiful Loggia on the opposite side of the way. The family Rucellai are descended from a certain Alemanno, a wealthy cloth merchant, who, when trading in the East, discovered a fine purple dye for wool, produced from a plant called orchel—*Lichen Roccella, Linn*: and thence, on his return to Florence, he obtained the name of Oricellai, or Rucellai. A descendant of Alemanno, Giovanni Rucellai, excited the jealousy of Cosimo de' Medici—Pater Patriæ—by his great wealth: he built the beautiful palace in the Vigna Nuova, as well as the Loggia in front, after designs by Leon Battista Alberti, whom he likewise employed to build the chapel of the Holy Sepulchre, in the neighbouring Church of San Pancrazio, and also the façade to Sta. Maria Novella. Giovanni's son, Bernardo, was a distinguished historian, and on the occasion of his marriage with a daughter of the house of Medici, a splendid banquet was given in the little Piazza before the palace. Bernardo and his son Cosimo were members of the Platonic Academy, who then held their meetings in the Rucellai Gardens, which had been laid out for the family by Leon Battista Alberti, on a piece of ground some little distance from the palace. The Rucellai had become ardent supporters of the elder branch of the Medici, but the representative of the family in the sixteenth century opposed the election of the Grand-Duke Cosimo, and was therefore sent into exile.

The palace contains a fine collection of pictures. The most remarkable is that of the Assumption of the Virgin, who lets down her girdle to St. Thomas, by Françesco Granacci, 1469—1543. The artist has treated the same subject in his picture now in the Uffizi Gallery, but Cavalcaselle considers the Rucellai picture the most favourable example of Granacci's manner. St. Thomas, St. John, St. James, St. Laurence, and St. Paul, stand below. According to Cavalcaselle, "There is soft gravity in the deportment of the saints conversing by the tomb, and the drapery is grand in the breadth of its cast. Two angels, supporting the glory of flaming rays, almost embody the grace of Filippino. But the muscular type and energetically forced motion of the St. Thomas rising from his knees to take the girdle handed down to him by the Virgin, as well as the enamelled surface of the panel, and its minute laboriousness, are derived from Michael Angelo, in emulation, perhaps, of the Madonna at the Uffizi, which seems to date from the first years of the sixteenth century."* The picture was painted for the Church of San Piero Maggiore; it is in oil on panel, and the figures are life-size. A Holy Family, by Granacci, in this gallery, appears to have been executed after the artist had studied the works of Raffaelle. There are, besides, a Madonna by Michael Angelo, and pictures by Carlo Dolce and other distinguished artists.

The Loggia before the palace, though walled up, and used as a magazine for pictures, has not lost the beauty of the original design. Beneath its arches one of the Rucellai arranged the marriages of three of his daughters at once; for it was the simple custom of those old Florentine merchants to transact public and private business in these appendages to their palaces, as well as to sit under their shade in the hot days of summer, to play chess and watch the gambols of their children.

By the Via del Moro we arrive at the Via della Spada,

---

* See "Crowe and Cavalcaselle," vol. iii. p. 538.

running parallel to the Vigna Nuova, and meeting where the house of Robert Dudley forms an angle opposite the Palazzo Strozzi. In the Via della Spada, behind the Palazzo Rucellai, is the former old Church of San Pancrazio, now used for courts of law. San Pancrazio was founded in 1078, when it stood beyond the first circuit of walls. In 1488 it was rebuilt by the Rucellai and Federighi families. The adjoining monastery was at one time inhabited by monks from Vallombrosa, whose residence here is commemorated by a fresco in the cloister by Neri de' Bicci, in which Giovanni Gualberto, the founder of the Order, is seen seated amidst bishops and saints. The fresco is a fair specimen of Neri de' Bicci's work. The Chapel of the Holy Sepulchre was built, as before mentioned, by Giovanni Rucellai, who employed Leon Battista Alberti as his architect, and sent one of his own retainers to Jerusalem to obtain the exact measurements. It is entered from the Via della Spada.

The Via Tornabuoni, the fashionable street of Florence, with its gay shops and Jockey Club, received its name from a family, whose history contains little remarkable, except that a lady of the house, Lucrezia Tornabuoni, noted for her literary attainments, became the wife of Piero de' Medici, and the mother of Lorenzo the Magnificent; and that Nicolò Tornabuoni, Bishop of Borgo San Sepolcoro, in 1560 introduced the use of tobacco into Tuscany, which was first known as the *Erba Tornabuona*.

In the centre of the Piazza SS. Trinità is an ancient Roman column, from the Baths of Caracalla, which was presented to the Grand-Duke Cosimo I. by Pope Pius IV. The statue of Justice, in porphyry, is the work of Françesco Ferucci, called Il Tadda, and was placed here to commemorate the final discomfiture of Cosimo's greatest enemy, Piero Strozzi, at the battle of Marciano, in 1554. It was probably not without intention that Cosimo, who had caused the murder of his father Filippo in the Fortezza del Basso, celebrated his triumph over Piero in the vicinity of the Strozzi Palace, and in front of the church where their ancestor, Palla Strozzi, lay buried.

The Church of the SS. Trinità is one of the most ancient buildings in Florence, and is supposed to have been commenced in the ninth century. The monks of Vallombrosa possessed a monastery here in 1091. The nave of the church was formerly divided into five aisles, but one on either side was enclosed in the thirteenth century, and broken up into chapels, when the entire building underwent alterations after a design of Andrea Pisano. In 1395 the belfry was added. The façade was the composition of Bernardo Buontalenti, who lived in the latter half of the sixteenth century, and removed the ancient mosaics which decorated the building, to make room for his own tasteless design. Above the principal entrance there is a small bas-relief of the Holy Trinity, by Giovanni Coccini, who also executed a good statue of St. Alexis over the door nearest the Arno. This statue is popularly believed to be the portrait of a pilgrim, who suggested the means by which the column in the Piazza was raised. St. Alexis, whom it is really intended to represent, belonged to the fifth century, and is said to have quitted a wealthy and luxurious home to live and die a beggar, and he thus earned the honour of canonisation.

Within the church, to the right of the central door, is a

shrine of white marble, resting on columns, carved with the most delicate arabesques and flowers, the work of Benedetto da Rovezzano, 1490—1550. In the first chapel of the right aisle is a bronze Crucifix of some merit, presented to the city of Florence by the religious confraternity of the Bianchi. The fifth chapel has a beautiful iron grating, behind which is an important picture by Lorenzo Monaco, considered, by Cavalcaselle, the best specimen of the master. The subject is an Annunciation : "The angel kneels, whilst the Virgin presses her right hand to her bosom, and raises her head to listen. Her form is long and slender, and her parted lips and the soft expression of her countenance, have an air of timid inquiry. The figure of the angel recalls one by Agnolo Gaddi, at Prato. The drapery has a certain breadth in the folds." The predella of the altar-piece is likewise described by Cavalcaselle as most carefully executed.*

At the end of this aisle is a lateral door, opening into the Via Parione, and a second door leading to the Sacristy, built in 1421 by Palla Strozzi. It contains his monument, which consists of a sarcophagus beneath an arch. Palla Strozzi was an accomplished scholar, who was banished to Padua with the Medici, with whom he likewise returned to Florence in 1434, and he built the first Palazzo Strozzi in the Piazza della Cipolle. Close to the door of the sacristy, and to the right of the high altar, is the chapel belonging to the Sassetti family, long since extinct, and which contains the monuments of Françesco Sassetti and his wife Nera Cosi, by Giuliano di San Gallo. They are simple

---

* See "Crowe and Cavalcaselle," vol. i. p. 555.

black sarcophagi, under an arch of white marble, ornamented with delicate sculpture, bas-reliefs, &c., representing below classical subjects. The most remarkable works of art in this chapel are the frescos on the walls by Domenico Ghirlandaio, some of which are still in fair preservation, although, from their situation in the church, they can only be seen on a very bright day. Next the altar are the portraits of Sassetti and his wife kneeling. Above are painted incidents from the life of St. Francis. In the three lunettes nearest the ceiling are represented the saint resigning his patrimony and assuming his serge dress and cord; Pope Honorius confirming the Rules of his Order; the saint in the presence of the Sultan. In the frescos below, St. Francis receives the Stigmata near his monastery of La Vernia in the Casentino. The Saint performs a miracle on a child of the Sassetti family, who had fallen from a window and was restored to life. The background represents the Palazzo Spini, and the bridge of the SS. Trinità. The funeral of the saint and the four sibyls, who are supposed to have predicted the advent of the Saviour, conclude the series. Beneath the portrait of Sassetti and his wife is the following inscription : " A.D. MCCCCLXXXV. XV."

In the Via del Parione, parallel with the river, is the entrance to the Palazzo Corsini, once forming part of the houses of the powerful Acciajuoli family, whose residences appear to have extended all along the Arno. The present building was after a design by Silvani.

The Corsinis were feudal nobles in the neighbourhood of Poggibonsi, when they removed to Florence in 1231. In 1342 the family were ruined by the failure of the Banks of Peruzzi, Bardi, and Acciajuoli. Tomaso Corsini, who a few years later was distinguished as a statesman, recovered the fortunes of his house, but, towards the end of his life, he retired to the Monastery of the Gaggio, beyond the Porta Romana, where he died in 1366, with a reputation for exalted piety. The father of the present Prince Corsini, Don Neri Corsini, Marchese Laiatico, whose monument is in Sta. Croce, is remembered by his countrymen for his patriotism in difficult times, and for his other virtues.

The Palace contains a good collection of pictures. In the first room there is a fine portrait by Sustermans of Cardinal Neri Corsini, whose brother Bartolommeo was created Marchese di Laiatico, in 1644, by the Grand-Duke Ferdinand II. There are several small pictures of interest —Cupid in a Garden, by Albano; Venus looking into a glass, by Titian; the Baptism of our Saviour, by Santi di Tito; a good specimen of the master, though the Christ is feeble; Tobit and the Angel, a small but very beautiful picture, by Andrea del Sarto; a Holy Family, by Palma Vecchio; the Suonatore, a replica, by Raffaelle (?) of his beautiful picture in the Sciarra Palace in Rome—the colour of the dress is, however, not identical; a very fine head of a dead Christ, by Cigoli, painful from the realistic representation of great bodily suffering; Venus with the dying Adonis, by Annibale Caracci—a good example of the master; a portrait attributed to Holbein; a Madonna surrounded by a garland of flowers, by Carlo Maratta.

The second room contains the most interesting pictures of the collection—the original sketch by Raffaelle for his portrait of Pope Julius II., with holes pricked for conveying the drawing to the canvas; a Madonna and Child, by Carlo Dolce, nearly a repetition of that in the Pitti gallery. In a recess at the further end of the room, facing the windows, is a large circular picture, by Filippino Lippi, the subject of which is a Holy Family, with angels who present flowers to the Child, whilst other angels sing from a scroll of music—the background is composed of a landscape with buildings, and the whole picture is carefully drawn, and the colour very agreeable; a Madonna and Child with angels, by Sandro Botticelli, though mannered, is sweet and tender; a fine head of Christ, in pastel, is by Cigoli—it was the study for an altar-piece in Sta. Croce; a Madonna and Child, in pastel, by Carlo Dolce, is very charming from the sweet modest expression of the Virgin; a Holy Family, by Mariotto Albertinelli, and another by Fra Bartolommeo, are most lovely—the hands in this last are beautifully painted; there is also a Holy Family, by Andrea del Sarto, and another by Sustermans. Within the room itself is a Holy Family, by Jacopo Pontormo, a good example of the master; another Holy Family, by Andrea del Sarto; and a St. Sebastian, by Carlo Dolce.

The room beyond is hung with family portraits—a charming group of children, by Cavaliere Pietro Benvenuti, the best Italian painter of the beginning of this century, represents the late Prince Corsini, his brother Don Neri Corsini, and their sister, an infant, seated on a dog. There is also a good portrait of Pignotti, the author of the "Fables," by Benvenuti.

In the last room is a wonderfully fine painting, by Sebastiano del Piombo—the Bearer of the Cross. The picture is cited by Vasari: it consists of three half-length figures, and is a fine composition. A portrait of Pollaiolo, by himself, is a very interesting picture, and one of the most valuable in this collection—it is highly finished; Poetry, by Carlo Dolce, a good picture.

From the Palazzo Corsini the Via Parione leads to the Via Borg' Ogni Santi, and, turning to the right, the Via del Fosso—a record of the ditch beyond the second circuit of walls—connects the Arno with the Piazza di Sta. Maria Novella. Before reaching the Piazza, we arrive at the Via Palazzuolo, in which is the old church of San Paolo, bearing the apocryphal date of A.D. 335. San Paolo was made a collegiate church in the tenth century, but in 1217 was bestowed on the Dominicans, who afterwards removed to Sta. Maria Novella. In 1516 Leo X. conferred the church on the dean and chapter of the Florentine Cathedral, with whom it continued until it finally became the property of the barefooted Carmelites. Some monuments of the Albizzi family, which had formerly stood in San Piero Maggiore, were carried hither, when San Piero was demolished in 1783. Beyond San Paolo, in the Via Palazzuolo, is the suppressed Convent of the Confraternità dei Vanchetone, so called because the members of this society were bound to walk silently in the religious processions which passed through the streets of the city— *Vanno chetone* —they go in silence. The confraternity was founded by a Cardinal Alexander de' Medici, in 1602, and was composed principally of artisans, especially silk weavers. The Medici arms are painted on the ceiling of their church, with subjects from the lives of the Saints, by Giovanni di San Giovanni. The church has a vestibule with two altars, one of which contains the image of the black Virgin of Loretto, presented by the Medici. It is spacious and elegant in form, but contains nothing remarkable, and has been recently appropriated for secular purposes by the municipality. There are some fine examples of wooden mosaic—*Intarsiatura*—in the sacristy; cupboards with small columns, every one with a different capital, picked out with gold, the work of Pietro Libri of Padua; a head of the Saviour, by Carlo Dolce; and a second, probably by the same master, though attributed to Salvator Rosa. The skeleton of a distinguished member of the order, Ippolito Galantini, is preserved, dressed, and crowned with a garland of lilies in silver; his portrait is in the saloon, reserved for the members of the society. There are two beautiful busts of boys, by Donatello, within the church, on either side of the sacristy. A wooden Crucifix over the altar is finely executed, though painful.

Nearly opposite the Church of San Paolo is the Hospital dedicated to the same saint, begun in 1451; the Porch or Loggia, in the Piazza di Santa Maria Novella, facing the church, was built after a design by Filippo Brunelleschi; and the series of medallions above, are by Luca and Andrea della Robbia; Vasari mentions them as fairly executed—"assai buono." The medallions at the end, near the corner of the Via del Fosso, contain the portraits of Luca and Andrea. It is supposed that Luca began the work which was finished by his nephews. On the site of the Loggia, the celebrated meeting between St. Francis and St. Dominick is said to have taken place, and the interview is commemorated in a relief by one of the scholars of Luca over a door at the end.

The hospital was at one time intended for the Pilgrims, or Pinzocheri, of the third order of St. Francis; and as, before the Council of Trent, all monasteries had a nunnery at no great distance, so likewise here was a convent of Pinzochere, who assisted the friars in the care of the sick until the monastery was suppressed in 1500, when the whole charge devolved on the nuns. Disputes, however, arose between them and the governors of the hospital, which ended in the nuns being deprived of their privileges, and the Grand-Duke Francis I. converting the building into a convalescent hospital, to which were sent the patients from all the other hospitals of the city, who were allowed to remain there four days, and to partake of eight meals. Pietro Leopoldo afterwards assigned the Loggia di San Paolo for girls' schools, in which useful arts were taught, and all that might conduce to make good mothers of families. Near this Loggia was the house of the eccentric librarian Magliabecchia.

The Piazza di Sta. Maria Novella was laid out in 1244, at the instigation of Pietro Martire, who wanted greater space for the multitudes who flocked thither to listen to his sermons; and as the open-air preaching of the Dominican Friars continued popular, the Piazza was still further enlarged at the expense of the city in 1331. The façade of the church, as has been already stated in this chapter, was built by Giovanni Rucellai, and his name is inscribed in large letters above the rose window. The Piazza was used on various festive occasions under the Republic. Chariot races were introduced here by the Grand-Duke Cosimo I., in 1563. The obelisks in the centre served for the *gugli*— goals—of the race. They were first made of wood, but the Grand-Duke Ferdinand I. ordered them to be rebuilt of mixed marble from Serravezza. The lily at the top and the tortoises on which they rest are by Giovan Bologna. In a small Piazza to the right, facing the church, is the

Croce al Trebbio, a granite column, the work of Giovanni Pisano, erected in 1308, to commemorate a battle which took place on this spot with the Paterini, or heretics, against whom the eloquence of St. Peter Martyr was directed in the Piazza di Sta. Maria Novella. The capital of the column supporting the cross, which is protected by a roof, is composed of rude images of the animals typical of the Evangelists, a favourite subject of the school, and of which there are examples in the pulpits of Pisa and Sienna. The column was at first crowned with a statue of St. Peter Martyr, as may be seen in a fresco in the large cloister of Sta. Maria Novella.

Between the Piazza Nuova and the Piazza Vecchia di Sta. Maria Novella, beside the church, is the Via degli Avelli, or the Street of Tombs, formed by a series of pointed arches, beneath which are burial places once belonging to some of the principal families of Florence. There is a tradition that the bones contained in these tombs were carried here from the cemetery around the Baptistery and Cathedral, when Arnolfo de' Lapi levelled the ground of the Piazza del Battisterio, and paved it with stone.

CHRONOLOGY.

	A.D.
Alberti, Leon Battista	b. 1398—d. 1480
Albertinelli, Mariotto	b. 1475—d. 1520
Andrea del Sarto	b. 1488—d. 1530
Benedetto da Rovezzano	b. 1490—d. 1550
Benvenuti, Cavaliere Pietro	b. 1769—d. 1844
Botticelli, Sandro	b. 1437—d. 1515

		A.D.
Brunellesco		b. 1377—d. 1444
Caracci, Annibale		b. 1560—d. 1609
Cigoli, Ludovico Cardi		b. 1559—d. 1613
Corsini family came to Florence		1231
,, created Marchesi di Laiatico		1644
Corsini, Tommaso		d. 1366
Cosimo I., Grand-Duke		b. 1519—d. 1574
Dolce, Carlo		b. 1616—d. 1686
Dominick, St.		b. 1170—d. 1221
Dudley, Robert, Duke of Northumberland		b. 1573—d. 1639
Francis, St.		b. 1182—d. 1226
Granacci, Françesco		b. 1469—d. 1543
Julius II., Pope		1503— 1513
Lippi, Filippino		b. 1460—d. 1505
Marciano, Battle of		1554
Maria Novella, Piazza di Sta., laid out		1244
,, ,, ,, enlarged		1331
,, ,, ,, chariot races		1563
Pancrazio, Church of San, founded		1078
,, ,, ,, re-built		1488
Paolo, Church of San		335
,, ,, ,, bestowed on the Dominicans		1217
,, ,, ,, Dominicans removed thence to Sta. Maria Novella		1516
Pinzochere Nuns of San Paolo suppressed		1500
Pius IV., Pope		1559— 1565
Pontormo, Jacopo		b. 1493—d. 1566
Robbia, Luca della		b. 1400—d. 1481
San Gallo, Giuliano di		b. 1443—d. 1517
Sebastiano del Piombo		b. 1485—d. 1547
Sustermans		b. 1597—d. 1681
Tobacco introduced into Florence		1560
Trinità, Church of SS.		1091
,, ,, ,, belfry built		1395
,, ,, ,, sacristy built		1421

CHAPTER XVI.

STA. MARIA NOVELLA.

THE Dominican Convent of Sta. Maria Novella was at one time, with the exception of the other Dominican Convent of San Marco, the most important religious institution in Florence. A small church, built in the ninth century by the family of Tornaquinci, stood on the ground occupied by the transepts of the present beautiful edifice. The principal entrance was in the Piazza Vecchia, beyond the Bacchiera gate, or postern, in the second circuit of walls, which was situated where the Via de' Banchi and the Via Panzani meet—a corner since known as the Canto de' Carnesecchi. This church was called Sta. Maria tra le Vigne—Sta. Maria among the Vines—until the tenth century, when it was enlarged by the canons of the Florentine Cathedral, and the name was changed to Sta. Maria Novella. It was about the year 1219 that St. Dominick sent a certain Giovanni da Salerno, or, as he was afterwards called, the Beato Giovanni, with twelve other Dominican friars, to introduce his Order into Florence. They first lodged in the Hospital for Pilgrims outside the Porta San Gallo; but when St. Dominick himself arrived there in 1221, the Papal Legate and the Bishop of Florence assigned the Church of

Sta. Maria Novella, as well as the adjacent land, to the Dominicans, on which they raised their monastery. They immediately commenced building, and the first stone of the new church was laid by the Legate, Cardinal Latino degli Orsini.* After a lapse of seventy years, two of the brothers, Fra Ristori and Fra Sisto, pupils of Arnolfo di Lapo, or Cambio, aided by contributions from several of the principal families of Florence, finished the church, which, from the elegance of its form and proportions, Michael Angelo called La Sposa, the Bride.

Sta. Maria Novella is one of the few churches in Florence whose façade is nearly complete. The base was begun in the middle of the fourteenth century, but the whole was only finished as we now see it in 1470. The architect, Leon Battista Alberti, ignoring all rules, has produced a mixture of German, Gothic, Greek, and Roman architecture, incrusted with black and white marbles, in the manner of the Baptistery and Cathedral, and the result is a composition of so much beauty and refinement, that though peculiar, it is impossible to deny its charm.

The inflated sails of the Rucellai forming the ornament in the frieze, and the decorations round the principal gate, are especially beautiful. Tall columns of black marble, with composite capitals, are on either side; within the lunettes over each of the three doors are frescos by Ulisse Ciocchi.† That in the central lunette represents the ceremony of the Holy Sacrament at the Feast of the Corpus Domini, when the

---

* The Pope then reigning was Nicholas III.
† Possibly the son of Giovan Maria Ciocchi, a Florentine painter of the seventeenth century.

Host was carried in procession to the Church of Sta. Maria Novella. In the foreground St. Dominick is kneeling, and is ministered to by angels. The lunettes over the other doors contain figures of Aaron with the manna, and Melchisedek with the shew-bread, and are both very mediocre paintings. On either corner of the façade are wheel-like patterns of great elegance, one of which is only half finished; below these, are astronomical instruments attached to the building. One is a marble gnomon, or dial; the other, armillas for the observation of the solstices. Both were made by Ignazio Danti (1537—1586). Ignazio was a Dominican monk from Perugia, who was employed by the Grand-Duke Cosimo I. for geographical as well as astronomical researches, and was the author of the maps in the Stanza della Guardaroba of the Palazzo Vecchio.

Cosimo proposed to draw a meridian line within this church, but his project was frustrated by his death. He had, however, already caused a hole to be pierced through the wall to allow the sun's ray to pass into the nave, and placed this gnomon, or marble quadrant, and the bronze equinoctial and meridian armillas, with an inscription in honour of himself, as well as a stone with a small line which marks the edge of the solar solstice in the winter of 1575. The first armilla was to indicate the moment of midday; the second that of the equinox; and they are so constructed, that when the sun is at midday or at the equator, the light strikes the concave of both armillas, leaving two thin threads of light on either side, and when these two threads are equal, it is exactly noon.

To the right, a small oblong-shaped cloister flanks the whole side of the church, as far as the Piazza Vecchia, and the external walls of two sides are formed by the succession of white marble monuments under pointed arches, which contain the coats of arms of the families to whom they belonged. These tombs have been recently repaired, and placed somewhat farther back than their original position, so as to widen the Via degli Avelli, which connects the Piazza Nuova and Piazza Vecchia of Sta. Maria Novella.

The interior of the church is in the form of a Latin cross, and, although not one of the largest, is one of the most beautiful buildings in Florence. The nave and aisles are divided by clustered columns of excellent proportions. In order to give an appearance of greater magnitude, Fra Ristori and Fra Sisto allowed wider intervals between the three first columns nearest the principal entrance, and raised the pavement two steps towards the choir, the whole width of the nave and aisles. Until the year 1568 a marble screen, with frescos and monuments attached to it, divided the church in half, and separated the male from the female worshippers.* By order of Cosimo I., Vasari destroyed this screen, and added the chapels along the aisles. The so-called Italian-Gothic style of the interior of Sta. Maria Novella is not correct according to architectural rules, but is nevertheless extremely beautiful.

On either side of the central door are frescos, transferred to their present position from the former screen. That to the right, facing the spectator, is an early Florentine representation of the Annunciation. Beneath, in three compart-

---

* This is still usual in the Church of San Zenone at Verona, where the ascent to the choir is by a numerous flight of steps.

VOL. II.   P

ments, are the Nativity, the Baptism of our Lord, and the Adoration of the Magi. The fresco to the left is a very remarkable painting by Masaccio. The subject is the Holy Trinity, but it has been much injured. The Saviour on the cross is supported in the arms of the Eternal, who is seen beneath an arch resting on Ionic columns and pilasters; the dove hovers over the head of the Saviour. The Virgin, who is represented advanced in life, points to her Son; St. John, on the other side, stands with his hands clasped; in front is the donor, in a red cap and Florentine mantle, and his wife dressed in black. The expression of these four heads, and the arrangement of their drapery, which falls in large folds, is very grand.*

Above the central door is a large wooden Crucifix, attributed to Giotto and his pupil Puccio Capanna, but Giotto is in reality supposed to have had very little, if any, hand in it. Below is a mosaic representing the Holy Family in the Stable of Bethlehem; above the Crucifix is the rose-window of stained glass, which has a Coronation of the Virgin, surrounded by a garland of angels.

Beside the door to the left is a large marble slab, the monument of one of the Vecchietti family, whose mansions were near the Mercato Vecchio. The first altar proceeding up the church has a picture of the Martyrdom of St. Lawrence, by Girolamo Macchietti, a pupil of Ridolfo Ghirlandaio. The modern monuments on either side to the Senator Ippolito Venturi and his wife, are by the sculptor Stefano Ricci. The four altars which follow contain pictures by Giovanni Battista Naldini (1544—1600), who was a pupil

---

* See "Crowe and Cavalcaselle," vol. i. p. 543.

of Pontormo and of Angiolo Bronzino. The subjects are—
The Nativity, the Presentation at the Temple, the Deposition from the Cross, and St. Francis preaching, with our Saviour in the clouds above. Both these last are highly praised by Borghini for composition and design. The chapel containing the Deposition from the Cross is dedicated to St. Thomas à Becket, and near it are two old monuments transferred here from the former screen, and which were erected to the memory of Tommaso and Ruggieri Minerbetti, liberal benefactors to the church, and whose family claimed kindred with the celebrated archbishop of Canterbury. The archbishop's family is supposed to have been so cruelly persecuted in England that they had to fly their country, and about the end of the twelfth century to have established themselves in Lucca, from whence they removed to Florence. The name of Minerbetti is supposed to be a corruption of that of Becket. Messer Ruggero Minerbetti fought on the Guelphic side in the battle of Montaperti, 1260, and thirty members of the family filled the office of Priors of the Republic between the years 1283 and 1531.

These monuments were made by Silvio da Fiesole, a pupil of Andrea da Fiesole, who lived towards the end of the fifteenth century: they are sarcophagi of white marble, beneath an architrave resting on Corinthian pilasters, and decorated with the arms of the family—three daggers on a shield—and with four very lovely cherubs' heads. Four doorways succeed one another along the wall of this aisle; they are decorated with carved stone cornices of similar design, and one of these opens on the Chiostro degli Avelli; the two which follow are built up, and the last leads to the Capella della Purità. Two marble busts above these doors are to the memory of Josephus Zenobi del Rosso, Professor, 1760; and Cosmæ Raynor Rossio Melocchio, Knight of St. Stephen, 1820. In the Capella della Purità is the Crucifix before which a celebrated Dominican nun, the Beata Villana, always prayed. There is nothing otherwise worthy of note in this plain square room. The next chapel has an altar-piece by Jacopo Ligozzi, a native of Verona, and pupil of Paolo Veronese (1543—1627), who lived long in Florence, where he was much employed by the Grand-Duke Ferdinand II. The subject of this picture is St. Raymond de Penáforte, a Spanish saint, raising a dead child to life. The groups, though not free from affectation, are graceful and well placed. The stone decorations on either side of the altar are extremely beautiful. One of these is the monument to a member of the Ricasoli family, and is the work of Romolo di Taddeo da Fiesole. Giovanni Battista Ricasoli, whose profile is represented in relief on this monument, was the counsellor and confidential friend of the Grand-Duke Cosimo I. Born in 1504, the godson of Pope Leo X., Ricasoli was educated for the Church, and was the fast friend of the Medici. He became chamberlain to Clement VII., and accompanied that pope to Bologna for the coronation of the Emperor Charles V. In 1533 he escorted Catherine de' Medici to Marseilles, when she went to marry Henry, the son of Francis I. The same year he was appointed by the Pope military commissioner, and was sent to Hungary against the Sultan Soliman. After the death of Clement VII. he attached himself to Ippolito de' Medici, and on his death by poison, he followed his cousin, Duke Alexander. When Alexander was murdered, in 1537, he attended the court of Cosimo I., and was created Bishop of Cortona, and sent on various missions to Charles V. at Madrid, and to Rome. In 1548 he accompanied Prince Francis (afterwards the Grand-Duke Francis I.) to Genoa, to do homage to Philip II., the son of Charles V., and was then sent to Flanders to demand succour from Charles against the French, who were coming to the aid of the Siennese, then besieged by Cosimo. From Flanders Ricasoli proceeded to England, and was present at the marriage of Philip to Queen Mary. He was afterwards employed at Rome, on the death of Pope Paul III., to procure the election of a pontiff favourable to Medicean interests. In 1557, Cosimo sent him to Henry II. of France, charged to administer a poison, prepared by the grand-duke himself, for his enemy, Piero Strozzi. This design was frustrated by Catherine de' Medici, and Ricasoli had to take flight; but from that time forth he was known as the "Vescovo dell' Ampollina."—the Bishop of the Poison-cup. The correspondence between Cosimo and Ricasoli, when at the court of Naples, still exists among the archives of the Strozzi family. Ricasoli fulfilled several other missions for Cosimo, but finding himself advanced in years, he thought it best to provide for his soul; and in 1561 took up his abode in Pistoia, to which See he had been appointed the previous year, and devoted himself to his episcopal duties. He died in 1572, and was buried in Sta. Maria Novella at Florence, where his nephews raised a monument to his memory. He was a patron of letters, and contributed to the foundation of the Florentine Academy: his manners were so attractive that he gained the affections of all connected with him, and had friends amongst the most illustrious personages of the day. When Charles V. bade him farewell, he not only embraced him, but—a rare honour—kissed his cheek.*

Turning into the eastern transept, there is a very interesting portrait-bust of the Archbishop Antonino in terra-cotta. A very ancient monument above this bust is to the memory of Tedice Aliotti, a bishop of Fiesole, who died in 1336; the monument is attributed to Lino or Tino of Sienna. The bishop reclines on a sarcophagus, which rests on three crouching lions, and has a relief of our Saviour rising from the tomb, with the Virgin and St. John on either side; a canopy above is supported on twisted columns and pilasters; still higher is an arch with the shield of the deceased, a lion rampant.

A large fresco much damaged, beyond the monument, and lower down, was painted in memory of Joseph, the Patriarch of Constantinople, who died in Florence in 1440, during the Œcumenical Council which was summoned by Pope Eugenius IV. in the hope of reconciling the Latin and Greek Churches. The patriarch is represented in his robes, with an image in his hand. Over this fresco is a monument to Fra Aldobrandini Cavalcanti of Florence, who died in 1269, and contributed largely to the restoration of the church: the friar, clothed in a bishop's robes, is represented in relief. The statuette of the Virgin and Child above, beneath an arch of black and white marble, is of the school of Nicolò Pisano. A flight of stone steps leads to the chapel belonging to the Rucellai family, and at the head

---

* "Genealogia e Storia della Famiglia Ricasoli"—Luigi Passerini, 1860.

of the steps is a marble sarcophagus, containing the bones of Paolo Rucellai, the father of Giovanni Rucellai, at whose expense the *facciata* of Sta. Maria Novella was constructed.

In this chapel is the celebrated Madonna of Cimabue, painted in 1240, and borne hither from his workshop in the Borgo Allegri in a festive procession. The Virgin, above life-size, is seated; she is clothed in a red tunic and blue mantle, which is drawn over her head as a hood; her feet rest on the step of the throne, which is carved in a rich pattern and gilt; over the back of the chair is a drapery equally rich in gold and embroidery; the throne itself is supported by six angels kneeling, three above each other, on either side. The infant Saviour is clothed in white, with a gold mantle over his knees.* It is from this picture we may date the impulse given to art, which developed the Florentine school of painting under Giotto. The features of the Virgin are straight and regular; her eyes are long and almond-shaped, but more open than is usual with masters of that period; her head is slightly inclined on one side towards her child, as she looks up with a soft and dignified expression; the mouth is peculiarly sweet, the hands and fingers are exaggerated in form and length, the head is too large; but she sits gracefully, her elbow resting lightly on the arm of the throne. The child's head is too small and his arms too long, but the expression of his countenance, as well as his attitude, possess dignity and power. The faces of the angels are singularly lovely.

In the right-hand corner of this chapel is the old monument to the Beata Villana, removed hither from a chapel

---

* See "Crowe and Cavalcaselle," vol. i. p. 204.

near that of the Purità. Villana was a Florentine lady of peculiar sanctity, who died in 1360. The daughter of a certain Andrea di Messer Lapo, a wealthy merchant who had his dwelling near the Piazza di San Felice, Oltr' Arno, she was devoted from her childhood to a life of religious contemplation, fasting, wearing a hair shirt, and spending day and night in prayer. Her parents insisted on her marrying a youth of the noble family of Benintendi, and after her marriage she was surrounded by all the temptations and pleasures of this life, in the midst of which she forgot her religious aspirations. One day, when dressed with unusual splendour, turning to look at herself in a mirror, she beheld, to her horror, a demon in her clothes. She called for another mirror, and a third, but in each, she saw herself more hideous. She accordingly changed her gay garments for her hair shirt, and hastened to the Church of Sta. Maria Novella, where, confessing her sins to one of the friars, she thenceforth returned to a life of penitence and prayer, assisting the poor, and seeing visions, until, worn out by abstemiousness, she died at the early age of twenty-eight. Many marvellous stories are told of the Beata Villana. Her son was buried in the tomb afterwards used by the Minerbetti family, and her grandson erected this monument to her memory. Vasari attributes it to Desiderio da Settignano; but more recent writers on art give it to Bernardo Rossellino, also known as Gambarelli. The saint appears as in sleep, reposing beneath a tent-like drapery, the folds of which are held back by graceful angels. In the centre are hands holding a crown, which radiates light. There are several pictures in this chapel, though none of transcendent merit. One of Sta. Lucia is by Benedetto Ghirlandaio, a brother of Domenico, but very inferior as a painter. This picture was executed for a Dominican monk, Fra Tommaso Cortesi, who is represented adoring the saint. The Martyrdom of St. Catherine is by Giuliano Bugiardini, a Florentine (1471 —1554), an assistant of Mariotto Albertinelli, and pupil of Domenico Ghirlandaio. He never became very eminent, and this is his best performance. The idea for the composition was taken from a design by Michael Angelo, for whom Bugiardini had the profoundest admiration; and a group standing apart on a terrazza is supposed to be by the hand of the great master himself. The saint is represented as a fair young girl, whose joy and thankfulness at being saved from a torturing death is well expressed. An early picture of an Annunciation has a lovely angel; and another painting, representing the Virgin appearing to St. Dominick, is treated almost precisely as in another picture in the Church of San Felice in Florence.

The first chapel to the left of the transept, and on a line with the high altar, is dedicated to the Holy Sacrament. A rude bas-relief on the pilaster supporting the arch, which is kept closed by an iron grating, represents St. Gregory blessing the founder of this chapel. The adjoining chapel belongs to the Strozzi family. At the back is the monument to Filippo Strozzi (the elder), who built the splendid palace in the Via Tornabuoni; he died in 1491, and Benedetto da Majano (1442—1498) was the artist employed to execute his monument. This sarcophagus is of black marble, and above it is a most beautiful relief in white marble of the Madonna and Child with four angels, surmounted by an exquisitely carved garland of roses and heads of cherubim. The arch beyond is also delicately carved in arabesques

There was formerly here the bust of Filippo Strozzi, which is now in the Strozzi Palace. The frescos on the walls of this chapel have been exceedingly injured by repainting; they were originally by Filippino Lippi, of whom Filippo Strozzi was the patron, but were not executed until after Strozzi's death. The subjects chosen by Filippino were incidents in the lives of St. Philip and St. John the Evangelist. St. Philip is represented exorcising a dragon, which had been worshipped as the god Mars by the inhabitants of Hieropolis, in Phrygia. The dragon has crept from beneath the altar, and emits such a poisonous breath that the son of the king has fallen dead in the arms of his attendants. Philip, aided by Divine power, is restoring him to life. The priests of the dragon, incensed against the apostle, crucify him, as represented in the lunette above; the moment chosen by the painter is when St. Philip, already nailed to the cross, is raised by cords. The action of the men who are pulling the cords is much praised by Vasari.[*] On the opposite wall St. John restores Drusiana to life. The saint is supposed to have passed a year and a day on the island of Patmos, and was returning to Ephesus amidst the rejoicings of the inhabitants, when he met a funeral procession issuing from the gates, and was told that Drusiana, in whose house he had formerly lodged, was dead. She was a woman much esteemed for her good works, and St. John, desiring the bearers to set down the bier, prayed earnestly for her restoration to life. His prayer was granted, and the apostle went home with her, and dwelt again under her roof.[†] Drusiana is represented in this fresco, rising from the trestle

---

[*] See also "Crowe and Cavalcaselle," vol. ii. p. 448.
[†] See "Sacred and Legendary Art," by Mrs. Jameson, p. 150.

on which she is carried; St. John is looking at her with a serious countenance; there is little elevation, but a great deal of dramatic power in the composition. The group to the right, of a child startled by a dog, is full of nature and truth, and the women and children here, as well as in the beautiful little group of Charity in the corner, are very lovely. The monochrome imitation of architecture round these frescos is not in very good taste. On the ceiling are the Patriarchs and their symbols. The painted glass of the window, with the Madonna and Child, St. John, and St. Philip, is very finely executed.

There was formerly a high altar here, the work of Baccio d' Agnolo, which was removed for the present altar, rich in mosaic work, but out of keeping with the rest of the building. Beneath it are the remains of the Beato Giovanni da Salerno, the Dominican who founded the church. On the pavement before this altar there was also at one time a slab in bronze with the effigy of Fra Leonardo di Stagio Dati, Prior of the Convent and Grand-Master of the Dominicans. This monument was executed in 1426 by Lorenzo Ghiberti, when part of the church was included in the choir, but, as it was much worn from the feet of visitors, it has been removed behind the altar and within the present choir, where it is placed in an upright position. This prior was a man of exemplary conduct, and was distinguished in letters; he was present at the Council of Constance, and was sent by Pope Martin V. to the Council of Pavia; the monument was decreed to him at the public expense, in recognition of his important diplomatic services.

The choir of Sta. Maria Novella, in the apse behind the high altar, was originally a chapel belonging to the Ricci

family; at their expense it was decorated with frescos by
Andrea Orcagna, to whom may perhaps also be attributed
the elegant architecture of the roof. These early frescos
were much damaged by a storm in 1458, when the Ricci,
unable to bear the expense of the repairs, yielded their rights
to Giovanni Tornabuoni, who some time afterwards employed
Domenico Ghirlandaio, then a young man, to repaint the
walls in fresco with scenes from the lives of the Virgin and
St. John the Baptist. Ghirlandaio had already gained a reputation by his beautiful frescos in the Sassetti Chapel of the
SS. Trinità, and Tornabuoni offered to pay him one thousand two hundred gold florins for this new work, with two
hundred florins more, if he was satisfied with the performance when finished. Ghirlandaio devoted four years to
the undertaking, but although Tornabuoni expressed his
satisfaction, he refused to pay him the two hundred additional florins; and Ghirlandaio, who esteemed his art more
than money, declared that to have succeeded in pleasing his
employer was to him of higher value than any payment.

The subjects on either wall are divided in seven compartments, in three parallel lines, with a lunette above. Separating each space, are painted architectural decorations,
executed with great elegance and richness of detail. In the
lower compartments, on the side which contains the life
of St. John the Baptist, are the Angel appearing to
Zacharias at the altar, and the Salutation of Elizabeth and
Mary; above, the Birth of John the Baptist, and Zacharias naming his child; still higher up, the Preaching in the
Wilderness, and the Baptism of Christ. In the lunette is
the Daughter of Herodias dancing before Herod; among
the spectators, in the fresco of the Angel appearing to

Zacharias, are portraits of several of the Tornabuoni family; Giovanni, at whose expense the frescos were painted, is next the angel. The four half-length figures at the right-hand corner are all portraits of distinguished literary men inhabiting Florence: the first, attired as a canon, is Marsilio Ficino; the second, with a red cloak, and black scarf round his neck, is Cristofano Landino, the commentator on Dante; the third, turning round, is Messer Gentile, a bishop of Arezzo; and the fourth, standing in the midst of the group and raising his hands, is Angelo Poliziano. The three half-length figures of youths, on the left, are Federigo Sassetti, Andrea de' Medici, and Gian Françesco Ridolfi, who all belonged to the Medici Bank. The lady in a gold brocade dress in the group of the Salutation was a celebrated beauty, Ginevra de' Benci, whose portrait Ghirlandaio also introduces in his frescos of the life of the Virgin. The small figures in the distance, standing on a terrazza overlooking the town, are said to have been drawn by Michael Angelo, who was a boy studying under Ghirlandaio when this fresco was painted.

In the lower compartment on the opposite wall, which contains the life of the Virgin, are Joachim's Expulsion from the Temple, and the Birth of the Virgin; above, the Virgin's Presentation in the Temple and her Marriage; and on the line, still higher up, the Adoration of the Magi, and the Massacre of the Innocents. In the lunette are the Death and the Ascension of the Virgin; but this last painting has been much damaged. In the compartment where Joachim is driven from the Temple there is a group of four men in the corner nearest the window; the old man behind with a bald head and a red cap is Alessio Baldovinetti, Domenico's master in his art; the artist has taken his own portrait in the man wearing a red cloak over a grey dress, with his hand resting on his hip; the third figure, with long black hair and thick lips, is the pupil of Domenico, Sebastian Mainardi of San Gemignano; and the fourth, seen in profile and wearing a cap, is the artist's brother, David Ghirlandaio. Ginevra de Benci, in her gold brocade dress, appears a second time, in the Birth of the Virgin.

Ghirlandaio accomplished a great work by covering so large a space with a design so rich, and executed with so much boldness. The men have all the character of portraits, and have the quiet dignity and sobriety of demeanour appropriate to citizens of a free Republic; the women are very lovely, pure, and refined, and have a modest grace and dignity which is extremely fascinating. The drawing of the figures and the grandiose arrangement of the drapery show the stride forward Ghirlandaio had made in art. The landscape, architectural reliefs, sculpture, and perspective of the pavement are all excellent, and kept in due subordination, as mere accessories to the principal subject. On either side of the windows are the portraits, life-size, of Giovanni Tornabuoni and his wife, in the costume of the day. Giovanni has taken care that his share in the decoration of the apse should not be forgotten, for he not only sat for his portrait in the frescos, but he has blazoned his coat of arms in the most conspicuous places, although the Ricci appended one condition to their cession of the chapel, that their coat of arms should be retained in its place. They sued him at law for the nonfulfilment of this compact; but Tornabuoni gained the suit by proving he had inserted the arms of the Ricci in an obscure corner behind the altar.

Above the portraits of Giovanni and of his wife are St. John the Baptist departing for the Wilderness, and an Annunciation; St. Francis before the Soldan, and the Death of Peter Martyr. Over the window is the Coronation of the Virgin. The window itself is in three divisions of richly coloured glass, the work of Alessandro Fiorentino, an expert master in his craft. In one division are six saints; in another, the Presentation in the Temple; and in the last, the Virgin in Glory. It was completed the year after the frescos. In the vaulted ceiling are the Evangelists.

The wood-carving of the stalls is by Giovanni Gargiolli.

CHRONOLOGY.

	A.D.
Aliotti, Tedice	d. 1336
Andrea da Fiesole	1465—1526
Baccio d' Agnolo	1462—1543
Baldovinetti Alessio	1427—1499
Benedetto da Majano	1442—1498
Bugiardini	1471—1554
Cavalcante, Fra Aldobrandi	d. 1229
Cimabue, his Madonna painted	1240
Council of Florence	1440
Danti, Ignazio	1537—1586
Ghirlandaio, Benedetto	1458—1497
" David	1452—1525
" Domenico	1449—1494
" Rldolfo	1483—1561
Giovanni da Salerno came to Florence	1219
Giotto	1276—1337
Landino Cristoforo	1424—1504
Ligozzi, Jacopo	1543—1627

	A.D.
Lippi Filippino	1457—1504
Macchietti, Girolamo, pupil of R. Ghirlandaio	1534—1592
Masaccio	1401—1428
Marsilio Ficino	1433—1499
Naldini, Giovan Battista	1537—1592
Poliziano, Angelo	1454—1494
Sta. Maria Novella finished	1470
Villana, Beata	d. 1360

CHAPTER XVII.

STA. MARIA NOVELLA—(*Continuation*).

THE first chapel to the left of the choir belongs to the Gondi family, and is encrusted with marbles, arranged after a design by Giuliano di San Gallo; it is dedicated to St. Luke, and is sometimes called the Chapel of the Crucifix, because it contains the crucifix of Filippo Brunelleschi, made after seeing a crucifix by Donatello, now in Sta. Croce, which he stigmatised as the representation of a peasant—*contadino*.*

The Gaddi Chapel is dedicated to St. Jerome, and was decorated by Giovanni Antonio Doscio, a pupil of Raffaello da Montelupo, in 1533. The columns of pietra-serena have very beautiful capitals. The altar-piece, of Christ restoring to Life the Daughter of Jairus, is a feeble production of Angelo Bronzino. On the sides of the chapel are reliefs by Giovanni dell' Opera, a pupil of Baccio Bandinelli: the Marriage of Mary and Joseph, and the Presentation in the Temple. Above, in the ceiling, are frescos of the Life of St. Jerome.

The chapel in the southern transept is reached by a

---

* See chapter on Sta. Croce.

flight of steps, in the same manner as the Rucellai Chapel opposite. It belongs to the Strozzi family, and is dedicated to St. Thomas Aquinas. Here are preserved the relics of a certain Beato Alessio degli Strozzi, who caused the chapel to be paved with marble about the middle of the fourteenth century. The walls are painted in fresco by the brothers Andrea and Bernardo Orcagna, and represent the Last Judgment, the Pains of Hell as described by Dante, and the Glories of Paradise, with a numerous assemblage of saints and holy personages. These frescos were probably executed prior to the altar-piece, which is also by Andrea Orcagna, and bears the date 1357. The Last Judgment is at the end of the transept, and covers the walls on either side and above the window. The Saviour in the clouds dispenses blessings and curses, and is accompanied by angels who bear the symbols of the Passion. To the left, the Virgin is kneeling; six of the Apostles are beside her; the Baptist is at the head of the remaining six to the right. Beneath the Virgin are patriarchs and prophets—Noah with his Ark, Moses and Abraham, saints and martyrs. In a corner of the foreground angels help one of the chosen, who is rising from the grave. The condemned, who are on the side below St. John the Baptist, show their despair by their gestures.

Although the painting on the wall to the left has suffered much from damp and restorations, enough of the fresco remains to enable us to judge of Andrea's composition. The Saviour and the Virgin—a sweet, yet dignified and queen-like woman—are seated side by side on a throne, and higher up on either side are fiery seraphim and cherubim; beneath, the angels play on musical instruments. The rest of the space is covered with a multitude of figures—apostles, prophets, saints, and martyrs, each accompanied by his or her guardian angel, who play on instruments, sing, or are engaged in prayer. An angel in the foreground is introducing a nun into Paradise. The Inferno—Hell—on the opposite wall, has been wholly repainted. Ghiberti, in his "Commentaries," attributes this fresco to Bernardo Orcagna.

A record in the Strozzi collection of documents mentions that a certain Tomaso di Rossello Strozzi, whose remains are laid beneath the chapel, ordered Andrea Orcagna to paint the altar-piece in 1354, on condition of its being finished in a year and eight months; but Orcagna was unable to fulfil that part of the contract. The panel is divided in five compartments. The Saviour, on a throne, is in the centre; above him are seraphim and cherubim. He presents the Gospel to St. Thomas Aquinas, who is led to him by the Virgin, and the keys to St. Peter, who is supported by John the Baptist. The saints kneel, and angels play musical instruments. St. Catherine and St. Michael are behind the Virgin, St. Lawrence and St. Paul behind the Baptist. In the centre-piece of the predella, our Saviour is saving St. Peter, who is sinking on the waters. On one side is the celebration of mass, on the other a king dying amidst the lamentations of a crowd of spectators, whilst a monk and two angels weigh the soul of the departed in a balance, and save it from the expectant demons. Cavalcaselle considers this altar-piece the finest panel picture by Orcagna.

St. Thomas Aquinas is represented on the coloured glass of the window, holding a head, from whence emanate rays which fall on a church he has in his other hand. Above are the Strozzi arms, and a Virgin and Child. The window was probably also designed by Andrea Orcagna. Beneath the staircase leading to the Strozzi Chapel, is the imitation of a sepulchre under a low arch, in which is an Entombment of Christ, attributed to Giottino. Above, is the portrait of Messer Fuligno di Carbone de' Galli da Campi, Bishop of Fiesole, who died in 1348, and was buried here. To the right of the staircase is a small door leading to the lower church and cemetery of the friars, entered from the cloisters, the walls of which are painted in frescos attributed to Greek artists who came to Florence in 1225, and to whom the Italian painters, among whom was Cimabue, were indebted for much of their skill in art. A small chapel contains a fresco of St. Anthony, and in the vaulting above is represented the Life of St. Benedict. In another chapel, dedicated to St. Martin, are paintings attributed to Jacopo da Casentino, of the fourteenth century. There is also, in a cloister adjoining this cemetery, a fine Robbia representation of Mary Magdalene in the Garden.

The door, on the left side of the staircase to the Strozzi Chapel, leads to the Bell-tower—Campanile—which was built by Fra Giovanni da Campi, a monk of Sta. Maria Novella, assisted by another friar, Fra Jacopo Talenti, in 1334. They were both well-known architects, and rebuilt the bridge of the Carraia when it had been destroyed by a heavy flood.

The Sacristy beyond was built after a design by Fra Jacopo Talenti, and intended for a chapel for the Cavalcanti family. It is now surrounded by presses of walnutwood, containing the priests' garments, reliquaries, &c. To the left of the entrance is a beautiful lavatory of terra-cotta, by Luca della Robbia—a Madonna and Child with angels, surrounded by a rich garland of flowers. Within the arch is a landscape, and on the pilasters delicately wrought arabesques, flowers, and fruit. The corresponding lavatory, by one Fortini, has heads of cherubim well executed. Above the door is a Crucifix, in relief, attributed to Masaccio, but more probably by a sculptor of that name, who lived in the fifteenth century. The window of old stained-glass here is very rich. In one of the presses is preserved, within a reliquary, the only remaining banner of the twelve which Peter Martyr presented in this church to the twelve captains whom he sent forth on Ascension Day, 1244, to destroy the Paterini, or Heretics, in Florence.[*] Here also is preserved the parchment bull[†] of Gregory IX., 1227, which confirmed the Order of St. Dominick. Leaving the sacristy, at the corner of the transept is a granite vase brought from the little village of the Impruneta, south of Florence, where once was a miraculous Virgin: it rests on a marble figure, the work of Michael Angelo.

The first altar in the aisle, after leaving the sacristy, contains the bones of the Beata Villana. Above it is a picture, by Dronzino, executed in 1592, of St. Hyacinth, a Polish missionary saint, who belonged to the Dominican order.

The Organ Gallery, of perforated marble, is a copy from the original, by Baccio d' Agnolo, which the monks sold, and which is now in the Kensington Museum, in London. There are no other works of interest in this aisle, except a monument by Andrea da Fiesole, who was assisted in his

---

[*] See vol. i. of this work, " Bigallo and Misericordia."
[†] Bull—*bolla*, stamped or sealed document.

work by his two scholars, Angelo Maso Boscoli and Silvio Cosini da Fiesole. This monument, which is a simple black marble sarcophagus, was placed here to the memory of a jurisconsult named Antonio Strozzi.

The marble pulpit, with bas-reliefs picked out in gold, was executed for the Rucellai family by Maestro Lazaro, after a design by Filippo Brunelleschi. The subjects are the Annunciation; the Birth of the Saviour; the Presentation in the Temple; and the Virgin in glory, letting down her girdle to St. Thomas.

The Cloisters of Sta. Maria Novella, which are entered from the church, are very large, and adorned with fresco paintings. The Green Cloister—Chiostro Verde—so called from the frescos around painted in terra-verde, was built early in the fourteenth century. On the wall, close to the steps leading to the church, is a painting in tempera, by Spinello Aretino, who died in 1400—the pupil of Jacopo da Casentino—representing Saints of the Dominican order: San Vincenzio Ferraris, a Spaniard, 1357—1455, and Santa Caterina of Sienna, with the archangel Raphael. The frescos round the cloisters contain scenes from the Old Testament. Those nearest the church, turning to the left, are by Paolo Uccello, and represent the Creation, the Expulsion from Paradise, the Building of the Ark, and the Deluge, which last is one of the most remarkable for truth to nature, powerful drawing, and perspective—a man clings to the Ark by his fingers, whilst others are drowning; among whom one in the foreground wears a primitive specimen of a life-preserver. The last of the series, executed by Uccello, is Noah's Sacrifice. They were all painted between 1446 and 1448, and are the more valuable as his genuine works are rarely found in the public galleries.* The remaining twenty-four frescos are by a still rarer artist, Dello Delli, 1404, but inferior in execution to Uccello. Near the gates close to the entrance to the old cemetery is a fresco, in a dilapidated condition, of the crucified Saviour, with the tree from the root of Jesse, the sun, moon, and a head of St. Thomas Aquinas, probably by a scholar of Giotto's.

Beyond the gates of the cemetery is a door with two beautiful windows, formed by an arch and twisted columns, belonging to the Spanish Chapel, so called because used on particular feast days by the Spaniards who came to Florence to attend Eleonora of Toledo, on her marriage with the Grand-Duke Cosimo I. The frescos were then cleaned. The altar-piece, by Alessandro Allori, represents St. James, the patron saint of Spain; and the tribune is painted in fresco by Pocetti. The chapel was built about the middle of the fourteenth century, at the expense of a certain Buonamico Guidalotti, a rich and devout Florentine citizen, for the purpose of celebrating the festival of the Holy Sacrament, or Corpus Christi, instituted in 1264 by Pope Urban IV. The architect employed by Guidalotti was a Dominican monk, Fra Jacopo da Talenti da Nipozzano, of the diocese of Fiesole, who has been already mentioned as having assisted in the construction of the sacristy. The architecture is simple; the roof groined, and supported by intersecting pointed arches. The spaces between the ribs, and the four walls beneath them, are richly decorated with frescos, which have been usually attributed to Taddeo Gaddi and Simone Memmi, of Sienna. There is some doubt whether Memmi painted any of these

---

* See "Crowe and Cavalcaselle;" Life of Paolo Uccello.

frescos, since when Guidalotti made his will in 1355, none of them were finished, and Simone Memmi died in 1345.* The subjects were selected by another Dominican, Fra Jacopo Passavanti,† a man of considerable literary eminence, whose writings are praised by Silvio Pellico. He was born at Florence towards the end of the thirteenth century, and was the grandson, by his mother, of Giovanni Tornaquinci, who contributed to the choir of Sta. Maria Novella, and who fell in battle, valiantly defending the Caroccio, on the Guelphic side, at Montaperti. Passavanti was sent by the Dominicans to Paris to complete his studies in Divinity and Humanity. He became the Superior in the Convents of Pistoia, San Miniato, and lastly Sta. Maria Novella, and died at the age of sixty in 1357. His monument is believed to be that beneath the Chapel of San Giovanni in the church, on which the figure of a monk may still be traced. He was the author of the "Specchio della vera Penitenza," a book of devotion, considered a model of purity and grace of style, worthy of Bocaccio, whom he preceded by ten years.

The series of frescos commence on the eastern wall, the subject of each ascending to the space above. The four frescos on the roof, and the whole of the wall to the left, are attributed to Taddeo Gaddi; that to the right to Simone Memmi. Vasari relates, that Taddeo was engaged to paint the whole chapel, and had only completed part when the

---

* Cavalcaselle considers these frescos overpraised, and that they are all by one hand, probably a scholar of the Siennese school who painted the fresco of San Ranieri in the Campo Santo of Pisa, possibly a certain Andrea di Florentia. See "Crowe and Cavalcaselle," vol. i. p. 375 ; vol. ii. p. 89.

† See Lord Lindsay's "Christian Art," vol. iii. p. 30.

Prior of Sta. Maria Novella invited Memmi, who had gained universal admiration by his frescos in Santo Spirito, to assist in this work. The subject on the eastern, or altar wall, is the Procession to Calvary, the Crucifixion, and the Descent into Hades. On the roof above is the Resurrection, painted by Taddeo Gaddi. Lord Lindsay observes, that it is the first instance in which the Saviour's body is made the source of illumination. On the western or entrance wall opposite, are frescos which fill up the space between the windows, the door of entrance, and the side walls; but they are so much injured by damp that they are hardly recognisable. They represent scenes from the lives of various Dominicans—St. Thomas Aquinas receiving the habit of his Order, the Murder of St. Peter Martyr, and several miracles performed by Dominican saints. On the ceiling above is the Ascension of our Lord, by Taddeo. On the northern wall is the Triumph, or Glorification, of St. Thomas Aquinas, also by Gaddi; and on the ceiling, the Descent of the Holy Ghost on the Apostles. This last approaches the style of the old Byzantine mosaics; the Virgin and Apostles are in a large building closed by folding doors, which various persons outside, in an Eastern costume, endeavour to open. In the frescos beneath, St. Thomas Aquinas sits in state; he is elevated above a screen containing fourteen stalls. The heretics Arius, Sabellius, and Averrhoes,* lie at his feet, and he is attended by saints of the Old and New Testament. The four Cardinal and the three Theological Virtues float

---

* Arius, born in Libya in the fourth century, died 336; Sabellius, born in the Ptolemaid, was condemned by the Alexandrian Council, 261; Averrhoes, born at Cordova, in Spain, in the twelfth century, died in Morocco, 1198.

above; and below, in the fourteen stalls, are the seven Profane and seven Theological Sciences, in the form of beautiful maidens, with their earthly representatives beneath them.

The subject on the southern wall is significant of the Church Militant, defended by the Dominican Order. The representatives of the Ecclesiastical and Civil Power, the pope and the emperor, are seated on thrones. The pope is Benedict XI.; he is accompanied by a cardinal and bishop; the emperor is Albert, and a king near him is supposed to be Philippe le Bel of France. To the left is the spiritual army of the Church; to the right, the attendants on the emperor. Among these is a supposed portrait of Cimabue in profile, wearing a hood and short cloak; Petrarch is near him, and Laura, with a burning heart, besides Arnolfo de' Lapi, Giotto, and Simone Memmi.* At the feet of the pope is a flock of sheep, symbolical of the faithful, as the black and white dogs which protect them are of the Dominican order. Immediately in front, to the right, are more of these dogs, killing wolves, representing the Inquisitors destroying the heretics who had worried the sheep of Christ. St. Dominick is again seen confessing a knight, beside whom are some dancing girls, and he points the way to Paradise to those who have already received absolution at his hands. St. Peter is in the gateway; behind him is Paradise, peopled by the blessed of all ages and both sexes, with the Saviour enthroned, and the Virgin Mary. Behind the pope and emperor, and other

---

* Cavalcaselle throws great doubts on the authenticity of these portraits. See "Crowe and Cavalcaselle," vol. ii. p. 86.

august personages, is the cathedral of Florence, with its first cupola. The lines over the perforated parapets are broken by statues of saints, prophets, or angels, which have all been removed, if they ever really existed. Above this fresco is St. Peter rescued from the waves, by Taddeo Gaddi, which is the finest of the paintings on the ceiling, and supposed by Cavalcaselle to have been painted by Taddeo's pupil, Antonio Veneziano.

The Chiostro Verde communicates with another and much larger cloister; and between the two is an altar with a painting, by Simone Memmi, of a Madonna and Child, and saints, in the Greek style. Beside the altar are two saints in fresco, by Bernardo Pocetti; and in a lunette above the gate, a Crucifix between St. Thomas Aquinas and St. Dominick, by Stefano Fiorentino, the pupil of Giotto.

The great Cloister of Sta. Maria Novella is one of the most spacious in Europe. Until recently a statue of the Beato Giovanni di Salerno stood in the midst, but this has been removed; it is surrounded by frescos representing incidents in the lives of saints of the order, separated by pilasters, on each of which is a portrait of a Dominican friar. The frescos in the lunettes are the best; and the fourth to the right represents St. Peter Martyr and his followers fighting with heretics in the Piazza della Croce al Trebbio. The column is crowned with a statue of Peter Martyr, as it once appeared. The thirteenth lunette, by Cosimo Gamberucci, has an historical interest, because it represents Fra Giovanni di Salerno founding the Church of Sta. Maria Novella, on the site of Sta. Maria delle Vigne, which is ceded to the Tornaquinci family, in presence of the papal legate. The twentieth lunette, by Santi di Tito, represents angels supplying the table of St. Dominick and his monks. Near a glass door which opens on the Farmacia, or dispensary of the friars, is a lunette by Giovanni Balducci, containing a fresco representing Sant' Antonino received by the Signory of Florence on the Ringhiera of the Palazzo Vecchio. It is interesting, both for the costumes of the period and because a picture of the Ringhiera. A chapel in the cloister, built by Messer Agnolo degl' Acciajoli, in 1303, when Bishop of Florence, was ceded by the friars to the Council of Eight, during the Ciompi Riots.

The principal entrance to the Farmacia is in the Via della Scala, where the stone framework of the door is carved in fruit and flowers by a modern artist. After passing through a corridor and anteroom, we arrive at a small vaulted chapel, with beautiful frescos by Spinello Aretino. The two frescos on the wall to the right of the window represent the Scourging of the Saviour, who looks reproachfully at his persecutors; and Christ bearing the Cross, in which the women who follow are pushed back by soldiers. Over these frescos, in a lunette, Christ is represented blindfold on a throne, and mocked by the Jews. Facing the window is a Pietà; the Virgin kisses the lips of the Saviour; the mourning women are behind her; St. John kisses his hand, and St. Peter is weeping at the feet, whilst gazing at the Saviour's face, and raising the cloth on which he lies; the other spectators look on in wonder and sadness. Next this fresco is a "Noli me tangere." The earnest, prayerful gaze of the Magdalene, and the thoughtful expression of the Saviour, are given with much beauty. Lovely angels tell the women at the tomb that Christ has risen. Above is the Crucifixion, in which St. Jerome's lion, seated, forms a curious balance to the fainting Virgin: the soldiers cast lots for the garment. On the wall to the left is the Last Supper, and Christ washing the feet of his disciples; and above is Christ with the tribute money.

Beyond this chapel are the rooms used for distilling from various flowers and herbs, as well as ante-chambers, where are sold perfumes, &c., manufactured by the friars. All this part of the former monastery looks on the great cloister. A large and lofty apartment, built in 1848, and richly gilt and ornamented, is reserved for the reception of royal personages. The pictures, busts, &c., which ornament these rooms, are not of any great value.

CHRONOLOGY.

	A.D.
Allori, Alessandro	1535—1607
Aquinas, St. Thomas	1226—1274
Baccio Bandinelli	1493—1560
Baccio d' Agnolo	1462—1543
Benedict XI., Pope	1303—1304
Brunelleschi, Filippo	1379—1446
Campanile of Sta. Maria Novella built	1334
Dello Delli	1404—1463
Donatello	1386—1466
Gaddi, Taddeo	1300—1366
Giottino	Living in 1395
Jacopo da Casentino	Middle of Fourteenth Century.
Memmi, Simone	1215(?)—1344
Orcagna, Andrea	1308(?)—1368(?)
Philippe le Bel of France reigned	1285—1314
Raffaello da Montelupo	1505—1567

	A.D.
Robbia, Luca della	1400—1482
San Gallo, Giuliano di	1445—1516
Spinello, Aretino	d. 1410
Uccello, Paolo	1397—1475
Veneziano, Antonio, elected to the Guild of Physicians and Apothecaries	1374

CHAPTER XVIII.

THE VIA DELLA SCALA.—GARDENS OF THE ORICELLARI.—STA. LUCIA.—BORG' OGNI SANTI.—LUNG' ARNO ACCIAJOLI.—BRIDGES.

THE Via della Scala has its name from a well-known Foundling Hospital in this quarter, Sta. Maria della Scala, which was called after a similar hospital in Sienna, with three staircases—*scale*, or *scalini*. The founder of the Florentine hospital, at the corner of the Via Oricellari and the Via della Scala, was a certain Cione di Lapo de' Pollini, or Cione, the son of Lapo, of the family of Pollini, whose marble bust is in the cortile of the Innocenti. In 1531 the building was ceded to the nuns of San Martino al Mugnone. In a chapel within the walls of the convent are frescos from the life of San Bernardo degli Uberti, and outside this chapel, which stands in a small piazza, is an inscription recording that here twenty thousand persons were buried during the plague of 1479. Sta. Maria della Scala, or San Martino al Mugnone, recognisable by the old style of rough masonry, is now used as a penitentiary. On the northern side of the Via della Scala, nearer the walls or boulevard, is the Conservatorio in Ripoli, once the Convent of San Jacopo in Ripoli, where was formerly a picture by Ridolfo Ghirlandaio, now in the Gallery of the Louvre at Paris. In the lunette over the door of this church is a fine example of Luca della Robbia ware; the subject, a Madonna and Child, with St. Dominick on one side and a saint on the other, surrounded by a beautiful garland of fruit. The treatment of this relief differs from most of Della Robbia's: the Child lies on his side, and is not as lovely as in other representations, but the Virgin and saints are grand and statuesque. Ripoli is a village near Florence, where the Dominicans first had an oratory, dedicated to San Jacopo. It finally became a convent of Dominican nuns, who removed to the Via della Scala in 1300.

The Via Oricellari crosses the Via della Scala; and, proceeding towards the Arno, the high iron gates on the right are the entrance to the Orti Oricellari, or Rucellai Gardens, where at one time the Platonic Academy, founded by Cosimo de' Medici, Pater Patriæ, held their meetings. A grotto and temple commemorate the exact spot; and the names of the academicians are inscribed on a column in the Garden; viz., Giovanni Rucellai, Angelo Poliziano, Lorenzo de' Medici, Pico della Mirandola, Nicolò Macchiavelli, Bernardo and Cosimo Rucellai, Luigi Pulci, Giovanni Corsini, Leon Battista Alberti. The palace in the midst of these gardens was built by Bernardo Rucellai, after a design by Leon Battista Alberti, who also laid out the ground. It underwent alterations at the hands of the architect Silvani in the seventeenth century, when it became the property of the Marchese Stiozzi Ridolfi, and was known as the Palazzo Stiozzi. It was not until after the death of Lorenzo de' Medici that the Platonic Academy was transferred here by the invitation of Bernardo Rucellai; and it was in these gardens that Nicolò Macchiavelli recited his famous discourses on Livy, and that the first Italian tragedy, *Rosamunda*, the composition of Giovanni Rucellai, was read in the presence of Pope Leo X. The beautiful Bianca Capello occupied this Palace before her marriage with the Grand-Duke Francis I. The huge statue of Polyphemus in the midst of the garden is by Antonio Morelli. There is likewise a statue of Pope Boniface VIII., which was on the first *facciata* of the Cathedral.

In a direct line with the Via Oricellari, and at the end of the broad street called the Porta Prato, is the Church of Sta. Lucia del Prato, which in 1251 was built in the midst of meadows by a Confraternity of Frati Umiliati, an Order founded in 1180, and first composed of Milanese who had been expatriated by the German emperors. During their exile in Germany they improved themselves in the manufacture of cloth, and on their return to Italy settled in Florence, where they built their church and convent on this spot, and carried on their trade. In 1547 the Grand-Duke Cosimo I. obliged them to sell their convent to the Scolopi, who were canons of San Salvatore, and whom the Grand-Duke had expelled from their own Convent of San Piero Gattolino, near the Porta Romana, to make room for the fortifications of the city. The Church of Santa Lucia is now under the patronage of the Torrigiani family.

In the first chapel to the right on entering, is a picture of St. Joseph with the infant Christ in his arms, and San Francesco di Sales and Sta. Teresa below; they are sweet in expression and soft in colour. Behind the high altar is a Nativity, by Domenico Ghirlandaio; a good picture, but in an obscure position. In the first chapel to the left is an Annunciation, by Pietro Cavallini, who painted the same subject in the SS. Annunziata. The Virgin is seated on a bench in a garden with a book beside her. She has a simple and innocent expression as she looks upwards at the dove which hovers over her; the angel kneels on the opposite side of the picture; and, though false in drawing, it is an interesting composition.

Beyond this quarter of the town is the Cascine, or Public Gardens of Florence, the fashionable promenade of the Florentine *beau monde*, and a favourite resort of all classes. Long avenues of fine trees and tall hedges of ilex and other evergreens afford shade and shelter in the hot days of summer; and in the evenings of May and June they are brilliant with thousands of fire-flies. The Arno, with a lovely view of the hills and villas beyond, is on one side of the Cascine, on the other, the magnificent range of Monte Morello and the Apennines. A casino, or farm, which once belonged to the grand-dukes, is now converted into a caffè, and the space before it is generally crowded with carriages.

The first palace of any importance along the Arno is modern; it was built by the celebrated actress Madame Ristori, but is now in the possession of the Marchese Fransoni, who belongs to an old Genoese family, and is nephew of the late Archbishop of Turin. The Palace contains several pictures of value, especially those of the early Florentine school, amidst which is a fine Botticelli; there are besides an unfinished Madonna by Francia, a most exquisite little picture of Christ amidst the Doctors, by Mazzuola, of Ferrara, and some interesting family portraits; a fine Vandyke, and a group consisting of a lady of the Fransoni family, with her son and daughter, by the most celebrated Genoese painter, Bernardo Strozzi.

In the Borg' Ogni Santi, the street parallel with the Arno, and at the corner of the Piazza Manin, is a Palazzo which belonged to the Quaratesi family, one of the oldest private dwellings in Florence, designed by Brunelleschi; this palace was at one time in the possession of the Gondi family, when it was painted by Andrea Feltrini in the peculiar Florentine manner, called *Sgraffiato*.

The Church of Ogni Santi, or San Salvador, was founded by the Padri Umiliati after their removal from Sta. Lucia. They had already purchased the space occupied by the present Piazza, which they converted into a pool, filled with water from the river, for cleansing the wool, and here they built their monastery and the adjoining church. In 1554 they were obliged to yield their rights to the Franciscans, who in 1627 rebuilt the church. A fresco was discovered this year—1872—behind the fine Luca della Robbia above the principal entrance; this fresco has been removed to Sta. Croce, but the Lucca della Robbia group is restored to its original position.

The interior of the church consists of a nave and transepts, in the form of a Latin Cross. In one of the transepts are two paintings which were originally by Andrea Castagno; St. Francis receiving the Confirmation of his Order, and the Death of the Saint. Both pictures have been repainted, and the later artist has converted St. Francis into San Bernardino, who presents his tablet with the name of Jesus on it to Pope Martin V., and whose body is exhibited to the public.

The only works of real artistic merit in the church are two frescos on either side of the nave; that to the left is by Domenico Ghirlandaio, and represents St. Jerome in his study; it is one of the earliest works of the master before his style was formed, and though faulty in drawing,—the leg of the saint actually appearing severed from his body,—there is a diligence and attention to detail, with variety of invention and power of expression, which show the promise of future excellence; the colour is clear and bright, and every detail, to the pattern of the table-cover and the various articles on the shelf above, are finished in a style which recalls early German or Flemish pictures.* The old man sits gracefully in a thoughtful attitude at his desk, which has the date 1480.

The fresco opposite is by Sandro Botticelli: St. Augustine in prayer; he looks upwards absorbed; beside him is an orrery: the hands and fingers are in Botticelli's peculiar manner; the saint is represented as an ordinary peasant—but the drawing is free and vigorous, the drapery falls in large and noble folds, and the colour is sober.†

The inside of the cupola over the tribune is painted by Giovanni di San Giovanni; and the life of St. Francis is represented in Pietra-Dura mosaic over the high altar: the bronze crucifix is by Cennini, a pupil of Tacca. The two marble angels on the gates of the choir are by Andrea Ferroni di Fiesole. The picture of San Bonaventura guided by an angel is by Fabrizio Boschi. The choir was built by Count Pandolfo Bardi; a Virgin in a dark situation over the entrance to the choir is by Bernardo Orcagna.‡

Within the sacristy, to the left of the choir, is an interesting picture of the Crucifixion, probably by Nicola di

---

* See "Crowe and Cavalcaselle," vol. ii. p. 464.
† Ibid, vol. ii. p. 415—420.   ‡ Ibid, vol. i. p. 453.

Pietro Gerini, the pupil and assistant of Taddeo Gaddi. Four angels hover above ; Mary Magdalene is at the foot of the Cross; the Virgin, St. John, and two monks on either side. This painting has also been attributed to Françesco da Volterra, of the school of Giotto and a pupil of Gerini.* In the left transept is a fine Crucifix by Giotto, and over the altar a wooden image of St. Francis in prayer.

The walls of the cloisters of Ogni Santi are painted by several good artists, and represent incidents and miracles in the life of St. Francis. Beginning from the door, the first five lunettes leading to the second cloister, and those on the side wall next the church, are by Giovanni di San Giovanni. The meeting of St. Francis and St. Dominick, and St. Francis receiving the Stigmata, are by Jacopo Ligozzi, who also painted all the lunettes on the northern and eastern walls. The door opening on the second or inner cloister conducts to the Refectory, where there is a noble Cenacolo, or Last Supper, by Domenico Ghirlandaio, bearing the date 1480, the same year that he painted the St. Jerome in the Church, when he was only thirty-one years of age. Although the arrangement is in accordance with the conventional rule, the composition is very original. The Saviour's head is extremely beautiful; and the absorbed expression of his countenance, serene yet serious, as if the treachery of his disciple was forgotten in the thought that the great sacrifice was shortly to be consummated, is truly sublime. St. Peter, beside him, true to the impetuous nature of this apostle, has taken on himself to reprove Judas, and points significantly with his thumb to the

---

* See " Crowe and Cavalcaselle," vol. i. p. 365—395.

Saviour. Perhaps to enhance the nobility of the head of Christ, the artist has erred in giving too much vulgarity to Peter, whose countenance nevertheless is very fine, animated, and expressive. The low, hardened villain, which Judas is represented, is well-expressed by his defiant attitude, and the sneer with which he meets Peter's angry reproof. St. John is asleep; his head is inferior to the same subject treated by other masters. Beyond him, one of the apostles leans his head on his hand, and appears plunged in melancholy reflections; his countenance and attitude are very beautiful, and are in contrast with the animation and questioning interest of the rest. Cavalcaselle remarks on this Cenacolo:—" It is not as yet here that Ghirlandaio impresses the beholder with his greatness as a composer; but the old symmetry of sitting apostles is already varied by a clearer exhibition of the moving thought in the assemblage, and great variety of individual expression and action is also apparent. But Ghirlandaio shows that his talent is not matured, especially in his handling of colour. Some roughness in the surface is caused by stippling. Some flatness is created by the absence of broad shadow; and the greatest depth being near the outline, communicates to the figures an unpleasant hardness, not diminished by the effort to define the forms with a wiry line. Sculptural grandeur, clearly within the painter's aim, is marred by too much arrangement of drapery, and the liquid general colour is of an unpleasant reddish tone."*

The Hotel de la Ville, on one side of the Piazza Manin, was the Palace of Caroline Murat. Not far from the Church

---

* See "Crowe and Cavalcaselle," vol. ii. p. 464.

of Ogni Santi is the Convent and Church of San Giovanni in Dio, adjoining which is the Hospital of that name on the site of the former houses of the Vespucci family. In one of these was born, in 1453, Amerigo Vespucci, who, from his discoveries north of where Columbus landed, gave his name to the Continent of America.

The Hospital of San Giovanni in Dio was founded by Simone, the son of Pietro Vespucci, in 1400. In 1587 it passed into the hands of the neighbouring Confraternity of San Giovanni in Dio, and was enlarged in 1735, at which time all the houses of the Vespucci were incorporated into the building. After the discovery of North America, the Vespucci were allowed the honour of attaching a Fanale to their houses, which has, however, been long removed, though an inscription records the birth-place of Amerigo Vespucci.

The first bridge across the Arno, after the Suspension Bridge at the further end, near the Cascine or Public Gardens of Florence, is the Ponte alla Carraia. The foundation-stone was laid in 1218 by a certain Lapo, a friend of Arnolfo di Lapo. It was then called Ponte Nuovo, to distinguish it from Ponte Vecchio, but it was afterwards known as the Carraia, from a postern or gate which stood at the entrance to the present Via Borg' Ogni Santi. The first Ponte alla Carraia was swept away by a flood in 1274, but it was rebuilt at the expense of the Padri Umiliati of Ogni Santi, and after a design of Fra Ristoro and Fra Sisto, the Dominicans who built Sta. Maria Novella. They laid the piles in stone, but constructed the bridge itself of wood, in consequence of which a fatal disaster took place during a theatrical representation conducted by the painter Buffalmacco, and given by the inhabitants of the Borgo San Frediano. The amusement consisted in an exhibition of the Infernal Regions upon the river; the advertisement ran as follows:—" *Chiunque avesse desiderato di aver nuove dell' altro mondo, si fosse portato al dì di calan di Maggio sul Ponte alla Carraia.** Boats were filled with persons dressed to resemble demons, who, amidst fire and smoke, uttered cries, to simulate the agony of the tormented. The bridge was crowded with spectators, when it suddenly gave way, all fell into the river, and, between fire and water, most of those who had come to learn something of another world, perished miserably. The bridge was rebuilt, but again destroyed by an inundation of the Arno in 1333; it was restored, but partially injured in 1557, and repaired by Ammanati in 1559, by order of the Grand-Duke Cosimo I. Within the last few years a chapel at the Oltr' Arno extremity has been removed, and the bridge widened.

The quay of the Lung' Arno Corsini connects the Ponte alla Carraia with the Ponte SS. Trinità. This bridge was founded in 1353 by Lamberto Frescobaldi, whose Palace is on the opposite side ; it was carried away by the flood of 1269, and reconstructed by Fra Ristori and Fra Sisto ; but it was again destroyed when the Ponte alla Carraia was swept away in 1333. Taddeo Gaddi began its restoration, which lasted until 1557, when it was destroyed for the last time, and rebuilt, as well as the Carraia, by Ammanati. It is considered one of the finest specimens of construction, and is much admired for the elegant curve of the arches. The

---

* Whoever desires to have news of the other world, let him come to the Bridge of the Carraia, on the Calends of May.

four marble statues above, life-size, represent the seasons: Winter is by Taddeo Landino; Spring and Autumn by Caccini, and Summer by Francavilla, a pupil of Michael Angelo. Francavilla was accused of having made the neck and right leg of his figure too long.

The Lung' Arno Acciajuoli, where once were the houses of the Acciajuoli family, extends from the Ponte della SS. Trinità to the Ponte Vecchio. The Acciajuoli family are supposed to have been workers in steel or iron at Brescia, who, about the year 1160, emigrated to Florence to escape the savage cruelty of Frederick Barbarossa. In 1313 one Dardano Acciajuoli was sent as Florentine Ambassador to King Robert of Naples. Their influence and power declined with the failure of the Bank of Bardi, Peruzzi, and Corsini; but they soon recovered their fortune. The year of this calamity (1342), Angelo Acciajuoli, a Dominican monk, was chosen Bishop of Florence, but he proved a traitor to his country, when he persuaded the Signory to invite Walter de Brienne Duke of Athens to take the city under his protection; afterwards, by a double act of treachery, he headed the conspiracy against him which ended by causing his own fall.

The most distinguished man of this family was Nicolò Acciajuoli, who, when on a journey to Naples for purposes connected with his trade, found favour in the eyes of Catherine, titular Empress of Constantinople, and wife of the Prince of Taranto. King Robert, perceiving the talents of Nicolò, encouraged this attachment, as he believed the Florentine merchant might be of use to his nephews, the sons of Catherine, and he appointed him Bailò or Governor of the Principality of Taranto. In 1338 Nicolò accompanied one of his pupils to Greece, and for three years he conducted a war against the Turks with consummate ability. King Robert on his deathbed named as his successor his grand-daughter, Joanna, married to Andrew, Prince of Hungary. Andrew was hated by the Neapolitans, and no less hated, it appears, by his wife, who caused him to be strangled in 1345. It is uncertain whether Nicolò was an actual accomplice in this deed, but he contrived to turn it to advantage, by persuading the widowed queen to marry his pupil, Lodovico, Prince of Taranto, when he took the government of the kingdom into his own hands, whilst maintaining Lodovico on the throne. When the King of Hungary threatened vengeance for the murder of his brother, Nicolò carried the Prince to Avignon, and only brought him back to Naples in 1348, when the plague had broken out in the south of France. In reward for these services, Nicolò was created Seneschal of Naples, and various rich estates in the kingdom were bestowed on him. Peace was at length concluded with Hungary through the mediation of the Pope, and Acciajuoli turned his attention to rid the country of brigands, and to recover Sicily from the Aragonese. When Naples was threatened with an interdict, Nicolò hastened to Innocent VI. and persuaded him to desist from this intention; the Pope was so fascinated by this extraordinary man, that he presented him with the Golden Rose, an honour hitherto reserved for royal persons, created him a Roman Senator, and sent him as his ambassador to Bernabò Visconti Lord of Milan. On his return to Naples, Acciajuoli enjoyed an almost sovereign power until his death in 1366. But though his life was thus spent abroad, he never forgot Florence, in whose neighbourhood he erected the splendid monastery of the Certosa, where he was buried, and where Andrea Orcagna raised a superb monument over his remains. Acciajuoli endowed there a college for fifty youths, who were to be instructed in the liberal arts, but this part of the monastery was never finished. Though proud of their great citizen, the Florentines jealously guarded against any attempts on his part to obtain power at home. They accordingly passed a decree that any citizen having jurisdiction in a city or castle out of Florence, should be excluded from holding office; but in order to mitigate the severity of this law they, at the same time, exempted him from the payment of taxes.

A bishop of the Acciajuoli family, who inhabited the palace on the Lung' Arno, which is now the Hotel dell' Arno, employed Pocetti to paint frescos, still in preservation in one of the rooms. The last of the family was Monsignore Filippo Acciajuoli, who died at Venice in 1834.

Close to the Palazzo Acciajuoli is the Ponte Vecchio, the oldest bridge in Florence, which, until 1080, was constructed of wood; in 1177 it was carried away by a flood, and rebuilt of stone; but it was again swept away by the great inundation of 1333, and was rebuilt by the painter and architect Taddeo Gaddi, and it has ever since resisted the violence of the Arno. From the year 1422 to the middle of the sixteenth century, the butchers of Florence had their shops here, but the Grand-Duke Cosimo I. dismissed them, and established the goldsmiths in their place; Vasari made use of the shops on the eastern side as a support for his gallery connecting the Palazzo Pitti with the Uffizi. The various coats of arms on the bridge are those of the Guilds which contributed to its repair, and an inscription commemorates a flood of the Arno. On the opposite side of the river, to the right of the bridge, was once the hospice of the Knights of Malta, which had been built in 1050 for the Templars. Near this spot, at a still earlier period, stood the column on which was the statue of Mars on horseback, at the foot of which fell young Buondelmonti, murdered by the enemies of his family; the statue of Mars was replaced by the group of Ajax and the wounded Patroclus, afterwards removed to the Loggia de' Lanzi. A small hospital was attached to the hospice of the Templars, which was afterwards ceded to the monks of San Miniato al Monte, and called the Oratory of the Holy Sepulchre; this was handed over to the Knights of Malta when the Order of Templars was suppressed in 1311. In this house the poet Ariosto lodged for six months i· 1513, the year Leo X. ascended the Pontifical throne, an event celebrated in Florence with peculiar magnificence. Ariosto came to study the Tuscan idiom, and was received by Nicolò Vespucci, the Superior of the Order, who had at the same time permitted Alexandrina Benucci, the beautiful widow of Titus Strozzi, to spend the months of her retirement from the world in this hospice. An attachment sprung up between her and Ariosto, which only terminated with the poet's death at Ferrara, in 1533.

CHRONOLOGY.

	A.D.
Acciajuoli came to Florence from Brescia	1313
,, bankrupt	1342
,, Nicolò in Greece	1338

	A.D.
Alberti, Leon Battista	1405—1472
Amerigo Vespucci born	1453
Ammanati, Bartolommeo	1511—1592
Ariosto died at Ferrara	1583
Botticelli, Sandro	1447—1510
Brunelleschi, Filippo	1379—1446
Castagno, Andrea	1396—1457
Cellini, Benvenuto	1500—1571
Feltrini, Andrea	1477—1540 (?)
Francia, Françesco	1450—1517
Gaddi, Taddeo	1300—1366
Gerini, Nicola	1385 (?)
Ghirlandaio, Domenico	1449—1494
Giovanni di San Giovanni	1576—1636
Joanna, Queen of Naples, reigned	1343—1381
Ligozzi, Jacopo	1543—1627
Lucia, Sta., in Prato built	1251
,, Frate Umiliati obliged to leave	1547
Macchiavelli, Nicolò	1469—1527
Mazzuola di Ferrara	1504—1540
Medici, Lorenzo de'	1448—1492
Mirandola, Pico della	1463—1494
Ogni Santi, Church of, built	1547
,, ,, Inhabited by Franciscans	1554
,, ,, rebuilt	1627
Poliziano, Angelo	1454—1494
Ponte alla Carraia swept away by floods in	1274
,, ,,	1333
,, ,,	1557
,, finally restored	1559
Ponte SS. Trinità founded by Frescobaldi	1252
,, swept away by floods	1333
,, ,,	1557
Ponte Vecchio built of stone	1080
,, destroyed by floods	1171
,, ,,	1333
Pulci, Luigi	d. 1490
Robert, King of Naples, reigned	1309—1343
San Giovanni in Dio founded	1400
Vandyke	1599—1641

CHAPTER XIX.

VIA DE' BARDI.—PALAZZO TORRIGIANI.—CHURCH OF SAN NICOLO.—PORTA SAN NICOLO AND PORTA SAN GIORGIO.

OPPOSITE the Templar's residence, at the corner of the Ponte Vecchio and the Via de' Bardi, is the Palazzo Manelli, where Bocaccio spent many an hour with his friend Françesco di Amanetti, who made a copy of the Decameron from the original manuscript.

The street following the course up the river from the Palazzo Manelli to the Piazza de' Mozzi is known as the Via de' Bardi; but the line of picturesque houses, of which it once consisted, have been in great part destroyed to form the new quay. Many a bloody battle took place in this long winding street, but the hardest fought was in the year 1343, when the nobles offered a stout resistance to the attack of the popular party, whom they had roused to anger by their insolent pretensions, even after they had lost all political power by the fall of the Duke of Athens, which they themselves had been the first to occasion.*

Among the buildings lately demolished was the little Church of Santa Maria sopr' Arno, once under the patronage of the Buondelmonti family, and connected with a

---

* See " Fantozzi Pianta Geometrica di Firenze," p. 233.

Porta San Nicoló.

romantic story, which is illustrative of old Florentine manners. The Buondelmonti, who were Ghibellines, held in abhorrence all the Bardi who belonged to the Guelphic party. It chanced, however, one day that Ippolito Buondelmonti, a handsome and accomplished youth, met in the Baptistery, or Church of San Giovanni, Dianora, the beautiful daughter of Amerigo de' Bardi, who inhabited a palace which, amidst late demolitions, is still left standing, and is better known as the Palazzo Tempi. Ippolito inquired her name, and from that hour sought every opportunity to pay his court to the lady, although he dared not declare his attachment from the enmity which subsisted between their families. This concealment preyed on his health, and his mother, with difficulty, extracted from him the cause of his malady. In her anxiety for the life of her son, she sought counsel from a lady related to Dianora, named Contessa, who contrived a meeting for the lovers at her villa outside Florence. A secret marriage followed, and Ippolito and Dianora were thus made happy. But one evening when Ippolito was on his way to visit his wife, carrying a rope ladder in his hands, he was observed and seized by the Bargello and his officers, who were going the rounds of the city, and mistook him for a robber. Rather than betray Dianora, Ippolito submitted to this accusation, and when his father Buondelmonti was summoned, his entreaties for the pardon of his son were all in vain. The following day, the flag of justice, the sign of a condemnation to death, was hoisted over the gate of the Palazzo del Podestà. Ippolito's one prayer was, however, granted—that, on his way to execution, he should be led past the house of Amerigo de' Bardi, in order, as he said, that he might seek a reconciliation with his enemies. Dianora was at the window when the procession appeared below, and rushing down the staircase she acknowledged Ippolito as her husband. The young couple and their parents were brought before the Podestà, who persuaded Amerigo de' Bardi to consent to the marriage, when peace was for awhile restored to the city.* On the façade of the Church of Sta. Maria sopr' Arno was an inscription—"*Fuccio mi feci*, M.C.C.XXIV."—supposed to have been placed here by Ippolito Buondelmonti in commemoration of his exploit, and of his having feigned himself a robber, as Fuccio was the name of a noted brigand of those times, who has been celebrated by Dante :—

>   .   .   .   "son Vanni Fucci
> Bestia, e Pistoia mi fu degna tana
> In qui son messo tanto perch' è fui
> Ladro alla sagrestia de' belli arredi." †
> *Inferno*, canto xxiv., v. 124—151.

A sarcophagus was attached to the outer wall of Sta. Maria sopr' Arno, where a certain Cavaliere de' Bardi was interred in the year 1342. A priest contrived to climb into it that night with the intention of robbing the dead of the jewels and money placed there. One of the bravos employed by the Duke of Athens happening to pass that way,

---

* This tale is preserved in a MS. in the Peruzzi family, who were partners with the Bardi in the bank of Bardi and Peruzzi.

† .   .   .   "I'm Vanni Fucci
Beast, and Pistoia was my worthy den,
So low am I put down, because I robbed
The sacristy of the fair ornaments."
Longfellow's Translation.

the priest, raising himself from the tomb, gave a shout, which so terrified the assassin, who imagined he beheld the ghost of the dead man, that he fled to his house, and declared that he would never again consent to go on the Duke's missions. This was reported to Walter de Brienne, who was so much enraged, that had not the man feigned sickness and declared he had seen a vision, he would not have escaped death.

The Palazzo Tempi, from the windows of which Dianora saw her husband led to execution, is most celebrated for a most beautiful Madonna by Raffaelle, possessed by the Tempi family, but now in the Gallery at Munich.

Behind the new Quay is all that remains of the Via de' Bardi. In the earliest times this street, under the name of the Via Pidiglioso, was inhabited by the most wretched population of Florence, until the Bardi, partners of the Peruzzi, in a bank which was the richest in Europe, took up their abode in this quarter, and built a street of palaces. The family were originally from the country, and settled in Florence in the tenth century. At the commencement of the quarrels between the nobles and popular party in the year 1215, the Bardi took the side of the Buondelmonti or Ghibelline faction, and it was not until much later that they became Guelphs. In 1338 the Bardi and Peruzzi Bank failed for the sum of 900,000 florins, which they had lent to Edward III. of England for his invasions of France, and which he refused to repay; but the Bardi soon recovered from this blow, and even after other losses they became as powerful as ever. When Walter de Brienne ventured to order the amputation of the hand of one of their followers, Ricci de' Bardi was so indignant at the infliction of a mode of punishment reserved for the common people, that he joined the conspiracy which caused the downfall of the tyrant: in reward for this service the Bardi as well as the rest of the nobles were admitted to a third share in the government, until their attempts to usurp greater power occasioned the privilege to be withdrawn. Bishop Acciajuoli of Florence was sent to announce to them the decree by which they were excluded from the government, but he was received with high words from Messer Ridolfi de' Bardi, who excited the populace against the democratic party in the state, whilst sending for arms and other assistance from Lombardy. The nobles of the Oltr' Arno barricaded the bridges, streets, and houses; the Nerli undertook the defence of the Ponte alla Carraia; the Frescobaldi and Manelli that of the SS. Trinità: the Rossi and Bardi defended the Ponte Vecchio and the Ponte Rubaconte. The Government succeeded in suppressing the rebellion on the right bank of the Arno, and attempted to pass the Rubaconte, but were repulsed by the Bardi, who were at length taken in the rear and forced into flight; they were received by the Quaratesi, and other nobles, but their houses, as before related, were sacked, and many of them burnt to the ground. With this destruction of the Bardi, the humiliation of the nobles was accomplished.

The wall which supports the gardens on the hill to the left, was built after the landslips had caused the fall of houses, and destruction of life and property; in the last, which occurred in 1547, Bernardo Buontalenti, then a child of five years old, was buried. When dug out, his forlorn condition excited the compassion of the Grand-Ducal family, from whom he received the education which made him the first architect of his day. Nearly opposite this wall is the Palazzo Capponi, formerly Uzzano, belonging to a younger branch of the Capponi family. It was built by Nicolò da Uzzano, after a design by Lorenzo de' Bicci. Nicolò was one of the most distinguished Florentines of the fourteenth century. He was born in 1350, and filled the office of Gonfalonier three times. Alike opposed to the ambition of the Albizzi and Medici, and foreseeing danger to the Republic from both these influential families, he prevented Giovanni de' Medici being chosen Gonfalonier, and it was only after Uzzano's death, in 1433, that Cosimo attained to power. Uzzano's only daughter, Ginevra, was married to a Capponi.

The bust of Nicolò d'Uzzano, in terra-cotta, by Donatello, is still preserved in the Palace which he built; it belongs to his descendant the Marchese Capponi; the head is full of life and truth, and is finished with marvellous care and attention to detail, even to every wrinkle in the face, the peculiar form of the ears, and a mole on the upper lip. The drapery is simple, and arranged in large folds. At the foot of the staircase of this Palace, in the entrance hall, are two ancient porphyry Lions, supposed to be Etruscan.

Next to the Palazzo Capponi is the Palazzo Canigiani, at one time the Hospital of Sta. Lucia, built in 1283. In this Palace was born Eletta de' Canigiani, who became the mother of Petrarch, and died in Avignon, at the age of thirty-eight.

The adjoining Church of Sta. Lucia degli Magnoli was founded by one Uguccione della Pressa, and finished by his son Magnolo, who gave his name of Magnoli to the church. In 1244 the patronage was bestowed by the Bishop of

Florence on the monks of San Miniato al Monte; but in 1425 the archbishop transferred this privilege to Nicolò da Uzzano, in recompense for having caused the principal chapel to be painted and decorated at his own expense. The beautiful distemper picture of the Madonna and Saints, by Domenico Veneziano, in the Uffizi Gallery, was once in Sta. Lucia degli Magnoli; but there is no good picture now remaining there. A graceful composition by Luca della Robbia is over the entrance door.

At the end of the Via de' Bardi is the Piazza de' Mozzi. The Mozzi was an ancient Guelphic family, who, from the thirteenth century, were the Pope's bankers; and when Roman prelates or any other church dignitary arrived in Florence they were lodged in their palace. Pope Gregory X. was entertained here, when he came to attempt the reconciliation of the Ghibelline and Guelphic parties in 1273; and when he laid the foundations of the Church of St. Gregory in this Piazza. The motto of the Mozzi family,— "Pax"—dates from Pope Gregory's visit. The fine gallery belonging to their palace was sold some years ago.

On one side of the Piazza de' Mozzi is the Palazzo Torrigiani, begun by Baccio d'Agnolo for the Nasi family, for whom Raffaelle painted his Madonna del Cardellino, now in the Uffizi Gallery. The Torrigiani belonged to the Guild of Vinattieri—Vintners—in the fourteenth century. One of the family, Benedetto di Ciardo, after having been twice Prior, was chosen Gonfalonier in 1380; but, wholly devoted to commerce, they only became distinguished in the seventeenth century, when a Torrigiani became Archbishop of Ravenna, and his brother was made a Senator: in 1657 he purchased the Barony of Decimio, which, in 1719, his son exchanged for a Marquisate. The Marchese Giovan Vincenzio had been brought up for the Church, and was made a Cardinal in 1753, and Secretary of State to Pope Clement XIII. At his death, in 1777, his nephew, Pietro Guadagni, the son of his sister, Teresa Torrigiani, succeeded to the title and name. A tablet has been lately placed over the door of that part of the palace which was inhabited by the late Marchese Carlo Torrigiani.*

The Palazzo Torrigiani contains one of the finest private collections of pictures in Florence.

No. 1., in a small entrance room, is a fanciful production of Botticelli's—a nymph in a wood hunted by a man on horseback and his dogs; two men are looking on. The subject is taken from one of Bocaccio's tales, so curiously illustrative of the manners of those days, and the light in which ladies were then regarded who refused to return the affection of their admirers, that we think it worth while to give a somewhat curtailed translation of the tale:—" In Ravenna, an ancient city of the Romagna, lived many noblemen and gentlemen, among whom was a youth called Nastagio degli Onesti, who, at the death of his father and uncle, inherited immense wealth. Being without a wife, he, as is usual with youths, fell in love with a daughter of Messer Paolo Traversari, a young maiden of far nobler birth than his own, but whom he hoped to persuade to love him by his virtuous acts. Yet, although his acts were most generous, lovely, and praiseworthy, they were not only fruitless, but rather seemed to injure him in her eyes, so cruel and savage

---

* The Marchese Carlo Torrigiani, already mentioned for his philanthropy, was grandson to the Marchese Pietro Guadagni.

was his mistress's behaviour towards him; which conduct was so hard for Nastagio to bear, that often, after having lamented in vain, he would fain have killed himself. But as often he tried to take courage and abandon her, or if possible hate her, as she hated him; but it seemed the more his hopes failed him the greater grew his love. As he persevered in lavishing vast sums on the lady, certain of his friends and relations began to fear that he would end by destroying himself and wasting his whole substance. They therefore entreated him, and advised him, to leave Ravenna, and to go for a while to another place, that he might diminish his expenses and cure his passion. Nastagio often ridiculed this advice, but at last consented, and ordered great preparations to be made as if he intended to visit France or Spain, or some other distant place. Mounting his horse, and accompanied by his friends, he then left Ravenna; and when he reached a place called Classis, three miles beyond the town, he told them that he had determined to remain there, and that they might return whence they came. Having pitched tents and erected pavilions, Nastagio began to lead the gayest and most splendid life, now inviting one friend, then another, to supper. It happened that in the beginning of May the weather was unusually fine, which brought the recollection of his cruel mistress to his mind, and, desiring all his servants to leave him that he might indulge in thoughts of her, he dragged himself along, step by step, lost in contemplation, until he reached a pine wood. Suddenly he heard a great weeping and loud lamentations as from a woman, which interrupted his pleasant thoughts; and, raising his head to see whence these arose, he beheld a most beautiful

damsel approaching him, running through the briers and
thorns towards the place where he stood, torn and scratched,
and crying aloud for mercy: and he also beheld a pair of
large and fierce mastiffs in pursuit, which, whenever they
reached her, tore her cruelly; and after them, a knight on a
black horse, with a rapier in his hand, using terrible words,
and menacing her with death. This sight struck terror into
Nastagio, who, taking compassion on the unhappy lady,
desired, if possible, to rescue her. Being unprovided with
weapons, he seized a branch of a tree, and thus approached
the dogs and the knight. But the knight called out from afar,
'Nastagio, do not interfere in this matter; leave the dogs
and me to deal with this wicked woman as she deserves:'
to which Nastagio replied, 'I do not know who thou art;
but this much I tell thee, that it is the basest cowardice for
an armed knight thus to seek the life of a helpless female,
and to set thy dogs at her, as if she were a wild beast; and
I shall certainly defend her to the best of my power.' The
knight then said, 'Nastagio, I am from the same land as
thyself, and when thou wert yet a little child, I, who was
called Guido degli Anastagi, was far more enamoured with
this woman than thou art with her of the Traversari; by her
pride and cruelty I was driven into such misery that, in my
despair, I slew myself with this rapier which thou beholdest
in my hand, and was condemned to eternal torments. Nor
was it long before she, who was enchanted to hear of my
death, died also, and for the crime of her cruelty, and for
her joy at my torments, of which she did not repent, as she
did not believe to have sinned but to have done well, she
likewise was condemned to the pains of hell; in which, as
she descended, the punishment assigned to her and to me

was for her to fly before me—and for me, that had loved her so fondly, to pursue her as my mortal enemy, and not as my mistress, and when I reach her to kill her, as I killed myself with this rapier; to tear out her hard and cruel heart, in which neither love nor pity ever entered, and give it to my dogs to eat; and, in no long interval, she rises again, to recommence her flight, and I and my dogs follow; and every Friday at this hour I arrive at this place, and here I punish her, as you will see; and do not suppose that we repose the other days of the week, but we arrive somewhere else, where she cruelly thought and acted against me; and I, who from a lover have become an avenger, am forced in like manner to pursue her, for as many years and as many months as she was cruel to me. Allow me, then, to fulfil the mandate of Divine Justice, nor oppose what thou canst not prevent.' Nastagio, hearing these words, was so terrified, that there was hardly a hair of his head which did not stand on end, as he gazed at the unhappy damsel, who timidly awaited her fate. The knight, like a mad dog, sprang upon her, who was held down by his mastiffs, and, whilst she cried for mercy, plunged his rapier through her breast. The damsel fell on her face to the ground, and he, seizing a knife, cut out her heart, and threw it to the mastiffs, who devoured it instantly. But before long the damsel rose suddenly again, as if nothing had happened, and began her flight in the direction of the sea, the dogs after her, and the knight, remounting his horse, renewed his pursuit; so that in less than half an hour, they disappeared, and Nastagio saw them no more. He remained there long in fear and pity, when it occurred to him that as this scene was to be repeated every Friday, it might be of use to him-

self. Marking the place, he returned to his servants, and
sending for his friends, he addressed them thus: 'You
have long urged me to cease from loving her who is my
enemy, and I am ready to do it, if you will grant me one
favour, which is this, that next Friday you persuade Messer
Paolo Traversari, and his wife and daughter, and all the
ladies of their family, and any others you please, to come
here and dine with me.' His request appeared a very
trifling one to those present, and, returning to Ravenna, they
invited all whom Nastagio wished to see; and, though it
was difficult to persuade the lady beloved by him, she
nevertheless went with the rest. Nastagio ordered a magnificent repast to be prepared, and had the tables placed
under the pines round that place, where he had beheld the
punishment of the cruel maiden, and so arranged that his
mistress should be seated exactly opposite where the deed
would be done. The last dish had just been brought, when
all began to hear the cries of the hunted damsel, and, in
wonder, asked what it meant. Rising from their seats to
see what it could be, they beheld the unhappy lady pursued
by the knight and dogs. The knight, addressing them, as
he had Nastagio, filled them with terror and wonder; and
when he repeated what he had done before, all the women
present—and there were a great many who had been relations
of the unhappy damsel, as well as of the knight, and remembered the story of his love and of his death—wept, as if
they too suffered with her: which scene being ended, and
the damsel and the knight having disappeared, all the spectators fell into many and various discourses on what they
had seen. But among those most terrified was the cruel
maiden beloved by Nastagio, who had distinctly seen and

heard everything, and was conscious that the scene was more addressed to her than any one else, remembering the cruelty she had always shown her lover; so that she already seemed to fly before his wrath, and to have the mastiffs at her heels. And such was her fear, that she herself told her father and mother she was ready to marry Nastagio, at which they were well pleased, and the following Sunday, Nastagio espoused her, and after the marriage they lived long and happily together.*

The next picture in the Torrigiani Gallery is a Magdalene, by Jacopo da Pontormo, extremely lovely, and the expression of sorrow and devotion very beautiful. Nos. 5 and 7, the Triumph of David, from a *cassone*, or bridal chest, painted by Benozzo Gozzoli. The figure of David, in No. 7, is very dignified, as he is borne along in a triumphal car after Saul. In No. 5 the perspective and horses recall Paolo Uccello's picture in the corridor of the Uffizi Gallery. Nos. 22 and 23, opposite—the Fable of Acca,—an Etruscan legend of the nurse of Romulus and Remus,—and the Expedition of the Argonauts, are by Paolo Uccello; both likewise belonged to a *cassone*. The subjects are treated with much animation, though the pictures have neither the elegance nor the beauty of the work of Benozzo Gozzoli.

Some of the finest pictures in the Gallery are in the second room—three noble portraits: No. 9, Girolamo Benivieni, by Leonardo da Vinci. Girolamo was a Florentine, born in 1452. He was the author of various sonnets and songs, chiefly of a religious character, many of which were

---

* See "Decameron" of Bocaccio, vol. iii. p. 387. Also Poetical Works of John Dryden, Esq., "Theodore and Honoria."

composed for the children who formed the celebrated processions of Savonarola to collect works of art of an immoral tendency, which they burnt in the Piazza della Signoria. Benivieni was an ardent admirer of Savonarola; after the siege of Florence he had the courage to address a letter to Pope Clement VII. reproaching him with the calamities he had brought on his native city, and demanding, as the sole compensation in his power, that he should give Florence a free government. Benivieni was noted for the sanctity of his life. He died in 1542, at ninety years of age. This portrait is wonderfully expressive: the poet has a noble countenance; he wears a black cap and dress. The background is a very sweet landscape, treated sketchily, in a pale greenish-blue colour. No. 7 is the portrait of Masaccio, by himself—a splendid drawing, careful, correct, and finished with surprising delicacy and truth. No. 11, a portrait of Luca Signorelli, likewise by himself—grandly drawn, forcible, and carefully finished, though hard in outline. No. 21, Pollaiolo—characteristic, though hard, angular, and somewhat stiff. No. 24, a very fine Spanish picture, a head of St. Anthony, by Ribera. No. 3, a picture, by Garofalo, of Christ and the Woman of Samaria. Over the door, No. 1, is the Riddle of Æsop, by the Cavaliere d'Arpino, from a drawing by Michael Angelo. A Madonna, by Ridolfo Ghirlandaio, is very sweet and soft, but rather feeble.

In the third room are two most beautiful paintings for a *cassone* by Filippino Lippi, representing the history of Esther. In the first, No. 8, Ahasuerus is seated on his throne; Esther kneels before him to invite him to the banquet; the surprise of Haman, who holds his hand to his mouth, is well given. The attendants of Esther, delicate and refined maidens, wait without; her own figure in white, walking away, is very lovely. In the background is seen the banquet. The sharp brilliancy of the lights in the open air, the distinct drawing of the small figures which yet preserve their distance and proper planes although the foreground figures and principal part of the story is kept in a comparatively subdued light, is very remarkable. Nos. 21 and 22, small pictures by Filippino Lippi, represent Esther, and the triumph of Mordecai. No. 7 is a very lovely Madonna and Child, generally attributed to Raffaelle, of his Florentine period; in composition it resembles the Cowper Madonna. The child lays across his mother's lap, and looks back with a most sweet expression, as he playfully holds her veil; the Virgin's head and hands are extremely beautiful and graceful.

No. 3 is a Deposition from the Cross, by Titian, painted in his old age—a noble production, wonderfully vigorous; the figure and head of Christ are especially beautiful. No. 12, a fine portrait of one of the Alberti family, by Paolo Veronese. No. 14, a very interesting portrait of the historian Françesco Guicciardini by an unknown artist.

In the furthest room is a fine Lucrezia by Guido Reni; a good portrait of Duke Alexander, the Moor; and a female portrait called Ginevra de' Benci, attributed to Leonardo da Vinci.

Returning through this apartment and crossing the first small entrance room, in a further suite, are several pictures of merit: Christ in the Garden of Gethsemane, by Passignano; Muleteers, by Salvator Rosa; and a very fine Hobbema.

Beyond the Torrigiani Palace, on the former Renai, now laid out in flower gardens, is a monument commenced by

Bartolini and finished by Romanelli, to the memory of Prince Demidoff, who, in conjunction with the Marchese Carlo Torrigiani, liberally assisted the cause of education in Florence. Behind the palace, where was once a picturesque line of houses, forming the back of the Via Bardi, are also now plats of flowers, and a broad paved road.

At the end of the Piazza dei Renai, facing the Torrigiani Palace, is the Palazzo dei Serristori, a family who were, from an early period, adherents of the Medici. Some, however, made an honourable exception; and Françesco Serristori, with his sons Guglielmo and Nicolò, attempted to liberate their country from the tyranny of the Grand-Duke Cosimo I. They were declared rebels, and the youngest, Nicolò, when taken prisoner at the battle of Montemurlo, was confined for life in the horrible subterranean dungeons of the Tower of Volterra. The Palazzo Serristori was occupied during the siege of 1528 by Malatesta Baglioni, of Perugia, to whom was confided the conduct of the defence, and who betrayed the city to the Imperialists. Malatesta consulted his astrologer on all occasions; and the room supposed to have been inhabited by this impostor, is all that remains of the palace, as it existed in the sixteenth century. In another palace of the Renai, facing the river, are some good frescos by Overbeck; the subject is the tribute paid to genius in every country.

Near the Palazzo Serristori is the Church of San Nicolò sopr' Arno. In the Piazza before this church the citizens met in 1529, and swore to defend their Republic to the last drop of their blood: after Florence had been surrendered to the Imperialists, it was in the Belfry of San Nicolò that Michael Angelo concealed himself, until

Pope Clement VII. promised to pardon him for having constructed the fortifications above Florence.

San Nicolò was one of the first twelve churches of Florence erected about the tenth century. Before 1184 it belonged to the monks of San Miniato al Monte, but in 1374 Gregory XI. placed it under the jurisdiction of the Bishop of Florence. On the external walls of San Nicolò is a tablet recording the height reached by the Arno during a flood in 1557. Over the high altar was once a picture by Gentile da Fabriano, painted for the Quaratesi family, much praised by Vasari, but of which nothing now remains except the side panels with saints which were on either side of the Madonna. Cavalcaselle observes :—" The side panels of the votive piece are still at San Nicolò, filled with a pretty graceful Magdalene in profile ; St. Nicolas, on whose cope scenes from the Passion are given with exquisite minuteness ; a fine St. George and a Baptist were in the old Siennese antique style ; the whole ornamented with profusion, flat and fused in tone, and with a rosy flesh tint shadowed in cool grey. In the gables of these panels are figures of canonized friars between angels." * In the sacristy is a much-injured fresco, attributed to Ridolfo Ghirlandaio, of the Virgin letting down her girdle to St. Thomas. St. Thomas is a graceful figure, and expresses in his action the gratitude and humility with which he receives the gift. A picture on panel, recently discovered in the church, but also now in the sacristy, is worthy of attention ; it is thus spoken of by Cavalcaselle :—" The Eternal, surrounded by

---

* See "Crowe and Cavalcaselle," vol. iii. p. 102. A faithful engraving from this picture may be seen in Rosini's "Storia Favola," xxxviii.

a glory of Cherubim of Umbrian type, sending down the dove of the Holy Ghost to the Virgin and Christ, both of whom kneel on a rainbow, spanning a golden heaven lighted by a sun in relief. The resurrection of Lazarus, in the foreground of a landscape, and St Louis of Toulouse, form the subjects of one side; whilst on the other are St. Cosimo, Damian, and a third saint together, and St. Benedict with a chained devil. It is more hasty than the Virgin of the Quaratesi, and strongly impressed with the defects of the Umbrian and Gubbian schools."

The Porta San Nicolò is the only gate remaining in its original height and form.

The Porta San Miniato, between the Porta San Nicolò and the city wall which skirts the gardens of the Boboli, leads to the churches of San Francesco and San Miniato, beyond Florence, and is now connected with the Porta Romana by the beautiful road of the Colli. In the Fondaccio di San Nicolò was the house of Doni, the patron of Raffaelle d'Urbino.

Returning from San Nicolò to the Via Bardi, on the top of the Costa, is a large building, now the Villa Petrovitz, but formerly a monastery of barefooted Augustinians. It was founded by the Grand-Duchess Christina of Lorraine in the sixteenth century, upon the demolished houses of the Sermanni family. A narrow passage leads to the Via della Costa, or Hill of San Giorgio; the ascent to the top is terminated by the Porta San Giorgio and the Fortress of the Belvedere. Halfway up this street, on the right, is a house once inhabited by Galileo Galilei; the sun-dial in the garden behind is supposed to have been constructed by the philosopher.

The Fortress of San Giorgio or Santa Maria in Belvedere was built by the Grand-Duke Ferdinand I., who employed Buontalenti for this purpose. The first stone was laid in 1590. Beneath it is a subterranean chamber, in which the Medici kept their treasures, and for which Buontalenti invented a lock which none could open without being made acquainted with the secret of its construction.

The Porta di San Giòrgio was built in 1324, and was so called from a little Church of St. George which once existed in that neighbourhood. On the side towards the country is a square marble tablet, on which is sculptured in high relief St. George and the Dragon. Within the arch is a fresco, better preserved than any other on the gates of Florence. The Virgin and Child are seated on a magnificent throne. On the right is St. George in armour leaning on a shield, on which is painted the arms of Florence, the Red Cross on a white field; and on the left is a saint with a pen and book, who either represents St. Sigismund or St. Maximilian. This fresco is attributed by Vasari to Bernardo Daddi, a scholar of Spinello Aretino.

Descending the hill, and passing the Augustinian Convent, the street divides into two narrow ways—that to the right leading again to the Via Bardi, near the Palazzo Tempi; and that to the left, a steep descent to the Piazza della Sta. Felicità. A small church at the entrance of this street, near the Costa, is called San Girolamo, and at one time possessed a painting by Ridolfo Ghirlandaio, but it is now Government property.

CHRONOLOGY.

	A.D.
Benivieni, Girolamo	1452—1542
Bocaccio	1313—1375
Botticelli, Sandro	1447—1510
Brienne, Walter de, Duke of Athens, died	1356
Buontalenti, Bernardo, buried under a landslip	1547
Donatello	1386—1466
Gregory X., Pope, in Florence	1273
Guicciardini, Francesco	1482—1540
Guido Reni	1575—1642
Lippi, Filippino	1457—1504
Lucia, Sta., de' Magnoli, under the monks of San Miniato al Monte	1244
,, the patronage bestowed on Uzzano.	1425
Nicolò, San, Sopr' Arno, built before	1184
,, meeting of citizens in Piazza	1529
Petrarch	1304—1374
Polaiolo, Antonio	1429—1498
Salvator Rosa	1615—1673
Signorelli, Luca	1441—1523
Spinello Aretino	1410
Uzzano, Nicolò	1350—1433
Vinci, Leonardo da	1452—1539

CHAPTER XX.

STA. FELICITA TO THE PIAZZA SODERINI.

IN the Piazza di Sta. Felicità, a column resembling that of the Trebbio is said to mark the spot where another discomfiture of the heretics—Paterini—took place. From this piazza, the remnant fled to the Gaggio, a nobleman's house, afterwards a monastery, beyond the Porta Romana, where they found protection. The Rossi family, mentioned by Dante, whose quarter was behind the Church of Sta. Felicità, were violent Papists, and led the fight and massacre. A terra-cotta statue of Pietro Martire was afterwards placed on the top of the column, but this has long since disappeared. The column itself was of much older date, and belonged to an ancient cemetery on this spot, where stood a little church dedicated to the Maccabees, as well as a celebrated convent of Benedictine nuns, which in 1059 was taken under the special protection of Pope Nicholas II. The nuns all belonged to noble families, and their convent was only suppressed, with other monasteries, on the entrance of the French into Italy early in this century. The church received its present form as late as 1736, when the adjoining Oratory of St. Mary Magdalene, of the twelfth century, was included within its walls. The tribune within belongs to the Guicciardini family, and a slab on the pavement, in front of the high altar, marks the burial-place of the historian Françesco Guicciardini. The loggia or porch in front was erected by Giorgio Vasari in 1564, to support the corridor, which he carried from the Uffizi to the Pitti Palace. Beneath this porch are monuments inserted in the walls, which were transferred there from the old cemetery. A figure in flat relief represents Barduccio Barducci, who died in 1414. He was a wealthy merchant on Exchange, and was twice Gonfalonier. His son Giovanni was of the Otto di Balià, who formed the Government of that period, and was the intimate friend of Donatello, who represented him as one of the prophets on the Campanile, which, from Barducci's bald head, is known as "Il Zuccone."* Below the monument of Barducci is the Mausoleum of Arcangiola Paladina, the daughter of a Pistoiese painter; she died in 1622, at the age of twenty-three, already famous for her skill in painting and music. The bust is by Agostino Buggiardini, a scholar of Giovanni Caccini. On the opposite side of the loggia is a well-executed monument to Cardinal Luigi de' Rossi, by Baccio di Montelupo (1445—1512). The statue is life-size and in repose, and the face extremely beautiful. The cardinal died in Rome, 1519; but his remains were brought hither for interment by order of Pope Leo X.

The Church of Sta. Felicità is in the form of the letter T, and has seventeen chapels, with marble altars. The first, to the right, is the Capella Capponi, built after a design by

---

* "The Gourd." See vol. i. chap. iii.

Filippo Brunelleschi, who also made the pillar to contain the holy water at the entrance to the church. Within this chapel is a Deposition from the Cross, by Jacopo Pontormo, who, according to Vasari, painted it without dark shadows, and in a clear and united colour, so graduated as to make hardly any distinction where the lights ceased and the half-tints began, or where the half-tints were followed by the shadows, thus producing great softness. The picture was destroyed by restorations in 1723. The four Evangelists are represented on the ceiling; three are by Pontormo, and one by Angelo Bronzino. The windows, with the arms of the Capponi, were executed by the celebrated French painter on glass, Guglielmo da Marcilla. Vasari relates that this chapel was decorated by order of Lodovico di Gino Capponi, who bought it from the Barbadori, for whom it was built by Filippo Brunelleschi.

In the fourth chapel after that of the Capponi is a fine picture executed by the living artist Cesare, representing the mother of the Maccabees mourning over her dead sons—a parallel story to that of Sta. Felicità. A painting by Taddeo Gaddi follows; it is in the same style as his fresco in the Baroncelli Chapel of Sta. Croce—the subject is a Madonna and Saints, and is in good preservation. The sacristy is supposed to have been built by Brunelleschi: it is in fine proportions, and has his favourite ornament of cherubs' heads round the cornice, which he adopted from the mosaic frieze of the Baptistery. A picture, attributed to Neri de' Bicci,* represents Sta. Felicità with her seven

---

* This picture was engraved for Mrs. Jameson's work on "Legendary Art."

sons, who all underwent martyrdom, exhorted by their mother to suffer any torments rather than abjure their faith. Sta. Felicità "is seated on a throne, a majestic colossal figure, holding in one hand the Gospel, which rests on her knee; in the other, the palm; while her seven sons, small in proportion and treated as accessories or attributes, are ranged on either side, the youngest standing in front." All have palms and golden glories, and wear rich dresses, and all but the youngest appear as warriors.* There are several other early pictures here, but none of any importance.

The most interesting works of art are in the chapter-house of the nuns, or Oratory of St. Mary Magdalene, where the frescos are attributed to Cosimo Ulivelli and Agnolo Gheri. Over the altar is a fine picture on panel of the Crucifixion, probably by Nicolò Gerini, who worked with Taddeo Gaddi. The Christ is feeble, and the grief of the angels who catch the blood is exaggerated to caricature; but the fainting Virgin, with the women round her, as well as the men with upraised hands, are very fine. The Magdalene at the foot of the cross, with lips apart, raises her eyes to the Saviour; the tall figure of St. John, whose drapery falls in large folds, the Centurion, who, with his finger on his lips, stands in silent wonder, and the old Pharisee behind, are extremely good. The eyes are small, but the faces are rounder and fuller than usual with Giotto. The predella below is by an inferior hand; it represents the Martyrdom of Sta. Felicità and her sons. On the ceiling are eight ovals, painted in fresco with much gran-

---

* See "Legendary Art," p. 381.

deur: the subjects are Christ and the Seven Cardinal Virtues; Faith, in the centre, is very fine. Within the cloister leading from the chapel are several frescos, which have been transferred here from other places: the Annunciation is pleasing, and the Visit of the Shepherds is interesting from the animation with which the story is told; the Madonna, seated beneath the projecting roof of a house, is very lovely.

From the Piazza di Sta. Felicità the Via Guicciardini leads to the Piazza dei Pitti, at the corner of which is the Palazzo Guicciardini, built by the architects Cigoli and Gherardo Silvani, who incorporated in this palace a small house where was born San Filippo Benizzi, one of the Order of the Servites, whose history, or legend, is recorded by Andrea del Sarto on the walls of the portico of the SS. Annunziata.

The records of the family Guicciardini date as early as 1199, when an ancient document mentions a merchant of that name, one Tuccio di Guicciardini. The grandson of this Tuccio made the fortune of the family, and Luigi, of a later generation, was Gonfalonier during the Ciompi riots of 1378. The historian Françesco, the godson of Marsilio Ficino, was born here in 1482. In 1511 he was sent ambassador to Spain, and on his return in 1515 he was chosen one of the Priors of the Republic. When deputed to meet Leo X., at Cortona, the Pope appointed him advocate of the Consistory, and afterwards governor of Modena and Reggio, and commissary-general of the papal forces. In 1527 he offended both the Florentines and Pope Clement VII.; the first by his attempt to restore the Medici to power, and the last by not having been sufficiently ardent in their cause. He therefore retired to Arcetri, near Florence, where he began his history. Guicciardini was the friend and tool of Duke Alexander, which is the greatest blot on his name; and when the duke was assassinated he assisted to raise Cosimo to the throne. Disgusted by Cosimo's resolution to reign alone and to reject all advisers, Guicciardini soon afterwards again retired to Arcetri, where he was occupied with his history until his death in 1540.

A tablet, on a house nearly opposite the Palazzo Guicciardini, records that here Nicolò Macchiavelli died, in the fifty-eighth year of his age, from the effects of a medicine he had prepared for himself. Macchiavelli was born in 1469, and was descended from a family who were Lords of Montespertoli, and belonged to the Guelphic party in Florence. In 1499 Nicolò was appointed chancellor of the great council, which had been shortly before instituted by Savonarola, and he was afterwards made secretary to the Republic. He was employed in twenty different embassies abroad, and among these were missions to the infamous Cesare Borgia. If the schemes of this prince for the unification of Italy found favour in his eyes, he nevertheless, in his celebrated work of the "Principe," painted the man who aspired to despotic power in the blackest and most contemptible colours. Taken literally, this essay has deservedly held up the author's name to obloquy; but, considered as a closely concealed satire—since the most astute of Florentine statesmen would hardly have been capable of the folly of advocating crime—and as an exposure of the degradation to which a human being must lend himself to obtain supreme power, Macchiavelli's work was no doubt intended to serve as a warning to mankind not to put their faith in princes. Accused of complicity in a conspiracy against Cardinal Giovanni de' Medici, afterwards Leo X., Macchiavelli was thrown into prison and put to the torture. He was only liberated at the intercession of Pope Leo himself, when he became Pope. The Macchiavelli houses extended back as far as the Fondaccio di Santo Spirito.

The Borgo San Jacopo was so-called from having been a borough of the city. At the corner of the Via Guicciardini were houses of the Cerchi family, whose principal residences were near the Piazza della Signoria. In this palace was included the tower of the Rossi family, and behind the marble bason of the fountain once stood the group of the Centaur, now under the loggia of the Uffizi, but which has been replaced by a mediocre statue of Bacchus belonging to a late period of art. Near the Cerchi Palace is the Palazzo Barbadori. It was for this family that Filippo Brunelleschi built the present Capponi Chapel in Sta. Felicità, as well as the palace itself. One of the family, Donato Barbadori, was employed in many important missions abroad, but finally he was implicated in a conspiracy, and was seized and beheaded.*

The Church of San Jacopo sopr' Arno is one of the twelve oldest churches in Florence; but, with the monastery attached to it, was wholly rebuilt in 1580, and in 1709 it underwent fresh restorations, when the stuccos were added inside the church, and busts of the Medici family placed on the façade of the monastery, in the Piazza Frescobaldi.

---

* See Macchiavelli, " Storie Fiorentine," lib. iii. p. 80.

The beautiful little portico of Corinthian columns in front of the church belonged to the earlier construction, and is composed of the remains of ancient monuments. According to the chronicler, Dino Compagni, it was in the Church of San Jacopo sopr' Arno that the nobles, led by Berto Frescobaldi, held a meeting in the year 1293 to protest against their exclusion from the Government by the popular party led by Giano della Bella, and where they determined to resort to arms rather than submit to the decree. The campanile of the church was built by Gherardo Silvani.

Opposite San Jacopo is one of the most perfect of the old Florentine towers remaining, which belonged to the Barbadori family. The inscription by one Sorbi, who placed the images in Luca della Robbia ware on the front, is modern. In the piazza beyond is the Palazzo Frescobaldi, which belonged to a family who were among the most turbulent of the Florentine nobles. Of German origin, they were all-powerful in Florence during the thirteenth and fourteenth centuries. Messer Lamberto di Fresco di Baldo caused a wooden bridge to be thrown across the Arno near his house, which was called the SS. Trinità, from the Church on the opposite bank. This same Lamberto bore the banner of King Charles of Anjou at the battle of Campaldino. The Frescobaldi were engaged in every battle of the Florentines, and gained great renown for their valour; but their domineering spirit awakened the jealousy of the citizens, and caused their exclusion from power in 1292, when, as already related, they called a meeting of nobles in San Jacopo sopr' Arno. Their indignation was still further aroused by the banishment of Messer Teglia Frescobaldi in 1303, who, in revenge, allied himself with Castruccio Castracani, Lord of

Lucca, and endeavoured to seize on castles belonging to the Florentines. The proscriptions which followed this act of treason were resented by the nobles in general, and Bardo dei Frescobaldi and Piero de Bardi conspired to overthrow the Government. Their schemes were discovered, and they were driven from Florence, only to return with the Duke of Athens. As the Frescobaldi afterwards joined the Bardi in another conspiracy to expel the Duke, they were for a time reconciled with the popular party; but the peace was of short duration, and the power of all the nobles was broken in the final discomfiture of the Bardi. To the greater honour of this family, it is recorded that the completion of Dante's poem was due to Dino di Lambertuccio Frescobaldi. Himself a poet, or "rhymer," and the friend of the great poet, Dino discovered and preserved the first seven cantos of the "Inferno," which Dante when sent into exile believed to have been lost; Dino sent them to him to the house of Moreollo Malaspina, in the Lunigiana, where Dante had taken refuge.

On the opposite side of the Piazza Frescobaldi, and facing the river, is one of the numerous palazzi belonging to the Capponi family. This palace was inhabited by Piero Capponi, already frequently mentioned for his heroic act in tearing to pieces a treaty destructive of Florentine liberty, and defying Charles VIII. of France to do his worst. Piero was killed in a war with Pisa, 1496, and bequeathed a greater name than fortune to his sons Nicolò and Giuliano. Nicolò was elected Gonfalonier amidst the rejoicings of the people, for the election of Nicolò Capponi was a signal for the restoration of order and the security of Florentine liberty. After the people had confirmed the election of the new Gonfalonier and Priors, a Franciscan and Dominican friar, according to custom, ascended the Ringhiera in front of the Palazzo della Signoria, carrying lighted torches, and followed by a canon of the Cathedral with the Gospels, to administer the oath to the new magistrates; after which ceremony the Signory, preceded by the trumpeters, walked in procession to the Baptistery to attend mass. On their return to the palace they were led to the apartments assigned them and sat down to a banquet, whilst the bells rang and the shouts of the people resounded in the piazzas and streets at the return of a popular government. A general illumination took place in the evening, the *fanali* or *lumieri* at the corners of the great palaces blazing with fireworks. The Mercato Nuovo, then an open space before the loggia was built, was cleared of its booths belonging to the silk merchants, and covered with an awning under which danced sixty youths and sixty maidens dressed in pearls and jewels; every maiden wore a garland of gold or silver, the manufacture of which made Ghirlandaio famous before he was more celebrated as a painter. The youths and maidens did not dance together, but separately, and at every new dance they all appeared in new dresses, which amusement lasted the whole night.*

One of the first acts of Nicolò Capponi, in imitation of Fra Girolamo Savonarola, was to propose that the people should acknowledge no sovereign but their Lord and Saviour Jesus Christ. In the course of time, however, Nicolò gave serious offence to some of the greater citizens; and among his offences was the marriage of his son to a daughter of the historian Francesco Guicciardini, instead of to a sister

---

* See " Marietta de' Ricci," vol. ii. pp. 144—151.

of Tommaso Soderini. Among his bitterest enemies were Françesco Valori and Jacopo Gherardi, who were jealous of his popularity; they contrived, by suspicions of treason, to have him dismissed from office, and he narrowly escaped with his life. But his patriotic endeavours to save his country from enemies, domestic and foreign, continued to the end of his life, which was shortened by grief at being unable to frustrate the schemes of Pope Clement VII. and the Emperor Charles V. for the destruction of the Republic. In a large room of this little palace are frescos by Pocetti commemorative of the history and patriotic deeds of the Capponi family.

Pursuing the quay along the river, the present Casa Molini, and the houses on the same side of the piazza beyond, belonged to the Soderini family, who from the earliest times exercised great influence in the Republic. It was here that one Nicolò Soderini received St. Catherine of Sienna, a remarkable woman, who was employed on various embassies, and whose genius and religious enthusiasm gained for her an extraordinary influence in her own and succeeding ages. The crucifix before which she worshipped is still preserved in the family of the Soderini. In 1502 Piero Soderini was created Gonfalonier for life, an honour unprecedented in the history of Florence. He was, however, a man of feeble resolution, and he vainly endeavoured to arrest the encroachments of the Medici; he was at last obliged to fly from Florence, and retired to Rome, where he died in 1522, and was buried there in Sta. Maria del Popolo, although a splendid monument in his honour, the work of Benedetto da Rovezzano, was erected in the Carmine at Florence. When Gonfalonier, Soderini employed Macchiavelli as his secretary, who has thus described his character—

"La notte che morì Pier Soderini
L' alma n' andò dell' Inferno alla bocca,
E Pluto la gridò, 'Anima sciocca,
Che, Inferno? Va, nel Limbo coi bambini.'" *

CHRONOLOGY.

	A.D.
Barbadori, Donato, beheaded	1379
Barducci, Barduccio	d. 1414
Benedictine nuns under the special protection of Pope Nicholas III.	1059
Benizzi, San Filippo	1247—1285
Bicci, Neri de, was alive in	1458
Bronzino Angelo	1502—1572
Brunelleschi, Filippo	1379—1446
Capponi, Piero	d. 1496
Cigoli	1559—1613
Ciompi Riots	1378
Felicità, Sta., reduced to its present proportions	1736
" Loggia built by Vasari	1564
Gerini, Nicolò	d. 1385 (?)
Guicciardini, Francesco	1482—1540
Jacopo, San, meeting of nobles held here	1292
Macchiavelli, Nicolò	1469
Montelupo, Baccio di	1445—1512
Paterini, their defeat	1182
Pontormo, Jacopo	1494—1557
Rossi, Cardinal Luigi de'	d. 1519
Silvani, Gherardo	1579—1675
Soderini, Piero, Gonfalonier	1502—d. 1522
Ullvelli, Cosimo	1625—1704

* "The night that Piero Soderini died,
His soul passed onwards to the mouth of Hell,
When Pluto cried, 'You foolish soul, begone!
What, Hell for you? Go, with the babes, to Limbo.'"

CHAPTER XXI.

FONDACCIO SANTO SPIRITO.—VIA MAGGIO.—CHURCH OF SAN FELICE.

PARALLEL to the quay already traversed, and leading back to the Piazza Frescobaldi, is the Fondaccio di Santo Spirito; and on a tablet to the left there is an inscription recording the birthplace of Françesco Ferruccio. The family of Ferruccio was from Piombino, and derived their name from *ferro*, "iron," having probably been workers in that metal. They were Florentine citizens in 1253, when one of the Ferrucci had a seat in the government. Françesco was born in 1489, and was destined for a merchant, but his inclinations were more for war and the chase, in which last occupation he spent much of his time in the Casentino, where he possessed land. He was sent on several missions to Malatesta Baglioni, then a celebrated leader of Free Companies; and he once had occasion to witness a signal defeat of this captain, in a vain endeavour to rescue Arezzo, which was attacked by the enemy: Ferruccio came to the rescue, when Baglioni was obliged to acknowledge the superior military skill of this Florentine merchant, and hated him accordingly. In 1529 Malatesta was invited to undertake the defence of Florence against the Imperialists, and Ferruccio volunteered to second his efforts by harassing the enemy and creating diversions outside the city; but his ability and success only increased the envy and spite of Baglioni, who finally betrayed Florence to the besiegers, and conspired to cause the overthrow and murder of Ferruccio at the Battle of Gavinana, among the mountains above Pistoia. In Ferruccio the Florentines lost the last defender of their Republic, and his name is still venerated among those of the greatest of their heroes.

Opposite this palace, at the corner of the Via de Serragli, is the Palazzo Rinuccini, now let out in apartments, and its rich gallery and library sold and dispersed. It was built by the architect Luigi Cardi Cigoli about the end of the sixteenth century, and the windows on the ground floor are much admired. The earliest record of the Rinuccini is when they built the Sacristy of Sta. Croce for their chapel, in 1294. They were frequently employed on embassies abroad; and in 1645 one of the family was sent as Papal Legate to Ireland, to endeavour to ameliorate the condition of the Catholics, who were barbarously persecuted by Cromwell. The Marchese Carlo Rinuccini was sent ambassador to Queen Anne to congratulate her on her accession to the English throne, and afterwards for the same purpose to George I.

/ Before the middle of the thirteenth century there were no houses of any importance on this side of the Arno, and when Buonaccorso Velluti, one of the ancestors of the present Duke di San Clemente, built himself a palace in this neighbourhood, his friends ridiculed his choice of a situation so remote from Florence. The first palace to the left after entering the Via Maggio is the official residence of the American Consul; it was formerly the Palazzo Firidolfi, a branch of the Ricasoli family; they were among the most valiant defenders of Florence against the Emperor Henry VII.—1312—and were in consequence placed under the ban of the Empire. The last male descendant died in 1818, leaving an only daughter, Lucrezia, who married a Ricasoli, and, as before stated, thus reunited the families after an interval of eight centuries. The two palaces which follow are Turco and Amerigo, and opposite them, No. 26, is the palace built for herself by Bianca Capello, and decorated with paintings in the Florentine manner. Her husband, one night when returning home, was murdered between this palace and the bridge. Bianca was the daughter of an old patrician family of Venice, and she was persuaded to form a secret marriage with a young Florentine named Piero Bonaventura. Fearing discovery by her parents, they escaped to Florence, where they lived in complete retirement in an apartment in the Piazza di San Marco. It happened, however, that Prince Francis, the eldest son and heir of the Grand-Duke Cosimo I., saw Bianca at a window, and was struck with her extraordinary beauty. The assassination of Bonaventura, which took place many years afterwards, was by some attributed to Francis, who had succeeded his father as grand-duke; and on the death of the Grand-Duchess Joanna of Austria, in 1579, he married Bianca, who was immediately adopted as a daughter by the Venetian Republic. She summoned her brother, Vittorio Capello, to join her in Florence, and he soon became the sole adviser and favourite of Francis, which so much excited the jealousy and hatred of the Medici family, that every means was employed to oblige Francis to dismiss Vittorio from his court. Bianca's voluminous correspondence with her brother, in her clear, bold handwriting, is still preserved in the Archives of the Uffizi. The dismissal of Vittorio did not, however, satisfy the enemies of the grand-duchess, who were resolved on her death; and one evening after she and the grand-duke had partaken of a supper at their favourite villa of Poggio-a-Cajano, both were seized with violent pains, and they died within a few hours of one another. Cardinal Ferdinand de' Medici, the brother of Francis, who succeeded to the throne, is accused of being the author of this crime, which accusation appeared the more probable by the contumely with which he caused the body of the unhappy grand-duchess to be treated, and her son only escaped persecution by leading a life of retirement in Florence.

Beyond the opposite Palazzo Amerigo is the Palazzo Ridolfi. The Ridolfi came to Florence from Ravenna, in the fourteenth century. Twenty-one of the family filled the office of Gonfalonier, and fifty-two that of Priors of the Republic. Nicolò de' Ridolfi was beheaded, in 1417, for having attempted to restore the Medici to Florence; but his son married a daughter of Lorenzo the Magnificent, and exercised great influence in the Government until his death, in 1525. His son again married a daughter of the celebrated Filippo Strozzi, and the favour he showed towards the Florentine exiles was the cause of his banishment by the Grand-Duke Cosimo I., when he found protection with Catherine de' Medici, Queen of France. From him are descended the present Ridolfi family. The most distinguished of the Ridolfi belonged, however, to another branch. Lorenzo de' Ridolfi governed the Florentine Republic towards the end of the fourteenth, and the beginning of the fifteenth centuries, assisted by Messer Maso degli Albizzi, and Messer Filippo Corsini, before Cosimo de' Medici attained to power; and it was these three men who raised Florence to the high position she afterwards held. In the year 1425, eight years after his cousin Nicolò de' Ridolfi had been beheaded for his friendship to the Medici, Lorenzo di Antonio Ridolfi was sent to Venice to solicit the Venetians to join in a league against Filippo Visconti, Lord of Milan. The cautious Venetians hesitated, when Lorenzo burst forth in these words:—" Venetians, last year the Genoese, when we abandoned them, created Filippo a prince; if you deny us your aid in our present difficulties, we will make him a king; and should we conquer, and you are left standing alone, none coming to your aid, however you may desire it, you will be the cause of his becoming emperor." Ridolfi then turned his back on the Senators and left the room, when they immediately consented to join the League.

The late Marchese Cosimo Ridolfi was one of the most honest and patriotic statesmen of Florence during the disturbed period antecedent to the union of Italy under Victor Emmanuel, which was the more to be admired in him, as he was tutor to the grand-ducal children. At the corner of the Via Maggio and the Via Marsili, is a house painted by Pocetti in chiaroscuro. This house was at that time possessed by the architect, Bernardo Buontalenti, and it was here that he received a flying visit from the poet Torquato Tasso. Tasso's poetry had been severely criticised by the Accademia della Crusca, and Ariosto preferred before him; he had felt the mortification acutely, when news reached him in Ferrara that his Pastoral of "Aminta" had been produced on the Florentine stage, with scenery by Buontalenti, which had secured for it the greatest success. Tasso instantly started for Florence, and rode up to this door in the Via Maggio. When Buontalenti appeared, Tasso asked, "Are you that Bernardo Buontalenti of whose wonderful inventions so much is spoken, and who contrived the machinery for a drama lately recited, the composition of Tasso?" "I am Bernardo Buontalenti," was the reply, "but not such as you have the kindness and courtesy to describe me." Upon this the poet embraced him, kissed his forehead, and with the words, "You are Buontalenti, I Torquato Tasso; adieu, my friend;" remounted his horse, and left Florence by the way he came. Buontalenti immediately informed the Grand-Duke Cosimo of this visit, but, though messages were sent to recall Tasso, it was too late, and he never returned to Florence.

Opposite this Palace is the Via Michelozzi, at the corner of which is the singular old Palace of the Michelozzi family, the upper storey overhanging the lower, and supported by brackets. One of the Michelozzi was Prior in 1386, and another was employed with Averardo de' Medici, the grandfather of Cosimo, to punish a rebellious town, in 1433. Giovan Battista di Tommaso Michelozzi, in the sixteenth century, placed the rich canopy over the high altar of the neighbouring Church of Santo Spirito. The celebrated architect belonged to another branch of this family. At the further end of the Via Maggio is the Casa Guidi, an old tower transformed into a modern mansion, and over the door is a beautiful inscription to the memory of the English poetess Elizabeth Barrett Browning, who lived and died here.

At the opposite corner, in the Piazza di San Felice, is the

church of that name, where many noble families have their burial-place; it belongs to a convent of Dominican nuns, called the Nuns of San Pietro Martire, who are permitted to afford protection to unhappy wives flying from their husbands. The Coro, or gallery, set apart for the nuns, above the entrance to the church, is supported by Doric columns. To the right of the door is a much injured fresco, grandly composed and with deep feeling, probably of the period preceding the schools of the Lippi and Masaccio? The Saviour is rising from his tomb; the Virgin, with one arm round his neck, and supporting his wounded arm with her other hand, kisses his face; St. John and Mary Magdalene kneel on either side.

On the opposite side of the church is a panel picture of three Saints, attributed to Piero di Cosimo, but rather resembling the style of the Pollaioli. St. Roch, in the centre, points to the plague-spot on his leg; on one side, is St. Anthony and his pig; on the other, St. Catherine; the legends of the Saints are given in the predella below: St. Anthony is chasing away his pig, the emblem of gluttony and a life of indulgence; St. Catherine is suffering martyrdom between two wheels; the legend of St. Roch in the centre is not sufficiently seen to ascertain its meaning. The colour and expression is very fine throughout.

A little further down the nave on the same side is a feeble picture, by Salvator Rosa, of St. Peter walking on the Sea. St. Matthew at the Receipt of Custom is by Cosimo Rosselli, and is a fair specimen of the master. The Madonna appearing to San Pietro Martire, by Ridolfo Ghirlandaio, aided by his favourite pupil, Michele, is also a good picture. The chapel which follows is dedicated to the Holy Wafer. Above it is a Madonna, in a lunette, which was brought here from the western entrance, where it is supposed to have worked miracles during a plague. A marble arch, with delicately carved foliage, encloses the whole. The Ancona, containing the wafer, has a Virgin and four saints, with adoring angels rising over the casket. Above is the Saviour rising from the tomb. To the right of the Virgin is an old and a young saint; to the left St. John the Baptist and another saint: angels fill up the interstices of the arch. A picture by Giovanni di San Giovanni represents an incident in the life of San Felice, when a bishop of Nola, who was dying of hunger and thirst, was relieved by him. The last picture on this side is so much injured, as to be almost incomprehensible. On the opposite side are,—a Virgin and Child, with saints; St. Anthony healing the Sick, by Ottavio Vanni; and St. Dominick, with other saints, by Vignoli, an artist of no great name. A fine Giottesque Crucifix is attached to the gallery for the nuns.

From the Piazza San Felice a street leads directly to the Piazza Santo Spirito, at the corner of which is another fine example of Florentine architecture of the sixteenth century, possibly after a design by Il Cronaca; a beautiful Fanale, similar to those on the Strozzi, Riccardi, and Pazzi Palaces, is attached to the corner. The Palace belongs to the family of Guadagni, whose gallery of pictures was adorned by two splendid landscapes by Salvator Rosa, which have been sold. The Guadagni derive their origin from Ser Guadagno di Guitto, a notary, who was one of the councillors of the Commune in 1204. From 1289 to 1528, the family reckon eleven Gonfaloniers and nineteen Priors. Bernardo Guadagni advised the exile of Cosimo de' Medici — Pater

Patriæ—in 1433; in revenge for which, Cosimo, on his return, not being able to seize on Bernardo, who had made his escape, treacherously seized on his son, and caused him to be beheaded. One branch of the family settled in France, where they were received with honour at the Court of Francis I.

CHRONOLOGY.

	A.D.
Buontalenti, Bernardo	1536—1608
Capello, Bianca	d. 1587
Cronaca, Il	1454—1509
Ferruccio, Françesco, murdered	1530
Ghirlandaio, Ridolfo	1485—1560
Giovanni di San Giovanni	1576—1636
Henry VII., Emperor, attacked Florence	1312
Pocetti, Bernardo	1542—1591
Ridolfi, Lorenzo de', ambassador to Venice	1425
" Nicolò de', beheaded	1417
Rinuccini in Ireland	1645
Tasso, Torquato	1544—1595
Vanni, Ottavio	1585—1643
Velluti Buonaccorso died	1296

CHAPTER XXII.

SANTO SPIRITO.

THE earliest Church and Monastery of Santo Spirito was built in 1292 by the Augustinians, who received such liberal contributions from the citizens that they were enabled to raise a temple of considerable size, which they adorned with paintings by Cimabue, Simone Memmi, and Giottino. After the expulsion of Walter de Brienne, Duke of Athens, in 1343, when the city was divided in quartieri—quarters—in place of the old division of sestieri, this important Augustinian monastery gave this quarter the name of San Spirito. The church, however, soon was found too small for the increasing population, and in 1433 a new edifice was commenced under the auspices of Filippo Brunelleschi. He proposed that the church should face the Arno, with a large Piazza before it; but the Capponi family, whose houses were along the river, made objections, and the plan was therefore altered. As Brunelleschi died in 1446, the building was not far advanced, and a calamity which occurred in 1470 caused a still further delay. Galeazo Maria Sforza, Duke of Milan, that year paid a visit to Lorenzo de' Medici, when a grand display of ceremonials was arranged for Easter Sunday in the Church of Santo Spirito; but, from the carelessness of some of the workmen, the building caught fire and was wholly consumed. It was recommenced according to the original design of Brunelleschi, which was followed as closely as possible. A contemporary anonymous author records that Brunelleschi was in the habit of only making a rough model of his architectural compositions, leaving the details vague and uncertain, and giving his directions to the masons as the work proceeded, altering and modifying his design. This fact must account for various defects in Santo Spirito, which some critics have attributed to one Antonio Manetti, a workman who had been a pupil of Brunelleschi, but who later set up as his rival, and ventured to disparage his designs. The church, nevertheless, is a noble example of Brunelleschi's compositions. The erection occupied above twenty years. The cupola was built after a design by Salvi d' Andrea, and was only finished in 1482, in which year, according to the diary of Luca Landucci, a Florentine citizen, a sermon was preached here. The sacristy was added in 1488, after a design by Giuliano di San Gallo, and the beautiful little vestibule which connects the sacristy with the church and cloister, was the joint work of Simone Pollajuolo, surnamed Il Cronaca and Giuliano di San Gallo. The sculpture within was executed by Sansovino (Contucci). The cupola of the sacristy was designed by Antonio del Pollajuolo. The belfry, which has been much admired for its perfect proportions, was the work of Baccio d'Agnolo.

The interior of Santo Spirito is very grand from the immense space, the extreme simplicity of the architecture, and its beautiful proportions. It is in the form of a Latin cross, 315 feet long, and 191 feet across the transepts. The aisles are carried round the nave and transepts by a line of handsome columns, of pietra-serena, with Corinthian capitals.

The chapels are raised a step above the pavement, a defect which Brunelleschi is said to have copied from the little Church of the SS. Apostoli, which he so greatly admired, that he refused to admit an error in the composition. Some of these chapels contain good altar-pieces. The first to the right of the entrance contains an Assumption of the Virgin, with saints, by one of the school of Piero di Cosimo. The second chapel contains a copy of Michael Angelo's Pietà at Rome, by his pupil, Nanni di Baccio Bigio. The third has a wooden statue of San Nicolò, in Tolentino, by Sansovino : the angels on either side are by Franciabigio, the friend of Andrea del Sarto. The rest of the chapels on this side of the nave contain nothing of importance.

In the right transept, however, are several interesting pictures. One of these, in the Capponi Chapel, is in a dark position, and represents a nun enthroned, supposed to be Santa Monaca, the mother of St. Augustine. She is giving the rules of her order to twelve other nuns ; angels kneel on either side. Cavalcaselle considers this picture to be in the style of the Pollaioli, although not one of the best specimens.* The nuns, who have very marked countenances, are portraits of ladies of the Capponi family.

The fourteenth chapel from the entrance belongs to the Nerli family, and contains a very beautiful picture by Filippino Lippi, painted in the artist's best manner. The Virgin is seated on a throne within a shrine, supported by pilasters, and adorned by lovely cherubs. The Christ-child on her lap is singularly beautiful ; one hand clasps his mother's fingers ; the other rests on a cross offered him by the little

---

* See "Crowe and Cavalcaselle," vol. ii. p. 397.

St. John, who appears full of earnest devotion. The finest part of the picture is St. Martin, who wears a bishop's stole, and presents the donator of the picture to the Virgin. The donator was Tanai de' Nerli, who belonged to one of the most distinguished families among the Florentine citizens; he was frequently employed on diplomatic missions, and made himself conspicuous by his persecution of Girolamo Savonarola; he even caused the bell of San Marco, which had been rung to rouse the citizens the night when Savonarola was seized, to be taken from the convent, and carried to San Miniato on an ass's back, as a sign of opprobrium. This fierce persecutor of a good and wise man is here represented kneeling humbly, and his countenance, as well as the action of his hands, express well the mingled wonder and reverence with which he approaches the mother of our Lord. On the opposite side of the picture St. Catherine presents the wife of Tanai de' Nerli to the Virgin, who turns her head towards her. In the landscape background is the gate of San Frediano, and Tanai, dismounting from his horse, gives the reins to an attendant, and kisses his little daughter who has come to the door of the house with a servant girl to meet her father. Cavalcaselle observes that no portraits of this time are more admirably real than these of the Nerli family—"Filippino never approached nearer than here to the ideal of simple and grand drapery. His precision in defining form is admirable, his ability in depicting popular life in distance astonishing for its realistic truth: his colour is a little raw but pleasant still, and modelled with great breadth and success."*

---

* See "Crowe and Cavalcaselle," vol. ii. p. 441.

The adjoining chapel has a copy of Perugino's picture of St. Bernard appearing to the Virgin, the original of which is in the Munich Gallery. At the angle of the transept, opposite the Capponi Chapel with the altar piece of Santa Monaca, there is another chapel, likewise belonging to the Capponi, and containing a marble monument behind an iron grating, to the memory of the first Gino Capponi, and erected by his son Neri, who is also buried here, as well as Piero, the grandson of Neri, celebrated in Florentine history. Gino was born in 1360, and rendered his name famous by the part he played in a war against Pisa, which city he conquered for the Florentines in 1404, and, when appointed governor, he gained the affection of the Pisans by his gentle behaviour. His son Neri, whose profile in basso-relievo by Simone di Betto is on this monument, was distinguished in the war carried on by the Florentines against the Duke of Milan, and by his spirited defence of the republic from the encroachments of Cosimo de' Medici. He died lamented by all his fellow-citizens in 1447. His grandson Piero was the champion of Florentine liberty, when threatened by Charles VIII. of France; and his spirited reply to that monarch's insolent declaration that if the treaty he had dictated were not signed he would sound his trumpets—"Then we shall sound our bells," will never be forgotten in Florence.* Piero Capponi was killed in 1496 in an assault against the Pisans; his remains were brought up the Arno in a funeral barge, and deposited in his house near the bridge of the SS. Trinità, from whence they were borne to the Church of

---

* See "Savonarola and his Times," by Pasquale Villari, translated by Leonard Horner, vol. I. p. 226.

Santo Spirito, accompanied by the magistrates and a vast multitude of the citizens. The church was lighted by innumerable tapers, and lined with four ranges of banners, bearing alternately the arms of the Florentine magistracy and of the Capponi family. A funeral oration was delivered over the coffin, proclaiming, in words of the highest praise, the distinguished life of the deceased, and the deep sorrow felt for the loss of the valiant soldier and eminent citizen. His remains were then deposited in the same tomb which his grandfather Neri had caused to be constructed for his illustrious great-grandfather Gino Capponi.* The opposite monument is that of Cardinal Luigi Capponi, a lineal descendant of Piero, who died in 1659.

In the nineteenth chapel, which is within the apse, there is an altar-piece with saints by Agnolo Gaddi. In this chapel is buried Piero Vettori, a literary critic of some reputation, born in 1499 at Florence. Although the Medici were the constant theme of his satire, the Grand-Duke Cosimo I., who had a just estimation for talent in every form, appointed him, in 1538, Professor of Classics; his lectures were attended by a vast concourse of students, who spread his reputation. He died in 1565.

The next altar-piece of a Madonna enthroned with saints on either side, is in the manner of Botticelli. Over the twenty-first altar are Martyrs, by Alessandro Allori; the predella is in the style of Botticelli, and contains a representation of the Pitti Palace as it appeared when first built. The twenty-fourth altar has an Annunciation by Sandro Botticelli: the twenty-fifth, a Madonna and Child, with

---

* See "Savonarola and his Times," &c. vol. ii. p. 93.

two angels, St. Bartholomew, and St. John the Evangelist. The twenty-seventh altar contains a good, though damaged, picture of the Madonna enthroned, with angels, St. Thomas, and St. Peter, with the date 1482. Cavalcaselle supposes these pictures to have been the joint production of Piero di Cosimo and Cosimo Rosselli, and he observes that "the styles of Ghirlandaio and Filippino are mingled with that of Cosimo Rosselli in both pictures."

The altar which follows is enclosed in a fine marble grating, the work of Andrea Sansovino. Cavalcaselle attributes the picture in the adjoining chapel to Raffaellino del Garbo; the subject is the Trinity, adored by St. Catherine and Mary Magdalene, who are on their knees. "The predella contains some pretty things, representing the Nativity between the Communion of St. Mary of Egypt and the Martyrdom of the Alexandrian Saint."* The same author adds, that he considers the picture "a carefully handled and gay specimen of his (Raffaellino's) painting—not the best example."

Over the thirtieth altar is again the Madonna enthroned with angels, St. Bartholomew, and St. Nicholas with his three loaves, attributed to Antonio Pollaiolo, but believed by Cavalcaselle to be another production of Piero di Cosimo and Cosimo Rosselli.

The thirty-second altar has Christ bearing his cross, in some respects identical with one of Ridolfo Ghirlandaio's best pictures, formerly in the Antinori Palace.

Near the door of the sacristy, beneath the organ, is another picture by Ridolfo Ghirlandaio, a Virgin and Child

---

* See "Crowe and Cavalcaselle," vol. iii. p. 417.

with St. Anna behind. Four saints stand on either side, and St. Mary Magdalene and St. Catherine kneel. The picture has been much damaged. There are no other pictures deserving notice in this church.

The choir in the centre, between the transepts, though a marvellously rich display of marbles, is, as a whole, heavy and ugly, and disturbs the architectural beauty of the building. It was placed here in 1599, during the reign of the Grand-Duke Ferdinand I., by the Senator Giovan Battista Michelozzi, already mentioned, who entrusted the work to Giovanni Caccini, the first artist in Florentine mosaic, or Pietra-Dura, a royal manufacture introduced and encouraged by the patronage of the Grand-Dukes Francis I. and Ferdinand I. The arms of the Michelozzi family are introduced in various parts. The choir, though rich in sculpture, is altogether in bad taste; the details, however, are worth studying. The altar is finely decorated with mosaics and bronze statuettes, and the carved wooden seats, and marble and bronze balustrade and candelabra very excellent in their kind.

The cloister beyond the sacristy is surrounded by frescos, representing scenes from the life of St. Augustine. An inner cloister is likewise decorated with frescos. A painting by Agnolo Gaddi was once here, but has been lately removed to the Bargello.*

It was in the Church of the Santo Spirito that Martin Luther preached when he came as an Augustinian friar to Florence, on his road to Rome. His name was inscribed in the books of the Monastery, but the library was dispersed

---

* See "Crowe and Cavalcaselle," vol. i. p. 472.

after the suppression of the monasteries by the French, towards the end of the last century. Many valuable works were then lost, and among them the writings of Bocaccio, bequeathed by him to the Augustinian friars.

CHRONOLOGY.

	A.D.
Allori, Alessandro	1535—1607
Brunelleschi, Filippo	1377—1444
Capponi, Gino	1360—1421
,, Neri	1457
,, Piero	1447—1496
Capponi, Cardinal Luigi	1659
Contucci, Andrea Sansovino	1460—1529
Cosimo, Piero di	1462—1528
D'Agnolo, Baccio	1462—1543
Franciabigio	1482—1528
Gaddi, Agnolo	1333—1396
Gallo, Giuliano di San	1443—1517
Garbo, Raffaellino del	1466—1524
Ghirlandaio, Ridolfo	1483—1561
Lippi, Filippino	1457—1504
Sforza, Galeazzo Maria	1444—1476
Spirito, Santo, founded	1292
,, new church commenced	1446
,, burnt	1470
Vettori, Piero	1499—1565

CHAPTER XXIII.

THE CARMINE.—PORTA ROMANA.—THE ANNALENA.

THE Piazza di Santo Spirito, which, until 1871, was an open paved square, has been recently laid out in gardens. Opposite the church at the entrance of the Via Sant' Agostino leading to the Carmine, is a house belonging to the Marchese Stufa, who possesses a most interesting bust of the Gonfalonier Nicolò Soderini, by Mino da Fiesole, which was discovered in a cellar. It is carefully finished in the manner of the old Florentine artists, full of life, and evidently a correct likeness, and every detail faithfully rendered, to the squint in the eyes and a mole on the lip. The Marchese has also three good reliefs in pietraserena, and a Madonna, which were found in the cellar with the bust of Soderini.

The corner of the Via Sant' Agostino and the Via de' Serragli is commonly known as the Canto della Cuculia, because this spot was once in the midst of the gardens belonging to the Velluti, frequented by the cuckoo. Here a triumphal arch was erected in honour of Charles V., when he entered Florence in 1515, and Ridolfo Ghirlandaio and his pupil, or son, Michele, exerted all their inventive powers and skill to make it more splendid. In a house near the

Canto della Cuculia a poor child was charitably received, who afterwards became the celebrated painter Filippo Lippi. His father was a butcher, and his mother died when Filippo was only two years old, when the boy was consigned to his aunt, who lived here, and kept him until he had attained his tenth year; her poverty obliged her to place her nephew in the neighbouring Monastery of the Carmine, where he was registered as an inmate, and where he remained until he was past twenty, in the year 1432, having been already entered on the books of the Carmine as a painter.

The Church and Monastery of Sta. Maria della Carmine was built for the Carmelite friars by Agnes, widow of Cione Tifa di Praniere Vernacci, in fulfilment of her husband's last will. The Soderini, Manetti, Nerli, Ferucci, and Serragli families gave generous contributions to the church, which was finished in 1475. In 1771 a great part of the building was destroyed by fire, and it was restored in its present form by Giuseppe Ruggieri, chiefly at the expense of the Marchese Lorenzo Niccolini. The monastery was built by Count Guido da Montefeltro, and enlarged by one of the Soderini.

The Carmelites pretend to derive their origin from Elijah, "who dwelt solitary in the midst of Carmel." In England they are called White Friars, from their mantles, which, by order of Pope Honorius III., were white, worn over a dark brown mantle.[*]

The Senator Giovanbattista Michelozzi, who built the canopy for the high altar of Santo Spirito, erected the covered

---

[*] See Mrs. Jameson, "Legends of the Monastic Orders," p. 429.

entrance to the cloister in the year 1600, and on that occasion the friars had the barbarity to whitewash and partially destroy a celebrated fresco in the cloister by Masaccio, which represented the Consecration of the Church, and contained portraits of the Archbishop Amerigo Corsini, Brunelleschi, Donatello, Giovanni de' Medici, Nicolò da Uzzano, Bartolommeo Valori, Lorenzo Ridolfi, and other celebrated men of the period. As much as remains of this fresco has been recently uncovered. A Florentine gentleman, in a red dress, is supposed to represent Giovanni de' Medici, the only virtuous citizen of the family which he founded. The face here is nearly obliterated, but the figure and action is refined and dignified, and the drapery arranged in grand yet simple folds; near him two friars converse with animation as they enter the church. Higher up, on the same wall, is a repetition of the favourite subject of hermitages, probably referring to the first hermits on Mount Carmel. One group is very amusing, and the figures composing it are evidently portraits. A stout jolly friar is seated on the ground, and turns towards the spectator with a broad smile; a younger monk addressing him, appears hardly able to keep his countenance. A piece of drapery which is all that remains of a third figure, descending the hill, would prove an admirable study for the young painter.

On another part of the same wall is the fresco of a knight and a nun, who are presented to the Virgin, by their patron saints. This fresco, though of an earlier date, is in better preservation. Cavalcaselle attributes it to Giovanni da Milano, the friend of Taddeo Gaddi. The expression of the nun is singularly sweet and earnest, and the saints behind are dignified. The remaining fresco of this cloister represent a series of events in the life of the prophet Elijah, whom the Carmelites claim as the founder of their Order.*

The interior of the church, which is in the form of a Latin cross, is spacious and lofty, but has no pretension to beauty. The roof is painted in fresco in a bad period of art. The pictures in the chapels on either side of the nave are all mediocre, except one by Pocetti, to the right, representing the Eternal appearing to the Virgin, who is mourning over her dead Son.

The southern transept contains the celebrated Brancacci Chapel, with the paintings by Masaccio and Filippino Lippi, which commenced a new era in Art, and formed the greatest painters of the Cinque-Cento period. Though preceding Raffaelle by nearly a century, Masaccio was well worthy of being his master; and when the youthful artist arrived in Florence, with ideas derived from the conventional types and formal, though correct, drawing of Perugino, he must have delighted in the freedom of hand, the close observation, and fine selection from nature, the dignity and grace of the figures, as well as the life and ease with which the story is told in these frescos. As a proof of Raffaelle's appreciation of these works, and of his unfailing industry, it is recorded that he copied them seven times.

Though injured by the fire of 1777, and in an obscure light, enough can still be distinguished to delight and astonish the spectators. Masaccio was born in 1402, and died in 1429, at twenty-seven years of age. When he had just commenced life as an artist, he was enrolled in

---

* Two heads from this fresco were long in possession of the poet Samuel Rogers, Esq., and are now in the National Gallery of London.

the Guild of Speziali—Apothecaries—who, as we have before mentioned, were peculiarly allied to the painters, from the chemical knowledge required in the preparation of colours. He travelled to Rome to paint a chapel in the Church of San Clemente, for the Cardinal di San Clemente; and on his return to Florence he painted the portrait of Giovanni de' Bicci de' Medici, and soon afterwards commenced his frescos in the Brancacci Chapel, by order of Felice di Michele di Piuvichese Brancacci of the quarter of Santo Spirito. The share attributed to another and earlier painter, Masolino, is denied by Cavalcaselle. Filippino Lippi, 1457—1504, finished what Masaccio's early death obliged him to leave incomplete. On the pilasters at the entrance are represented Adam and Eve under the Tree of Knowledge and the Expulsion from Paradise. The walls of the chapel are divided in twelve compartments, including these two frescos—St. Peter heals Tabitha, and cures a cripple at the Gate of the Temple. He preaches and baptizes; the youth who has just thrown off his garment, and stands shivering with cold, is a figure which, according to Lanzi, formed an epoch in Art. Peter and John heal a cripple; the houses in the background have windows constructed for blinds, before the use of glass; the two Florentine youths converse in the centre of the composition: their draperies are finely drawn, and the colouring is soft and agreeable. Peter rescued from Prison; the expression of the angel, who, with a smile on his countenance, is listening to the apostle, is singularly sweet. The grand figure of St. Paul standing before the prison is by Filippino Lippi, and was introduced by Raffaelle into his cartoon of Paul preaching at Athens. Peter finding the Tribute Money in the

Fish's Mouth, is a large compartment, in which the composition is divided in three separate events; Andrew calls Peter; Peter seeks for the money in the mouth of the fish; and in the centre and principal group, the Saviour, a calm and dignified figure, is seated in the midst of the apostles: Peter is eagerly expostulating with him. The heads of the apostles are very fine, and may have suggested to Raffaelle his group in the cartoon of "Feed my Sheep." A grand range of mountains forms the background, not unlike the Carrara, as seen from the Mediterranean. Below this fresco, St. Peter raises a youth to life, a scene from the apocryphal history of the apostles. The story is thus given by Mrs. Jameson:—" Simon the magician challenged Peter and Paul to restore to life a dead youth, who is said to have been a kinsman or nephew of the Roman emperor. The sorcerer fails of course. The apostles resuscitate the youth, who kneels before them. The skull and bones near him represent the previous state of death. A crowd of spectators stand around and behold the miracle. All the figures are half the size of life, and quite wonderful for the truth of expression, the variety of character, the simple dignity of the forms and attitudes." *

Masaccio died when at work on this picture, and the central group of the composition was finished many years later by Filippino Lippi. The kneeling youth is said to have been a portrait of Françesco Granacci, who was born in 1469, and was, when painted, apparently about sixteen. Among the spectators are several portraits. The first head on the left is Marco Soderini, who died in 1485; the poet

---

* See "Memoirs of the Early Italian Painters," by Mrs. Jameson.

Luigi Pulci is on his right, and the two on each side of monks are Piero Guiccardini, the father of the historian, and Piero del Pugliese.

Opposite is one of the finest composition of the series, Nero condemning Peter to Death, with the Apostle's Crucifixion, attributed to Filippino Lippi. Nero is seated on a throne, his head crowned with laurel; to the right, behind his extended arm, are three portraits; that to the right of the pro-consul is Antonio Pollajuolo; the third from Nero is Masaccio, and resembles the portrait by himself in the Uffizi Gallery, from which it may have been taken. There are also portraits to the left of Nero; one is probably Filippino, with a bald head, seated. At the further end of the composition St. Peter is crucified with his head downwards: the cross is supported by two half-nude executioners, who are letting down the saint by a rope; Botticelli's portrait is among the spectators with sorrowful countenances. Filippino likewise executed the remainder of the frescos in this chapel. As Mrs. Jameson observes:—" In considering these works, their superiority over all that painting had till then achieved or attempted is such that there seems a kind of break in the progression of Art, as if Masaccio had overleapt suddenly the limits which his predecessor had found impassable; but Ghiberti and his gates explain this seeming wonder. The chief excellencies of Masaccio were those which he had attained, or at least conceived, in his early studies in modelling. He had learned from Ghiberti not merely the knowledge of form, but the effects of light and shade, in giving relief and roundness to his figures, which, in comparison to those of his predecessors, seemed to start from the canvas. Masaccio added a precision in the drawing of the naked figure, and a softness and harmony in colouring the flesh, never attained before his time, nor since surpassed, till the days of Raphael and Titian. He excelled also in the expression and imitation of natural actions and feelings. . . . Add the animation and variety of character in his heads—so that it was said of him that he painted souls as well as bodies—and his free-flowing draperies, quite different from the longitudinal folds of the Giotto school, yet grand and simple, and we can form some idea of the combination of excellence with novelty of style which astonished his contemporaries." *

The artists who, Vasari informs us, studied here, besides Raffaelle, were Leonardo da Vinci, Michael Angelo, Andrea del Sarto, Fra Bartolommeo, Perugino, and Baccio Bandinelli.

In a chapel of the Sacristy of the Carmine some interesting frescos have been recently discovered beneath the whitewash, which are supposed to have been by the hand of Agnolo Gaddi. The subject is the legend of St. Cecilia, with her husband, St. Valerian, and their friend, St. Tiburtius. St. Cecilia is a most lovely woman, and the same fair face, with the delicate features, long golden hair, and dignified, yet sweet and serious expression, are preserved with portrait-like fidelity in every representation of the saint. In the lunette on the wall to the left, facing the high altar, is the Marriage of Valerian and Cecilia; below is the banquet, in which the servants bring in meat, whilst Cecilia plays on her organ; and at the opposite end she is seen conversing with her husband. In the lunette above the window an

---

* See "Memoirs of the Italian Painters," by Mrs. Jameson.

old man is seated on a martyr's tomb, and points out St. Urban to Valerian. In the lunette on the wall to the right of the altar, Valerian is instructed in Christianity by an old man, and is baptized by St. Urban. In the second division, on the left wall, Valerian is seen in prayer crowned by angels; Tibertius is instructed in Christianity by Valerian and Cecilia, and is baptized. On either side of the window, Valerian and Tibertius distribute alms and bury the dead; they are led before the Prefect; on the right wall they are on the way to execution, when they convert their jailer and all his family; they are prepared for death by Cecilia, and are executed. On the lowest compartment, to the left, Cecilia distributes alms, and is taken prisoner; on her road to execution she instructs the bystanders, and four thousand persons are converted. On the right wall, opposite, Cecilia is beheaded, and the blood is collected as it flows from her neck; her figure here is especially graceful; she is buried in the catacombs, and her house is consecrated as an oratory by St. Urban.

In the choir of the church, which was built by the Soderini family, is the monument by Benedetto da Rovezzano, to the memory of the celebrated Piero Soderini, who was Gonfalonier of Florence in 1502, and who died and was buried in Rome. It consists of a plain dark green marble sarcophagus beneath an arch of white marble, richly decorated with delicate carving, and skulls which have a circle of hair like that of monks. On the supports and other parts of the monument are larger skulls, with hair starting from the head, giving them a still more ghastly appearance; figures of men, animals, genii with scrolls of acanthus leaves, and imitations of antique arabesques are included among the ornaments; and lower down, leopards, the papal keys, and the favourite Florentine decoration of festoons of fruit.

. In the northern transept, which belongs to the Corsini family, built in 1675, is the tomb of Sant' Andrea Corsini, to whom the chapel is dedicated. The painted ceiling is by Luca Giordano. The ponderous marble relief of the apotheosis of the saint is by Foggini; one one side, represented in a similar manner, is the story of a victory of the Florentines over a famous leader of Free Companies, won by the prayers of Sant' Andrea; on the other, the Virgin accompanied by Angels, appears to the Saint. Andrea Corsini died in 1373; he was first a Carmelite friar, and afterwards Bishop of Fiesole, and was canonized by Urban VIII. in 1629.

From the Carmine to the Walls is inhabited by the lowest population of Florence. The Porta San Frediano, built in 1324 by Andrea Pisano, is one of the finest gates in the city. The remains of the Ante-Port may be traced on the outside wall. It was here that Charles VIII. of France made his entrance into Florence in 1494. "On the day appointed, the 17th November, the Signory were in attendance in a balcony erected near the San Frediano gate. Many of the young Florentines of the first families went out to meet the king, who, at two o'clock in the afternoon, made his solemn entry. As he approached, the Signory rose, and Lucca Corsini, to whom the duty had been assigned, advanced to read an address that had been prepared. But just at that moment rain began to fall, the horses would not stand, but pushed against one another, and the whole ceremony was thus thrown into confusion: Gaddi alone, who was steward of the palazzo, had, however, sufficient presence of mind to make his way, and contrived in the hubbub to say a few words to the king in French, suited to the occasion, after which Charles went forward under a rich canopy. . . . On each side of him rode the Cardinals San Piero in Vincola and of San Malo, together with some of his marshals. The royal body-guard followed, consisting of a hundred archers selected from amongst the handsomest youths of France, and two hundred knights of France on foot, in splendid dresses, and armed; then came the Swiss guard, with their brilliant uniforms of various colours, having halberts of burnished steel, their officers wearing rich plumes on their helmets. . . . The centre consisted of the Gascons, short, light, active men, whose numbers seemed to multiply as they marched forward. But the most splendid appearance of all was made by the cavalry, in which were to be found the most noble young men of France: they had engraved armour, mantles of the richest brocade, banners of velvet embroidered with gold, chains of gold, and ornaments of the same precious metal. The cuirassiers presented a hideous appearance with the horses looking like monsters, from their ears and tails being cut short. The archers were extraordinarily tall men; they came from Scotland and other northern countries, and they looked more like wild beasts than men." * Such was the accompaniment of one of the greatest sovereigns in Christendom, whom Pier Capponi awed into submission by the mere force of his firm and courageous patriotism.

---

* See "Savonarola and his Times," by Pasquale Villari, translated by Leonard Horner, Esq., vol. L p. 219.

Between the Porta San Frediano and the Porta Romana, beneath the walls, was the old Cemetery of the Jews, who were not permitted to lie within the city; the small stones amidst the grass still remaining, mark the graves of this persecuted people. Within the walls, at the corner nearest the river, is a Tabernacle, attributed to Domenico Ghirlandaio, which is all that remains of a convent which once stood here. The subject is a Madonna and Child, St. John the Evangelist, and Mary Magdalene. Beyond this point, outside the city, is the last remaining of the Tiratoii, or buildings adapted for stretching and drying cloth, once belonging to the most influential Guild in Florence. The Church of San Frediano is as old as the ninth century, when it stood in the midst of fields, before the third circuit of walls included the borough. The Soderini were granted the patronage by Pope Paul II., in 1462. The present church is wholly modern; it occupies the area of the old convent of the Carmelites of Santa Maria degli Angioli and Santa Maria Maddalena de Pazzi; the nuns ceded their convent, in 1628, to the Cistercian friars, and received in exchange the convent in the Borgo Pinti. The cell of Santa Maddalena de' Pazzi has been converted into a chapel.

Returning to the Piazza Soderini, the Via de' Serragli continues as far as the Porta Romana. To the right, on entering this street, is one of the finest palaces in the city, built by the Marchese Ubaldo Feroni in 1770, after a design by Zanobi del Rosso. The palaces on the other side are supposed to have belonged to the extinct family of the Serragli. The name of the street was probably derived from them, and not, as some have supposed, from barricades raised in it. Further on, to the left, a long line of houses formed the palaces of the Salviati, who were descended from a celebrated physician in the thirteenth century, Maestro Salvi by name. Twenty-one of the family sat as Gonfaloniers of the Republic, and sixty-three held the office of Priors; the most celebrated was Françesco, who held the archbishopric of Pisa at the time of the Pazzi conspiracy, and who joined Jacopo and Françesco Pazzi in their attempt against the lives of Lorenzo and Giuliano de' Medici. The archbishop was hung from a window of the Palazzo della Signoria. This palace is supposed by some to have been inhabited by him, but the fact is doubtful.

To the right is the suppressed Convent and Church of Santa Elisabetta, in which was included a poor dwelling where San Filippo Neri was born, in 1515. The tabernacle at the corner is attributed by some to Pocetti, by others to Giovanni di San Giovanni. Near the Gardens of the Villino della Torre, between the Via de' Serragli and the Via Romana, is the little Church of Ser Umido, built on part of the site of the larger church of San Piero Gattolino, which was demolished by Cosimo I. It was in San Piero Gattolino that the Padri Scopetini took refuge during the siege of 1529. After its destruction, in 1547, a poor man called Messer Umido, who earned his livelihood by the sale of old iron, resolved to collect money to build a church in its stead; he persevered and succeeded, and the church of his erection is still known as San Piero di Ser Umido.

On the opposite side of the Via de' Serragli are the extensive gardens and villas belonging to the Marchese Torrigiani. The grandfather of the present owner built a high tower in the centre,—the crest of the family being a tower,—from whence a fine panorama of all the country round can be obtained. His son, the Marchese Carlo, who inherited the garden, and bequeathed it to his nephew, the present owner, placed there a good statue of his father by the living artist Fede.

At the farther end of the Via de' Serragli is the Church and Seminary of La Calza, which has had a succession of inhabitants. In 1323 it was an hospital belonging to the Order of the Knights of Jerusalem, and it was at that time called San Nicolò de' Frieri. In 1392, certain ladies of the Order of St. John of Jerusalem were allowed to use the building for their convent. They were removed during the siege, when the convent was given to the Ingesuati from the Porta Pinti, when the name was changed to San Giusto della Calza, from the stocking-like material of the cowl worn by these monks. They enlarged the church and monastery, and enriched it by various pictures; but the Ingesuati were suppressed by Clement IX. in 1688, and the convent was finally sold to the Congregation of Priests of San Salvatore, and changed its name again to San Giovan Battista della Calza. The church was probably indebted to the Ingesuati for the picture by Perugino over the high altar. The crucified Saviour is in the same attitude with that in Sta. Maddalene de' Pazzi, though without its refinement and grace; on one side is the Beato Giovanni Colombini, of Sienna, and St. John the Baptist; a vigorous figure, but more in the hard style of Andrea Castagno, and by some attributed to Luca Signorelli. The Magdalene on her knees contemplates the feet of the Saviour, and strives to draw out the nails; she has a beautiful, expressive face; St. Jerome, who presses eagerly forward, looking up in the Saviour's face, is likewise very fine; behind him, St Francis, is a repetition of Perugino's usual figures, soft in expression, and carefully drawn. The colour is very sweet throughout, but wants cleansing and refreshing to bring out the tone, which, in its present condition, is dead and hard.

In the Refectory is a Cenacolo by Franciabigio; the heads are good, though feeble; the drawing of the figures careless, and the whole painting is in a damaged condition.

The Porta Romana, which is on the old high road to Rome, was formerly known as the Porta di San Piero Gattolino. It was by this gate that Pope Leo X. and the Emperor Charles V. made their entry into Florence in 1536. They passed up the Via de' Serragli to the Canto alla Cuculia, where the triumphal arch was prepared by Ridolfo Ghirlandaio, to the Piazza San Felice, by the Via Maggio to the Ponte SS. Trinità, thence to the Via de' Martelli, by which they reached the Palazzo Medici, now Riccardi, where they took up their abode. Fra Bartolommeo, in his youth, lived near the Porta Romana, and thence obtained the name of Baccio della Porta.

Opposite the Porta Romana is a nearly effaced fresco by Giovanni di San Giovanni, which the artist is supposed to have painted in one night. Mars, Pallas, and Mercury, with the Graces, dance to the music of Apollo's lyre. Florence is represented as a majestic female seated on a throne, habited in the sacred vestments of St. Stephen, pope and martyr. Beside her are female representatives of Sienna and Pisa, as well as Flora, and the four seasons, with Amorini; the River Arno is above the architrave.

Turning into the Via Romana, and passing the Church of Ser Umido, before arriving at a gate of the Boboli Gardens, is a house with a tablet recording the dwelling of Giovanni di San Giovanni. The opposite Casa MacDonald is on the site of what was once the large Convent of Annalena, founded by the unhappy widow of Baldaccio dell' Anguillara, whose tragical fate was recorded in the chapter on the "Palazzo della Signoria," and who owed his death to Cosimo de' Medici's jealousy of Neri Capponi, whom he wished to deprive of the services of so able a commander. The Convent of Annalena belonged to Dominican nuns until they were suppressed in 1808. It extended as far back as the Via de' Serragli, where for many years the American Hiram Powers, one of the greatest of living sculptors, had his studio.

CHRONOLOGY.

	A.D.
Benedetto da Rovezzano	1478—1552
Brunelleschi, Filippo	1379—1446
Carmine built	1475
" destroyed by fire	1771
Charles VIII. of France	1494
Charles V., Emperor, entered Florence	1575
Corsini, Andrea	d. 1373
" Amerigo, first Archbishop of Florence	1420
" Chapel in Carmine built	1676
Donatello	1386—1466
Francavilla	b. 1548
Frediano, San, under the Soderini	1467
Gaddi, Agnolo	1333—1396
Ghirlandaio, Domenico	1449—1494
" Ridolfo	1483—1561

320   WALKS IN FLORENCE.

	A.D.
Giordano, Luca	1632—1705
Giovanni di San Giovanni	1576—1636
Lippi, Fra Filippo	b. 1412—1469
„ Filippino	1457—1504
Masaccio	1402—1427
Medici, Giovanni de'	1360—1429
Neri, San Filippo	b. 1515
Perugino	1446—1524
Pisano, Andrea	1345
Pocetti	1542—1591
Pollaiolo, Antonio	1429—1498
Porta San Frediano	1024
Pulci, Luigi	d. 1490
Ridolfi, Lorenzo, at Venice	1425
Salviati, Francesco, Archbishop of Pisa, hung	1478
Soderini, Marco	d. 1486
„ Piero, Gonfalonier	1502
Urban VIII., Pope	1625—1644
Uzzano, Nicolò d'	d. 1432
Valori, Bartolommeo	1354—1427

CHAPTER XXIV.

THE BOBOLI GARDENS.—PALAZZO DEI PITTI.

THE gate opposite the site of the former Convent of Annalena is one of the entrances to the Boboli Gardens, which were laid out by order of the Grand-Duke Cosimo I., when he purchased the Palazzo dei Pitti for his wife, Eleonora of Toledo. Buontalenti and Tribolo were the architects commissioned to make the designs for this magnificent garden, which was given the name of Bogoli, or Boboli, from a family who had once houses in this quarter. Tall trees and hedges of bay, cypress, olive, ilex, and other evergreens, divide the ground into endless walks, shady pathways, and groves adorned with statues of unequal merit, and varied with water containing gold fish. Above all towers the noble stone pine, and beneath are banks of roses and grassy lawns, which refresh the eye, fatigued by the glare of the city. In the midst of a large sheet of water near the Porta Romana, is a group of statuary by Giovan Bologna, placed on what is called the Isoletto, from whence the ground rises abruptly; and an avenue of tall trees and hedges, with statues at intervals, leads to a plateau, commanding, towards the south and west, splendid views of the town and surrounding country. The little meadow on the plateau is called L' Uccellaja, probably from having at one time been a bird-snare, so common around Florence. A little higher is a winding staircase, the entrance to the Garden of the Cavaliere, where there is a casino or villa, with a small garden, from whence is obtained a distant view of hill and valley in the direction of Arezzo and Rome. Returning to the Boboli, a narrow path conducts to the highest point, directly above the palace, facing which is a statue of Dovizia—Abundance—supposed to have been a portrait of the Grand-Duchess Joanna of Austria, the first wife of Francis I. This statue was commenced by Giovan Bologna, and finished by his scholar, Tacca. To the right is the Fortress of San Giorgio, overlooking the garden; immediately below is the Fountain of Neptune, in the centre of which is a good statue of the sea-god throwing his trident, executed in 1565 by Stoldo Lorenzi, an artist who is little known, but who was probably a scholar of Giovan Bologna. Near the Fortress of San Giorgio is the Tower of the Belvedere; and a rapid descent by various paths, as well as by the broad way which leads directly from the Fountain of Neptune, conducts to the semicircular space behind the palace, called the Amphitheatre; stone benches rise one above the other, on either side, and here various spectacles were formerly exhibited for the diversion of the grand-ducal family. An Egyptian Obelisk and Porphyry Bason occupy the centre. The path to the left leads to the apartments usually occupied by the king in a wing of the palace, opposite the Uccellaja, at the foot of which is a statue of Pegasus by the modern sculptor Costoli. Beyond are the gates of Annalena and of the Porta Romana. The path to the right of the Amphitheatre conducts to the usual entrance to the gardens, beneath the palace. Opposite this gate is a grotto, built by Buontalenti, to receive four large unfinished statues by Michael Angelo, which the artist had intended to form part of his Monument to Pope Julius II., and which were presented to the Grand-Duke Cosimo I. by Leonardo Buonarotti, the nephew of Michael Angelo. The statues of Apollo and Ceres, at the entrance of the Grotto, were executed by Baccio Bandinelli; Paris and Helen are by Rossi da Fiesole; and in the small inner grotto, painted by Pocetti, is a marble bason supported by four satyrs, and surmounted by a figure of Venus, the work of Giovan Bologna.

The Palazzo dei Pitti was commenced in 1441, by Luca Pitti, one of the wealthiest and most influential citizens of Florence, a rival of the Medici rather than of the Strozzi, but who did not yield the palm to either, in his ambition to play a leading part in the government; he was, at any rate, resolved that his palace should exceed both of theirs in size and magnificence. When Piero de' Medici lost his father Cosimo Vecchio, Luca Pitti conspired with Agnolo Acciajuoli, Nicolò Soderini, and Dioti-Salvi Neroni, to wrest the power from his hands. The marriage of Piero's son, Lorenzo, with Clarice Orsini, belonging to one of the greatest of the Roman families, still farther aroused the vigilance of his enemies, and this marriage added mortification to Luca Pitti's jealousy, since he had intended his own daughter for the young Medici.

Luca's faction obtained the name of Del Poggio, because the Pitti Palace was built on the hill of San Giorgio, whilst the Medici Palace, in the plain below, gave the name Del Piano to their opponents. Fortunately for Piero, Luca Pitti appears to have been of as weak and irresolute a character as his own; and after the final discomfiture of the Pitti and their party, and the banishment of all who had followed their banner, Luca was allowed to remain in Florence, where he lived with a suspicion of treachery attached to his name, despised and shunned by all, and left to wander in solitude through his vast palace.

The building was begun by Maestro Fanelli, a clever builder, after a design by Filippo Brunelleschi. The façade is divided into three tiers, and constructed of enormous blocks of stone. On the lowest part are lions' heads finely executed, from one of which flows the purest water in Florence, carried hither by pipes from the mountains near Pratolino. At the death of Brunelleschi, in 1444, the palace was only finished as far as the second row of windows, and the loggia, which, according to the original design, was to have crowned the edifice, has never been added. The roof was placed by Fanelli, but the wings were not even begun when Luca Pitti died. His descendants were unable to meet the expenses of so vast a building, and in 1549 Buonaccorso Pitti sold it to Eleonora of Toledo. On a house in the Fondaccio di Santo Spirito, which at that time belonged to the Pitti, may still be seen a sketch of the palace as it was when they abandoned it to their rivals the Medici. Ammanati added the wings, and enclosed the beautiful little court behind, where he built a grotto, with niches containing three groups of statuary: Hercules and Antæus, Hercules leaning on his club, and Pluto with Cerberus. At one end of the surrounding colonnade is a mule in black marble, supposed to commemorate the animal employed to carry the materials for the erection of the palace. Above the grotto is a bason with *putti* playing musical instruments.

THE BOBOLI GARDENS.—PALAZZO DEI PITTI.

To the right of the palace entrance, beneath the colonnade, is the Royal Chapel, adorned with frescos by Luigi Ademollo, an artist of mediocre powers. The high altar is richly decorated with arabesques and pictures in flat and raised pietra-dura. In front of the table is the Last Supper, and beautiful statuettes are inserted in niches at the sides, where rubies and other precious stones are scattered over a ground of lapis lazuli. Above the altar is a Crucifix in ivory, by Giovan Bologna. In the sacristy are copies of the famous Magdalene of Correggio, at Parma, as well as of other pictures.

Returning to the colonnade, and passing to the left of the entrance, there is a small court in which is the statue of Ajax supporting a dying warrior, a repetition of the group under the Loggia de' Lanzi, and, judging by its merits, probably the original work. In the anteroom beyond is a bust of Luca Pitti, the founder of the palace, and three drawings of the original design for the Palazzo dei Pitti, with the loggia on the top, as intended by Brunelleschi. The adjoining chamber contains the splendid collection of old plate.

Within a glass case in front of the entrance are tazze, by one of the school of Benvenuto Cellini, each containing a relief representing a different subject. In a cabinet to the left is old church plate, and beyond, in another cabinet, a *cassetta* or casket for the holy wafer, when exhibited on Maunday Thursday; it is worked in rich enamel, and set with enormous emeralds. Two beautifully silver-gilt and enamel goblets, with delicately wrought handles, are by Benvenuto Cellini; but one of the greatest treasures in this room is a large niello by Maso Finiguerra, in the centre of which is the Madonna and Child, and around are scenes from the Life of our Lord.

A mosaic table of fine workmanship is placed under glass in the middle of the room. Two silver salvers are by Benvenuto Cellini, on one of which is the Rape of Proserpine; on the other, Orpheus. In the same cabinet are goblets and a flask of fine enamel, also by Benvenuto. Farther on is a little image of the Infant Saviour, in pietra-dura, which belonged to the Grand-Duke Cosimo I.; also a beautiful crozier. Opposite the entrance is a bronze-gilt candelabrum, supported by satyrs, and standing on a pedestal of tortoiseshell, the work of Giovan Bologna. A little dog, in ivory, by Donatello, is in a case between two miniature wax-heads by the celebrated modeller in wax, Zumbo; one of these represents the Sufferings of Purgatory, the other the Tortures of Hell. In the window is a bronze Crucifix by Giovan Bologna, a relief by Tacca of the Crucifixion, and a very fine Limoges enamel with the history of our Lord. The finest crucifix here is in a cabinet near the entrance; it is in ivory, and by Donatello. Christ is represented looking upwards in the agony of prayer; at his feet is the skull.

On the first floor of the palace a suite of rooms are exhibited, once occupied by Pius IX., but they contain nothing of importance. The state apartments beyond are richly decorated, and the ball-room, though too narrow for its height and length, is very handsome; it has lately been fitted up with much taste and magnificence for the receptions of Victor Emmanuel.

As the Palazzo della Signoria is the monument of early republican government in Florence, so the Palazzo dei Pitti is associated with the period when she was under the rule of sovereign princes. When we remember that this city, which played so prominent a part in European politics, and in the progress of civilisation, was torn by factions within her walls which not unfrequently converted Florence into a battle-field, we may well marvel at the strength of her Republic, and at the sagacity of her civic rulers, which could maintain her independence during seven centuries, and raise their city to the first rank in commerce, literature, and art. On one side were ranged haughty nobles, glorying in their supposed superiority of birth, supported by an armed peasantry whom they summoned to their aid from their castles in the country, abetted by the German emperors, who claimed suzerainty over nearly the whole peninsula, and reinforced by wealthy citizens who preferred titles and power to liberty; on the other side, simple merchants, strong only in union for the preservation of their just rights, and supported by the Church, which in those days represented Italian nationality. It was not until the citizens themselves consented to bow beneath the sway of one of their own order, and Florence had submitted to become the slave of Medicean ambition, that she fell from her high estate, and gradually sank as much below the level of other communities as she had once soared above them. Cruelty, rapacity, and superstition were the characteristics of the princely inhabitants of the Pitti, from Cosimo I. to Giovan Gastone.

Some curious observations on the condition of Florence in the seventeenth century, under Ferdinand II., may be found in a letter from one of the clerks of the English Privy Council, written in 1650, of which the following is an extract:—

"This letter comes to kisse your hands from fair Florence, a Citie so beautifull that the great Emperour (Charles V.)

said that she was sitting to be shewn and seen, onely upon Holidays. She marvailously flourisheth with Buildings, with Wealth, and Artisans; for it is thought that in Serges, which is but one commodity, ther are made two millions evry year. All degrees of people live here not onely well but splendidly well, notwithstanding the manifold exactions of the Duke upon all things: For none can buy here Land or Houses, but they must pay eight in the Hundred to the Duke; none can marry or commence suit in Law but ther's a Fee to the Duke; none can bring as much as an Egg or Sallet to the Market, but the Duke hath share therinna. .... Add herunto that the Duke himself in som respect is a Marchant, for he sometimes ingrosseth all the Corn of the Country, and retails it at what rate he pleaseth," &c., &c.

In 1765, with the accession of Pietro Leopoldo, the son of Francis II. of Lorraine and the Empress Maria Theresa, Tuscany became an Austrian province, and all the unappropriated revenue was claimed by Vienna. Pietro Leopoldo was imbued with the admirable theories of government of his brother the Emperor Joseph, and he endeavoured to enforce them on a people degraded by two centuries of despotic rule, and who had therefore neither previous training nor education to accept the new ideas willingly. Many of his good works nevertheless remain, and have borne fruit; but after a reign of twenty-five years he was called to the throne of Austria, and the Council of Regency opposed and abolished his measures, and set at nought the principles he had vainly attempted to inculcate; another proof, if such were wanting, that true liberty cannot be given by an individual, but must spring from the heart of the people. In 1790 Pietro Leopoldo sent his second son, Ferdinand, to Tuscany as

Grand-Duke — his principal adviser, Fossombroni, was celebrated for the reforms he introduced, but, in 1805, Ferdinand was obliged to abdicate in favour of the Duke of Parma, and Buonaparte shortly afterwards placed his sister Elisa on the throne of Tuscany, with the title of Queen of Etruria; her reign ended in 1814, when Ferdinand resumed the crown. He died in 1824, and was succeeded by his son Leopold II., the last Austrian grand-duke. Though Leopold was a man of mild temper, irreproachable character, cultivated mind, and a patron of literature and science, the general condition of the country did not greatly improve under his rule; and in a time of revolution the fears of the government prevented all communication between city and city, even for commercial purposes, whilst the Bargello was crowded with political prisoners, some of whom were among the best and most able men, as well as belonging to the first families. Finally, an Austrian army was invited by the grand-duke himself into the country to protect him against his own subjects. Since the accession of Victor Emmanuel, Tuscany, with the rest of Italy, has not only enjoyed a parliamentary government, but communication between the cities has been promoted, and commerce improved, though the most enlightened principles of free trade have not yet crossed the Alps, whilst agricultural meetings have been instituted, and education is actively assisted both by the legislature and by private individuals. More than all this, these benefits have not been conferred or dictated by the sovereign or his ministers, but have emanated from the representatives of the people and from the people themselves.

Tuscany cannot yet bear a comparison with countries which have long enjoyed a democratic constitution, but a steady and rapid progress may be traced during twelve years of freedom. If there is still a young nobility who waste their substance whilst their country demands the energies of all her sons, and if the religious sentiment has been weakened in the mass of the people by the misconduct or mistakes of those who should have been their guides, there are some even among the nobles whose active exertions for good may in time leaven the whole lump, and the education which is to train the heart as well as understanding to higher views of right and wrong, must eventually reawaken a deeper religious sentiment, whilst leading the child to the knowledge and love of God.

Under the government of which Victor Emmanuel is the constitutional head, the Tuscan people have little reason to regret that they have ceased to be an Austrian province, and that the Palazzo dei Pitti is no longer inhabited by an Austrian prince, the last of whom has been thus described by the Tuscan poet, Giuseppe Giusti:—

> "Il Toscano Morfeo vien lemme-lemme,
> Di papaveri cinto e di lattuga,
> Che per la smania d' eternarsi asciuga
> Tasche e Maremme.
>
> "Co' tribunali e co' catasti annaspa,
> E benchè snervi i popoli col sonno,
> Quando si sogna d' imitare il nonno
> Qualcosa raspa." *

---

* "The Tuscan Morpheus gently moves along,
With poppies and with lettuce garlands crowned,
Eager for immortality he drains
Our pockets and the Marshes.

"In courts of law and taxes feels his way,
And whilst in sleep he drowns his people's sense,
Whene'er he dreams to imitate his grandsire
He rasps the crust."

CHRONOLOGY.

	A.D.
Ademollo, Luigi	
Ammanati, Bartolommeo	1511—1592
Brunelleschi, Filippo	1379—1446
Cellini, Benvenuto	1500—1571
Cosimo I., Grand-Duke, began to reign	1537
Donatello	1386—1466
Eleanora of Toledo married to Cosimo I.	1539
Ferdinand III.	1790—1824
Francis II.	1737—1765
Giovan Bologna	1524—1608
Joanna of Austria	1565
Julius II., Pope	1505
Medici, Piero de'	1416—1463
Michael Angelo	1475—1564
Pietro Leopoldo, Grand-Duke	1765
Pitti, Luca	1395—1472
Tribolo	1485—1550

PUBLIC GALLERIES AND MUSEUMS OF FLORENCE.

THE ACADEMY.

First Room.

AT the corner of the Via Ricasoli and the Piazza di San Marco is the Accademia delle Belle Arti, once the Hospital of St. Matthew, which now contains the finest examples of early Florentine art.

The entrance-hall has four reliefs by Luca della Robbia: over the principal door is St. Augustine; facing it, the Madonna and Child, with St. Francis and St. Ursula; over the door to the right, the Resurrection; and opposite, the Virgin lowering her girdle to St. Thomas. Within the cloister, leading to the rooms for academical study, are various reliefs of the Robbia school, and statues by Tuscan artists. Among these are the models for Virtue trampling on Vice, and for the Rape of the Sabines, by Giovan Bologna; an unfinished torso for a figure of St. Matthew, by Michael Angelo; a colossal horse's head belonging to the antique group on Monte Cavallo, at Rome, and casts from the Boar and Dogs, of the Uffizi.

A corridor to the right of the entrance-hall is lined with casts of modern statues, and leads directly to the Library. Midway, a door to the left opens on a vast room, which formerly served as the Female Ward of the Hospital, but which is now the principal Picture Gallery :—

No. 1. The Life of Mary Magdalene: a curious example of early Italian art, retaining the conventional Byzantine type, which had been imported from Constantinople (the ancient Byzantium) through Venice.

No. 2. The Madonna Enthroned, by Cimabue: in many respects this picture resembles his more celebrated and better preserved painting in the Rucellai Chapel of Sta. Maria Novella. We find here little variety of expression or action: the heads lean either towards the right or left shoulder; but there is a certain majesty in the tranquil form of the Virgin becoming the Queen of Heaven, and Cimabue has given her more animation than in pictures of the Byzantine school; in the heads of the prophets below, the spectator is reminded that Cimabue was the master of Giotto. The unaffected earnestness with which the sacred subject is treated, gives this work a higher interest than it deserves for mere technical skill; Cavalcaselle observes, "that it may rank higher than that of the Rucellai as regards composition and the study of nature; but the old types are more obstinately maintained; and, above all, the colour has been so altered by time and restoring that the excellent qualities of Cimabue in this respect can hardly be traced any longer. Cimabue here gave the Virgin a more natural attitude and a less rotund head, but a weightier frame, stronger outlines, and a less careful execution than before. He characterized with a wild energy the two prophets in the centre niche, and gave them individuality and expression."*

No. 15 is another large altar-piece, painted by Cimabue's pupil, Giotto. Though not a favourable specimen of this great Florentine artist, it exhibits the progress made in a few years; there is a nearer approach to nature, and less of the old conventional type. The drawing is carefully studied; a feeling for beauty is shown in the head of the Virgin, as well as in some of the surrounding angels, and the Child is fuller and rounder in form; but the type throughout has less dignity, and is heavier than in earlier paintings; the Virgin's mantle is arranged in large massy forms, following the outline of the figure beneath. Giotto painted this picture for the Frati Umiliati of the Church of Ogni Santi.

No. 3. Santa Umiltà, the foundress of the convent which stood on the site now occupied by the Fortezza del Basso; the picture is by an unknown author, but of the Giottesque school, and represents various incidents in the life of the saint; it is cleverly composed, and tells the story well.

No. 4 to No. 13 are small panel pictures attributed to Giotto, representing the Life of St. Francis, which once adorned the presses of the sacristy of Sta. Croce; they are, however, supposed more probably to have been painted by Taddeo Gaddi; the reasons for this opinion are thus stated by Cavalcaselle: "It is evident that the compositions are Giotto's, and executed according to his maxims—that the attitudes, the action, are likewise his—that the subjects are,

---

* See "Crowe and Cavalcaselle," vol. i. p. 206.

in fact, more or less repetitions of the frescos of the upper Church of Assisi, but that the execution is sketchy, conventional and decorative—that the feeling of the great master is absent, whilst the heads, features, and extremities are of the false and ever-recurring forms peculiar to Taddeo in the Madonnas of 1334 and 1335, and the frescos of the Baroncelli family." The series includes the whole history of St. Francis, but it is not arranged in chronological order. They are as follows :—He abandons his father to consecrate himself to a religious life, under the protection of the Bishop of Assisi; the Dream of Pope Innocent III., in which St. Peter points to St. Francis supporting the falling church; St. Francis asking for the confirmation of his Order from the Pope; he ascends to Heaven in a car of fire; he appears to his martyred disciples; he receives the confirmation of his Order from Pope Honorius IV.; he holds the Infant Christ in his arms on Christmas-eve; he appears to his disciples in church, and shows them the stigmata, or marks of the nails on his own hands and feet; he receives the stigmata—a composition identical with Giotto's fresco of the same subject, lately discovered on the walls of the interior of Sta. Croce; his Death. Every variety of natural and appropriate movement and attitude is displayed in these little pictures.

No. 18 to No. 29. The Life of our Saviour, another series of panel pictures belonging to the sacristy of Sta. Croce, and likewise attributed to Giotto, but more probably the work of Taddeo Gaddi: these are in some respects inferior to the Life of St. Francis; they are harder in outline and less beautiful, if we except the Adoration of the Kings, and the Presentation in the Temple, which in treatment resembles the same subject by Andrea Pisano on the bronze gates of the Baptistery.*

No. 14. The Virgin appearing to St. Bernard, by an early unknown artist. It is clear in colour, and sweet and true in expression. The two heads behind St. Bernard, looking over him, are full of character and in excellent contrast.

No. 16. A damaged picture, by Giovanni da Milano, in which may be observed a closer attention to natural forms and power of expression, with further abandonment of conventional types; there is, however, exaggeration, amounting to caricature, in the heads of the Virgin and the Magdalene.

No. 17. The Presentation in the Temple, by Ambrogio Lorenzetti of Sienna. A feeble picture much repainted; but the architectural drawing and the perspective of the Temple are executed with great care and finish; restorations and varnish have, however, nearly obliterated all traces of the master's hand.†

No. 30. An Annunciation, by Lorenzo Monaco. The Virgin timidly shrinks back at the approach of the angel. Vasari describes this new and original treatment of the subject by Giotto in the Badia. The picture he alludes to, however, has long disappeared, with all Giotto's paintings in that church; but this Annunciation, which was removed from the Badia in 1812, so exactly corresponds with Vasari's description, that it is probably the same, although he has mistaken the author. The attitude of the Virgin is repeated in the picture by Lippo Memmi of Sienna, in the

---

* See "Crowe and Cavalcaselle," vol. i. p. 145.
† Ibid., vol. i. p. 310.

corridor of the Uffizi Gallery (No. 9). On each side of the Annunciation are pictures of saints—St. Catherine and St. Anthony, and St. Proculus and St. Francis. St. Proculus is not unlike the representation of a warrior saint in the picture, No. 14. The angel of the Annunciation with his wings of many colours, his hands folded on his breast, and a flame on his head, is very graceful.

No. 31. A large composition of many figures attributed to Taddeo Gaddi, the favourite pupil of Giotto, but more probably the work of Nicolò di Pietro Gerini, an artist of his school, who occasionally painted with Taddeo, but was greatly his inferior; the date of his last picture is 1401. This Entombment, as described by Cavalcaselle, "does not improve on acquaintance, being at first sight more pleasing than on closer examination. The draperies are overcharged with line and folds, and gay changing hues appear to have been preferred by a painter who can be no other than Gerini."[*]

No. 32. An interesting picture of the Adoration of the Kings, by Gentile da Fabriano, an Umbrian painter, born in the latter half of the fourteenth century, who exercised considerable influence on the school of early Venetian Art. His works have been compared with those of Fra Angelico, but Gentile used gold only to add ornament to his pictures, and not, as Fra Angelico, to suggest an idea of heavenly glory; he imitated embroidery and rich stuffs, thus destroying the poetry or illusion of his picture. Gentile's "masterpieces are only remarkable for their longing softness, their affectation of grace, their laborious fusion, and for a profuse ornamentation inherited from the Umbrian and

---

[*] See "Crowe and Cavalcaselle," vol. ii. pp. 21, 22.

Siennese schools; . . . . . the tenderness, and finish, and care," with which he, as well as Fra Angelico, prepared and used their materials, is one of his greatest merits.* Gentile was first employed in Bergamo and Venice, from whence he came to Florence in 1422. This picture was painted in 1423. The attempts at foreshortening, and the portrait-like character of the heads, as well as the multitude of figures, men, horses, dogs, birds, and apes, recall Paolo Uccello and the Pesellini; whilst the Umbrian tenderness of treatment, and Venetian rich colouring and love of ornament, indicate the various schools in which the artist had studied. The Holy Family is insipid, but the three kings are in natural attitudes, and have much beauty of expression.

No. 33. The Madonna and Child surrounded by Angels and Saints in Adoration, by Agnolo Gaddi, the son of Taddeo, and the pupil of Giovanni da Milano, from whom he derived a certain realistic tendency, or the endeavour to imitate nature closely, without selection; he sometimes even descended to caricature in his attempt to portray violent emotion; as Agnolo advanced in the knowledge and practice of his art, he ceased to follow his master in this respect, and even developed greater powers in composition than his father Taddeo:—"As a draughtsman he was free and bold, defining everything equally . . . . he frequently failed to define form truly, and, whilst the best of his figures are still below the standard of Giotto, certain forms are purposely and persistently false. The eyes are straight and narrow, and the nose expanded flatly at the end, and the mouths generally droop at the corners. . . . . In the draw-

---

* See "Crowe and Cavalcaselle," vol. ii. pp. 96—101.

ings of hands and feet he bestowed more care, but he evidently never possessed the clear comprehension of the nature of the forms he depicted. His hands are defective and coarse; the fingers are short, broken and angular at the joints, and mechanically executed. . . . . As a colourist Angelo was bold. His tones are bright, clear, light, and transparent, and he shows a feeling for the true nature of harmonies. His idea of relief was greater than that of Taddeo." This picture was painted for the Church of San Pancrazio, in Florence. "The Virgin has a vulgar face, but a graceful action; the draperies are massive and fine." *

No. 34. A Deposition, by Fra Angelico, executed with the utmost care and finish. The brilliancy of the colour, without shade or chiaroscuro, becomes flat and gaudy in a picture of these dimensions, and is not as well adapted for the representation of an earthly scene, as when meant to symbolize celestial purity. The worshipping angels in the sky are here not devoid of grimace. The body of the Saviour is covered with dark lines, to denote the strokes of the rod with which he had been scourged, and is feeble in drawing and colour; the group of females on the left is the most interesting part of this picture, especially the woman without a glory, dressed in black and with a white veil, who holds one end of the sheet in which the body of the Saviour is to lie. The best male heads are, a man in a black cap in the centre, evidently a portrait; Nicodemus, standing below; and the two who are detaching the body from the cross. St. John is a very graceful figure, and is full of feeling. The hands are all delicately executed. The miniatures of saints, set in

---

* See "Crowe and Cavalcaselle," vol. i. pp. 463—473.

the frame of this picture, are admirable both in expression and colour. Those above are by Lorenzo Monaco, but not equal to the rest by Fra Angelico. It is with some hesitation we venture to differ in our estimation of this picture from so high an authority as Cavalcaselle, who writes:—
"Nothing can be better than the nude in its fleshy, flexible forms, which show the scars of the previous flagellation, nothing truer than the movement. The group to the right is remarkable; the heads revealing a point of contact between Angelico and the works of Masolino di Castiglione, as regards character and drawing; and the landscape, betraying the usual defects of perspective. Yet composition, design, and colour combine to create the harmony, which was the great gift of Fra Giovanni."

No. 35. An altar-piece, painted for the Church of Sta. Felice, in Florence, by Spinello of Arezzo, assisted by Nicolò Gerini, the author of the Entombment, No. 31, and by his son, Lorenzo di Nicolò Gerini. The Coronation of the Virgin is by Lorenzo, and is not unlike a picture by an unknown artist in the Uffizi Gallery (No. 15), which has been attributed to Spinello. The compartment to the right is by Nicolò, and represents St. Peter, St. John the Evangelist, St. James, and St. Benedict. That to the left is by Spinello; St. John the Baptist, St. Matthew, Sta. Felicità, and St. Andrew; they are grand and dignified figures, especially that of St. Felicità. Below are half-length figures of St. Jerome and St. Peter; St. Luke and St. Thaddeus; St. James the Less and St. Philip; St. Simon and St. Bartholomew; St. Thomas and St. Paul; St. Gregory and St. Lawrence. At the base of the central panel are words to this effect—This picture was painted for the chapter of the Convent of Sta. Felicita, and (paid for) by money of the said convent in the time of the Abbess Lorenza de Mossi (Mozzi), in the year of our Lord, 1401. Cavalcaselle observes:—" But for this record it would be difficult to assign to each of these painters his share in the entire work. That of Spinello is undoubtedly beneath his usual powers, and in harmony with the third-rate talent exhibited by Lorenzo and Nicolò." *

No. 36. A Madonna and Child, by Masaccio; above, St. Anna and Angels: probably an early picture by the master, painted for the Church of St. Ambrogio. Masaccio was apt to neglect minute details, and to aim principally at life and movement; his figures were sketched in rapidly. This picture is an imperfect specimen of the master.

No. 37. St. Jerome, attributed to Andrea Castagno, but more probably by Filippino Lippi; the two accompanying pictures, Mary Magdalene and St. John the Baptist, which have all the defects and none of the merits of Andrea, are evidently by an inferior hand.

No. 40. A Madonna and Child, by Fra Filippo Lippi, with little to recommend it, except the infantine grace of the child.

No. 41. The Coronation of the Virgin, an important picture by the same master. Fra Filippo's own portrait, as a friar of the Carmine, is on the right; he wears a red scarf, and his hands are joined in prayer as he ascends the steps of the celestial temple, in which are assembled angelic beings who witness the coronation of the Virgin, represented as a young and modest girl, not daring to raise her eyes

---

* See "Crowe and Cavalcaselle," vol. ii. p. 18.

to the Eternal, who is crowning her, but looking towards one of the slender angels who support the band or scroll that descends from the Saviour. Groups of angels crowned with roses, among whom are scattered aged saints, sing hymns on either side of the throne; below them, and nearer the spectator, are similar groups and small children. The type is the same throughout; heavy-featured, round faces, with light hair, but they have the charm of a sweet simplicity united with grave earnestness of demeanour, and their attitudes are graceful. The draperies are drawn and composed with care and judgment. An aged monk in white, in the foreground to the left of St. Anthony, has a fine portrait-like head. The picture has been much damaged, and has been repaired in most parts.*

The predella below, No. 42, belonged to the Barbadori altar-piece, which was executed for the Church of Santo Spirito, and is now in the Louvre at Paris; the colour of this predella has been injured by time, but it has far greater claim to admiration than the picture above. It was painted when Fra Filippo was only twenty-six years of age; and as the Barbadori picture is said to be one of the greatest efforts of his genius, so this predella has a refinement of feeling and grandeur of composition which we miss in the large picture, No. 41. The Annunciation is treated in a novel manner. The angel kneels gracefully, the curve of his wings follows the inclination of his body, and forms an arch over his head: he presents a lighted candle to the Virgin, whose dignified and noble presence is unlike the simple peasant girl the painter usually represents her.

---

* See "Crowe and Cavalcaselle," vol. ii. p. 327.

No. 43. The Baptism of Christ, by Andrea Verocchio. The aërial distance, the sky, and landscape, are very beautiful. The outline of the figures is extremely fine, though hard, and the anatomy in that of the Baptist is too much defined; this, probably, is occasioned by the unfinished state in which Verocchio left the picture. The features of the Baptist, as well as of the Saviour, are rather coarse and vulgar, but the expression noble; the soft and delicate beauty of the kneeling angels is due to Leonardo da Vinci, the pupil of Verocchio, who was so disgusted at his own inferiority that he is said from that time forth to have renounced painting.

No. 44. St. Jerome kneeling in Prayer, attributed to Fra Filippo, but more probably by his son, Filippino Lippi, in his decline.*

No. 46. A very fine picture by Sandro Botticelli, painted at the period when his works display the influence of the Pollaioli. The hands of the Virgin, especially her left, are executed with the utmost truth and finish; the child is most lovely and graceful, though both mother and child have the angular movements characteristic of Botticelli. St. Cosimo and St. Damian kneel in the foreground; the first turns to the spectator, the last looks up at the Virgin; both are noble heads. St. Francis, who is behind St. Catherine, is extremely fine; the other saints are more remarkable for the beauty of their draperies than their persons. The colour is full and powerful.

The predella below, No. 48, is by the younger Pesellino, and represents the Birth of the Saviour, the Martyrdom of

---

* See "Crowe and Cavalcaselle," vol. ii. p. 347, *note*.

St. Cosimo and St. Damian, and St. Anthony of Padua discovering the heart of a dead usurer in his money chest; this last is the finest of the three compartments. According to Cavalcaselle—"a gentle and natural animation pervades all the figures. The females on the foreground are in good proportions, and the whole is drawn and executed with neatness, precision, and freshness, and without vulgarity."

No. 47. The Coronation of the Virgin, one of Botticelli's finest works. Angels, hand in hand, dance in a circle round the glory which surrounds her; they are light and graceful, with floating hair, and draperies which quiver in many folds in the breezy air—one angel especially, clothed in crimson, bending forwards as if preparing to join in the movement, is most lovely. Of the four saints below, St. John the Evangelist, holding his Gospel in one hand and raising the other in ecstasy, is in an awkward attitude; St. Augustine, who writes in a book, is very grand; the two others are St. Jerome and St. Eloy or St. Lo. The extremities are admirably drawn. No. 49, the predella to this picture, is also by Sandro Botticelli. Beginning at the left hand, St. John the Evangelist is seated on the island of Patmos; St. Augustine in his study; St. Jerome in the Wilderness; and last, and finest, St. Lo as a blacksmith, shoeing the leg he has cut off from a white horse beside him, whilst Satan, disguised as a lovely female, stands by, watching the operation.

No. 50. The Visits of the Shepherds and the Magi, by Domenico Ghirlandaio, a highly finished picture. The Virgin is especially beautiful; she kneels with a sweet smile: her hands joined as in prayer, and her whole soul absorbed in the contemplation of her child, who lies on the hem of his mother's garment, with his finger to his lips; the traditional goldfinch, the scarlet of whose head is the symbol of sacrifice, stands perched of a stone near. A group of peasants, the shepherds of sacred story, one of whom carries a lamb, converse together; Joseph shades his eyes from the light, and looks up at the angel who is descending with the good tidings to another group of shepherds, who are seen on a distant hill tending their flocks. A gay procession of riders, every horseman attended by his *Fante*, or footman, wind along the road below, and pass through a triumphal arch dedicated to Pompey the Great; these are the Magi, or Kings from the East. Near the Holy Family, the ox and ass drink from a sarcophagus, on which is an inscription to another Pompey, an augur. The landscape is very beautiful; the river, town, the church, with a spire, and the pale, quiet colour throughout the background, resembles that in Ghirlandaio's equally fine picture of the same subject in the Church of the Innocenti.

No. 51. An Adoration of the Shepherds, by Lorenzo Credi; though the glazes have been injured, which occasions some crudeness, the warm under-tint of brown prevents any real harshness in the clear, pure colour, and gives a delicious harmony to the whole; the devotional and animated expression of the angels and shepherds, the graceful attitudes, delicately drawn hands and refined type of the heads, as well as of the figures, betray the influence of Leonardo da Vinci. The shepherd carrying the lamb on his arm is especially beautiful; he stands in a natural and easy attitude of repose, and the tender expression of his countenance corresponds with the action symbolical of Him "who gathers the lambs with His arm, and carries them in His bosom."

No. 52, A Madonna and Saints, by Sandro Botticelli; the upper part of this picture, according to Cavalcaselle, is a modern addition by Veracini.*

No. 53. Christ in Prayer in the Garden of Gethsemane, by Pietro Perugino; one of the loveliest compositions of the Umbrian School, and painted for the Gesuati of this city, who had their monastery beyond the Porta Pinti, where they were celebrated for their manufacture of coloured glass. Perugino worked much for the friars during his residence in Florence, from 1492 to 1499. The sleeping St. John, in this picture, is of a beauty so akin to the compositions of Raffaelle, that it is difficult not to assign it to the pupil rather than the master; but no such doubt exists in the mind of the modern critic, who thus describes the picture: "One sees how well Perugino has placed the Redeemer on an elevation, kneeling and praying, whilst an angel brings the cup. The three apostles lie sleeping on the foreground, as Iscariot, in the distance, leads the soldiers to the capture. With much thought in the composition, and much freshness in the types, the picture gains an additional charm from the hour with which Perugino marks the time of action. The sun has just set, and the strong reflection still rests on the Saviour and apostles, who detach themselves in gloom from the pale horizon of the sky. In this twilight the forms are finely brought out by well-modelled relief." †

No. 54. A Trinità, by Luca Signorelli of Cortona, in his grand style. The Virgin's head and throat are beautifully modelled; the archangel Michael weighing human souls in the balance is noble in composition and drawing.

---

* See "Crowe and Cavalcaselle," vol. ii. p. 424.
† Ibid, vol. iii. p. 200.

St. Anastasius is a splendid head, and the attitude of the hands, as well as those of St. Augustine, is natural and easy. The picture is painted in simple full colour: the angel Gabriel is, however, a heavy figure, and inferior to the rest of the composition.

No. 55. An Assumption of the Virgin, by Perugino: a choir of angels play on different musical instruments; below are the Cardinal San Bernardo dei Uberti, San Giovanni Gualberto, St. Benedict, and the archangel Michael. The artist has inscribed his name below, with the date, A.D. MCCCCC. The gorgeous and spotty colouring is disagreeable at first sight, but the picture grows on the spectator as the wonderful beauty and life in the countenances reveal themselves, especially those of St. Benedict and Giovanni Gualberto; the hands are executed with the utmost finish, and the landscape is very lovely, fading away in the light horizon. The Virgin, gazing upwards, is one of Perugino's finest conceptions of the subject. The picture was painted for the monks of Vallombrosa, when Perugino executed the frescos in the Sala del Cambio, at Perugia; and a few years later than the picture of Christ in the Garden of Gethsemane.

No. 56. The Crucifixion—the Virgin and St. Jerome on either side of the cross; likewise by Perugino. The sun has set, and to enhance the solemnity of the hour a low tone of colour pervades the picture. The figures are executed somewhat carelessly. The Madonna is the same which Perugino painted in his masterpiece, the Crucifixion of Sta. Maddalena de' Pazzi, only inferior in expression.*

---

* Passavant observes on this picture, "They are on the whole beautiful figures, which in many respects recall those in the Sala del

No. 57. A Descent from the Cross, by Perugino and Filippino Lippi, painted for the SS. Annunziata. Filippino had only finished the upper half of the picture when he died, in 1514, and Perugino was requested to finish it. The earnest upward gaze of the kneeling Magdalene is very beautiful, as well as Filippino's work, the head of Christ, and the old man above, disengaging the body from the cross.

No. 58. An Entombment, by the same artist. St. John, Mary Magdalene, and the Saviour, are the most beautiful parts of the picture, which was executed for the Gesuati, beyond the Porta Pinti, and transferred to the convent of the Calza during the siege of Florence.

Nos. 59, 62, and 63 belong to an altar-piece on panel, painted by Andrea del Sarto for the Church of the Hermitage, at Vallombrosa, in 1528. No. 59. Four Saints, life size—St. Michael; St. John the Baptist; San Giovanni Gualberto, the founder of the Vallombrosian Monastery; and Cardinal Bernardo degli Uberti. The head and attitude of St. John, with his arm raised in the act of preaching, is very grand; the lines of composition are flowing, and there is great breadth of chiaroscuro, and a deep rich colour, low in tone, and in harmony with the solemn and majestic figures composing the picture. The two charming little arch boy angels of No. 62 are full of life and vivacity. No. 63 is the Predella for this altar-piece. Breadth and harmony of chiaroscuro and colour, the free,

---

Cambio (of Perugia); but we discover the first trace of that hasty treatment which unfortunately always acts disadvantageously in his later works." See Passavant, "Rafael von Urbino," vol. i. p. 496.

bold dash of the pencil, and aim at effect rather than finish, mark the later Florentine school, distinguished from the careful drawing and attention to detail of earlier masters. St. Michael, as usual, is seen weighing human souls, entirely indifferent to the touch of the expectant demon by his side. San Giovanni Gualberto, passing unscathed through the fire, is a very grand composition; and the decapitation of John the Baptist is equally fine. The last compartment, likewise very admirable, represents Cardinal Bernardo degli Uberti. The two circular pictures of Madonnas on each side of the boy angels, No. 64, are by Fra Bartolommeo, and are sketched without outline.

No. 61. A fresco by Andrea del Sarto—Christ seated on his tomb, life size; a noble figure, grand in drawing and in position; the relaxation of all the limbs, and the prostration of extreme debility, is given very finely; the colour is soft and transparent.

No. 65. The Virgin enthroned, attributed to Fra Bartolommeo. The infant Christ exchanges his heart with that of St. Catherine; he stands beside his mother, and is singularly graceful and beautiful in form and action. This is, however, the repetition of a picture sent to France, and is probably the work of Bartolommeo's pupil, Fra Paolino.

No. 66. The Virgin and Child appearing to St. Bernard, by Fra Bartolommeo. St. Bernard, on his knees, is finely composed and executed; the head is full of deep feeling, the drapery falling in majestic folds, and drawn with care and precision. The rest of the picture is soft and feeble, from the absence of the last glazes or transparent colours, but its merits in composition, grace, and elegance are worthy of high estimation.*

No. 67. The Resurrection, by Raffaellino del Garbo, the pupil of Fillippino Lippi, who, as described by Cavalcaselle, has "affectation in forms, mannerism in drawing, and flatness," but who has also the merit, especially in some of his Madonnas and Saints, of grace, correctness, and clear, brilliant colour. This picture is not a good specimen of the master, either in composition or colour. Behind it is a small fresco in *terra verde*, by Andrea del Sarto, painted when this room was an hospital for women.

No. 68. The body of the Saviour supported on the knees of his Mother; Mary Magdalene, St. John, St. Dominick with another friar, designed by Fra Bartolommeo and coloured by Fra Paolino. The arms and hands of the Christ are very finely drawn.

No. 69. San Vincenzio, by Fra Bartolommeo, executed in 1516, when he painted the San Marco, now in the Palazzo dei Pitti; very fine in chiaroscuro and colour, as well as composition.

No. 70. A feeble representation of the Trinity, by Mariotto Albertinelli, the friend of Fra Bartolommeo. The outline and general effect of the figures have been injured by fresh gilding in the background.

No. 72. Also painted by Albertinelli for the Monastery of St. Julian, representing the Madonna enthroned, with St. Dominick, St. Nicholas, St. Julian, and St. Jerome. "The figures are firm and well proportioned; the chiaroscuro well defined, the colour a little bold."†

---

* See "Crowe and Cavalcaselle," vol. iii. p. 443.
† Ibid, vol. iii. p. 488 and *note*.

No. 73. An Annunciation, painted by Mariotto Albertinelli for the company of St. Zenobius, in 1510, and thus described by Cavalcaselle:—" In order to suit this subject for its position, he placed the panel on the altar, and studied the perspective as well as the play of light and shade on the spot; and as he had some peculiar notions as to the propriety of combining marked relief with fusion, he tried a number of experiments with little satisfaction to himself. The result, as we now see it, was an excessive lucidity of colour, obtained by a copious use of strong varnish in the oils, and a substance at once viscous, flowing, and difficult to model. Time dealt severely with this example, and what it has spared has suffered from restoring; but besides, Mariotto gave evidence of an extravagant fancy in the confused arrangement and strange dresses of the angels surrounding the apparitions of the Eternal: thus casting into the shade the finer points made in the fair types of the Virgin and angel. The subsequent removal to the gallery, where the effect of a low centre of vision is negatived by hanging below the line, combines such other disadvantages as to give Mariotto's work an unfavourable aspect."*

No. 75. The Virgin in Glory, with Saints, by Françesco Granacci, painted at the same period with his picture of the Virgin and St. Thomas in the Uffizi Gallery. The Madonna is very dignified, and is surrounded by four beautiful angels. The saints below are St. Catherine, St. Bernard, St. Giovanni Gualberto, and St. George; they are earnest and noble in expression, but the picture has been damaged, and is gaudy in colour.

---

* See "Crowe and Cavalcaselle," vol. iii. pp. 487, 488.

No. 78 to 82 are heads in fresco, by Fra Bartolommeo and his scholars, of which the finest are St. Peter Martyr and a monk.

The remaining pictures in this room are not of sufficient interest to detain the visitor.

Second Room.

Three rooms of this gallery are kept closed, but admittance is obtained by application at the door.

First in the catalogue, as well as in age, is a Coronation of the Virgin, attributed to Ugolino, of Sienna. The dates of this artist's birth and death are uncertain, and nothing is positively known of him, except that he lived early in the fourteenth century, and that, although a native of Sienna, he painted principally in Florence, where he executed the miraculous picture of the Virgin for Or San Michele, which has long since disappeared. The only other painting which can, with any degree of certainty, be assigned to Ugolino, is a fragment of an altar-piece for Sta. Croce, which was sold to England. The picture belonging to the Academy is of doubtful authenticity, and has been given to a contemporary of the Gaddi's, half a century later than Ugolino. Another early painter, Luca Bonaventura Berlinghieri, has a picture here, No. 28, a Crucifixion. Berlinghieri's name is known less as an artist than from having assisted in a treaty between Luca and Pisa in 1228. A portrait by him of his contemporary, St. Francis of Assisi, which exists at Pescia, was once assigned to Margheritone or Arezzo, whose painted Crucifix is in Sta. Croce.

No. 9. A picture of the fourteenth century by an unknown

artist; the predella is by a superior hand; the life of the Virgin is well told, and her marriage is treated in an original manner; she stands under the porch of the Temple to receive the ring from Joseph.

There are several pictures in this room by the Bicci, both Lorenzo and Neri, marking the decline of the Giottesque school. Neri's best production is, No. 41, a Madonna and Child, with St. Catherine, St. Agnes, Sta. Lucia, and St. Margherita. In the lower part of this picture is a Crucifixion and two angels; in the predella, the dead Saviour mourned over by the Virgin and the Disciples; also St. Andrew, St. James, St. Jerome, St. Anthony with his pig, St. Augustine, and another Bishop.

No. 35, a picture in three compartments, by Spinello of Arezzo. The Virgin and Child are in the centre; the Child allows a goldfinch to peck his finger; four angels are in adoration. On one side are St. Paulinus and St. John the Baptist; on the other, St. Andrew and St. Matthew, who dips his finger in the ink bottle brought him by an angel. The head of the Virgin is sweet, and she bends gracefully. Spinello painted this picture in 1391.

No. 34. A curious painting by an unknown artist, representing the marriage of Bocaccio Adimari and Lisa Ricasoli, in 1420. The family of the Adimari, whose palaces occupied a considerable part of the present Via Calzaioli, towards the Piazza del Battisterio, were then at the height of their power, and one Alemanno, probably the uncle of the bridegroom, was Cardinal and Archbishop of Pisa: he died in 1422. The lady was of no less illustrious parentage; her family settled in Florence about 1306; several of them had served under the Emperors Frederick Barbarossa, Henry VI., and Otho IV. The costumes of the period are here exhibited; the procession is moving from the Loggia dei Adimari towards the Cathedral, which is represented as a red brick building, with a belfry seen above the awning. Sta. Maria del Fiore was not finished earlier than 1419, and we may therefore suppose it possible that this marriage may have taken place a few years sooner than the date assigned, for the artist appears to have given a faithful representation of the surrounding buildings, viz., the Baptistery, before which ladies are seated to witness the show, and a gate beyond, probably the postern of the Spadai, or sword-makers. A carpet is spread over the old pavement of Florence; beneath the Loggia, servants are carrying golden dishes for the banquet, and musicians are seated near; one plays the trombone, the rest are the trumpeters of the Republic, and have banners with the red lily of Florence attached to their trumpets.

No. 24. An Allegory of Spring, one of Sandro Botticelli's most celebrated works. It was painted for Cosimo de' Medici's Villa of Castello, near Florence, at the same time with the Venus, now in the corridor of the Uffizi Gallery.* Both the subjects, and their treatment, are in accordance with the taste of the period, when Greek classics were in fashion, although Greek art was imperfectly understood. The influence of Fra Filippo Lippi may be traced in Botticelli's slender figures, and the influence of the Pollaioli in his love of ornament.† In the midst of a grove, Spring is seen attired in a white garment, sprinkled over with bunches of

---

* See Uffizi Gallery Corridor.
† See "Crowe and Cavalcaselle," vol. ii. p. 418; "Vasari," vol. v. p. 113.

flowers. She holds a bow in one hand, and raises her dress with the other to receive the flowers poured into it from the lips of a nymph, who flies from a genius of the wood. These two last figures resemble the Zephyrus and Aurora in the picture of Venus rising from the Sea. In the midst of the grove, Venus stands clothed in a white dress, over which is thrown a red mantle, lined with blue and gold. Botticelli has been more successful in producing his idea of beauty in the goddess than in Spring. She stands gracefully, with her head slightly bent; Cupid hovers above, and aims his arrow at the Graces, who dance in a circle, their hands entwined, whilst gazing at a youth wearing the cap of Mercury and gathering the roses above his head. The Graces are draped in white, and their movements appear slow and languid. The colour of this picture has been much damaged.

Nos. 19 and 20 are by Fra Angelico; the Madonna and Child with Saints. Though both pictures are faded, the charm of the master remains in that peculiarly grave dignity and grace which he imparts to all his figures; the hands are delicately drawn: an Angel in No. 20, to the right of the spectator, is especially lovely: No. 22 is another but feebler production by Fra Angelico.

No. 16. A Visitation of Elizabeth to Mary, by Giacomo Pacchiarotti, of Sienna, born in 1474. He appears, according to Vasari, to have been much esteemed in his native city, though almost all the numerous pictures he executed have long since disappeared. He joined in revolutionary disturbances within Sienna, and was consequently banished. This picture is one of three, which are all that remain to show his powers as an artist. "Though light and washy in colour,"* and somewhat insipid, there is a pleasing simplicity in the composition: a triumphal arch, and long paved way form the background, and the Holy Spirit as a dove is hovering in the clear blue sky above the principal group.

Returning to No. 6, a Crucifixion with a kneeling Magdalene, is attributed to Andrea del Castagno, but Cavalcaselle considers it to have been painted by Luca Signorelli, and used as a church standard: it is very fine, though the attitude of the Magdalene is rather theatrical.

No. 17. A Madonna and Child with Saints, by Domenico Ghirlandaio, is the finest picture in this room. It is powerful in drawing and expression, and painted in full bright colours. The head of the Virgin is very lovely. The four splendid figures of saints are—St. Thomas Aquinas, St. Denis the Areopagite; St. Clement, who was the third Bishop of Rome, and therefore represented as Pope!† and St. Dominick. St. Thomas, one of the greatest theologians of the Roman Catholic Church, has a countenance expressive of conscious power; acute, yet dignified: he was descended from the sister of Frederick Barbarossa, who married a Count of Aquino. Their grandson was educated in the schools of the Benedictine friars of Monte Cassino, but he took the Dominican habit in Naples. He was remarkable for self-command, for his calm deportment, and for his humility as well as learning; he refused all Church preferment, and died in 1274, in a Cistercian abbey at Fossa Nova, near Rome, on his way to Lyons, to complain

---

* See "Crowe and Cavalcaselle," vol. iii. p. 378.
† See Mrs. Jameson's "Legendary Art," p. 371.

against Charles of Anjou.* St. Denis is here represented with a red collar round his neck, to signify his death by decapitation; he stands on the other side of the Virgin; he has been confounded with Dionysius the Areopagite, or judge of the Areopagus, at Athens. St. Denis was sent to France, by Pope Clement, to preach the Gospel, and was beheaded during the persecution under Trajan. He is said to have risen after his execution, and, carrying his own head in his arms, to have walked two miles, accompanied by angels singing, until he reached a hill outside Paris, since known as Mont-Martre, where St. Denis and his fellow-martyrs were buried. The body of the saint was afterwards transferred to the Abbey, which bears his name. St. Dominick, who is next to St. Thomas Aquinas, has an earnest, noble countenance; he looks back at the spectator.

In the predella below are scenes from the lives of these holy personages. One of the loveliest represents the Legend of St. Clement. Condemned to banishment during the persecution by Trajan, he was obliged, with other Christian prisoners, to break stones: they were all suffering from thirst, when St. Clement knelt down and prayed, upon which a lamb appeared to him, standing on a rising ground; the vision was unseen by the saint's companions in misfortune, but on their digging where he directed them, a stream of water gushed forth. The contrast between the calm yet fervent expression of St. Clement, and the indifference of the other captives, who are busily at work, is admirably given. Next the Legend of St. Clement is an

---

* See Mrs. Jameson's "Monastic Orders," p. 392.

anecdote relating to St. Thomas Aquinas: he was reading aloud to the brethren in the Refectory of the Convent, when the Superior corrected his pronunciation; St. Thomas meekly acquiesced, although he knew himself to have been in the right; only observing afterwards, "the pronunciation of a word is of small importance, but humility and obedience are of the greatest." The saint is represented seated; he wears a white dress, and has a beautiful expression of mingled dignity and resignation. The centre compartment of this predella has the Entombment of the Saviour; beyond, is the Legend of St. Dominick. On Ash-Wednesday, in the year 1218, Dominick, with Cardinal Stefano di Fossa Nova, was in the Chapter-house of the Convent of St. Sixtus, in Rome, when news was brought that the Cardinal's nephew had been thrown from his horse and killed. The body was carried into the Chapter-house, where the prayers of St. Dominick restored the youth to life. The last scene in the predella represents the execution of St. Denis, who is walking off with his own head.

No. 36. A Crucifixion, by Antonio del Ceraiolo, a pupil of Lorenzo Credi. The devotional expression of the countenance of St. Francis is fine. Darkness spreads over the sky, and only a streak of light is visible on the horizon. The landscape has a green tone throughout. The painter belonged to the latter half of the fifteenth and the beginning of the sixteenth century.

Beyond this room are two of smaller size, but containing some of the greatest treasures of the collection.

No. 1 comprises a series of small pictures intended for a predella to an altar-piece, by Luca Signorelli; they represent the Last Supper, the Garden of Gethsemane,

and the Flagellation, and are late works of the master,
treated with freedom and great power, though slight and
sketchy.

A predella by Neri de' Bicci follows.

From No. 22 to No. 29 are pictures by Françesco
Granacci, the pupil of Domenico Ghirlandaio, and the
friend and admirer of Michael Angelo and Raffaelle. These
pictures represent the life and martyrdom of St. Apollonia.
The figures are too tall and slender, but nevertheless they
have grace, movement, and dramatic appropriateness; the
saint herself is very lovely.*

No. 9. Two Angels, attributed to Granacci.

No. 13. A Holy Family, by Lorenzo Credi, executed
for the Church of SS. Annunziata, and painted in the clear,
hard colour peculiar to the artist. The child is puffy and
heavy, as are also the forms of that still more original artist,
Fra Filippo Lippi, to whom is attributed the Holy Family,
No. 12, next that of Credi. This defect does not, however,
exist in the picture. No. 26, also in Lippi's early style, when
he was still under the influence of Fra Angelico.† The
Virgin kneels in adoration of the infant Saviour; the Holy
Spirit descends, and two hands above are typical of the
Creator, from whom the Dove has flown. St. John the
Baptist as a boy is seen to the right, pointing to the Christ,
and looking back, as if calling others to follow; to the left
is a Camaldoline monk. The wilderness, represented by
rocks, trees, and rivers, covers the whole background, leaving no space for sky. The Madonna has the high forehead,

---

* See "Crowe and Cavalcaselle," vol. iii. p. 539.
† Ibid., vol. ii. p. 322.

the pale delicate colour, and serious, yet pure, innocent and girlish expression usual with the representations of the Mother of the Saviour in the religious school of Florentine artists; two angels kneel above.

No. 47 and No. 48, are also by Lippi; both interesting pictures, especially that of the Annunciation; St. Anthony is hard and defective in drawing, especially in the hands and feet.

No. 25 is a damaged, though very interesting picture, by Sandro Botticelli, of Tobias led by the angel Gabriel; though the forms are angular, the movements are free, and the composition grand.

The most important works in the room are by Fra Angelico. No. 11 to No. 24 include two series of small panel pictures, principally by this master, which once adorned the doors of the cupboards containing the sacred plate in the monastery of SS. Annunziata. The subjects are all taken from the life of the Saviour, except one mystical representation of the Wheel in the vision of the prophet Ezekiel. These pictures were executed by order of Piero de' Medici, the son of Cosimo, Pater Patriæ, about 1433. The animation and dramatic power, as well as traditional type, in these small compositions, recall the Giottesque school, whilst there is a superior refinement, beauty, and tenderness, with greater vigour than usually characterizes Fra Angelico. In the Visit of the Magi, the Virgin is one of his purest and most lovely conceptions of the Mother of the Saviour. The Worship of the Shepherds, the Presentation in the Temple —St. Anna seen on one side—the Flight into Egypt, the Raising of Lazarus—the treatment of which is peculiarly Giottesque—the Last Supper, which, though not supposed to be by Angelico, is represented in an original and beautiful manner: these are among the best. In the panel where the Saviour bears his cross to Calvary, his mother is pushed back by the Roman soldiers, who bear on their cloaks the scorpion, the sign of the Gentiles.

No. 19, a predella by Fra Angelico, containing six scenes from the lives of St. Cosimo and St. Damian; the subject was chosen in compliment to the artist's patrons, the Medici; this was also painted for the SS. Annunziata.

No. 20, a Madonna with the Child clothed, standing on her knee, by Fra Angelico.

No. 37 and No. 38 are miniatures by the same painter, representing the Crucifixion, and Christ rising from the tomb; in the background are the instruments of the Passion; the kiss of Judas; the ear of the high priest's servant, &c.

The gem of this collection is the Last Judgment, by Fra Angelico—No. 41. Every figure in this wonderful picture is in itself a perfectly beautiful miniature, yet each necessary to the rest, and forming, as a whole, a most harmonious and lovely composition. A deep blue sky, gradually fading to a thin, white horizon, composes the background, and a double line of tombs divides the lower part of the picture. The Saviour above is feebly imagined and coldly executed; he is seated in glory, and turns the back of his left hand to the condemned, whilst extending towards the blest the open palm of his right, in which the wound is still perceptible. Around the Vescica Pisces in which he is seated, are fiery seraphim; lovely infant heads with wings. Beyond them is a garland of still more angelic beings, some of whom wear the "helmet of righteousness," and the "whole armour of God." Near these the Virgin is seated in a robe of silver, embroidered in gold; and, with her arms crossed on her bosom, she bends meekly towards her Son. Opposite her is St. John the Baptist, his hands clasped reverentially. On either side are patriarchs, prophets, and saints, seated in a half circle; St. Dominick concluding that on the right; St. Francis on the left. In the centre St. Michael bears the cross on his shoulder, whilst attendant angels arouse the dead by the sound of the trumpet.

The condemned on the right of the spectator are hurried to torments by demons; some stop their ears, others gnaw their own hands, and this part of the picture, as well as that still further on to the right, representing every degree of physical torture, and ending with that inflicted by Lucifer himself, is in accordance with the traditions of an ignorant and barbarous age, and which, though immortalised by Dante, would be simply disgusting, if it was not also ludicrous. But no genius save that of Fra Angelico could have painted the happiness of the blessed with such truth of expression, nor have described every variety of emotion which we may suppose possible at such a moment. Some look up with grateful love to the Saviour; others embrace one another, or are embraced by their guardian angels; one, overcome with joy and wonder at the glorious vision opening before him, can advance no farther, but kneels, with eyes entranced, fixed on the gates of Paradise, to which the celestial being at his side points the way. Angels crowned with roses, and with glittering wings, move in a mystic dance amidst flowers, whilst others float onwards in a stream of golden light, and enter the Heavenly Jerusalem.

Carlo Dolce has painted an ideal portrait of Fra Angelico,

No. 27; a good picture, but seen to disadvantage beside the powerful head of Girolamo Savonarola, represented as Peter Martyr, by Fra Bartolommeo. Though the features are plain, the sweet, patient, and devout expression of the eye and mouth is singularly beautiful; and whether this picture be a genuine portrait or an imaginary likeness, it conveys a true idea of the character belonging to this real martyr to his faith.

No. 39 and No. 42 are miniatures by Sandro Botticelli; the first represents scenes taken from the life of St. Augustine; the second, Herodias with the head of John the Baptist in a charger, and Christ rising from the Tomb.

Two splendid heads of Vallombrosian monks, seen in profile, are attributed to Perugino, but are more probably by Raffaelle. That turning to the right is a portrait of Don Blasio, General of the Order; the other Don Balthasar, Abbot of Vallombrosa. Raffaelle may have painted these pictures when visiting Vallombrosa on his way from Urbino to Florence. The heads are sharply defined on a dark background, and modelled with the utmost care in good relief; every feature, including the ears, is drawn with individuality; and yet this close attention to exact form is kept duly subordinate, or made to assist the higher aim of the artist in truth of expression. Light, shade, and colour, have here each their relative importance. The lovely Madonna del Cardellino, now in the Tribune of the Uffizi Gallery, is said to have been painted for this Abbot of Vallombrosa.

Beyond the room containing these pictures is a small collection of drawings, or cartoons, by eminent painters. The Apostles Peter and Paul, by Fra Bartolommeo, are the original designs for paintings now in the Quirinal, at Rome.

No. 8 and No. 9. Mary Magdalene and Christ appearing to the Marys, by the same master.

No. 18, a Holy Family, and No. 23, St. Dominick, also by Fra Bartolommeo.

No. 5. A Virgin and Child, attributed, with great probability, to Raffaelle.

No. 21, a still more lovely drawing of the subject, likewise attributed to him, but doubtful.

No. 2 is a copy of Raffaelle's Madonna della Gatta. A colossal female head, said to be intended for the Virgin, is by Correggio. There are also drawings by Lorenzo Credi, Pocetti, Bronzino, Baroccio, and Cigoli.

A custode, from the Accademia, will accompany the visitor who may desire to see the celebrated works of Andrea del Sarto, at the Scalzo, in the Via Cavour. This building was at one time part of the dwelling of Ottaviano de' Medici, situated near the gardens of San Marco; and in a room above, the Scalzi, or "Barefooted" Friars held their meetings. These friars were called Scalzi because, when they bore the crucifix in public processions, they always walked barefoot. The house had a cortile, or court, with cloisters resting on columns; and when Andrea del Sarto was beginning life as an artist, and living with his friend, Franciabigio, near the Mercato del Grano, they were both employed by this confraternity to adorn the walls with frescos in chiaroscuro. The subject chosen was the Life of St. John the Baptist, to which saint the confraternity was dedicated. The only joint work of the artists was the Baptism of Christ, which, though full of feeling, and a wonderful production for two young men, is the least well executed of the series. The rest of the frescos were painted with a certain rivalry, which gave a stimulus to the work. Andrea was often called away by other engagements, and therefore these paintings are spread over a lapse of years. In 1517 he executed the borders round the fresco of the Baptism of Christ; all the rest of the friezes were the work of Franciabigio, who also painted St. John taking leave of his father Zacharias when departing for the desert, and the meeting of the Saviour and St. John. In 1517 Andrea finished the compartment of St. John baptizing in the Desert. In 1520 he painted the allegories of Faith and Charity, and, soon afterwards, Herodias dancing before Herod, the Martyrdom of St. John the Baptist, and Salome presenting his head to her mother Herodias; the Angel appearing to Zacharias; and the allegory of Hope. He finished the fresco of Zacharias in 1523, when he painted the panel picture of the History of Joseph for the Borgherini family, now in the Pitti. In 1524 Andrea resumed his work at the Scalzo, and painted the Visit of Elizabeth to Mary; and in 1526 he executed his latest fresco, the Birth of St. John. We have here an opportunity of tracing Andrea del Sarto's progress in his art during the eleven years that he painted in this cloister. In the Preaching of St. John we see the influence of Ghirlandaio; in the Baptism of St. John, and St. John before Herod, that of Albert Dürer. The Angel appearing to Zacharias was painted just before the Madonna del Sacco, in the SS. Annunziata; and the two latest and largest frescos preceded Andrea's Last Supper, in the Monastery of the Salvi. These frescos have all been much injured by damp and exposure to weather, before the Cloister was protected by glass. In 1735, the Confraternity of the Scalzi was suppressed by the Grand-Duke Pietro Leopoldo, who sold all the building, except the Cloister, which from that time forth was attached to the Academy of Fine Arts.

THE PITTI GALLERY.

Large Rooms.

THE collection of pictures in the Pitti was made wholly by the Medici, who, about the year 1640, after they had become sovereign princes, brought them to this palace, which was then converted into a royal residence. Pietro da Cortona, and another artist, Cyrus Ferri, were employed to decorate the magnificent suite of rooms which were destined to contain the *chefs-d'œuvre* of the greatest masters in painting. All these pictures belong to the best period of Tuscan art, and to the second Revival; but in the smaller rooms, parallel with the suite towards the Piazza, are excellent specimens of works by earlier artists.

The numbers begin with the pictures of the latest school; and in the furthest room, which is called the Sala di Venus, Pietro da Cortona, wishing to flatter the reigning Medici, painted on the ceiling allegorical scenes and personages symbolical of the virtues of their ancestor, the Grand-Duke Cosimo I., who appears as a youth, protected and specially favoured by the gods.

Two splendid Sea Pieces by Salvator Rosa, Nos. 4 and 15, are placed opposite one another. The sea and sky have the glow and melting softness of Claude Lorraine, but the figures are more carefully drawn and are grouped naturally in easy attitudes; those especially in No. 4, to the right, are admirably placed; the drawing is spirited, and the colour forcible. No. 2, Duplicity, composed of two figures, is by the same master; but this picture has neither the wild picturesque beauty nor dash of the pencil usual with Salvator, and is insipid in its sobriety. Nos. 9 and 14, two Landscapes by Rubens, are in a very different style from the sea-pieces of Salvator, though they are painted with equal freedom. The town, on a bay, with mountains in the foreground, No. 9, is apparently taken from Genoa. No. 14 is a Flemish scene, fresh in breezy clouds, cornfields, hedges, and trees.

No. 11. A good picture, by Françesco Bassano, of the Martyrdom of St. Catherine. Françesco belonged to the Venetian school, and was the son of the more celebrated Jacopo, and the brother of Leandro Bassano. He was inclined to exaggerate the chiaroscuro of his pictures.

No. 16. A fine Portrait of an Old Man, by Rembrandt.

Nos. 17 and 18 are by Titian. No. 17, the Marriage of St. Catherine, is an inferior repetition of the picture in the National Gallery of London; and No. 18 is a very lovely Portrait of a Lady in the Venetian costume, who has been alternately called a Duchess of Urbino, the daughter of Palma Vecchio, and Titian's mistress. When the picture was carried to Paris, in the last century, the background was entirely repainted, and part of the veil which hung behind the face was destroyed.

No. 13. A good Florentine picture of the second Revival, by Matteo Rosselli—the Triumph of David. The movement of the figures is well expressed, but the heads, though not without beauty of feature, are insipid, and the clear bright colour has a certain prettiness, inappropriate to a subject taken from sacred story. Matteo Rosselli and Jacopo da Empoli may be regarded as the colourists of this school; they endeavoured to modify the exclusive attention paid to anatomy and drawing, which, in the hands of the followers of Michael Angelo, had become pedantic and exaggerated.

No. 10. A graceful picture of Narcissus at the Fountain, by Françcsco Curradi: Narcissus is represented as a peasant-lad.

No. 21. Sta. Martina, by Pietro da Cortona.

No. 22. Apollo flaying Marsyas, by Bilivert.

No. 27. The Saviour appearing to St. Peter on the Water, by Cigoli. Though in an obscure place between the windows, it is one of the best pictures in this room, and is a work of considerable power, with more nature and expression, and less of the model, than is usual with this school whose principal merit is correct drawing and strict obedience to rule.

The ceiling of the next room, the Sala di Apollo, was chiefly painted by Cyrus Ferri.

No. 36. The Portrait of the Archbishop Bartolini Salimbeni, by Girolamo da Carpi, of the Ferrarese School, 1494—1566. The archbishop was of the Florentine family whose palace, now forming part of the Hôtel de l'Europe, in the Via Porta Rossa, is still distinguished by the Salimbeni poppy. He was appointed administrator of the Pisan Church by Pope Leo X., and Archbishop of Malaga by Charles V., and he was buried in the Campo Santo of Pisa.

Nos. 37 and 38 are indifferent examples of pictures by Paolo Veronese and Jacopo Palma of Venice.

No. 29. A Holy Family, by Angelo Bronzino. The head of the Virgin is a fine portrait, in his usual style, and not unlike Bianca Capello.

No. 40. A Madonna and Child, by Murillo. The Child stands on his mother's knee and rests his right arm on her breast. The Virgin has the modest, girl-like simplicity usual with Murillo, and more than his ordinary refinement of type.

No. 41. The Hospitality of St. Julian, by Cristofano Allori. The legend of St. Julian is as follows :—As an act of penance the saint became a ferryman, and one night he brought a youth across the river whom he discovered to be a leper. The wife of St. Julian, however, received the sick man into their house, and they laid him on their bed. The next morning the leper was transfigured before them, and appeared as an angel, bringing pardon for past sins.* This picture is considered as the *chef-d'œuvre* of Allori. The original drawing for the man with the oar in his hand is in the Gallery of the Uffizi.

No. 42. A Head of Mary Magdalene, by Perugino ; very sweet in expression, drawn and painted with great softness, although rather the portrait of a lovely woman than the ideal representation of a penitent sinner.

No. 43. A Male Portrait, by Franciabigio, the friend and brother-artist of Andrea del Sarto. The black under-tint has come to the surface, and injured the picture, which is finely executed, and has an agreeable landscape background.

No. 46. St. Francis in Prayer, by Cigoli ; full of deep

---

* See Mrs. Jameson, "Legendary Art."

feeling; the rocky scenery of La Vernia forms the background. This is one of the most beautiful and touching pictures by the master.

No. 49. The Infant-Prince Leopold de' Medici, afterwards Cardinal, by Tiberio Titi, a Florentine. This prince was the son of the Grand-Duke Cosimo II., by the Grand-Duchess Maria Maddalena, of Austria. He devoted his life to the study of literature and art, and made the collection of portraits for the Gallery of the Uffizi. He died in 1675.

No. 51. A Deposition, by Cigoli; carefully drawn and composed, but the figures are in attitudes which recall the model, therefore the picture, whatever claim it may have for admiration of the correct drawing and colour, does not awaken sympathy or interest in the subject.

No. 54. A fine Portrait, by Titian, of the poet Pietro Aretino, who was born in 1492, the illegitimate son of a gentleman of Arezzo. He wrote a treatise against the system of Papal Indulgences, which caused his banishment from his native city, but Pope Clement VII. allowed him to reside in Rome, where his talents ensured him a favourable reception. Though his satirical writings were directed against those in power, and obtained for him the name of "the Scourge of Princes," he contrived to secure the favour and patronage of the greatest monarchs of the age: Francis I. lavished gifts on him, and Charles V. presented him with a valuable gold chain. He composed a paraphrase of the Seven Psalms, and several religious works. Some of his publications had, however, an immoral tendency, and caused so much scandal that the Pope was at length obliged to banish him from Rome. He was intimate with the Grand-Duke Cosimo I., to whom he sent this picture, in which the gift of the emperor is represented. He writes to Cosimo, "Surely I breathe here; the blood circulates, and I see my living self in a painting; had I given the artist a few more crowns he would have bestowed more pains on the material of the dress, the silk, the velvet, and brocade; I say nothing of the chain, for it is indeed painted, *sic transit mundi*.

In the same letter, Aretino alludes to the picture, by Titian, of Giovanni delle Bande Nere, the father of Cosimo, under whom Aretino had served, and who had made his peace with the Pope. The two portraits appear to have been painted about the same time; but Aretino declares the artist had kept that of Giovanni unfinished, because he was tempted to Rome by the offer of greater remuneration from Paul III. (Alexander Farnese).

No. 55. Portrait, by Baroccio, of the Infant-Prince Frederick, of Urbino, the son of Françesco Maria II., Duke of Urbino, and of the Princess Claudia, daughter of the Grand-Duke Ferdinand I. Frederick of Urbino was father of the Princess Vittoria della Rovere, who married her cousin the Grand-Duke Ferdinand II., and brought the valuable collection of pictures to Florence, as her dowry.

No. 56. The Madonna del Rosario, by Murillo.

No. 58. A Pietà, by Andrea del Sarto, one of his finest compositions; the colouring is rich, the drawing masterly, especially in the foreshortening, and in the body of the Saviour, which is extended on a white cloth; the impression left on the spectator, however, is cold, from the absence of appropriate feeling in the countenances and actions of the figures, which appear to have been painted separately from models. Cavalcaselle describes this picture as, "a composition according to the correct rules, very dramatic and powerful, in which even the merit of originality cannot be denied. The Michael Angelesque fibre in it shews strength; and the cleverness with which Andrea presents a scene, in its movements forcible yet human and familiar, in its expressing realistic, yet sufficiently elevated, is greatly to be praised."[*] This picture was painted, in 1524, for a convent in the Mugello, where Andrea had sought refuge from the plague, then raging in Florence.

No. 59 and No. 61 are portraits of Maddelena and Angelo Doni, by Raffaelle. The lady was of the wealthy family of Strozzi, and was married to a rich Florentine, Doni, the patron of Raffaelle. There is nothing ideal in either portrait; both are faithful renderings of truth. The hands are studied carefully, and the dress and jewels are finished with attention to detail; the landscape background is clear and pure, and, though light, retreats behind the full-coloured forms. The countenances of Doni and his wife are serious; Maddalena's is expressive of goodness, whilst there is more force and talent in the face of Angelo. In both there is a defect in the perspective, the farther eye being placed too high. They were painted during Raffaelle's second visit to Florence, when he was still very young, and had not yet attempted portraits.[†]

No. 60. Portrait of Rembrandt, by himself.

No. 62. A Holy Family, by Andrea del Sarto, painted in

---

[*] See "Crowe and Cavalcaselle," vol. iii. p. 571.
[†] See Passavant, "Rafael von Urbino," vol. i. p. 94; vol. ii. p. 52.

1521 for Zanobi Bracci, when the artist was employed by Ottaviano de' Medici in the decorations of the Palace of Poggio a Caiano for Pope Leo X. The children, especially St. John, are easy and graceful; the Virgin gazes at her son with a sweet, happy countenance; the colour is rich and warm, and the group natural, without any attempt at scientific display.

No. 63. Portrait of Pope Leo X., by Raffaelle; to the right of the Pope is his cousin, Cardinal Giulio de' Medici, afterwards Clement VII.; on his left, Cardinal Luigi de' Rossi, the Pope's secretary. The Pope is seated at a table with an illuminated missal and a silver bell; though large and coarse in person, he is represented as the man of cultivated and luxurious tastes and habits; his attitude is dignified, and his hands beautiful. The picture was painted about 1518; there is a copy by Andrea del Sarto at Mantua so exact that it deceived Raffaelle's scholar, Giulio Romano, who supposed it was the original which Ottavio de' Medici, by order of Pope Clement VII., had promised to bestow on the Duke of Mantua.

No. 64. A Pietà over one of the doors, by Fra Bartolommeo. The expression of the dead Christ is touchingly beautiful, mild, dignified, and sad. The gentle resignation of the sorrowing Virgin, and the passionate grief of the Magdalene, who clasps his feet, are given with the simple truth of nature. The colour is pure and correct. "The group realises at once all the precepts considered as final in the sixteenth century. It is a modification and an advance upon Perugino's, combining all the tenderness of the Umbrian, with greater selection, astonishing individuality, pure nature, and refined feeling. It is not possible to cite an instance in which a lifeless form is rendered with more flexibility or with more anatomical accuracy." *

No. 66. Andrea del Sarto, by himself.

No. 67. The Magdalene, by Titian; wonderful in colour; a lovely Venetian woman looking upwards in prayer, and half covered by the soft waving tresses of her golden hair.

No. 72. The Portrait of a Man in Black, by Cristofano Allori.

The Sala di Marte has a representation on the ceiling of Mars, accompanied by Hercules, Victory, &c., to signify the warlike achievements of the House of Medici.

No. 76. Portrait of John Churchill, Duke of Marlborough, by Adrian Van der Werff.

No. 79. The Madonna della Seggiola, by Raffaelle, painted entirely by his own hand, probably in the year 1510, when he was engaged with the fresco of the School of Athens in the Vatican. The Virgin is not divine, but she is the perfection of womanly beauty and modesty, as well as of maternal tenderness. The Child is grand in form and expression, although the rounded limbs and features and the clinging action are wholly infantine; the earnest, yet child-like worship of the little St. John is no less appropriate and excellent. The composition is simple, the colour rich, and the heads of the Virgin and Child are highly finished, whilst the rest of the picture is painted with great freedom, yet softness, produced without scumbling, and leaving the outlines distinct.†

---

* See "Crowe and Cavalcaselle," vol. iii. p. 471.
† See Passavant's "Rafael von Urbino," vol. i. p. 294; vol. ii. p. 294.

No. 80. The Portrait of a Belgian anatomist, Andrea Vesale, by Titian. Vesale was accused of homicide, and condemned to death, for having opened the body of a Spanish gentleman. He had been invited to Spain by the Emperor Charles V., and Philip II. commuted his sentence to banishment.

No. 81. A most lovely Holy Family, by Andrea del Sarto, which, though entirely different in thought and treatment from the Madonna della Seggiola, is not unworthy of its place beside the work of Raffaelle. The Virgin is simple and dignified, though without classical beauty; and the children are animated and drawn with grace and power. The Christ sits astride on his mother's knee, and looks back to listen to the eager words of St. John, who leans over the lap of Elizabeth. The colours are agreeable, and melt into one another; the outline is almost lost; there is great breadth as well as softness in the chiaroscuro.

No. 82. The Portrait of Cardinal Guido Bentivoglio, by Vandyke, may be compared with the portraits of Titian, not only in the quiet dignity, character, and elegance of composition for which Vandyke was remarkable, but in truth of flesh tints and warmth of colour, in which in this instance the Fleming is not far short of the Venetian master. Cardinal Bentivoglio was born at Ferrara of an ancient Bolognese family in 1519. When only nineteen years of age he was appointed secretary to Pope Clement VII., and was sent later by Pope Paul V. as Papal Nuncio to Flanders. Though one of the Judges of Galileo at Rome, he had not the power to prevent his condemnation. He wrote the "History of the War in the Netherlands," and his own memoirs, and died in 1644.

No. 83. Luigi Cornaro, a splendid portrait of a Venetian nobleman, by Titian. Cornaro died at the age of ninety-six. His youth was spent in dissipation, but he early reformed his life, and in 1558 he wrote a treatise on sobriety. He was greatly and universally respected, and was held in high honour by his fellow-citizens. The large, penetrating, dark eyes, and the finely-cut movable nostrils, bespeak a quick and fiery nature, whilst the high forehead, thoughtful brow, the firm lips, and dignified deportment, to which may be added the well-ordered dress, are significant of a wise and resolute character, as well as of that taste and refinement which belong to a true gentleman. The picture is full of life, and it is impossible to say what is most worthy of admiration—the correct drawing, the reality of the flesh tints, or the great painter's power in expressing the mind of the sitter.

No. 85. A fine picture, by Rubens, with portraits of himself and his brother and of the philosophers Lipsius and Grotius. They are seated at a table, with a bust of Seneca in a niche behind them, and a landscape background. Whilst Rubens was celebrated as a diplomatist as well as painter, his brother and Justus Lipsius were equally remarkable as philologists. Lipsius became professor of history at Leyden, and subsequently at Louvain; he was appointed historiographer to Philip II., and created a councillor of state by the Archduke Albert; in his old age he abjured the Protestant religion, and died a Roman Catholic in 1606. Hugo Grotius, the son of a burgomaster of Delft, in Holland, was born in 1583, and was sent, when a youth, in the Dutch ambassador's suite to France; he was already so distinguished for learning that King Henry IV., as a token of his admiration, bestowed on him a gold chain, at the same time calling him "the marvel of Holland." He was afterwards condemned for his religious opinions to imprisonment in the fortress of Loevenstein, from whence he escaped by the assistance of his wife, and fled to France, where he received a pension from the king. After a vain attempt to return to Holland, he entered the service of Queen Christina of Sweden and her minister Oxenstiern, and died at Dantzic in 1645. In this picture, the artist, Peter Paul Rubens, is seen in three-quarter face, with red moustaches, his hand resting on his hip; his brother Philip is beside him; he has light hair and moustaches, and holds a pen. Justus Lipsius has a long beard and short hair; his forefinger rests upon a book. Grotius is in profile, with moustaches and barberoyale. The character and power displayed in this picture gives it a place beside the noble portraits of Titian, though the rich and varied colours in which Rubens delighted hardly suit the gravity of the persons represented.

No. 86. An Allegory, by Rubens, in which he has revelled in wondrous sunlights and bright colours. The subject is Peace and War. The restless spirit and gigantic power of the master is displayed in size of muscle, violent action, contrasts of storm and sunshine, astonishing breadth of light and shade, in deep full colour and warm shadow, intended to give full value to the dazzling brilliancy of his lights on the fair skins of women and children. There is nothing to interest or please in this picture, and its sole attraction is the example it presents of the qualities peculiar to Rubens. The original sketch is in the National Gallery of London, bequeathed by the poet Samuel Rogers.

No. 87 and No. 88 are two oblong paintings containing

many figures, and both charming in colour, by Andrea del Sarto; they represent the History of Joseph, and may be considered as one picture. In the first is Jacob and Rachel with Joseph, who is relating his dreams to his parents; Jacob sending Joseph to his brethren; the brethren putting Joseph into the well; they sell him to the merchants, and one of them in the foreground is showing his blood-stained garment to their father. In the second painting Pharaoh is seen asleep: the curtains of his bed are sustained by two boy-genii; behind are seen the fat and lean kine, and in front the ears of corn; at the top of the staircase leading to Pharaoh's palace Joseph is led to prison, and again below he is brought before Pharaoh; Pharaoh listens to Joseph's interpretation of his dreams; Pharaoh names him governor, and bestows on him a gold chain; two children are playing with a dog in the foreground, and there is a lovely landscape background, with architecture, figures, &c. Both these pictures, as well as similar pictures in the Uffizi Gallery, No. 1,249 and No. 1,282, by Jacopo Pontormo, were painted for Françesco Borgheri upon his marriage.

No. 90. The Ecce Homo, by Cigoli. The noble dignity and patient suffering expressed in the Christ is more touching from the contrast with the vulgar countenances of his persecutors; the traces of the scourging are given with painful reality; the picture is finely drawn and coloured, and is an excellent example of the master.

No. 92. A fine Portrait, by Titian, of a young Venetian Gentleman; the type is peculiarly characteristic of the race; finely cut long features, oval contour, blue eyes, and reddish brown air, with that grave dignified demeanour which gives an air of nobility to the Venetian of every class.

No. 93. St. Francis in Prayer; a good study of an Italian Peasant, by Reubens; inferior in poetic sentiment to the same subject treated by Cigoli, No. 46.

No. 94. The Holy Family, by Raffaelle, known as the Madonna dell' Impannata, from the white cloth—*panno*—used instead of glass for the window in the background; the composition is wholly by Raffaelle, as well as the painting of the head of the Child, whom Elizabeth is restoring to the Virgin; the rest of the picture was probably painted by one of Raffaelle's scholars; the expression of Elizabeth is fine, and full of feeling; the other female heads, as well as that of St. John, are feeble and cold.*

No. 95. The Sacrifice of Abraham: a good picture by Cristofano Allori, Il Bronzino; in colour resembling the painting of Matteo Rosselli.

No. 96. Also by Bronzino: Judith with the Head of Holofernes, which is said to have been painted from the artist's own head. Judith is supposed to be a portrait of Bronzino's mistress, and the old woman her mother. The arms of Judith, extended and foreshortened, are finely drawn, and her head and figure are grand and powerful. The golden silk of which her dress is composed is painted with marvellous clearness and vigour, and the whole colour is rich and harmonious.

No. 97. An Annunciation, by Andrea del Sarto: good in colour, but feeble in composition; Joseph stands beside the Virgin, who starts back as two angels approach, one of whom bears the lily. This picture has been much repainted.

---

* See Passavant's "Rafael von Urbino," vol. i. p. 186; vol. ii. p. 394.

No. 92. A Magdalene, by Cigoli.

No. 106. A good Portrait of Galileo when old, by Sustermans; the end of his telescope is seen below, near the frame: this likeness of the philosopher appears to have been taken later than the portrait in the Uffizi Gallery.

The Sala di Giove has a statue, in the middle of the room, representing Victory, by the modern sculptor, Consani: the goddess is seated on a rock, and is inscribing upon her shield the words "Montebello, Palestro," &c.

No. 110. A sketch for part of the picture of Bacchus and Ariadne, by Titian, in the National Gallery of London.

No. 111. Over the door, the Conspiracy of Catiline, by Salvator Rosa; and

No. 135. A Battlepiece, by the same artist.

No. 112. Another Battlepiece, finely treated by Jacopo Cortese, called the Borgognone, a native of France, who also painted the same subject (No. 133) with even greater power. These and two others in this gallery are among his finest productions.

No. 113. The most celebrated picture in this room is the Three Fates, by Michael Angelo. They are all taken from one old woman, represented in different attitudes; Clotho holds the spindle, off which she spins the thread of life; Lachesis twists the yarn in her fingers, and Atropos prepares to cut it with her scissors. A romantic tale is told relating to this picture. During the siege of Florence, in 1529, when Michael Angelo was conducting the defensive operations, an old woman is supposed to have presented herself before the municipality, and offered her son to fight for his native city; the great artist, it is further said, was so struck with her countenance, that he has recorded it in this picture. The story is, however, probably a fiction, and it is even uncertain whether the picture itself is by the hand of Michael Angelo. "Severe, keen, and characteristic," as Kugler describes it, he does not consider it a genuine work of the master; there is a want of variety of attitude and countenance, and even of exaggeration of form, as well as a certain meagreness, which Michael Angelo would hardly have imitated, far less invented.

No. 116. Portrait of Vittoria della Rovere, the wife of the Grand-Duke Ferdinand II., by Sustermans. The artist has represented her in the costume of a Vestal Virgin.

No. 118. Portrait of Andrea del Sarto and his wife; not an authentic picture.

No. 123. The Virgin in Glory, with four Saints below, by Andrea del Sarto. The kneeling St. Catherine, a bright happy-looking girl, is the best figure in the group; the male saints are feeble. The Virgin above has no pretension to beauty, but is well placed; two kneeling and sitting cherubim with scrolls in their hands, on either side of her, are the best part of the picture; the colour, as usual with this master, is very agreeable, but the upper part is so much more feeble than the lower, they hardly seem to belong to one picture; and, as it was finished ten years after Andrea's death, by a certain Vincenzio, called Morgante Bonilli, of Poppi, this difference may be easily accounted for.

No. 124. Another and most beautiful Annunciation, by Andrea. The Virgin stands in an attitude of meek suspense, looking back at the angel: she holds a book in her left hand, and raises the forefinger of the right, as if questioning. The archangel, a lovely and graceful figure, kneels and looks at her with earnest appealing gaze; two angels stand behind; the architecture and landscape background is extremely beautiful, and the warm colour in the foreground is carried out by the red mantles of the figures leaning over the balcony in an adjoining house. Cavelcaselle thus describes this picture: "The mode in which the angel is presented recalls Fra Bartolommeo. But the movement and lines, though soft and gentle, are unconstrained and free, as in Del Sarto's own creation, the Nativity, at the Servi. The Virgin is most dignified in air and pose. Decorum and grave beauty are almost as combined as in Della Porta, without the emptiness which grew to a defect with Andrea's later years; the colour is rich, and in good keeping with a landscape full of atmosphere."

No. 125. St. Mark, a colossal figure by Fra Bartolommeo, painted at the same time with the San Vincenzio of the Academy, which Kugler preferred to this picture. St. Mark is a gigantic and powerful figure, grand in drawing and composition. He is seated in a niche, holding his gospel and pen with both hands, whilst looking back, lost in contemplation. The picture was placed over the entrance to the choir of St. Mark, but after the demolition of the choir, which was in the centre of the church, it was bought by Prince Ferdinand de' Medici, and in 1799 was taken to Paris, where it was transferred from wood to canvas.

No. 37. A Meeting of Huntsmen, by Giovanni di San Giovanni, a Florentine painter of the Second Revival. The heads are very spirited.

No. 138. Portrait of Guidobaldo II., Duke of Urbino, grandfather of Vittoria della Rovere, by Federigo Zucchero, a painter of the Roman School (1543—1609).

No. 139. A Holy Family, by Rubens. The colour of the children is very lovely.

No. 140. The Portrait of a Lady, by Leonardo da Vinci. A most exquisitely finished painting; the drawing is careful, though the left eye is somewhat too high; the lips are just closed, the eyes calm, the nostril delicate; her grave and gentle deportment are significant of self-restraint; the head is gracefully bent, and the perfect simplicity and dignified composure mark a woman of noble mind and training. Her hands are very beautiful; she holds a missal in her left. The landscape, seen between two open arches, represents a walled town—probably Florence—and distant hills.

No. 144. The Battle of Montemurlo, in which the Grand-Duke Cosimo I. destroyed his enemies, and secured his seat on the throne of Tuscany. The picture is by Giovan Battista Franco. A nude figure, to the right, may have been copied from a small picture in the National Gallery of London, attributed to Michael Angelo; and the Ganymede above appears also to have been borrowed from other pictures.

The fifth room of this suite is called the Sala di Saturno. The god is represented on the ceiling, with Mars and Prudence—the work of Pietro di Cortona.

Nos. 145, 146, and 169. The Virgin and Child, with an Angel, and two other Holy Families, are by Domenico Puligo, a pupil of Andrea del Sarto.

No. 147. A Nymph and Satyr, by Giorgione.

No. 149. A fine Portrait of Cardinal Hippolito de' Medici, by Jacopo Pontormo. His hand rests on the head of a dog, which is painted with much life and power. Hippolito was the natural son of Giulio de' Medici, Duke of Nemours, whose monument by Michael Angelo is in the Sacristy of San Lorenzo. Hippolito was educated by his uncle Leo X.; and although his tastes led him to prefer a secular to an ecclesiastical career, he was forced to enter the Church and accept a cardinal's hat. He died—it is supposed by poison—in 1535.

No. 150. Very beautiful Portraits of Charles I. of England and Henrietta Maria, by Vandyke.

No. 151. The Portrait of Pope Julius II., by Raffaelle, a repetition of the fine portrait in the Uffizi Gallery (No. 1,131).

No. 152. The Death of Abel. A powerful picture by Schiavone.

No. 154. John the Baptist when a child, asleep, watched over by Elizabeth. One of the most lovely compositions of Carlo Dolce. The tranquil sleep of infancy is beautifully given, and the colouring and chiaroscuro have the fulness and power of Ludovico Caracci. No. 155. Sta. Rosa, by the same artist, has his usual qualities of sweetness and finish, with insipidity.

No. 158. The Portrait of Cardinal Bernardo Dovizi of Bibbiena, by Raffaelle. A most wonderfully life-like picture of an astute, polished ecclesiastic, mild but immovable; his hands are very elegantly formed, and rich with jewels. The picture is only in part by Raffaelle, who executed another some years later, which is now in the Museum at Madrid. The cardinal was the son of poor parents in the Casentino, a valley behind the mountains of Vallombrosa, and he took the name of Bibbiena from his native city. He began life as tutor to the sons of Lorenzo de' Medici, who had already secured the services of his brother as secretary. When Bibbiena's pupil became Pope Leo X.—1515—he was created a cardinal. He died suddenly at Rome in 1520. Paolo Jovius, the historian, whose monument is in the Cloister of San Lorenzo, attributes the death of the cardinal to poison in a dish of new-laid eggs.

No. 159. Christ rising from the Tomb, with the Evangelists on either side, by Fra Bartolommeo. In his left hand the Saviour holds the sceptre, with the globe surmounted by the cross, and raises his right to bless. His countenance is mild and noble, his attitude dignified, and the flowing lines of his white drapery add to the majesty of his appearance. With the exception of a defect in the right arm, the drawing is very fine. The arm of St. Matthew is boldly foreshortened; St. John is beside him; St. Luke and St. Mark on the other side; all four are powerful figures; the draperies are grandly composed, and we may perceive in them the examples Raffaelle followed in his later works. The two little angels below, who support a picture of the world on which rests the sacramental cup, are most lovely; the colour is sober, but fine. This picture was painted soon after Fra Bartolommeo had lost his best-beloved friend, Mariotto Albertinelli, in 1515.*

The paintings of Giorgione are so rare, and can so seldom be authenticated, that both the pictures in this room— No. 147 and No. 161—are doubtful. The last represents Moses taken from the Nile, and presented to Pharaoh's daughter. It is fine in colour, and has an exceedingly lovely landscape background. The figures are drawn with

---

* See "Crowe and Cavalcaselle," vol. iii. p. 466.

spirit and grace, and the picture is probably a sketch for some larger work, or it may have belonged to a bridal chest, or other piece of furniture.

No. 162. The Portrait of Françesco Maria della Rovere, Duke of Urbino, and father of the Grand-Duchess Vittoria della Rovere, by Federigo Baroccio.

No. 163. An Annunciation, by Andrea del Sarto, the third in this gallery; it was painted for Giuliano della Scala, to be placed in a chapel of the SS. Annunziata. The curtains at the side were added later. It is a feeble picture, and injured by restorations.

No. 164. The Deposition from the Cross, by Pietro Perugino; a noble yet simple composition, in the tender, sweet, and earnest manner of the Umbrian School, with careful and somewhat academical treatment. It was in this picture that Perugino, in 1495, presented an example of landscape painting to the Florentines, such as had never before been seen in Florence. Vasari speaks of the brilliancy of the general tones and of the backgrounds; they are still preserved in all the charm of freshness, in spite of time and repairs. The Umbrian School directed their attention especially to landscape, and Perugino made the best of his opportunities in studying earlier and contemporary masters in the same line. According to Cavalcaselle, when describing the picture, "He fitted trees and shrubbery so cleverly, that in spite of all the calculations which it reveals, the result seems a spontaneous creation of nature. . . . . He also made the lines of the country complementary to those of the figures, which he ceased to place with Umbrian symmetry and regularity, in order to put them together pyramidally. . . . The Saviour's body, still full of the flexibility of life, but supine in death, is supported in its winding-sheet on a stone by Joseph of Arimathea; the head is held up by the Magdalene, the left arm by the Virgin. Mary Cleofas looking over the heads of both, completed the pyramid, with Mary Salome kneeling at her side, between the Virgin and a youth who stoops to raise the corners of the cloth at the Redeemer's feet; St. John and the wife of Zebedee, Nicodemus, and two others, stand to the right and left. The Virgin shows her maternal love in an agony of grief without grimace. In the Magdalene sorrow and sympathy are united in the face and action; Joseph of Arimathea turns away his head, overcome by the melancholy of the scene, while the youth at the Saviour's feet is less affected. . . . As a study of nude the Redeemer is finely proportioned, without the false conventionalism so often conspicuous in the hands, feet, or articulations of earlier and later creations, and without their stiffness, length, or lameness. One sees in it, as in the surrounding mourners, the forerunner of that splendid work of the sixteenth century, the Pietà of Fra Bartolommeo "* (No. 64 of this gallery).

No. 165. The Madonna del Baldacchino, by Raffaelle, executed on his return from Rome, after he had painted his first large composition of the Entombment of Christ. He had studied the grand treatment of drapery with Fra Bartolommeo, and in return he had imparted to him the knowledge of perspective, which he had acquired in the school of Perugino; in this picture, which he painted for the Florentine family of Dei, to be placed in Santo Spirito, Raffaelle endeavoured to imitate Fra Bartolommeo; and it may be

---

* See "Crowe and Cavalcaselle," vol. iii. p. 196.

compared with the Madonna by Bartolommeo in the Academy—No. 65. The Virgin, seated on a throne, holds the Child on her knee, who looks back naïvely at the Apostle Peter, standing beside St. Bruno; St. James the Less and St. Augustus are on the opposite side. Two angels support the canopy above the Virgin and Child, and two other most lovely infants stand below, one having his arm round the other's neck, and sing praises. The picture was left unfinished, which is evident from the weak face and figure of St. James, and was sold by Raffaelle's scholars, Giulio Romano and Giov. Françesco Penni, to Baldassare Turini, who conveyed it to his city of Pescia, from whence it was afterwards brought to the Pitti. The head and figure of the Virgin is extremely lovely and graceful, and quite in Raffaelle's own style, and it is only in the composition and draperies that we discover the influence of Fra Bartolommeo.*

No. 167. Apollo and the Muses dancing in a circle on the top of Mount Parnassus, by Giulio Romano; a truly magical group, which seems to float in the graceful movement of the dance; a golden sunlight in the background.

No. 171. The Portrait of Tommaso de Phœdra Inghirami, by Raffaelle. The faithful adherence to nature in portrait is shown in the squint and the coarse features, as much as in the large, fat, yet delicately white hands of Inghirami, all painted with the highest finish. The clever expression of the face compensates for want of beauty; the drawing is careful, and the composition and colour simple. The dress

* See Passavant's "Rafael von Urbino," vol. i. p. 125; vol. ii. p. 89.

is that worn by Inghirami when he acted as secretary to the conclave of cardinals which elected Giovanni de' Medici Pope, as Leo X. Inghirami belonged to an ancient family of Volterra, and when only an infant he lost his father, and was brought to Florence, where he was placed under Medicean protection. At thirteen he was sent to Rome, where his remarkable powers were developed, and he was celebrated for his great learning. On one occasion he performed in Seneca's tragedy of Hippolytus, before the Cardinal di San Giorgio; the part assigned Inghirami was Phœdra; the piece having been interrupted by an accident to the machinery, he came forward and amused the company by improvising Latin verses; he was applauded and called for in his character of Phœdra, and the name was ever afterwards attached to his own. Passavant remarks the full daylight effect of this picture, and the fine modelling, with the tenderest fusion, which strikingly recall Hans Holbein's method, although Raffaelle could not have seen any work of the German master, since Holbein was at that time only fifteen years of age. The flat treatment of the accessories leads to the conclusion that this part of the picture is by the hand of a scholar.*

No. 172. The Dispute of the Holy Trinity, one of Andrea del Sarto's most celebrated pictures, equally fine in composition, drawing, colour, and expression. The head and action of the youthful St. Lawrence, who stands in the centre and carries his gridiron, is extremely beautiful and dignified. St. Augustine and St. Peter Martyr pursue the discussion

---

* See Passavant's "Rafael von Urbino," vol. i. p. 212; vol. ii. p. 164.

with animation; St. Francis listens with a meek countenance;
he has one hand on his breast, in the other he carries his
Institutes; St. Sebastian, half undressed, kneels at the feet
of St. Augustine—his back is finely painted; St. Mary
Magdalene, a lovely portrait of Andrea's wife, holds her
vase of ointment, and kneels beside St. Francis, with lips
apart, listening. The emblem of the Trinity descends upon
the group. Cavalcaselle writes of this picture in the following terms:—" In order to show that he (Andrea) was
at home in every mood, he accepted a commission from
the monastery of San Gallo, and thought out the noble altar-
piece (of the Pitti) of the Fathers disputing on the doctrine
of the Trinity, in every line of which stern power and boldness are discerned. Yet, as usual, there is abundance of
the atmosphere and vapour which are now his peculiar
characteristics. He seems, at this moment, to have been
looking at some of Fra Bartolommeo's latest emanations,
such as the solitary St. Vincent, now at the Academy, or
some statues of Michael Angelo; for the masks are expressive and resolute, the attitudes are grandiose, the forms
are well proportioned, weighty, and nobly draped." *

No. 174. The Vision of Ezekiel, by Raffaelle, one of his
noblest compositions, though painted on so small a scale.
It is not only exquisitely finished in all the details, but composed, drawn, and coloured with a grandeur which is not
surpassed by any of his larger paintings, whether in oil or
fresco. The countenance and attitude of Jehovah are truly
majestic, and the Lion, the Ox, and the Eagle, the symbols
of St. Mark, St. Luke, and St. John, partake of the solemn

---

* See " Crowe and Cavalcaselle," vol. iii. p. 562.

grandeur which pervades the picture; the youthful angel in adoration, typical of St. Matthew, is a noble as well as lovely form, and no less fine are the infant-angels who support the arms of the Eternal; a glory, composed of faintly traced angels' heads, descends in rays from above; and far beneath, the world is seen at early dawn in a mysterious and beautiful twilight. Ezekiel is walking below on the earth. The picture was painted for Count Vincenzio Ercolani of Bologna.

No. 178. Cleopatra, by Guido Reni; a painting possessing wonderful breadth and delicacy in the shadows and half-tints.

The Sala dell' Iliade is painted by a recent artist, Luigi Sabatelli. In the centre is a very lovely statue of Charity, by the Tuscan sculptor, Bartolini; it is gracefully composed, and the flesh tenderly modelled; the drapery falls in large and well-arranged folds, but the hair is stiff and inferior in execution. The composition is the same as a group of the Cinque-cento period in the Bargello.

The two principal pictures facing one another in this room are by Andrea del Sarto, No. 191 and No. 225; both represent the Assumption of the Virgin. No. 225 was painted for the Cathedral of Cortona, and greatly to the disgust of the inhabitants of that city, it was brought to Florence in 1609 by command of the Grand-Duke Ferdinand II. The Madonna is seated above in the clouds; her hands are clasped in adoration; her eyes are cast down. Three boy-angels bear her upwards, and proclaim the glad tidings to the Apostles below, whilst five lovely cherubs' heads form a garland around her of exquisite beauty. St. John gazes earnestly upwards; the rest of the Apostles, among whom

is a kneeling saint, gather round the Virgin's tomb. The
Bishop, St. Nicholas, with his three typical balls beside him,
turns to the spectator. These figures have too much the air
of academical studies placed in groups, though the artist has
thrown much expression in each of the heads; the colour is
very brilliant, yet harmonious.

No. 191 is in many respects different, and on the whole
superior to the picture just described. Vasari gives its
history as follows:—Bartolommeo Panciatichi, a Florentine merchant, settled at Lyons in France, desired to leave
a remembrance of himself in that city. He accordingly
ordered a painting of the Assumption of the Virgin from
Andrea del Sarto. The panel chosen by the artist, however, split several times whilst he was at work. Andrea
became discouraged, and after leaving and resuming this
picture at intervals, he at last abandoned it altogether, and
it was still unfinished at his death. The son of Bartolommeo
Panciatichi, however, held it in high estimation, and had
it conveyed to his villa, which stood on the site of the present Palace of the Poggio Imperiale, beyond the Porta
Romana of Florence. From thence it has been brought to
the Palazzo Pitti. The Madonna in this picture appears
wrapt in heavenly thoughts, and looks upwards, one hand
extended as in prayer, the other holding her mantle. A
boy-angel below the clouds from whence she is ascending
raises his finger, and tells the Apostle she has risen. The
early morning is dawning in a pale, grey sky. St. John
and two other Apostles have heard the news; their attitude
is full of earnest devotion and wonder. The others who
look into the tomb are figures of inferior merit. The painter
has introduced his own portrait among the Apostles. The

standing cherubs round the Virgin are very graceful and lovely. Cavalcaselle writes of No. 225 :—"A more quiet and orderly distribution than No. 191, and something more reminiscent of Fra Bartolommeo. The Virgin is raised up to heaven most gracefully, and there is an atmosphere almost like Correggio's in the glory." Of No. 191 he writes :—"A master-piece for lightness, vapour, and finish, and of a good 'sfumato.'"

No. 184. Andrea's own portrait when young, by himself.

No. 185. The only positively genuine picture by Giorgione in this gallery, and one of the few in existence; it represents a group of musicians. The centre figure plays on a spinnet or piano, whilst looking back at a man behind; his fingers are pressed firmly on the keys, as if pausing whilst listening to the friend, who is laying one hand on his shoulder to arrest his attention: though in shade, the mild expression of this man's countenance is not lost. All the force and brilliancy of the picture is, however, concentrated in the head of the central musician, but the light is carried on to a third person standing on his right. There is great breadth of chiaroscuro, and no sudden transitions, but a uniform golden or rich sunset glow throughout the composition.

No. 186. The Baptism of Christ, by Paolo Veronese.

No. 188. Salvator Rosa when young, by himself; and No. 218, a Warrior, by the same artist, painted with breadth and vigour, though a coarse, ugly figure.

No. 146. St. Benedict and Saints, by Paolo Veronese; and No. 216, a portrait by him of Daniel Barbero, a Venetian Ambassador to England: the hands are magnificently painted, the attitude easy; the fur of the dress treated with great breadth, dashed in without attention to detail, but the more effective from the contrast with the high finish of the head and hands; a noble example of Venetian painting.

No. 199. A Holy Family, by Françesco Granacci; an agreeable picture, sweet in expression, especially the Infant Christ, but not a fine specimen of the master.

No. 202. The Angel refusing the Gifts of Tobias, by Bilivert; this is one of the best works of the Revival, good in drawing, though too florid in colour.

No. 208. The Madonna enthroned, with Saints, by Fra Bartolommeo. The two angels at the foot of the throne, with a violin and guitar, are most lovely, and full of religious feeling; nothing can exceed the sweet infantine grace of the Christ, who places a ring on the finger of St. Catherine; the attitude of the Virgin is somewhat affected, but she holds the Child tenderly, whilst turning her head towards Sta. Reparata, a sweet, modest-looking young maiden, clothed in green and red, kneeling at her feet. The saints standing on the right of the Child are very fine, especially St. George; St. Bartholomew carries a knife, the symbol of his martyrdom by being flayed alive; three Augustinian monks, probably portraits, are behind. The flying angels who support the canopy are painted with the utmost truth and beauty, and the light striking on one of them is very effective. There are five heads among the crowd of spectators who converse together, and all are in natural attitudes; the colour of the picture is dark and rather heavy. Cavalcaselle considers this the finest of Fra Bartolommeo's creations during the period that he was assisted by his friend Mariotto Albertinelli. It was painted in the year 1512. "In composition, drawing, and relief, it was beyond his own power to come nearer perfection. Great as the charm had been with which he had invested the group of the Virgin and Child in the altar-piece of Bishop Hurault" (in the Louvre), "he now infused new elements of beauty into it by increased grace in the shape and air of the Virgin, and by contrasting the turn of her head and frame with that of the Infant. In balancing the positions of the kneeling St. Catherine at the foot of the pedestal, and seating two boy-angels with viol and guitar on the steps of the throne, he reared the well-known pyramid of distribution. He placed a fine St. Michael" (St. George?) "in armour, and a St. Bartholomew erect, in weighty position, as mainstays on the foreground, uniting them by a circular chain of spectators in converse on the floor of the semi-dome. In rivalry with Raphael at times in bold foreshortening, he prodigally wasted his science in the reproduction of form and drapery, poising four lovely seraphs in flight under the festoons of the dais. The whole is thrown on the panel, as Vasari says, in so gallant a style as to leave the impression of a living scene. Yet it is more by truthful transition of neutral light and shade, than by colour, that Fra Bartolommeo obtained effect, the tone being reduced almost to a monochrome by the use of lampblack."*

No. 214. A good copy of Correggio's Madonna and St. Jerome, by Baroccio, though partaking of the prettiness of the copyist.

There are several fine portraits by Titian in this room. No. 200. Philip II. of Spain, a picture presented by that monarch to the Grand-Duke Cosimo I., with a portrait of

* See "Crowe and Cavalcaselle," vol. iii. p. 454; Vasari, "Vite dei Pittori," vol. vii. p. 158.

Philip's father, the Emperor Charles V., also by Titian, which is in another room of the palace. This mean and vulgar features and countenance of Philip have received a certain air of dignity from Titian's pencil.

No. 201. A second splendid portrait of Hippolito de' Medici, by Titian; the young Cardinal is here represented as a Hungarian magnate, in the costume he wore when sent as papal legate to the Emperor Charles V. The face is peculiarly Italian, as well as indicative of the passions fostered by the unhappy circumstances of his life; a young and chivalrous spirit forced to bend to the yoke of the priesthood: the quick, penetrating eye beneath the raised eyebrow, and the dilated nostril, express a high temper, whilst the fine and delicate smile on the lips tells less of pleasure than repressed feeling.

No. 215. A beautiful portrait of an unknown gentleman, by Titian; the dress, consisting of a black velvet coat and short mantle, is almost lost in the background, whilst the white at the throat and wrists is kept low in tone. Although the architectural background is carefully defined, it is subdued in colour, and gives relief to the figure, which stands easily; the hands are beautifully composed, easy, graceful, and drawn and coloured with truth; the head is fine, but the picture is placed too high to judge of all its merits.

No. 221. Portrait, by Titian, of Constance Bentivoglio, the daughter of Hercules Bentivoglio, a captain of Free Companies, who fought for Florence. The lady married first, in 1512, Lorenzo Strozzi of Ferrara, and secondly, Filippo Torniello, of Novara.

No. 219. The Virgin adoring the Infant Jesus, by Perugino.

No. 220. Jesus and Saints, by Annibale Caracci.

No. 223. Portrait of a man, by Hans Holbein.

No. 224. Portrait of a lady in the Florentine costume, by Ridolfo Ghirlandaio; hard in outline, sharp, clear, correct, with much animation in the countenance. This picture is not unlike that of Maddalena Doni, by Raffaelle—No. 59—particularly in the treatment of the hair, though this work of Ghirlandaio is inferior in finish.

No. 228. The Saviour, a head by Titian, extremely fine, though not equal to the Tribute Money, now in Dresden, which it in some respects resembles.

No. 232. Portrait of Vittoria della Rovere and her son, painted as the Madonna and Child, by Sustermans; the maestro di casa, or head steward of the duchess, stood for Joseph.

No. 230. The Madonna del Collo Lungo (long neck), by Parmigiannino. The painter, according to Vasari, was so delighted with his own work that he left it in an unfinished state. Not only the neck of the Virgin, but all the figures, including that of a man, as well as a column in the background, are drawn out to an extraordinary length. There is much sweetness of expression, mingled with affectation, in this picture.

No. 235. A Holy Family, by Rubens.

No. 237. A Madonna and Saints, by Rosso Rossi, who lived 1496—1541. This picture was painted for the family of Dei, and was placed in their chapel at the Santo Spirito, when the Madonna del Baldacchino was removed.

Rich tables of Florentine mosaic, and valuable vases of black marble and gold, adorn every room of this suite.

Small Rooms.

A square room to the back of the palace is called the Stufa, or Stove. Pietro da Cortona painted the walls in fresco, with allegories representing the Ages of Man, from sketches by the younger Michael Angelo Buonarotti, the nephew of the great sculptor. Matteo Rosselli added the Virtues on the ceiling in 1622. Two celebrated bronze statues of Cain and Abel, by the modern sculptor Dupré, are the treasures of this room. They are finely composed and modelled, and are no less remarkable as an example of Florentine bronze casting by Passi. Cain is placed in the centre of the room; the body of Abel lies prostrate, as if from the violence of the fall. It is to be regretted the two statues are not placed near one another, so as to form one group.

The adjoining room contains one of the most celebrated pictures of the collection, No. 266, the Madonna del Gran Duca, by Raffaelle—so called because it was always kept in the private apartments of the grand-duke; and it is even said that the grand-duchess directed her prayers to this picture when she desired the birth of a son. The Virgin is singularly modest and sweet; the contour of her face and the delicate form of the mouth, as well as the soft, downcast eyes, are pre-eminently beautiful, even among Raffaelle's Madonnas, although this picture belongs to the artist's Florentine period, and is neither so classical as the Madonna della Seggiola, nor so sublime as his greatest creation, the Madonna di San Sisto; but for simple, noble loveliness and purity, this representation of the Virgin is unrivalled; the light which seems to pass from her face melts in her soft fair hair and in the blue-grey of her mantle, until lost in the dark background; her hands are rather large; she holds the Child tenderly, who is less lovely in face than his mother, but his flesh and limbs are beautifully painted and modelled. Towards the end of the last century this valuable work was in the possession of a poor widow, who sold it to a picture-dealer for twelve crowns; from thence it found its way to the Gallery of the Grand-Duke Ferdinand III., who carried it with him wherever he went. When bought from the widow it was in a perfect state, but it has since that time twice undergone the process of cleaning. This was the first picture Raffaelle painted when he visited Florence, after leaving the school of Perugino.*

No. 245 is also attributed to Raffaelle. Passavant believes this female portrait to be the model from which he painted or rather idealized the Madonna di San Sisto. The fine Roman head and bust and the sleeve of the dress he supposes to have been executed by Raffaelle himself, but the rest of the picture to have been finished after his death by an inferior hand. This portrait was in the Palace of the Poggio Imperiale until 1824, when it was brought to the Pitti.†

No. 256. A Holy Family, by Fra Bartolommeo: the composition is very Leonardesque; the infant St. John crouches at the feet of Elizabeth, who smiles as if amused; the Virgin is not elevated in feeling, but the colour of this picture is agreeable, though it has suffered from cleaning and restorations.

---

* See Passavant's "Rafael von Urbino," vol. i. p. 85, vol. ii. p. 35.
† Ibid., vol. i. p. 225, vol. ii. p. 336.

No. 265. A fine half-length figure of St. John the Baptist, by Andrea del Sarto, painted for the King of France, but kept back by Ottaviano de' Medici, and finally placed in this collection.

No. 243. Portrait of King Philip IV. of Spain on horseback, by Velasquez.

No. 255. An admirable portrait of a gentleman, by Van der Helst.

No. 258. Another fine portrait of a gentleman, by the Venetian, Tinelli, a scholar of Titian and Bassano. Tinelli enjoyed a high reputation, and was patronised by Louis XIII. of France.

No. 244. Portrait of a young man, by Franz Pourbus, an excellent Flemish painter of the school of Floris. He painted Henry IV. of France and Marie de' Medici; the hands are finely drawn.

Passing along a short passage, and leaving a boudoir adorned with statues to the left, the first room arrived at is the Sala di Ulisse.

No. 307. Another fine picture, by Andrea del Sarto—the Madonna and Child, with St. Lawrence, St. Paul the Hermit, St. Sebastian, and St. Mark behind, and in the foreground St. John the Baptist and Mary Magdalene. The Infant Christ is full of dignity; heads of cherubim support the Madonna. "A fine, easily-handled work of the master, in well-fused tones."*

No. 311. An interesting portrait of Charles V., by Titian, painted at the same time with his son Philip II. for the

---

* See "Crowe and Cavalcaselle," vol. iii. p. 571, and p. 572. *note.*

Grand-Duke Cosimo I. The emperor is advanced in years, and has a worn and unhappy countenance.

No. 297. A very fine portrait of Pope Paul III., by the Venetian, Paris Bordone. His long, thin figure, gaunt features, and his sharp, querulous countenance, though full of intelligence, are indicative of an unhappy, restless old age. Paul III. (Alexander Farnese) was chosen Pope in 1554 at sixty-eight years of age. His chief aim was to check the progress of Lutheranism. He had been married before he took sacred orders, and he asked and obtained the hand of Margaret of Austria, the illegitimate daughter of the Emperor Charles V., for his grandson, Octavius Farnese. The benefits which he bestowed on his relations were only repaid by ingratitude, and thus embittered the latter years of his life; he died at the advanced age of eighty-four. Though a correspondent of Erasmus, he established the Inquisition at Naples, and confirmed the Order of Jesuits.

No. 287. A good male portrait, by Santi di Tito.

Nos. 306 and 312. Two good landscapes, by Salvator Rosa.

No. 300. An old man, likewise by Salvator Rosa.

No. 324. Portrait of George Villiers, Duke of Buckingham, the handsome favourite of James I. and Charles I., by Rubens, assassinated by Felton in 1628. The picture is full of life, a face uniting beauty and talent.

Several pictures in this room are by Cigoli—No. 291, St. Francis; No. 301, portrait of a man; and No. 303, the Supper at Emmaus.

There are also pictures by Cristofano Allori; and No. 289, a fine picture by Ligozzi: the Virgin appearing to St. Francis.

The Sala di Prometeo contains some fine specimens of the early Florentine school.

No. 338. A Madonna and Child, by Fra Filippo Lippi, which has great sweetness and refinement; the flesh tints are painted with a gentle gradation, and the hands of the Madonna, as well as the Child, are well drawn. The Virgin holds a pomegranate in her left hand, which the Saviour grasps with His right. In the background St. Anne is seen in bed, and the infant Virgin is in the arms of an attendant; at the bedside is a woman followed by a female servant with a basket on her head; two other females with a child bring offerings. The meeting of Joachim and Anne is also represented.

No. 388. The death of Lucretia, by Fra Filippo Lippi.

No. 347. A Holy Family and Angels, attributed to Filippino Lippi. The Virgin is kneeling before the Child in a garden of roses; she is very tender and graceful; the Child is in a playful attitude; one of the angels throws flowers. Cavalcaselle remarks: "This piece, which pleases at first sight, will not bear close inspection, as it wants the finish and feeling noticeable in Filippino. It reminds one of the rounds by Botticelli, without being assignable to him either. It is a production of some subordinate."*

No. 357 is by Botticelli. The Virgin stands holding the Infant Jesus down to receive the embrace of the little St. John, whose child-like tenderness and graceful figure constitute the principal charm of this picture. There are rose-bushes in the background.

No. 353. A portrait by Botticelli, of Simonetta, a lady

---

* See "Crowe and Cavalcaselle," vol. ii. pp. 333, 334.

celebrated for her beauty, which is certainly not remarkable in this picture. She has regular features, but her long neck and awkward figure are not improved by a cap and gown as ugly as they are simple. La bella Simonetta was beloved by Giulio de' Medici.

No. 369. Ecce Homo, by Antonio da Pollaiolo; and No. 384, St. Sebastian, by the same master, of which Cavalcaselle observes: "In the usual coarse forms and proportions in the parts, but still displaying and reminding of a study of the antique, and coloured with the bright tones impregnated with much vehicle, which mark the Prudence in the Uffizi."

No. 354. A Holy Family, attributed to Lorenzo Credi. The Madonna worshipping the Child, who is laid on the ground, his head resting on a bundle of faggots. In the distance is a bright sunny landscape; the ox and ass are in one corner; Joseph is looking on. This picture is probably of the school of Credi.

No. 365 is by Mariotto Albertinelli. The Virgin kneels before the Child, who receives the nails, the instruments of his sacrifice, from an angel; both the Christ and the angel are very graceful, and the Virgin is pleasing. "A brilliant easel piece, charming for the combination of the qualities of Leonardo and Credi, for noble seriousness in the face of the Virgin and the pleasing plumpness in the shape of the Infant Christ; the landscape of Ferrarese minuteness in detail, like that of Fra Bartolommeo's Vision of St. Bernard."*

No. 377. Ecce Homo, by Fra Bartolommeo. A head in

---

* See "Crowe and Cavalcaselle," vol. iii. p. 486.

fresco, resembling that of the half-length figure in the Academy, No. 78; the expression is sad though sweet, and there is a peculiar tenderness about the mouth.

No. 341. A small picture, by Pinturicchio, the Visit of the Magi; interesting from the variety of heads and expression.

No. 344. The Grand-Duke Cosimo III. when a Child, by Sustermans; a charming portrait, natural and simple.

No. 345. A Holy Family, by Baldassare Peruzzi of Sienna.

No. 346. The Magdalene borne to Heaven by Angels, by Taddeo Zuccaro; the groups of cherubim and angels extremely lovely.

No. 359. The Holy Family, by Domenico Beccafumi of Sienna; the children are pleasing.

No. 362. A Holy Family, by an artist of the school of Francia of Bologna.

No. 363. A very lovely Holy Family, by Garofolo; very charming, though not divine.

A long, narrow corridor connects these rooms with a suite farther in the interior of the palace, called the Corridor of the Columns, from two valuable columns of oriental alabaster which are placed here. Six pictures in pietra-dura represent Painting, Sculpture, Architecture, and Music, the Pantheon of Rome and the Tomb of Cecilia Metella. The collection of miniatures in water-colour and oil was made by Cardinal Leopold de' Medici in the course of his travels through Europe, but, unfortunately, there is no catalogue, nor means to learn whom they represent. The first room following the corridor is called the Sala della Giustizia. The rich Stipo, or Ebony Cabinet, inlaid with precious marbles in the centre, was formerly used by Cardinal Leopold de' Medici, when officiating at mass.

One of the most interesting pictures is No. 408, a portrait of Oliver Cromwell, by Sir Peter Lely. The story connected with this picture adds to its interest. When the persecution of the Waldensian Protestants, whose sufferings Milton has immortalised in his beautiful Ode, had reached its height, the Lord Protector of England determined to arrest its course. He accordingly sent a message to the Pope, Alexander VII., that if these barbarities did not cease, he would send the English fleet up the Tiber. The result was an order to the Duke of Savoy to stay his hand. The Grand-Duke of Tuscany, Ferdinand II., was so struck by the courage and character of Cromwell, that he requested him to sit for this picture, which Lely, then a young man, painted.

No. 401. A fine portrait of the Canon Pandolfo Ricasoli, by Sustermans. He belonged to the Order of Jesuits, but was accused of immoral practices, and was condemned by the Inquisition to be walled up alive.

No. 403. Portrait of the Grand-Duke Cosimo I., by Angiolo Bronzino.

No. 404. Portrait of the Grand-Duchess Vittoria della Rovere, by Carlo Dolce.

The ceiling of the Sala di Flora was painted by the modern artist Marini. In the centre of the room is Canova's celebrated statue of Venus, which was intended to replace the Venus de' Medici, when this antique statue was carried to Paris.

No. 415. Portrait of Ferdinand II., by Sustermans.

No. 423. The Adoration of the Shepherds, by Titian.

No. 427. The Calumny of Apelles, by Franciabigio, who, like Sandro Botticelli, revived the subject treated by Apelles.

No. 430. The Madonna and Child, by Cigoli.

No. 431. A landscape, by Agostino Tassi, the master of Claude Lorraine, a very rare master.

No. 434. Portrait, by Bronzino, of the Engineer Luca Martini, who drained the Tuscan Marshes by order of the Grand-Duke Cosimo I.

No. 437. The Repose in Egypt, by Vandyke, painted in the manner of his master, Rubens.

No. 447. A supposed portrait, by Giovan Bologna.

In the Sala dei Putti, No. 453, Peace burning the weapons of war, by Salvator Rosa : a very fine landscape, which might have furnished a study to our own Gainsborough ; the same effects of light on sky and water, the broad touch in the trees, dark-brown shadows in the foreground, and simple chiaroscuro with little colour.

No. 458. Portrait, by Franz Dowen, of the Electress Palatine Anna Maria de' Medici. She was daughter of Cosimo III., and sister of the last Medicean Grand-Duke Gian Gastone ; she survived all her family, dying in 1743. She is again represented by the same artist, No. 459, in a hunting costume ; a third time, No. 466, and again, No. 467, with her husband, the Elector Palatine.

No. 472. A beautiful little landscape, by Ruysdael ; No. 481, a good picture by Breughel, of a Madonna encircled by a garland of flowers. There is also a Madonna, by Andrea del Sarto.

Returning to the Sala di Prometeo, a room to the left is called the Galleria Pocetti, as the ceiling was painted by that artist. At the end is a bust of the first Napoleon in marble. The pictures contained in this room are not of sufficient importance to deserve notice.

TABERNACLES.

THE only remaining specimens of pictorial art to be noticed are the Tabernacles at the corners of the old streets and alleys, which once formed a conspicuous feature in Florence. Many of these were painted by the best masters, and enclosed in frames of marble carved with much elegance. The best have been removed to the galleries, and though a few good pictures are still left in their original positions, they are hardly to be distinguished behind the glass, thickly engrained with dust.*

Some of the most important are as follows :—

The Cinque Lampade in the Via degli Alfani, already mentioned.

Charitable Persons bestowing Alms on Prisoners, by Fabrizio Boschi, at the corner of the Bargello, also mentioned above.

The Virgin and Joseph adoring the Child, by Pocetti, opposite the Church of San Procolo.

Christ bestowing Alms on Prisoners, by Giovanni di San Giovanni, in the Via del Palagio, where was once the prison of the Stinche.

In the Via de' Tintori, at the corner of the wall opposite

---

* See vol. i. p. 197.

the Church of San Giuseppe, is a Tabernacle, by Jacopo da Casentino, which has, however, been much repainted.

Beyond the Porta Sta. Croce is a Madonna, by Domenico Veneziano.

The Madonna and Child appearing to a Cardinal, and children, who worship below, by Alessandro Gherardini, is near the Pia Casa di Lavoro di Montedomini.

Between the Via San Piero Maggiore and the Via dell' Agnolo, near the market of San Piero Maggiore, is an Annunciation, by Giovanni Balducci.

In the Piazza di San Martino, near the Institution for the Poveri Vergognosi, is a fresco representing the good Bishop Antonino distributing alms, by Cosimo Ulivelli.

A tabernacle at the corner of the Via Larga and the Piazza di San Marco, a good deal repainted, is by Gherardo, a celebrated miniature-painter of the sixteenth century.

In the Via Chiara, between the Via Nazionale and the Via Sant' Antonino, are two tabernacles—one by Gianozzo Manetti, of a Holy Family, and the other a Crucifixion, with the Virgin and St. John, the Magdalene kneeling in the background, by Pocetti.

In the Via della Ruote, between the Via San Gallo and the Via Caterina, is the Marriage of St. Catherine, by Domenico Puligo; the Virgin is standing with her Son in her arms, who is giving the ring to St. Catherine, and St. Peter Martyr is beside them.

The Martyrdom of St. Catherine, near San Bonifazio, is by Ferrucci.

In the Via Nazionale is the Luca della Robbia, already mentioned.*

---

* See vol. ii. p. 184.

On the house in the Via de' Ginori, which once belonged to Taddeo Taddei, the friend of Raffaelle, was a tabernacle by Giovanni Sogliani, now transferred to the corner of the Via del Bisogno; it represents the Crucifixion, with the Virgin and St. John below, and weeping angels above.

To the left of the Church of Sta. Maria Nuova, Christ is represented with a mother and three children, by Giovanni di San Giovanni; and at the entrance to the cortile there is another tabernacle—Christ with the Woman of Samaria, by Alessandro Allori.

At the Canto de' Carnesecchi, at the corner of the two roads which lead to the old and new piazzas of Sta. Maria Novella, is a fresco of the Virgin and Saints, by Domenico Veneziano, which was so much admired that it excited the envy of Andrea del Castagno, and led to his assassination of Domenico.

Behind the Hospital of San Paolo, near the Piazza di Sta. Maria Novella, is a Virgin and Child enthroned, with St. Peter and St. Paul on either side and angels above, by Anton Domenico Bamberini.

The tabernacle at the corner of Santa Maria Novella, at the head of the Via della Scala, is by Françesco Fiorentino, a pupil of Don Lorenzo Monaco, which, though injured, exhibits delicacy in the execution, and is pleasing in colour.*

In the Via Palazzuolo, near the Via del Prato, is a fresco of Christ when a child, walking between his parents, by Giovanni di San Giovanni.

A Virgin and Child, by Carlo Portelli, is in the Via delle Terme.

---

* See "Vasari," vol. ii. p. 214, note 3.

TABERNACLES.

South of the Arno: a Virgin and Child appearing to a Bishop, with two angels seated in front, by Cipriano Sensi, is in the Via Maffia, leading from the Via Michelozzi to the Via Fondaccio Santo Spirito.

In the Via della Chiesa is a Bishop kneeling, with a Mother and Children, by Cosimo Ulivelli.

A Holy Family, with St. Roch and other saints, and with a cardinal on his knees, by Filippino Lippi, is in the Via de' Preti, in the neighbourhood of Santo Spirito.

Two Monks glorified, the Saviour above, by Domenico Ghirlandaio, is in the Via della Caldaia, near the Via de' Preti.

A Virgin and Child, with two angels, by Pier Dandini, is in the Piazza Santo Spirito.

Among these, it is probable that the best may still be removed to the galleries. The purpose of these tabernacles, to awaken the religious sentiment in the people, is fulfilled, and the stimulus has lost its effect; the devout worshipper is no longer seen in prayer before them, and the crowd of indifferent passengers hurry past without even appearing conscious of their existence.

MANUFACTURE OF PIETRA-DURA.

IN the Via degli Alfani is the establishment for the manufacture of articles in Florentine mosaic, or pietra-dura, which was at one time a royal monopoly, like that of Sèvres china in France, and was chiefly used for gifts to sovereigns and other exalted personages.

The art of producing pictures of fruit, flowers, and even landscape and figures, by uniting stones of various colours cut into the required shape, had been practised in Lombardy before it was introduced into Tuscany by the Medicean Grand-Dukes Cosimo I. and Francis I. When Ferdinand I. fulfilled the intention of his father and brother, by erecting the Mausoleum of San Lorenzo * for the interment of the Medicean family, he desired that the walls should be incrusted with marbles and precious stones; and for this object he founded the royal manufactory of pietra-dura. About the year 1580, six Milanese masters in the craft had been invited to Florence to teach the art of what is now called Florentine mosaic; and in 1597, the first attempt at figure on record was made in a portrait of

---

* See vol. i. chap. viii.

Cosimo I., executed by Messer Françesco Ferrucci.* It was not until the year 1600, however, that the Royal Institute for the manufacture of pietra-dura commenced operations; and, in 1601, the Grand-Duke ordered a portrait in this material of Pope Clement VIII.—Aldobrandini of Florence—which portrait is still to be seen in the Corsini Palace at Rome. The artist placed at the head of the establishment was the architect Costantino de' Servi, who was specially enjoined to superintend the excavation of the stones, whether imported from other parts of Italy or from abroad, and to see them sawed, to discover any flaws, and select those best adapted for the ornaments destined to enrich the Medicean Mausoleum. According to Baldinucci, Costantino was remarkable for his skill in works of both high and low relief, and still more in flat mosaic. Describing the difficulties of the art, Baldinucci proceeds thus :—
"The work is so excellent in its kind, that it not only resembles a picture, but reality; with this difference, that whereas it is the aim of a good painter to mix and diffuse his colours, so as to form an indefinite number of half-tints, all differing essentially from the original colour, the artist in *commesso* † cannot multiply his material, nor melt one colour into another, but he must adopt the stone as nature has made it. In order to convey the colour by insensible gradations from the highest light to the deepest shadow, he must seek out the most delicate tints which nature has produced, and observe the infinite number of shades dis-

---

* Not to be confounded with the sculptor in porphyry of the same name, who died a few years previously.

† The term used for this kind of mosaic.

coverable on the hardest gems and other stones. To accomplish this, he must be well acquainted with the painter's art, so as to be able at once to recognise in the stones or gems those he can adapt for his purpose, and whether intended for deep shadow or half-lights, to retain always present and fresh in his memory, the kind of stone necessary to produce the effect."

The pietra-dura and gold reliefs, statuettes, and column: now in the Gem Room of the Uffizi Gallery, were all intended for the Medici Chapel, and were manufactured here. In imitation of the Royal Mausoleum, the Senator Giovan Battista Michelozzi, forty years later, placed the choir in Santo Spirito, richly adorned with pietra-dura mosaic.

The art was carried from Florence to the East, when Ferdinand I. sent four artificers to the Great Mogul to procure a variety of silices, which abound in Northern India; and where, it is supposed, they assisted in the decorations of the Taj Mehal, the famous tomb of Akbar, at Agra, on which Orpheus is represented playing the violin, with beasts who listen; the whole encircled by garlands of flowers and fruit of every description. Similar decorations in the Palace of Shah Jehan, at Delhi, are likewise attributed to Italian artists.

The works in pietra-dura mosaic reached their highest perfection in the reign of Ferdinand II., when foreign countries became eager to emulate Florence in this manufacture, and Florentine artists were invited both to France and Naples. The greatest advance was made in the production and variety of half-tints and shadows—due, however, principally to a French goldsmith and gem-carver, Luigi Siriès, who left the service of Louis XV. in 1722, and settled in Florence, where he was appointed Director in the Pietra-dura Establishment. He confined the art to ornamental uses, for which it is in reality adapted, and ceased to represent figure and landscape, which, however wonderfully achieved, only prove the impossibility in this material to vie with the painter's art. The large tables with a porphyry ground in the Pitti Gallery, and with representations of shells, flowers, &c., delicately shaded, are the work of the brothers Luigi and Carlo Siriès.

On the staircase leading to the Museum is a bust of the founder, Ferdinand I. Within are specimens of the old Florentine mosaic, chiefly intended for the altar of San Lorenzo. The artist now employed for the designs is Signor Odoardo Marchionni, who has introduced a harder material than paragona, which is allied to marble, and formerly used for the ground of the mosaic. About thirty-eight persons are employed in the establishment, which is wholly supported by the Government, though no longer a monopoly, as individuals are now permitted to follow the art on their own account; but as the materials are expensive, shell is often used instead of chalcedony in the pietra-dura sold in shops. Both the designs and execution have lately been greatly improved. A collection of the stones in use, such as agates and siliceous substances, are arranged according to the countries whence they are obtained, so as to enable the workmen to select those best fitted for the purpose. They are cut with wire saws and emery powder, which last is also used to polish the stone. Most of the work is inlaid and flat, as statuettes and raised relief are now rare.

EGYPTIAN MUSEUM—ETRUSCAN REMAINS.

IN the Via di Faenza, not far from the Piazza della Indipendenza, is the Egyptian Museum, to which the collection of Etruscan remains, formerly in the Gallery of the Uffizi, has lately been transported.

Early in the sixteenth century this building was a convent belonging to the nuns of San Onofrio, but it had long been applied to secular uses, when in 1826 the proprietor, by trade a coach-builder, wishing to increase the light in the large square room, formerly the Refectory of the convent, began whitewashing the walls. In the course of the work traces of painting appeared beneath the dirt and coats of whitening; an artist was summoned to assist in cleansing this away, and a beautiful cenacolo, or fresco, of the Last Supper was discovered. As Raffaelle visited Florence from 1504 to 1505, and is supposed to have been employed by the nuns to decorate the walls of their convent, the work was at once assigned to him; and this opinion appeared confirmed by the refined beauty of the heads, and the careful drawing of the hands, feet, and drapery, to which may be added the period to which the painting certainly belongs, and the inscription of Raffaelle's name, now indistinctly seen on the border of Saint Thomas's dress:—

RALVR·ROMMDV
Raf. Urt.   M.D.V.

The following description of this fresco, at the time of its discovery, was written by an eminent connoisseur in Art :*—"The heads generally are pretty well varied, but much on a level, in the stiff, hard style of the early masters; the countenances wanting in expression, excepting that of Christ and that of Judas. The Saviour is not *divine*, but a man acquainted with sorrow; mild, benignant, and melancholy. His countenance is very sweet. The head of Judas is full of spirit, but has rather the air of a fierce captain of banditti than of a scoundrel betraying his Master, and selling his faith. The draperies are in general pretty broad, but the remarkably fine master-work is in the painting of the hands and feet; these are admirable, and the position of the former surprisingly varied. On the hem of the garment of one of the disciples are to be found these characters, or something near it—' RAF. VRBJ. x MDXV.' No man except Raffaelle was ever admitted within these walls."

Doubts have since arisen as to the authorship of this fresco, and Cavalcaselle attributes it to other pupils of Perugino, stating that it had been painted over, and that "the colour is that of a practised coarse hand, which is neither Raffaelle's nor Perugino's." It is not, however,

* The late Lieutenant-General Sir Henry Bunbury, Bart., K.C.B.

impossible that when the fresco, originally by Raffaelle, was restored by an inferior hand, the inscription may have been injured in the process, which would account for its present indistinctness. The obscure position of this inscription, which can only be discovered after a close inspection, would not have been selected by an impostor; and the character of the heads may be compared with other works of Raffaelle at this period—his Madonna del Gran Duca, and Madonna del Baldachino, both in the Gallery of the Pitti, as well as with the portraits of Angelo Doni and his wife Maddalena Strozzi, &c., &c. The head and figure of St. James, with his hands beautifully placed in repose, of St. Thomas and of St. John, are very Raffaellesque. Around the room —besides original drawings and studies for this fresco, which are likewise attributed to Raffaelle—are other drawings, photographs, and engravings, showing the varied and yet similar treatment of the subject by artists of different schools and countries.

In the corridor from which this room is entered are various Papyri and Egyptian remains; and, turning to the left, a door opens on a large hall containing a valuable collection of Egyptian antiquities. At the end of this hall is a very interesting bas-relief, engraved and painted on the stone which closed the burial place of King Sethos I. (Ramases), and which was removed by Belzoni. The goddess Hather, the supposed nurse of Sethos, makes him touch her necklace, to express he was her cherished son. The necklace is coloured, and of a flexible material, fastened at intervals by a ribbon. Imitations of this style of necklace will be found on the statues of Etruscan *Cippi*, as well as chains which resemble that round the neck of the king.

To the right of the relief is a curious stone cage, which once held the sacred Hawk of the Egyptians. In the centre of the room are large sarcophagi and statues, whilst along the whole length of the wall, from the door, are ranged mummies under glass. Over a closed door at the end is a picture of all who were engaged in the Franco-Tuscan expedition to Egypt, 1828—1829. Champollion, who was at the head, is seated, dressed as an Egyptian; on his right is the Director Rosellini; both are listening to explanations from a sheik. To the left of this picture is a case containing Egyptian masks or busts in high relief, and an ancient encaustic portrait of a very lovely Egyptian girl. A small case near contains corn grown from the seed found in a mummy. Among the various utensils, articles of clothing, sculpture, &c., which fill the cases down this side of the room, there are most interesting bas-reliefs, showing the whole process of making pottery.

Leaving this room at the end of the corridor is a smaller room, containing the rest of the Egyptian collection. In the centre is a War-chariot of the simplest construction, which was discovered in a tomb. No iron has been employed, but the wheels as well as the body of the vehicle are all wood, bound together with thongs of leather. The chariot is composed of a half-circle of wood filled in with straw plait—the only modern addition—on which the charioteer could stand; a larger hoop, supported in the centre by a wooden pole, was for the reins; the shafts are long, and a very simple kind of harness is suspended from the end of the shafts. Two fine mummy cases are placed on each side of the room, and many smaller ones are ranged round the walls. In the window are two black stone altars, and a small statue in the same material near the door represents a priest or god, holding an inscription before him. Cases No. VI. and VIII. are filled with recent acquisitions. Case VI. has gold ornaments, a chain of amulets, statuettes of Egyptian women washing clothes, and bronzes of various periods. Case VIII. contains articles from the Island of Cyprus; a mixed assemblage of Greek, Phœnician, and native Cypriote manufacture. Some of the vases do not differ in form from those of Greece proper or Etruria; two or three are unique in shape. The symbol of Cyprus—a series of circles from small to large—is to be found on almost all. One shelf is fitted with glass, among which some of the beads are precisely the same as those found in Etruria. Another shelf has terra-cottas, most of which are small busts, and several are unmistakably Greek; the Phœnician are in very rude art, and have the tall pointed cap usually worn by that people. The Cypriote busts have a peculiar physiognomy, and, according to Asiatic custom, are crowned with wreaths or diadems, such as are seen on the heads of Etruscan monumental figures.

Beyond this Egyptian room is a small corridor with shelves, on which are placed Etruscan ash-chests, coloured; one of these has the representation of a youth falling in battle, very spirited. The female figure to the left of the entrance, and another to the right when leaving this corridor, wear the virginal wreath, and belonged to monuments of unmarried women. The fluted vase to the left, with a relief round the rim representing a race, has been lately added.

In the centre of the first Etruscan room is a bronze statue, above life-size, of an orator, with his arm raised, as if addressing an audience. He is attired in a tunic with

short sleeves, and a mantle which hangs in large and simple
folds; an inscription in Etruscan character, on the border
of his tunic, has the name of the orator or of the sculptor,
Aulo Metello. The buskins, or shoes, are fastened by
leathern thongs twisted round the leg; the head is noble
and animated, with the eager expression, plain features, and
square intellectual brow commonly seen in Tuscany. The
exaggerated length of the right arm is owing to imperfect
repairs. The statue was discovered at Sanguinetto, near
the Lake of Thrasymenus; it is a proof to what perfection
the art of bronze casting, as well as of modelling, was
brought by the Etruscans. All round this room are ranged
cippi, or chests, which contained the ashes of the dead;
there is one exception, where a statue, life-size, is placed
over a sarcophagus containing the body of the deceased.
These statues, which probably bore some resemblance in
face to the person when alive, are in general in short
proportions to fit the lid of the ash-chest, and are of a conventional type; the reliefs below are generally very superior.
We are reminded in these monumental figures of their
Asiatic origin: the men wear garlands or coronals, and
chains or necklaces like those of the Egyptian Sethos and
the goddess Hather; these chains are sometimes twisted in
their coronals, instead of being hung round their necks;
they have besides rings on their fingers, and hold the patera
or sacrificial cup; sometimes they have a tablet or diptych
in their hands; the females are generally represented with a
fan formed like a palm-leaf, or they have mirrors. In the
window is a statue of a reclining female, more than usually
elegant; she has a bracelet and armlet on her right arm,
not unlike the silver bracelets worn by Hindoo women.

The favourite subjects of the reliefs on these cippi are taken from Greek story, and the composition and even the execution of several are worthy of Greek artists. Incidents from the tale of the siege of Thebes, the Calydonian Boar, the fight with the Minotaur, the Rape of Helen, the Trojan War, and the events in the history of Ulysses, are frequently repeated. Many of the subjects are simply typical of death; the separation of a husband and wife, and of parents from their children,—winged demons wait to convey the soul away in a chariot with horses; in some instances a female is anointing a seated figure, as for sacrifice; in others, a victim is kneeling at an altar. Nearly in the centre of the wall, and facing the window, is a monument on which is represented a group of persons lifting the body of the deceased into a car; the sinking figure, the actions of those around, and the whole composition might have formed a study for a Deposition from the Cross to an artist of the Cinque-cento period.

The second room is smaller, but contains a choice collection of cippi; one especially, which faces the entrance to the Hall of the Orator, a little to the right, has two warriors sinking to the ground after a fatal combat; each is supported by his genius or guardian spirit, whilst between them, seated on a rock, is a third winged genius, holding the sword of justice. The expression of the fainting heroes, particularly of the warrior nearest death, is extremely beautiful. Above them is placed another relief, with a similar subject, repeated on one of the cippi in the Hall of the Orator, though inferior in execution. Two nude statues of Proserpine, with stones for arms, are on each side of the door leading to a further room. The following subjects are represented on cippi in this room:—The soul departing in a chariot; a group of persons starting on a journey—the females in a waggon, the men on horseback; a family is taking leave of a dying person; Ulysses and the Syrens,—possibly signifying that those on the voyage of life must, like Ulysses, be deaf to all the seductions which might detain them here,—this subject is very common; pointed columns are also frequent, though the meaning is not satisfactorily explained; a beautiful relief of the story of Orestes and Pylades—they are at the tomb of Agamemnon, and Electra, the sister of Orestes, is followed by a slave, who bears a tray, or *focolaro*, so often met with in Etruscan tombs. Where a dolphin is represented, it refers to the story of the Tyrrhenean pirates, whom Dionysius or Bacchus, the god whose rites are symbolical of immortality, turned into dolphins. Snakes or hippocampi were considered by the Etruscans emblematical of the passage of the soul from one state of existence to another; and the same idea is applied to all amphibious animals, fabulous or real, when represented on these tombs.

In the centre of this room is the bronze Chimæra found near Cortona, when the fortifications of the city were repaired in 1554; it is cited by Vasari as a proof of the perfection of Etruscan bronze casting.* The inscription on the paw may signify the name of the artist; the characters mark the period, as some letters in the Etruscan alphabet are known to have been a late innovation. When first discovered, the Chimæra was conveyed to Florence, and placed in a room of the Palazzo Vecchio, inhabited by the

---

* See Vasari, " Vite dei Pittori," vol. i. p. 199.

Grand-Duke Cosimo I. The myth of the Chimæra or Fire-breathing monster,—therefore the more appropriately represented in metal,—was first invented in a volcanic district of Asia Minor, from whence a colony was planted in Etruria; but it seems difficult to account for the form given to it of a lion with a dragon or serpent's tail, and a goat's head springing from the back. The Chimæra, as here represented, has been wounded by Hercules, the chosen hero of the Etruscans, and the whole action of the animal and of its three heads express pain.

The small room beyond contains armour discovered a few years ago in a tomb near Orvieto. It has been moulded to the form of the wearer, and the grieves and every part is finished with the utmost precision. The remains of gilding are still to be traced on the bronze. Cabinets with various instruments, strigils, &c., surround the room, and in the window is a most exquisite bronze pail, suspended on a hook, with a relief around it. The subject is a Bacchanalian procession. An outline drawing of this beautiful composition is exhibited on the wall.

At the entrance to a second suite of rooms are two rude though expressive terra-cotta figures; on one side is a most beautiful bronze statue of Pallas Athenæ with the Ægis. The repairs have been badly made, and are easily detected. The statue is worthy of the utmost praise for elegant proportions and finish of detail. Around, placed under glass, is a collection of small bronzes. In the case to the left is a representation of a dead stag, hanging head downwards; there are likewise statuettes of warriors, winged horses, chimæras, &c. Opposite this case a very early period of art is represented in the long, shapeless figures of gods, taken from an Etruscan temple, the bells of which are exhibited below. A third case has a collection of various instruments, such as handles, and the strigil used to scrape the oil from the persons of gladiators preparing for the games. Lastly, a case of other utensils, handles, &c., which exhibit a high state of art ; one handle is formed of two genii supporting a wounded man ; a second, of a warrior who raises another sinking in death.

The long corridor, which connects this cabinet with another at the farther end, is filled with Etruscan inscriptions ; these are chiefly on tiles, which were used to close up the graves of the dependants or friends of a great family, and who were buried in the walls or the embankments on either side of the passage or staircase leading to the principal tomb. Other inscriptions belong to cippi. On the top of three ranges of shelves are placed round or conical stones, which were used to mark the burial-places in the Etruscan cemetery.

The cabinet beyond contains a collection of most exquisite gold ornaments, some unique of their kind—such as a pair of earrings formed of a lion's head, grand in its small proportions, and, hanging from its jaws, is a little filigree basket, with a dove at the top. In another case there is a small but valuable collection of Etruscan coins, beginning with the large, clumsy bronze money, having the wheel of Etruria, and ending with a fine Greek work on the silver coin, besides two or three rare and valuable gold pieces, bearing the head of the chimæra ; these last have been contributed to the Museum by the Marchese Carlo Strozzi. The wheel, which often appears on the monuments as well as coins, is a symbol peculiar to Etruria ; and even in these days the inhabitants of certain villages in the neighbourhood of Cortona are known as the *Ruotelesi*, or the people of the wheel. Another case in this room contains articles in ivory and glass. In the third and fourth cases are exhibited bronze instruments, spear-heads, hatchets, fibulæ, or clasps, and flint arrow-heads.

The next room contains objects in terra-cotta; some very spirited heads or masks are in the case to the right; one, of an old woman with a single tooth and blind of an eye, is especially remarkable; also a relief of a ship with rowers and pilot, as well as a very elegant little torso of a youth.

Opposite are vases of white terra-cotta, richly ornamented, and evidently of a late period; others are black, fluted, with a fine polish; on some of these is a very beautifully executed representation of a hunter and dog. Terra-cottas of animals in very rude workmanship, horses, &c., not unlike the toys sold to this day in the streets of Florence, and ex voto offerings of arms, feet, &c., are in the last case to the left; whilst opposite are Canopi, or ash-chests, with the head and arms of a man.

The last two rooms of this Museum contain a small but choice collection of Etruscan vases, beginning with those in the farther room near the entrance-hall. The cases are divided by two shelves, and within the lowest division is a narrower shelf, on which are ranged the smallest vases. Below are imperfect or unimportant vases and terra-cottas of various kinds.

The earliest Etruscan pottery in Case I. is rude in material and in construction. The third little jar from the right is one of the oldest specimens of pottery in existence,

Forms of Etruscan Vases.

and was found at Sovana, near Pitigliano. The fourth and sixth vases are peculiar, from the perpendicular lines on their surface. All these early vases have been baked in the sun. The curious vessel on the bottom shelf of Case II. is supposed to have been intended to hold live animals, pigeons, or rabbits. In Case II. the vases are of an improved form, and we find the black ware peculiar to Chiusi, the ancient capital of Etruria. Jugs with one handle (Œnochoe) (*see* No. 7 of illustration), mixing-jars—wide-mouthed vessels with two small handles, for mixing the wine with water, and known as Stamni (*see* No. 9), and cups (Cylix) (*see* No. 6), have on them representations of wild animals, sea-horses, &c., typical of immortality. On the lowest shelf is a curious and ugly vessel with many mouths.

As these vases have been all found in the vaults or chamber-tombs of Etruria, it is supposed their forms were imitations of vessels in common use; but their peculiar ornaments are symbolical of Etruscan ideas of immortality. They were probably manufactured for the funereal banquets held in these abodes of the dead.

On the top shelf of Case IV. is a very fine Canopus; the human head is supposed to represent the manes or soulless body of a dead person, and is found on Greek gems with Mercury, the guide of souls to the infernal regions. Upon the jugs below are seen the symbolical bird, the dove or cock; the last suggesting the re-awakening of the spirit. On the lowest shelf, a kind of stove and dishes are ornamented with heads of a very Egyptian type.

In the centre of the top shelf, Case V., is a very large water jar, a vessel with three handles (Hydria) (*see* No. 10);

and on either side, jars for wine or oil with two handles (Amphoræ) (*see* No. 2)—one of these has a man and horse in relief repeated all round. Two fine cups without handles are on the next shelf, with an Œnochoe, having likewise subjects in relief; below is a two-handled cup (Cantharus) (*see* No. 5), good in form, and with a delicate fan-like ornament in white. On the bottom shelf is a large circular Focolaro, a sort of tray containing various vessels left exactly as they were found in the tomb whence it was taken. These focolari are supposed by some to have been placed in the tombs of mothers of families, and the vessels within to represent household or kitchen utensils; besides cups, bottles, ladles, &c., there is generally a tablet, which may have been used to write down the orders for the day.

Case VI. On the second shelf are five remarkable Œnochoe. The central vase has a lid in the form of a bull's head, and round it is a relief representing a man seizing a bull by the horns with one hand, whilst with the other he grasps one of the animal's forelegs,—probably Theseus conquering the ferocious Marathanian bull; above are heads of lions and of the Chimæra. The four remaining Œnochoe have human faces and winged griffins in relief around, with the bird at the top. Below this shelf is a large Œnochoe with tigers carrying off their prey; in the upper part are Egyptian heads. On either side of this vase are Focolari.

Case VII. Two large Œnochoe and a Hydria with the cock at the top; round these vases are reliefs of wild animals. In the middle of the second shelf is a singular-shaped vase, like a tunny fish, with a human face, having Egyptian curls hanging down at the end; on either side are very singularly-shaped small Œnochoe; lower down are cups with a heating apparatus beneath them; also curiously shaped vessels, supposed to support the arm when writing. On the bottom shelf is a large dish with two handles, and two Focolari, one of which has also two handles.

Case VIII. A Hydria and Œnochoe, both of which have the cock at the top, and two circular bowls; on the bottom shelf is a very large Focolaro, ornamented by human heads with ram's horns; there are likewise flat dishes with beautifully twisted handles and doves, and, where the handles join the dish, Egyptian heads. These dishes rest on small round stoves.

Case IX. Amphoræ with reliefs; on the shelf of small vases is a dish, composed of three cups, probably for condiments to be placed in the middle of the table. There are, besides, two circular bowls, and another large Focolaro, with human heads, without the ram's horns; the eyes are half-closed, and the mouths are smiling; the chins are singularly long, and the cheek-bones high.

Case X. A large circular Focolaro with the usual accompaniments, and two more round bowls.

Case XI. A singular vessel or mixing-jar, in the form of a gourd.

Next this case is the entrance to a low chamber, constructed to resemble the Etruscan tomb recently discovered near Orvieto, with copies of the paintings on the walls, and vases on a low shelf around. The bronze gilt armour and vases in a room already described were taken from this tomb. An ancient bronze candelabrum is placed in front, with candles attached to it, in the same manner as the painted candelabrum on the wall of the compartment to the right. The paintings represent what may be supposed to be the funereal banquet. Meat is hung up, and cooks engaged in the preparations are seen to the left. On the right, Pluto and Proserpine and guests are seated at the feast. One young man with a vase in his hand is singularly beautiful and Greek in character.

Returning to the first room, Case XII. contains another gourd-shaped vessel with a lid, the edge of which is moulded like the lotus leaf.

Case XIII. On the second shelf is an Œnochoe, with a head of Egyptian type seen in profile, and animals in relief.

Case XIV. The material, as well as designs, of the vases exhibited in this case, and in Case XV., belong to the finest period of black pottery. The polish is singularly clear and bright, the shapes are simple and elegant; some are fluted, but most of them smooth. The smaller vases, lamps, œnochoe, &c., are exceedingly beautiful. There are also two Pateras (saucers), with a hollow protrusion in the centre for the insertion of the middle finger, precisely like those seen in the hands of male figures on the Etruscan cippi.

Case XV. A sieve of very fine workmanship; a beautifully fluted cup is on the second shelf, and among these elegant vases a jug of an old and singular form (*see* No. 4).

A small marble chair in the window of this room was found in a tomb with a canopus upon it.

The vases in the adjoining room are all supposed to be of Greek origin, though found in Etruria, and probably of Etruscan manufacture. The works of art of this singular people prove them to have attained a high degree of civilisation, but nothing remains of their history beyond a few inscriptions, difficult to decipher, in an extinct language,

EGYPTO-ETRUSCAN MUSEUM. 431

and the scanty records, or references made to them by Roman authors. They appear to have been a mixed race of colonists from Asia, Egypt, and Greece, who had intermarried with the Italian aborigines; and everything, however trifling, which can throw light on their manners and customs, and on their ideas of religion, has an additional interest when associated with the character of their descendants, inhabiting the same country.

The earliest pottery which had any pretension to artistic form was made in Corinth, and the few specimens that remain, may be recognised by a rude representation of the Corinthian Rose, of which one or two may be seen in Case I. A Corinthian is supposed to have first imported the art to Etruria. The Etruscan vases of the earliest period, in the same case, are of a yellow or pale ashen colour, and have a dull opaque surface; they are decorated with designs in brown, crimson, purple, and white. The figures are ranged within horizontal bands round the vase, and are Asiatic in character, whilst the lotus-leaf of Egypt forms a conspicuous ornament: the subjects are chiefly the combats of wild animals—lions, leopards, bulls, goats, swans, the sphinx, chimæra, and griffin, all representing a chaotic age; whenever the human form appears, it is stiff and conventional, and the names are written over each, in early Greek or Etruscan characters.

The second style of vase-painting was probably of Athenian origin, as Athens was celebrated for beauty of design, and a portion of the city was assigned to the potters, whose works must have been held in high estimation, since they were given as prizes in the games. It is not surprising that works of art so fragile have almost all perished during the centuries of barbarian rule in Greece; and only a few, which have been assigned by conjecture to Athens, may still be seen in the museums of Europe. The period of painted Greek vases commences earlier than any known Greek sculpture, and ends about the reign of Alexander of Macedon, B.C. 360. They were used first in the celebration of the rites of Bacchus and Ceres, the divinities of wine and corn, whose ceremonies were symbolical of immortality; for as the skin of the grape must be broken to produce wine, and the corn must be sown in the ground and die before bread can be made, so the body of man must perish before his spirit can be set free. These painted vases were sometimes used to contain the wine thrown on the funereal pile, and were afterwards placed in the tomb; others contained the ashes of the dead; others, again, were the gifts of friends, and these have the name, and the Greek word ΚΑΛΟΣ, Beautiful, equivalent to "Hail," inscribed on them: many of the vases were used as rewards for the victors in the public games. The ground of these vases of the second period is red, and the figures black, with the occasional use of white for the faces and hands of females, and even purple in the draperies. The drawing is dry and stiff, but with life, movement, and dramatic effect sometimes bordering on caricature; the subjects are chiefly taken from the exploits of Hercules, the favourite Etruscan hero. The large eyes represented on two small Cylice and on the Patera, in Case I., have been variously explained; some suppose them to represent the eyes in the peacock's tail, well-known in Christian legends to be typical of immortality; others believe the vases which have eyes, belonged to ships, as eyes were commonly painted on the prows of Greek vessels, and continue to be so on the trading ships of Greece or Dalmatia to this day; a celebrated vase in the British Museum has the eye on the ship of Ulysses, who is passing the Syrens. This peculiarity may have arisen from the resemblance a ship bears to the dolphin.

The subject on an Amphora of early date in Case I., lowest shelf, is a hero and his charioteer starting on a journey. Mars and Minerva are beside him. An old white bearded man is seated at the horses' heads. On another Amphora, Mercury (bearded) is represented leading Juno, Minerva, and Venus to Paris. A third Amphora has Apollo seated beside a palm-tree, and playing on a lyre, whilst a female turns to listen, and raises her hands to her head.

Case III. An Amphora from Vulci. The drawing is archaic but true. Hercules carries a pole on his shoulder, at the ends of which two youths are suspended with their heads downwards. These youths are the two Cercopes or Gnomes who robbed Hercules in his sleep. The hero has his club in one hand. He is preceded by Mercury, the god of thieves, as well as conductor of souls to Pluto, who turns round, raising his right hand. Mercury wears his cloak and winged Petasus or cap, and holds his caduceus in his left hand. A goat is beside him.

Case IV. On the second shelf an Œnochoe, on which Minerva is represented seated. She is attired in her ægis and helmet, and carries her lance in her left hand, whilst raising her right to receive the libation which Hercules offers her in a cantharus; above hang his bow, quiver, and club. On an Olpe or jug, of a peculiar shape, No. 12, Ariadne is seated on the bull. The word Olpe signifies a leathern flask, and was used for jugs without spouts. The Olpe belongs generally to an early period. Two Œnochoe have representations of warriors fighting over a dead body, and three female figures with stars above them, carrying a cornucopia and grapes, probably the Hesperides, from whom Hercules stole the golden apples.

Case V. A very singular Hydria, with a chequered pattern round the mouth. On the lid is an assembly of the gods; below are bacchanalian figures saluting a superior personage by raising the hand to the forehead in the Indian manner. In the central band is a dance of satyrs. The colours are black, white, and red. Another Hydria of early or archaic times represents the legend of Triptolemus, the favoured of Demeter or Ceres, the inventor of the plough and of agriculture, and the hero of the Eleusinian mysteries. Demeter had given Triptolemus a chariot with winged dragons, and seeds of wheat which he sowed over the earth. He is always represented as a youthful hero, sometimes with the Petasus (the felt cap worn by ploughmen and fishermen, the same as that worn by Mercury, with the addition of wings), with a sceptre and ears of corn, and with a chariot drawn by dragons. On this vase Triptolemus is represented with winged horses. Lower down he is attended by a female figure with a cup. In another part of the vase Hercules is seen strangling the lion, and Triptolemus again in his chariot, besides warriors and a female carrying a vase. On the small shelf is a beautiful little Cantharus with two handles.

The third and best style of ceramic art consists of red figures on a black ground. The designs do not at first differ widely from those of the second period, and the style may be divided into early and late. The early is stiff and archaic, but vigorous; the late, in which the art of drawing has attained greater elegance, as well as freedom, may be assigned to three hundred years before our era, or from the end of the Peloponnesian War to Alexander the Great. The early or strong style belongs to the age of Phidias; the more graceful is cotemporary with Parrhasius and Apelles. Inscriptions gradually disappear, and scenes of domestic life, or the gentler tales of heroic legend, are substituted for the labours of Hercules and the feats of Achilles.

Case V. A large and very beautiful Hydria. A warrior is dancing on a board, whilst a lovely female is seated before him; her attendants play on musical instruments in a band. Below, a female flies from a youthful warrior, and two other maidens turn towards a dignified old man, as if to appeal to him for protection.

A fine Stamnos has a representation of a ceremony during the feast of new wine. A table, on which are two Stamni, is placed before an image of Bacchus, and females with cups and ladles are mixing the wine with water. Their drapery falls in straight folds, but is very elegant. The Feasts of Bacchus or Dionysius are favourite subjects on Greek or Etruscan pottery; for the god was held in peculiar veneration in Lydia, whence a colony had settled in Etruria.

Near the Stamnos just described, is an Amphora on which Mercury is represented pursuing a nymph; and on another Stamnos, Hercules plays the double pipe to Pan, who carries his club, whilst a Faun falls backwards in wonder at the sight.

On a Pellice, a vase rarely found in Etruria, and belonging to the most perfect style of art (*see* No. 1.), is the figure of a man binding up the arm of a youth, in very fine drawing.

Case VII. contains a Celebe, or wide-mouthed vessel, generally found in Sicily or Magna Grecia (*see* No. 11.); this Celebe belongs to the Phidian period, and the drawing of a Centaur and Lapitha is full of vigorous movement, life, and strength. A beautiful little Amphora has the genius of Harmony, and on a companion vase is a nymph with ribbons; both were intended for marriage presents. A fine Cylix, or shallow cup (*see* No. 6.), has two Fauns playing the double pipe and dancing before a child, over whom a male figure with two sticks appears to be performing an incantation; a female with her back turned to this group has the same child, on whom she is placing an ass's head; two other females, with sticks and a cup, converse, or are engaged in a ceremony. This design may allude to some legend of the sorceress Circe; the composition and drawing are excellent. On a fine Crater, Neptune is covering Encelades with the Island of Sicily; both figures are very powerful in drawing, and belong to the Phidian period. Within this crater is a second vase to contain the ashes of the dead, which was originally closed by the beautiful Rhyton or drinking cup, shaped like a horse's head, hanging above. Within the rim of this Rhyton is a delicate little drawing of male and female figures. A Celebe in this case has again the subject of the feast of new wine; two male and two female figures with cups and the double pipe.

The cases which follow contain some vases of greater interest, found in the recently discovered tombs of Orvieto, the copy of which is next the first room of vases. A Stamnos with yellow figures on a black ground, and with a dull surface, has a spirited and beautiful drawing of Hercules or Herakles, as an infant, strangling the serpent sent to destroy him by Juno Hera. His mother, Alcmena, noble in person and attired in majestic drapery, has her spindle in her left hand, whilst extending the right to her heroic son; Ificles, the half-brother of Herakles, here called Iolaus (who was in reality the son of Ificles), flies for protection to a woman, who is probably an attendant or nurse. Zeus or Jupiter, and Hera, look on with displeasure from behind. On the other side of this vase, Priam is represented kneeling at the feet of Achilles to beg for the body of Hector; Achilles, seated in the centre, turns towards Pallas-Athenæ-Minerva, who wears the ægis, but has laid aside her helmet; the owl is seated on her spear. A female between Athenæ and Achilles, with an amphora and œnochoe in her hands, possibly Briseis, appears to intercede. The Trojan hero lies dead at the feet of Achilles; Priam wears his royal mantle and the fillet round his head; a youth, to whom it is difficult to assign a name, is between him and Achilles. The horses behind, fed by a groom, are probably meant to signify the cruel fate of Hector, since they have been taken from the chariot of Achilles. The groom or slave has an entirely different type of face from the Greco-Etruscan.

A second vase, in the form of an Amphora, has the representation of a soul urged on by a Demon towards Charon, who has yellow and white wings on his shoulders and heels, and horns on his head; he is seizing on the soul of a woman enveloped in a mantle; behind Charon is Cerberus. The figures are short and clumsy, though animated, and the contrast is well given between the calm and wondering aspect of the soul and the fury of the demons. Another

Amphora has twisted handles; the design is a combat of Centaurs.

The rest of the vases within the cases in this room illustrate the fourth period, or that of the decline; the ground is left pale red, or reddish yellow; the designs are overloaded with ornament without regard to symmetry, and the drawing is careless and incorrect. This style extends nearly to the end of the Roman Republic, a few years before the Christian era.

In the window is a large Amphora of white terra-cotta, round which is painted three dancing nymphs. On each side are Amphoræ of immense size, in one of which was found the ashes of the dead. The soul is represented seated within a shrine, and a horse ready to convey it away. On one vase is a winged genius with an old man, possibly Pluto or Vulcan, who is admonishing the departed soul; friends bring gifts; the head or manes of the deceased is represented on the handles and neck of the vase. The lid of one vase has been lately restored.

In the middle of this room is the celebrated François Vase, discovered by Monsieur François near Chiusi, in 1845, also called the Vase of Peleus, from the principal subject; a lost fragment was long afterwards discovered by the Marchese Carlo Strozzi, which is now placed below it. It is in the second style, black figures on a light ground; in the central band is the marriage of Peleus, the father of Achilles, to Thetis, on Mount Pelicon; the gods are here represented taking part in the marriage solemnity. The uppermost band has the hunt of the Calydonian Boar, and Theseus slaying the Minotaur; the second contains the legend of the Centaurs and of Achilles. Below the marriage of Peleus is the story of Troïlus, and Vulcan's return to Olympus; the fifth band is filled with wild animals; the sixth has the Pigmies and the Cranes.

In the glass case below are also several curious and elegant small vases of various periods. A beautiful Patera has the representation of a banquet; two youths prepare for the games, and are holding the stragil with which they have scooped off the oil anointing their bodies; a fillet is bound around their heads; above the principal figures, who recline on couches, hang all the utensils for the banquet. The subject is repeated on the same vase.

MUSEUM OF NATURAL HISTORY.

THE palace in which the Natural History Museum of Florence is preserved originally belonged to the Bini family, but passed through several hands until the year 1795, when the Grand-Duke Pietro Leopoldo purchased the building from the Torrigiani. He employed the Abate Felice Fontana to begin a collection of objects illustrative of natural history, and afterwards appointed him Director of the Museum, which was opened to the public in the year 1780. In 1807 the Queen of Etruria, Elisa Buonaparte—Bacciocchi—added a School of Public Instruction, and founded Chairs of Astronomy, Physics, Anatomy, Zoology, Mineralogy, Botany, and Chemistry, which were maintained until the restoration of the Grand-Duke Ferdinand III. in 1814, when this admirable institution was suppressed. It was, however, restored in 1833, after the accession of the late Grand-Duke Leopold II., with the exception of the Botanical Chair, which was only reinstated in 1842. Since the accession of Victor Emmanuel in 1859, the institution for more advanced studies—*Studii Superiori*—has been founded, and Chairs of Geology, Metallurgy, and Mining added. Courses of lectures are annually delivered. The present Director or President of the School and Museum, is the eminent botanist, Professor Filippo Parlatore.

The Palæontological Museum is on the ground-floor, where there are also rooms devoted to the chemical and philological department. Within the court of the building is a fine block of lignite, and another of lead ore from Sardinia. The two singular globes, one terrestrial, the other celestial, placed at the entrance, were constructed by Matteo Neroni, and by Ignazio Dante, the author of the maps in the Palazzo Vecchio and of the astronomical instruments on the façade of Sta. Maria Novella. These globes were brought here from the Palazzo Vecchio.

On the first-floor are the collection of physical instruments, as well as the Botanical Museum. Immediately to the right, at the head of the staircase, is a small temple consecrated by the last Grand-Duke Leopold II. to the memory of the celebrated Galileo Galilei, the inventor of experimental philosophy, who was born at Pisa in 1564, and died in Florence 1692. His statue here is by Aristodemo Costoli, a Florentine sculptor, recently deceased; it is placed in the centre of the Tribune. The walls, decorated with stucco, are also painted with frescos representing incidents in the life of the philosopher; and around are busts of his disciples or fellow-workers. Some of Galileo's most valuable instruments are exhibited in cases or niches. Among the most interesting are the two first telescopes constructed by himself in 1609, when he held the Chair of Mathematics in Padua. The Venetian Senate, as a reward for this invention, confirmed him in his professorship for life. It was by means of one of these telescopes that he discovered the satellites of Jupiter. The Grand-Duke Ferdinand I. of Tuscany desired to possess this instrument, but it was only after the death of Galileo that it became the property of his son Cosimo III.

In another niche is the first microscope invented by Galileo, and presented by his disciple Vincenzio Viviani, b. 1622, d. 1703. The telescopes which belonged to Torricelli, Viviani, and other physicists are all likewise preserved here, as well as the powerful crystal lens made by Brezans of Dresden, and placed on a wooden pedestal, which thirteen years after the extinction of the Accademia del Cimento was used by Averani and Targioni, the pupils of Viviani and Redi, in their experiments on the combustibility of the diamond, and of other precious stones, and which in our days was also employed by the celebrated Sir Humphrey Davy, in his researches into the chemical components of the diamond.

Viviani, the favourite pupil of Galileo, has been already mentioned in a previous chapter; but Evangelista Torricelli, the inventor of the barometer, has a name of even greater celebrity. A native of Faenza, born in 1608, he was educated in the Jesuits' College of that city, until his uncle, a Camaldoline friar, anxious for the further development of his remarkable talents, sent him to Rome. Torricelli there formed the acquaintance of Castelli, a pupil of Galileo, and, some years later, the great philosopher invited him to Florence, and received him as a son. After the death of Galileo, which took place within three months afterwards, Torricelli was appointed his successor as Court Mathematician, and was chosen a member of the Accademia della Crusca, but he died at the early age of thirty-nine.

Averani, a Florentine, born in 1645, was educated at the Jesuits' College in Florence, where he displayed an almost universal genius; equally distinguished in literature and science, he was appointed Professor of Greek at Pisa, where he died in 1707.

Targioni Tozzetti, a celebrated physician and botanist, was born in 1712, and died in 1783. At twenty-three years of age he was appointed Professor of Botany, under Micheli, at Pisa, and afterwards Director of the Botanical Garden in Florence, where he completed the catalogue of plants. Having been made Librarian to the Magliabecchian Library, he arranged the vast number of volumes bequeathed to the city by that eccentric book-collector. Targioni having resigned his place as Director of the Garden, was appointed Physician to the Grand Ducal family. He travelled in Tuscany to collect materials for his great work on the agriculture, natural history, art, and antiquities of his native country; he suggested measures for the drainage of the marshes, and to prevent the frequent inundations from the Arno; but his most important work was his last, on the progress of physical science.

Francesco Redi, the last whose name is mentioned in connection with the Tribune of Galileo, was born at Arezzo in 1626, and educated at Pisa; he practised as a physician in Florence, and was one of the most remarkable observers of his time. His attention was chiefly directed to the study of insect life, but he threw light on other subjects of natural history: he also contributed to maintain the purity of the Tuscan idiom, and is best known abroad by his graceful poem, " Bacco in Toscana," in which he gives a description of the vines of Tuscany. Redi died in 1694, and was buried at Arezzo.

In rooms on the same floor with the Tribune of Galileo

are other physical instruments of historical interest: an inclined plane, said to have been used by Galileo; the tube of Torricelli, placed on a wooden frame, and inscribed *Tubo di Torricelli Firenze, anno* 1604; a chromatic scale invented by Nobili, whose monument is in Sta. Croce, and a medallion drawn and coloured by means of electro-chemistry. The first galvanometer, likewise constructed by Nobili, as well as his first thermo-electric pile. Besides instruments of inferior value, there is a case containing all required for experiments on attraction by electric currents and the lode-stones. Lastly, a large lode-stone, with wires, to obtain the electric spark, produced by magnetic action; on the stand is inscribed, *Sotto gli auspici di Leopoldo II., diede la prima scintilla il* 30 *Genn.*, 1832. *A. L. Nobili e Y Antinori.*

Among the collection of modern instruments, which is gradually increasing, is a galvanometer by which the late distinguished Professor Matteucci first discovered the currents of magnetism in animals; Matteucci presented his library of scientific books and periodicals to this Museum.

Facing the staircase is the room assigned for lectures on botany, surrounded by a valuable botanical library of five thousand volumes, handsomely bound, bequeathed by Mr. Philip Barker Webb, whose portrait in oil is over the door opposite the entrance. Mr. Webb travelled over a large portion of Europe and Asia Minor, accompanied by Monsieur Berthollet; they published a valuable work on the Canary Islands, which they also visited. In the winter of 1848 Mr. Webb arrived in Florence, and he was so much impressed with the value of the botanical collection, as well as with the interest taken in the Museum by the Grand-Duke

Leopold II., that, at his death, he bequeathed his own large and rare collection of dried plants to this prince, and desired by his will that a house he had recently purchased in Paris should be sold, and the profits invested to purchase an annual sum for additions to the botanical section of the Museum.

Beyond the lecture-room is an exhibition of the natural products used for medicine and art, arranged by the present Director, Professor Filippo Parlatore. Though not equal in size to the similar collection in Kew, founded by the distinguished botanist the late Sir William Hooker, it is as complete. Professor Parlatore began this collection, as well as the Herbarium of Central Italy, in 1842, and obtained specimens of flowers, fruit, and seeds from the botanical gardens attached to the Museum, as well as from Italian and foreign botanists. When the Professor was one of the jurors at the great Exhibitions of Paris and London of 1855, 1862, and 1867, and at the Italian Exhibition of 1861, he obtained great additions to the collection; and when chosen Director of the Museum he sent a circular to the Italian Consuls in all parts of the world, to request their assistance in contributions of natural products from every place in which they were stationed. By these means the collection of vegetable products has become singularly rich and important, including specimens preserved in spirits of wine; woods, starches, sugars, oils, gums, resins, balsams, textile fibres, &c., with manufactures of all kinds, such as ropes, cloths, hats, fans, carpets, boxes, and articles of dress, as well as everything applicable to medicine or the industrial arts. There are, besides, drawings and photographs of various useful, important, or singular plants: the dragon tree of Teneriffe, the Mexican cypress, the raphia palm of Madagascar, the palm which produces the vegetable ivory, the kauri pine of New Zealand, &c.—a section of the trunk of this pine is exhibited which is nearly eight feet in diameter.

Besides these, there is a very rich collection of cereals and grasses, such as serve for brooms, matting, &c.; the Italian reed, *Arundo donax*, so familiar to every traveller crossing the Alps into Italy; the sheaths of the Indian corn, which, from their elasticity, are used for under-mattresses—*Sacconi;* the *Coix lacryma*, Job's tears, the seeds of which are used for rosaries; the papyri of Syria and Syracuse—*Cyperus Syriacus*—on which Professor Parlatore has published a pamphlet to prove this papyrus to be a different species from that of Abyssinia and Nubia; also the tubers of the *Cyperus esculentus*, eaten in Sicily, and from which a refreshing drink can be obtained.

Among the specimens of the bulrush tribe are Typha found in marshes all over Europe, and used in Tuscany to protect the oil and wine flasks, and for ropes; also specimens of *Typha angustifolia, L.*, which the Sicilian peasants use for candles; and the product of the Palmi di San Pier Martire—*Chamærops humilis, L.*, from Algeria and Sicily.

The Oricello, or Orchell, is a lichen most worthy of notice, because of the beautiful amaranth colour obtained from it, and from which the family of Rucellai, or Oricellai, who first introduced the dye into Florence, took their name. There are good specimens of lichens which grow on the lavas of Etna and Vesuvius, collected by Professor Parlatore; and a fine specimen of the *Pietra Napoletana* of the Apennines, or Fungus Stone, which, when soaked in water for a certain time, produces good edible fungi, and whose nature has occasioned much discussion among naturalists.

All these products are arranged in the natural order, beginning with the Cryptogams, proceeding to the Monocotyledons, and ending with the Dicotyledons. The families to which the plants belong are marked on the cases, and each specimen has the common as well as scientific name attached, with its locality, the name of the donor, and the date.

The wax preparations are especially interesting; in one case is a magnificent representation of the anatomical structure of the Truffle; also of the Fungus, *Oidium Tuckeri*, which causes the vine disease, made under the direction of Professor Amici; as well as that of the minute fungi which attack both the vine and the rose: some of the most beautiful of these wax specimens represent the fecundation of the Gourd and Orchids.

This collection is one of the richest in Coniferæ and Gnetaceæ, illustrated by Professor Parlatore in his monograph of these families of plants, which forms part of the great work—the *Prodromus*—of De Candolle. There are also various specimens of cottons, with coloured illustrations; and woods and fruits of Borneo, contributed by Signor Odoardo Beccari, who is now engaged in a second voyage for the discovery of objects in Natural History. China, Japan, and Australia, are all here represented, with rare specimens from Central Africa, Angola, and Benguela, added by the German naturalist, Mr. Welwitsch.

Beyond the room containing this collection of plants and vegetable products, is the valuable Herbarium of the Museum, which owes its existence to Professor Parlatore.

Several small Herbariums of peculiar value are kept in the Director's private apartment, all of which have been collected by botanists prior to Linnæus.

The Herbarium of Andrea Cesalpino is supposed to be the oldest in existence; its date is about 1563. Cesalpino was born at Arezzo, in 1519, and became Professor of Botany and Medicine in his native city: he was afterwards chosen physician to Pope Clement VIII., and died in Rome in 1603. He was one of the first who arranged his specimens according to classification founded on the organization and fructification of the plant. His Herbarium, preserved in the Florentine Museum, was made for one of the Tornabuoni family, as appears in a letter written by him from Pisa in 1563. The specimens, which are very small, are pasted on half-sheets of strong, coarse, white paper, which Professor Parlatore has had bound into folio volumes. Each specimen has its Greek, Latin, and Italian name, written by Cesalpino himself; there is no attempt at systematic nomenclature, and nothing of system visible in the arrangement, but an index in the collector's handwriting is prefixed to the volume. This Herbarium belonged to the Palatine Library until 1844, when the Grand-Duke Leopold II. presented it to the Museum of Natural History.

The Herbarium of Pier Antonio Micheli is no less valuable. Micheli, born in Florence in 1699, died in 1737. His volumes of manuscripts and drawings were purchased for the late Professor Targioni Tozzetti; among these last are a vast number of coloured drawings of fungi: Micheli was the first to discover these were real vegetables, and he has been called the precursor of Linnæus. His Herbarium was bought from the Targioni's family by the

Grand-Duke, in 1845, to increase the collections in this Museum.

A small volume is preserved here, containing a few plants, with their names in autograph, by Linnæus, Thunberg, Swartz, and Acharius.*

The central Herbarium of the Florentine Museum is very rich in European and African specimens, and is arranged with the utmost care and ingenuity, so as to enable the student to find any specimen he requires with the greatest facility. The plants are in sheets of paper made up into separate packets; and each packet, containing certain families, is placed between boards, fastened together by straps and buckles. Within every sheet are various specimens of the same species, and these are arranged within the packet according to geographical distribution, beginning with plants growing in the most northern latitudes, and gradually proceeding south, or, in like manner, from east to west. Every plant has a label attached to it, with its name, locality, the name of the donor, and the date of its discovery, inscribed; thus enabling the student to compare the specimen with observations on the subject, published prior or subsequent to the date here given. This label is fastened with pins to a half folio sheet of paper, to avoid the use of gum or cement, so injurious to the specimen. The packets are laid

---

* Charles de Linné (Linnæus), born at Roeskilde, Sweden, 1707; died in 1778.

Charles Peter Thunberg, Swedish botanist, pupil of Linnæus, professor at Upsala; died 1798.

Olaus Swartz, born 1760; died 1817.

Eric Acharius, born in Sweden 1757, one of Linnæus's best pupils; died at Upsala in 1819.

on shelves in niches, resembling Columbaria, around a very large chamber. The system followed in the arrangement of the whole is that of De Candolle.

The adjoining room contains the Herbarium of Mr. Webb, comprising 1,062 packets of plants, which include 80,000 species. Besides Mr. Webb's Herbarium there are those of Pavon, Labillardière, Desfontaines, and Mercier. Pavon made his collection in Peru and Chili. Labillardière accompanied La Perouse on his expedition to New Holland. He was taken prisoner by the Dutch, and his collections were brought to England; but, through the generous intervention of Sir Joseph Banks, they were restored to Labillardière without being opened; lest, as Sir Joseph wrote to Jussieu, "a single botanical thought should be taken from him who had gained them at the risk of his own life." Labillardière died in 1834, and his Herbarium was bought by Mr. Webb. It is especially valuable, because containing the description of each plant in Labillardière's own handwriting, afterwards published in his works.

René Desfontaines was the master of De Candolle; he collected 1,600 species in Tunis and Algeria, and discovered 300 new ones. Mr. Webb purchased his Herbarium for 6,000 francs. Philippe Mercier was a Genoese.

The Botanical Museum has also a rich collection of fossil plants, some of which are wanting in the botanical cabinets of the capital cities of Europe. This collection was begun by Professor Parlatore, and possesses already more than 4,000 valuable specimens. Among these, the most noteworthy are the fossils of the Carboniferous formation from the mines of Mercurio di Iano, near Volterra, and the fossil plants from the vicinity of Sinigaglia; those of the Travertine and of the Miocene formation of Tuscany, and from many formations in other parts of Italy, including the Permian formation of the Brescian territory. The splendid collection of large palms from the country around Verona and Vicenza formerly belonged to the naturalists Massalongo and Visiani; the impressions of plants from the lava of the Island of Lipari; those from the supposed Carboniferous strata of the Tarantaise which shine like silver, because covered by a strata of talc, are all important; as well as the great collection from the Miocene of Switzerland, illustrated by Professor Heer, with many fossil impressions from the Carboniferous strata of France, Belgium, England, and Germany; those from the Tertiary of New Zealand, and the models in plaster of many fruits and unique specimens, with stems of trees from all parts of the world.

The celebrated wax anatomical preparations of this Museum are among the most interesting objects here. This art was first brought to perfection by a Sicilian noble, Gaetano Giulio Zumbo, born in Syracuse, 1656. The report of his wonderful skill in wax-modelling having reached the ears of the Grand-Duke Cosimo III., Zumbo was invited to Florence; some time later he left Tuscany for Marseilles, where he lived under the patronage of Louis XIV., and died in 1703.* The anatomical preparations of the structure of the torpedo, illustrate the experiments made by Tain and Matteucci on animal electricity. The representations in wax of the magnified anatomy of the lobster, cuttlefish, earth-worm, and the tongues of molluscs, are well

---

* Several small waxen figures of Zumbo have already been mentioned in the description of the Bargello and Pitti Palace.

deserving of attention; there is likewise the egg in the several stages of the 'chicken's development; the anatomy of various types of vertebrated animals, the cat, goat, rabbit, codfish, &c. In adjoining rooms are exhibited specimens of human anatomy, among which are wax models of the muscles, ligaments, and cartilages, and of skeletons; the last are, however, of small value, since the reality can be so easily procured.

The zoological, anatomical, and mineralogical collections are all on the second floor. The visitor passes through a succession of small rooms containing a large collection of insects, under the care of Professor Targioni Tozzetti, who represents the third generation of a race of illustrious naturalists; beyond the insects, are corals and madrapores; and finally the Mammalia of Italy, admirably prepared. In one room is a remarkably fine example of the Tuscan wolf; also a good specimen of the wild boar of the Maremma, the moufflons or wild sheep from Sardinia and Corsica, and very fine specimens of fish from the Mediterranean, both stuffed and preserved in spirits; the globo-cephalus, with its skeleton, and the pilot-whale found at Orbitello.

The collection of birds is tolerably large, and remarkably well preserved.

The palæontological collection from Central Italy is extremely valuable. It was first formed by order of the government from materials already existing in the Museum, and in the third Scientific Congress held in Florence, a resolution was passed, to add minerals and geological specimens from all parts of Italy, to be arranged geographically, according to the geological divisions of the Peninsula,—the fossils following the rock specimen of each formation, and the minerals in like manner illustrating the formation, and arranged according to a consecutive system. That part which exhibits the minerals of all countries is very rich, though less remarkable for number or variety than for the beauty of the specimen. Those from the Island of Elba are among the most valuable of the whole collection. The Museum has been lately enriched by the addition of that of Prince Demidoff.

The geological collection, under the direction of Professor Cocchi, is in two divisions—the general collection, and that intended to exhibit the rock formations of Italy. The most important specimens belonging to the first of these divisions are those from Hungary—Kaiserstühl—and those from Egypt recently presented to the Museum. As an appendix to these collections, is a yet incomplete collection of geological specimens applied to the useful arts, the most important of which are the Italian marbles, cut and polished, which received the Premium at the London Exhibition of 1861.

The Palæontological Museum of Central Italy, on the ground-floor, consists chiefly of fossil mammiferi. It is also remarkable for fossils from the Tertiary deposit, the Pliocene portion of which, Professor Cesare d'Ancona is now illustrating. An important part, for the beauty and number of the specimens, are the fossils from the Pietra-forte, Upper Cretaceous, as well as of fossils of the Secondary formation in Tuscany, almost unique of their kind, and collected by the exertions of Professor Cocchi.

The general collection has been noticed by some of the most eminent European naturalists, especially by the late Dr. Hugh Falconer, who has published numerous observations on the fossils of the Florentine Museum.

The celebrated fossil human skull from the neighbourhood of Arezzo is preserved here, as well as other specimens of great value, such as those of the—

Elephas meridionalis	named by	Nesti.
Rhinoceros Etruscus	„	Falconer.
R. Megarhinus	„	Christof.
Hippopotamus major	„	Cuvier.
Bos Etruscus	„	Falconer.
Equus Stenonis	„	Cocchi.
Sus	„	Sp.
Cervus dicranios	„	Nesti.
Cervus ctinoidas	„	Nesti.
Bos primigenius	„	Blum.

The recent discoveries on animal physiology by means of vivisection, by the distinguished German Professor Schiff, though open to animadversion from those who consider that no addition to human knowledge can justify the means employed, have greatly added to the scientific reputation of the institute attached to this Museum.

The Museum is chiefly distinguished—for its collection of Physical Instruments; for Mr. Webb's Herbarium and Library; for the fossil bones from the Val d' Arno Superiore, and Inferiore, contained in the Palæontological Museum; for the complete collection of Vicentine Fossils, and for the wax models of anatomical structures.

Attached to the building, and adjoining the Boboli, is the Botanical Gardens. It was commenced by the Grand-Duke Pietro Leopoldo, a few years after the foundation of the Museum, and was considerably enlarged by Ferdinand III., whose favourite study was botany, and who therefore added the hot-houses, and enriched the garden with a collection of foreign plants, some of which were imported by the Botanist

Raddi, sent by Ferdinand to explore the vast Empire of
Brazil. Under the direction of Professor Ottaviano Targioni Tożzetti, and by the aid of the gardener Berni, and
afterwards of the gardeners Giuseppe and Antonio Piccioli,
the gardens were entirely re-formed and nearly doubled in
extent; and in 1842, when Professor Parlatore was called
to the Chair of Botany, they again underwent improve-
ments to adapt them better for scientific study. One part
of the garden is assigned to the sexes of plants, illustrative of the natural system; another to represent the flora of
China and Japan, and to assist in the study of geographical
distribution; another part to plants from the temperate and
frigid zones of America and Europe.

This garden is especially distinguished by the great number of specie, which have increased from 826, which they
were in 1842, to above 111,000. There is a fine collection
of Palms, Cycadeæ, Conifers, Tree-ferns, Aroideæ, Orchids,
Draconæ, Maranite, &c. Among the rare plants are, the
Pachira, Anda, Hura, Psidium, Pandanus and Cycas, Arau-
caria, and various species of Cinnamon, Quassia, Cinchona,
Ipecacuanha, Coca, Nux vomica, Nepenthes, Bursera gum-
mifera, Anacardium, Mango, &c.

It is to be hoped that in the new arrangements making in
the Museum, the Director may be allowed to improve, and
add to the hothouses, which are few, small, and ill constructed.

CHRONOLOGY.

	A.D.
Acharius, Eric	b. 1757—d. 1819
Averani	b. 1645—d. 1707
Botanical Chair	1842
Cesalpino, Andrea	b. 1519—d. 1603
Desfontaines, René	
Galileo Galilei	b. 1564—d. 1642
" his first telescope	1609
Labillardière	d. 1834
Linnæus	b. 1707—d. 1778
Michele, Pier Antonio	b. 1699—d. 1737
Museum commenced	1775
" opened to the public	1780
" School of Public Instruction founded	1807
" " " suppressed	1814
" " " restored	1833
" Institute of Studii Superiori	1859
Redi, Francesco	b. 1626—d. 1694
Swartz, Olaus	b. 1760—d. 1817
Targioni Tozzetti	b. 1712—d. 1783
Thunberg, Peter	d. 1798
Torricelli, Evangelista	b. 1608—d. 1647
Viviani, Vincenzio	b. 1622—d. 1703
Zumbo, Gaetano Giulio	b. 1656—d. 1703

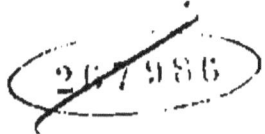

INDEX.

Abate, Neri, vol. i., 198
Academy of Fine Arts, vol. ii., 241
" Platonic, vol. i., 74; vol. ii., 240
Accademia degli Apatisti, vol. ii., 88
" del Cimento, vol. i., 241
" della Crusca, vol. i., 240; vol. ii., 174
" Filarmonica, vol. ii., 80
Alfieri, Vittorio, vol. ii., 87
Alighieri, Dante, vol. i., 129; vol. ii., 27, 136, 141, 174, 180
Altafronte, Castle of, vol. ii., 4
Anthologia, the, vol. i., 186
Antonino, Bishop, vol. i., 73, 218, 290; vol. ii., 157, 169, 177, 614
Archives, the, vol. i., 338
Ariosto, Lodovico, vol. ii., 252
Athens, Duke of, vol. i., 193, 317, 308; vol. ii., 10.

Baccano, Il, vol. i., 173
Baglioni, Malatesta, vol. ii., 269, 286
Banca Nazionale, vol. ii., 88
Baptistery, the, vol. i., 23
" Gates of, vol. i., 28
Bargello, the, vol. i., 314
" Chapel of, vol. i., 329
" Office of, vol. i., 326
Bastianini, Girolamo, vol. ii., 164
Beatrice, Countess, vol. i., 126
Benivieni, Girolamo, vol. ii., 178, 266
Beniai, San Fillppo, vol. ii., 116
Benvenuti, Pietro, vol. ii., 200
Bianca Capello, vol. i., 339; vol. ii., 141, 288

Boccaccio, vol. ii., 32, 854, 761
Boniface VIII., vol. ii., 82
Borsi, Pietro, vol. i., 93, 107
Bracciolino, Poggio, vol. i., 85, 117; vol. ii., 185
Browning, Mrs. Ella. B., vol. ii., 99, 291
Bruni, Leonardo Aretino, vol. ii., 31

Calcio, game of, vol. ii., 9
Calimala, term of, vol. i., 172
Canto della Coculia, vol. ii., 304
" della Farina, vol. i., 232
" alla Paglia, vol. i., 120
Capanna, Puccio, vol. ii., 210
Capello, Bianca, vol. i., 239; vol. ii., 141, 288
Capitano del Popolo, his residence, vol. i., 178
Capponi, Niccolò, vol. ii., 282
" Piero, vol. ii., 10
Captains of Guelphic party, vol. i., 117
Carnesecchi, vol. i., 244; vol. ii., 10
Caroccio in Mercato Nuovo, vol. i., 174
Casa Casuccini, vol. i., 106
" Guidi, vol. ii., 291
" Londi, vol. i., 101
" Pia di Lavoro, vol. ii., 76
" Stufa, vol. ii., 104
Cascine, the, vol. ii., 242
Cavalcante, Guido, vol. i., 86
Cecco d' Ascoli, vol. ii., 45
Cemetery, ancient, of Cathedral, vol. i., 61
" round Baptistery, vol. i., 86
" of Jews, vol. ii., 315

438   INDEX.

Cemetery, Protestant, vol. II., 98
Church of S. Ambrogio, vol. ii., 93
  ,,   S. Andrea, vol. l., 106
  ,,   SS. Annunziata, vol. ii., 113,
          122
  ,,   S. Apollinare, vol. l., 300;
          vol. ii., 1
  ,,   S. Apollonia, vol. ii., 183
  ,,   SS. Apostoli, vol. i., 180
  ,,   Badia, vol. l., 306
  ,,   S. Barnaba, vol. ii., 263
  ,,   S. Biagio, vol. l., 175
  ,,   S. Carlo, vol. i., 196
  ,,   S. Cecilia, vol. l., 229
  ,,   S. Croce, vol. II., 35
  ,,   S. Elisabetta, vol. ii., 316
  ,,   S. Felice, vol. ii., 299
  ,,   S. Felicità, vol. ii., 274
  ,,   S. Firenze, vol. ii. 2
  ,,   S. Frediano, vol. ii., 135
  ,,   S. Gaetano, vol. ii., 186
  ,,   S. Giovannino, vol. ii., 149
  ,,   S. Giovannino dei Cavalieri,
          vol. ii., 187
  ,,   S. Jacopo sopr' Arno, vol.
          ii., 280
  ,,   S. Jacopo tra Fossi, vol.
          ii., 2
  ,,   S. Jacopo in Ripoli, vol. II.,
          240
  ,,   S. Leonardo in Arcetri, vol.
          i., 222
  ,,   S. Lorenzo, vol. l., 124
  ,,   S. Lucia degli Magnoli,
          vol. II., 259
  ,,   S. Marco, vol. II., 175
  ,,   S. Margherita de' Ricci,
          vol. i., 304
  ,,   S. Maria sopr' Arno, vol. ii.,
          254
  ,,   S. Maria dei Battilani,
          vol. ii., 181
  ,,   S. Maria in Campo, vol. II.,
          87
  ,,   S. Maria della Carmine,
          vol. II., 305
  ,,   S. Maria del Fiore, vol. i.,
          50
  ,,   S. Maria Maggiore, vol. II.,
          185
  ,,   S. Maria Nipoticosa, vol. i.,
          193

Church of S. Maria Novella, vol. ii.,
          ,. 207,
  ,,   S. Maria sopra Porta, vol. i.,
          175
  ,,   S. Maria degli Ughi, vol. i.,
          189
  ,,   S. Martino, vol. i., 290
  ,,   S. Michele, vol. i., 196
  ,,   S. Michele delle Trombe,
          vol. i., 295
  ,,   S. Michele del Visdomini,
          vol. i., 303; vol. ii., 88
  ,,   S. Nicolò sopr' Arno, vol.
          ii., 269
  ,,   Ogni Santi, vol. II., 243
  ,,   Or San Michele, vol. i., 196
  ,,   S. Pancrazio, vol. ii., 194
  ,,   S. Paolo, vol. ii., 201
  ,,   S. Piero Gattolino, vol. ii.,
          316
  ,,   S. Piero Maggiore, vol. i.,
          306
  ,,   S. Piero Scheraggio, vol. i.,
          198, 221, 256
  ,,   dei Pretori, vol. II., 181
  ,,   SS. Procolo e Nicomede,
          vol. II., 84
  ,,   S. Reparata, vol. i., 5, 49
  ,,   S. Romolo, vol. i., 113
  ,,   S. Salvador, vol. i., 120
  ,,   S. Simone, vol. ii., 81
  ,,   S. Spirito, vol. II., 205
  ,,   S. Stefano, vol. i., 178
  ,,   S. Tommaso, vol. i., 162
  ,,   SS. Trinità, vol. ii., 196
  ,,   Ser' Umido, vol. ii., 316
  ,,   S. Zenobius, vol. i., 64
Cimabue, workshop of, vol. i., 117
Ciompi, Riot of the, vol. i., 319
Collegio Eugeniano, vol. i., 313
Column of S. Felicità, vol. ii., 274
  ,,   of Mars, vol. i., 19
  ,,   in Mercato Vecchio, vol. i.,
          163
Compagni, Dino, vol. i., 48; vol. ii., 82
Company of the Bigallo, vol. i., 98
  ,,   . Buonuomini di S. Martino,
          vol. i., 118, 201
  ,,   Laudesi di S. Maria, vol.
          i., 198; vol. ii., 73
  ,,   S. Luke, vol. ii., 126
  ,,   Misericordia, vol. i., 92

Company of the Scalzi, vol. ii., 364
" Umiliati, vol. ii., 241, 242
" Vanchetone, vol. ii., 201
Convent of S. Ambrogio, vol. ii., 93
" Annalena, vol. ii., 319
" S. Caterina, vol. ii., 142
" S. Clemente, vol. ii., 181
" S. Egidio, vol. ii., 90
" S. Maddalena de' Pazzi, vol. ii., 99, 103
" S. Marco, vol. ii., 154
" S. Maria degli Angeli, vol. II., 135
" S. Maria Novella, vol. ii., 206
" Monte Domini, vol. II., 78
" Montecelli, vol. II., 76
" S. Rocco. vol. ii., 181
Corsini, Don Neri, vol. ii., 32
Council of Greek and Latin Churches, vol. ii., 9
Croce al Trebbio, vol. ii., 204

Dante (see Alighieri)
Dante da Castiglione, vol. i., 119, 128; vol. II., 157
Danti, Fra Ignazio, vol. i., 276
Davanzati, Bernardo, vol. i., 188
Donati, Forese, vol. i., 178
" Piccarda, vol. ii., 77
Dudley, Robt., Duke of Northumberland, vol. ii., 192
Duomo, the, vol. i., 50
" Opera del, vol. i., 114

Esecutore della Giustizia, vol. i., 261
Etruscan origin of Florence, vol. i., 1

Family of Acciajoli, vol. i., 180; vol. ii., 249
" Adimari, vol. i., 192
" Alberti, vol. ii., 7
" Alessandri, vol. i., 102
" Amidei, vol. i., 178
" Amieri, vol. i., 167
" Bardi, vol. ii., 357
" Bischieri, vol. i., 50
" Buondelmonte, vol. i., 178; vol. ii., 355
" Capponi, vol. II., 108, 299
" Corsini, vol. ii., 198
" Falconieri, vol. i., 50

Family of Fransoni, vol. II., 242
" Frescobaldi, vol. ii., 280
" Ginori, vol. ii., 153
" Gondi, vol. II., 225
" Guadagni, vol. ii., 293
" Guicciardini, vol. ii., 275, 278
" Guidi, vol. ii., 85
" Infangati, vol. I., 189
" Lambertesca, vol. i., 176
" Lamberti, vol. i., 170, 178
" Macci, vol. i., 193
" Marucelli, vol. ii., 141
" Medici, vol. i., 223
" Michelozzi, vol. ii., 291
" Nerli, vol. ii., 297
" Pandolfini, vol. II., 182
" Pazzi, vol. i., 175
" Perozzi, vol. II., 8
" Pitti, vol. II., 323
" Ricasoli, vol. ii., 153
" Ricci, vol. ii., 220
" Ridolfi, vol. II., 289
" Rinuccini, vol. i., 278; vol. II., 287
" Rondinelli, vol. ii., 186
" Rossi, vol. ii., 274
" Rucellai, vol. ii., 193, 215
" Serristori, vol. ii., 369
" Soderini, vol. II., 284
" Strozzi, vol. II., 212, 216, 230
" Tornabuoni, vol. ii., 193, 220
" Torrigiani, vol. ii., 260
" Vacca, vol. i., 230, 257
" Velluti Zati, vol. II., 38, 110, 287
" Vespucci, vol. II., 247
Fanali, or Lanterna, vol. II., 7
Ferucci, Francesco, vol. ii., 196
Ficino, Marsilio, vol. i., 74
Fiesole, Etruscan city of, vol. i., 2
Filicaia, Vincenzio, vol. ii., 34
Florence, origin of name, vol. i., 3
" topography of, vol. i., 9
Fortezza del Basso, vol. ii., 184
" S. Giorgio, vol. ii., 271
Foscolo, Ugo, vol. ii., 29
Fossombroni, Vittorio, vol. ii., 35

Galilei, Galileo, vol. II., 36, 271
Galleries, Public, of Art, vol. i., 316; vol. ii., 332

Galuzzi, vol. i., 101
Game of Calcio, vol. ii., 9
,, Palla e Maglio, vol. ii., 111
Gardens of Boboli, vol. ii., 321
,, Medici, vol. ii., 142
,, Orti Oricellari, vol. ii., 240
,, Torrigiani, vol. ii., 117
Gherardo, Bishop, vol. i., 125
Ghetto, the, vol. i., 159
Ghibellines and Guelphs, vol. i., 191
Giotto, Campanile of, vol. i., 62
Giovio, Paolo, vol. i., 151
Giudici alla Ruota, vol. i., 330; vol. ii., 4
Gonfalonier, Office of, vol. i., 201
Grand-Duke Cosimo I., vol. i., 113, 231; vol. ii., 208
Grand-Duke Ferdinand I., vol. i., 146
,, Pietro Leopoldo, vol. ii., 138
Grazzini, Anton Francesco, vol. i., 83
Guilds, vol. i., 117
Guild of Advocates, vol. i., 211
,, Butchers, vol. i., 177, 210
,, Farriers, vol. i., 205
,, Flax Merchants, vol. i., 168, 204
,, Foreign Wool Merchants, vol. i., 172, 212
,, Furriers, vol. i., 204
,, Hosiers, vol. i., 200
,, Merchants on Exchange, vol. i., 164
,, Notaries, vol. i., 212
,, Physicians and Apothecaries, vol. i., 162, 203
,, Silk, vol. i., 176, 200
,, Smiths, Carpenters, and Masons, vol. i., 208
,, Swordmakers, vol. i., 209
,, Vintners, vol. i., 180
,, Wool, vol. i., 172, 206
Guittone, Fra, of Arrezzo, vol. ii., 135

Hospital of S. Bonifazio, vol. ii., 182
,, Foundling—the Innocenti, vol. ii., 130
,, S. Maria Nuova, vol. ii., 89
,, S. Maria della Scala, vol. ii., 210
,, S. Matthew (see Academy of Fine Arts)

Hospital of S. Paolo, vol. ii., 202
,, Templars and Knights of Malta, vol. ii., 252

Inquisition, Office of the, vol. ii., 45

Landino, Jacopo, vol i., 213
Lando da Gubbio, vol. i., 116
Lapo, Arnolfo di, vol. i., 315; vol. ii., 15
Latini, Brunetto, vol. ii., 186
Library of S. Croce, vol. ii., 44
,, Laurentian, vol. i., 152
,, of S. Marco, vol. ii., 171
,, Marucelliana, vol. ii., 142
,, National, vol. i., 239
Lions of the Republic, vol. i., 256, 261
Loggia degli Adimari, vol. i., 193
,, of Bigallo, vol. i., 99
,, de' Lanzi, vol. i., 222, 225

Macchiavelli, Nicolò, vol. ii., 39, 279
Magliabecchia, Antonio, vol. i., 239
Manetti, Gianozzo, vol. i., 66, 71
Manin, Daniel, vol. ii., 35
Marsili, Luigi, vol. i., 82
Marzocco, the, vol. i., 268
Marzuppini, Carlo, vol. i., 72; vol. ii., 15
Matilda, Countess, vol. i., 7, 119
Medici, Card. Alexander de', vol. ii., 201
,, Bernadetto de', vol. ii., 145
,, Cosimo de', vol. i., 359; vol. ii., 171
,, Giovanni de', vol. i., 111, 126, 137
,, Giovanni delle Bande Nere, vol. i., 121, 129, 296
,, Giuliano de', vol. i., 141
,, Lorenzo de', vol. i., 27
,, Lorenzo, Duke of Urvino, vol. i., 142
,, Orlando de', vol. ii., 121
,, Ottaviano de', vol. ii., 142
,, Piero Il Gottoso, vol. i., 137
,, Salvestro de', vol. i., 318
,, Tombs of the, vol. i., 140—146
Mercanzia, Office of the, vol. i., 211
Mercato Nuovo, vol. i., 124
,, Vecchio, vol. i., 160
Mirandola, Pico della, vol. ii., 94, 278

Monti, the, (Public Funds), vol. i., 170
Mugnone, course of the, vol. i., 11
Murate, Prison of, vol. ii., 79
Museum, Egyptian, vol. ii., 416
" Etruscan, vol. ii., 450
" Natural History, vol. ii., 440

Neri, S. Philippo, vol. ii., 316
Niccoli, Nicolò, vol. i., 151; vol. ii. 271
Niccolini, Gio. Bat., vol. ii., 143

Order of the Servi, vol. ii., 113
Orlandini Baldassare, vol. i., 281
Orso, Bishop Antonio de', vol. i., 75

Palio, the, or Cloth of Gold, vol. i., 302
Palazzo Acciajuoli, vol. ii., 251
" Albizi, vol. i., 106
" Alessandri, vol. i., 302
" Antellesi, vol. ii., 11
" Antinori, vol ii., 185
" Arcivescovile, vol. i., 119
" Barbadori, vol. ii., 280
" Barberini, vol. ii., 11
" Buonarotti, vol. ii., 81
" Canigiani, vol. ii., 259
" Capello, vol. ii., 288
" Capponi, vol. ii., 108
" Capponi Oltr' Arno, vol. ii., 282
" Capponi, Uzzano, vol. ii., 259
" Castellani, vol. ii., 4
" Cerchi, vol. ii., 280
" S. Clemente, vol. ii., 110
" Conte Bardi, vol. ii., 83
" Conti Galli, vol. i., 301
" Corsi, vol. ii., 167
" Corsini, vol. ii., 198
" delle Cento Finestre, vol. ii. 186
" Feroni, Oltr' Arno, vol. ii., 315
" Feroni, Spini, vol. i., 184
" Feruccio, vol. ii., 287
" Firidolfi, vol. ii., 288
" Fransoni, vol. ii., 248
" Frescobaldi, vol. ii., 218, 280
" Gherardesca, vol. ii., 107
" Ginori, vol. ii., 151

Palazzo Gondi, vol. ii., 3
" Guadagni, vol. ii., 203
" Guicciardini, vol. ii., 278
" Guidi, Conti, vol. ii., 83
" Gulgni, vol. ii., 139
" Manelli, vol. ii., 140, 254
" Martelli, vol. ii., 150
" Michelozzi, vol. ii., 291
" Montalvo, vol. i., 300
" Murat, Caroline, vol. ii., 246
" Nonfinito, vol. i., 297
" Orlandini, vol. ii., 186
" Panciatichi, vol. ii., 99
" Pandolfini, vol. i., 231; vol. ii., 282
" Pazzi, vol. i., 300; vol. ii., 88
" Pitti, vol. ii., 323
" Pucci, vol. ii., 140
" Quaratesi, vol. i., 298; vol. ii., 243
" Riccardi, vol. ii., 146
" Ridolfi, vol. ii., 289
" Rinuccini, vol. ii., 187
" Rucellai, vol. ii., 192
" Salimbeni, vol. i., 188
" Salviati, vol. ii., 116
" Seristori, vol. ii., 11, 169
" Simone di Firenzuole, vol. ii., 303
" Spini, vol. i., 183; vol. ii., 198
" Strozzi, vol. i., 188; vol. ii., 187, 240
" Tempi, vol. ii., 257
" Torrigiani, vol. ii., 260
" Uguccione, vol. i., 231
" Valori, vol. i., 306
" Vecchio, vol. i., 255, 273
Pandects of Justinian, vol. i., 157
Panzano, Michele da, vol. ii., 90
Passavanti, Fra Jacopo, vol. ii., 232
Paterini, the, vol. i., 95; vol. ii., 204
Pedro, Don, di Toledo, vol. i., 85
Peter Martyr, vol. i., 96; vol. ii., 204, 279
Piazza del Cimatori, vol. i., 299
" di S. Croce, vol. ii., 9
" di S. Maria Novella, vol. ii., 203
" della Signoria, vol. i., 221
" SS. Trinita, vol. ii., 195
" Vecchia, vol. ii., 185
Pietra-dura, vol. ii., 412

462 INDEX.

Pitti Gallery of Painting, vol. ii., 367
Podestà, Office of the, vol. i., 314
Poliziano, Angelo, vol. i., 74, 85; vol. ii., 178
Ponte alla Carraia, vol. ii., 247
" alle Grazie, or Rubaconte, vol. ii., 5
" SS. Trinità, vol. ii., 248
" Vecchio, vol. ii., 251
Pope John XXII., vol. i., 44
" Leo X., vol. ii., 118
" Martin V., vol. i., 120
" Paschal II., vol. i., 126
Porta Bacchiera, vol. ii., 206
" a Balla, vol. ii., 88
" San Frediano, vol. ii., 313
" San Gallo, vol. ii., 180
" alla Giustizia, vol. ii., 76
" San Miniato, vol. ii., 272
" delle Pere, vol. ii., 8
" Romana, vol. ii., 318
" San Giorgio, vol. ii., 271
" Vladomini, vol. ii., 88
Porte (Gates) of Florence, vol. i., 14
Portinari, Folco, vol. i., 295

Quarters of Florence, vol. i., 11, 262
Quay Lung' Arno Acciajuoli, vol. ii., 247
Quay Lung' Arno Corsini, vol. ii., 248

Races, Horse, vol. i., 297
Ranieri, Bishop, vol. i., 46
Ricasoli, Giovan Batt., vol. ii., 212
" Pandolfo, vol. ii., 45
Ringhiera, the, of Palazzo Vecchio, vol. i., 267
Ripa Fratta, Fra Lorenzo, vol. ii., 267

S. Bernard, Chapel of, Palazzo Vecchio, vol. i., 278
S. Bernardino, vol. ii., 83
S. Louis of Toulouse, vol. ii., 22
Sacchetti, Francesco, vol. i., 217
Savonarola, Girolamo, vol. i., 139, 260; vol. ii., 164, 174
Scala, Bartol. della, vol. ii., 107
Soderini, Nicolò, vol. ii., 304
" Piero, vol. ii., 104, 318

Stinche Vecchio, (Prison), vol. i., 257; vol. ii., 80
Strozzi, Filippo, vol. ii., 184, 187
" Palla, vol. ii., 197
" Strozzo, vol. i., 24, 44
Stufa, Ugo della, vol. i., 123

Tabernacles, at corners of streets, vol. i., 197; vol. ii., 408
Tabernacle of "Cinque Lampade," vol. ii., 140
Tamburo, the, vol. i., 261
Tasso, Torquato, vol. ii., 290
Theatre in Uffizi, vol. i., 237
Tiratojo, vol. ii., 315
Torrigiani, March. Carlo, vol. ii., 184
Toscanelli, Paolo, vol. i., 62
Towers, old, of Florence, vol. i., 10
" of Roscoli, vol. i., 315
" La Castagna, vol. i., 292
" Cerchi, vol. i., 294
" Guardamorto, vol. i., 94
" Palazzo Vecchio, vol. i., 258
Tozzetti, Targioni, vol. ii., 25
Turpin, Archbishop, vol. i., 181

Uberti, Farinata degli, vol. ii., 64
" Uberto degli, vol. i., 198
Uccellatojo, bird-tower, vol. i., 10
L'Uffizi, the, vol. i., 234
" Gallery of Paintings, vol. i., 346
Ugolino of Sienna, vol. i., 197
Uzzano, Nicolò d', vol. i., 30, 180; vol. ii., 141, 259

Valori, Baccio, vol. i., 306; vol. ii., 104
" Francesco, vol. i., 318
Vettori, Piero, vol. ii., 300
Via Borgo Allegri, vol. ii., 79
" degli Albizzi, vol. i., 257
" de' Bardi, vol. ii., 254
" Cacciajoli, vol. i., 193
" Calzaioli, vol. i., 192
" del Corso, vol. i., 206
" San Gallo, vol. ii., 181
" Ghibellina, vol. ii., 79
" Borgo de' Greci, vol. ii., 9
" Borgo San Lorenzo, vol. i., 122
" Oricellari, vol. ii., 240

Via dei Pittori, vol. I., 105
  „ della Sapienza, vol. ii., 148
Vieusseux, Gian Pietro, vol. i., 185
Villa Petrovitz, vol. II., 271
Villani, the, vol. ii., 84
Vindomini, Cerettieri, vol. i., 193
Viviani, Vincenzio, vol. ii., 66, 71

Walls, circle of, vol. i., 12
  „ of city, vol. i., 194
Wills, Countess, vol. i., 306

Zecca, the, or Mint, vol. I., 116
Zenobius, Bishop, vol. i., 3, 79, 118, 177;
  vol. ii., 177

THE END.

Uniform with this Work.

WALKS IN ROME.

By AUGUSTUS J. C. HARE.

Third Edition. 2 Vols. Crown 8vo., 21*s.*

"The best handbook of the city and environs of Rome ever published. . . . Cannot be too much commended."—*Pall Mall Gazette.*

"This book supplies the peculiar sort of knowledge which the traveller in Rome evidently needs. He does not want a mere guide-book to mark the localities, or a mere compendious history to recall the most interesting associations. He wants a sympathetic and well-informed friend who has himself been over the places described, and has appreciated them with the same mingled sentiments of inquisitiveness, reverence, and inexplicable historical longing with which the traveller of taste must approach a city of such vast and heterogeneous attractions as Rome."—*Westminster Review.*

"This book is sure to be very useful. It is thoroughly practical, and is the best guide that yet has been offered."—*Daily News.*

"Mr. Hare's book fills a real void, and gives to the tourist all the latest discoveries and the fullest information bearing on that most inexhaustible of subjects, the city of Rome. . . . . It is much fuller than 'Murray,' and any one who chooses may now know how Rome really looks in sun or shade."—*Spectator.*

"Whoever has a visit to Rome in contemplation should not fail to read Mr. Hare's book before starting. He will enter upon his explorations with double interest and intelligence. Whoever is already familiar with the city, and comes across these 'Walks,' will think himself transported again to the old scenes."—*Scotsman.*

"The real richness of Rome as well as its interest are known only to those who stay a long time there; but for such or even for those whose visit is a brief one we know no single work that can replace this of Mr. Hare. We heartily recommend it to past and future visitors to Rome; they will find it a condensed library of information about the Eternal City."—*Atlantic Monthly.*

WANDERINGS IN SPAIN.

By AUGUSTUS J. C. HARE.

With Illustrations. Crown 8vo, 10*s.* 6*d.*

"This charming book is written with all the ease and grace peculiar to Mr. Hare."—*Morning Post.*

"Since the publication of "Castilian Days," by the American diplomat, Mr. John Hay, no pleasanter or more readable sketches have fallen under our notice."—*Athenæum.*

"In Mr. Hare the reader finds a guide who is full of fact and incident, who conveys abundance of information in a happy style, and, in a word, is as conscientious as he is pleasing."—*Daily Telegraph.*

"A delightful work. Each of the scenes described will henceforth, in the minds of readers, be associated with Mr. Hare's account of their beauty, their past, and the thoughts they suggest."—*Conservative.*

"Many books have recently been written about Spain and its people, but this one is specially succinct, clear, and readable; and should certainly be purchased by any one intending to make a Spanish tour."—*Nonconformist.*

STRAHAN & CO., 56, LUDGATE HILL, LONDON.

Works by Alfred Tennyson, D.C.L.,
POET-LAUREATE.

Poems. Small 8vo, 9s.

Maud, and other Poems. Small 8vo, 5s.

In Memoriam. Small 8vo, 6s.

The Princess. Small 8vo, 5s.

Idylls of the King. Small 8vo, 7s. Collected. Small 8vo, 12s.

Enoch Arden, &c. Small 8vo, 6s.

The Holy Grail, and other Poems. Small 8vo, 7s.

Gareth and Lynette, &c. Small 8vo, 5s.

Selections. Square 8vo, cloth extra, 5s.; gilt edges, 6s.

Songs. Square 8vo, cloth extra, 5s.

Library Edition of Mr. Tennyson's Works, in Six Post 8vo. Vols., 10s. 6d. each.

Pocket-volume Edition. Eleven Vols., 18mo, in neat case, 50s.; in extra binding, 55s.

The Window; or, the Songs of the Wrens. With Music by A. Sullivan. 4to, cloth gilt extra, 21s.

STRAHAN & CO., 56, LUDGATE HILL, LONDON.

www.ingramcontent.com/pod-product-compliance
Lightning Source LLC
Chambersburg PA
CBHW051239300426
44114CB00011B/808